JCCs of North America

MIFGASH

EXECUTIVE LEADERSHIP FORUM

This book is presented as a gift

to JCC professionals

who attended

JCCs of North America

Mifgash: Executive Leadership Forum

from

JCC Association
of North America

January 2023 • Atlanta, Georgia

Advance Praise for *Never Alone*

"This book can be read on two levels. One is the series of public issues that Natan Sharansky addresses with strong conviction: his belief that Palestinian democracy must precede Palestinian statehood; his consequent opposition to the Oslo agreement and the Gaza withdrawal, then to the Iran nuclear accord; his euphoria at the airlift of Ethiopian Jews to Israel; his distress at the rise of anti-Semitism and at the religious and political rifts among Jews in Israel and the Diaspora. The other level is more significant, at least to me, having known Natan for about forty-five years. It is the personal and intellectual journey that he describes as he explains himself. Here is an exceptional man, schooled in Soviet doublethink, then finding his Jewish identity and his ideology as a free-thinker, separated from his new wife for a dozen years and locked for nine in the Gulag before rising to high Israeli leadership. Trauma victims know that recovery often depends on good people's support. That he had, giving him power to make from his suffering a lodestar that guides his judgments. You might disagree with him here and there, but you cannot help liking him, because you cannot help looking through the issues into his heart of idealism."

> —**David K. Shipler**, former *New York Times* bureau chief in Moscow and Jerusalem and author of seven books, including the best-selling *Russia: Broken Idols, Solemn Dreams* and the Pulitzer Prize–winning *Arab and Jew: Wounded Spirits in a Promised Land*

"Those of us who have been political prisoners wonder: 'Yes, we have exited our cell, but does it ever leave us?' After ten years it is still with me—and while reading this very impressive book I felt the same from my friend, Natan Sharansky. For me, his art expresses my deep feelings.... Just as we broke the lock to go out of the cell, we have to break out of the political box of thinking to solve the problems of the Middle East. So, yes, I agree with the book's message, we need democracy throughout the region, along with mutual economic programs, to make real peace.

"This book is a very important social and human message for peace and civility in the Middle East. We are partners and will continue to struggle together for the future of our region. That is our historical duty as peoples of the Middle East and also our personal responsibility, hand by hand, to send this message. That is what has been done in this book, and I have the honor to thank you, my very dear brothers: in this struggle, you will never be alone."

> —**Dr. Kamal Allabwani**, founder of the Syrian Liberal Democratic Union and Syrian Prisoner of Conscience, 2001–2011

NEVER ALONE

NEVER ALONE

PRISON, POLITICS, *and* MY PEOPLE

NATAN SHARANSKY
and GIL TROY

PUBLICAFFAIRS

New York

PublicAffairs
Hachette Book Group
1290 Avenue of the Americas, New York, NY 10104
www.publicaffairsbooks.com
@Public_Affairs

Printed in the United States of America

First Edition: September 2020

Published by PublicAffairs, an imprint of Perseus Books, LLC, a subsidiary of Hachette Book Group, Inc. The PublicAffairs name and logo is a trademark of the Hachette Book Group.

The Hachette Speakers Bureau provides a wide range of authors for speaking events. To find out more, go to www.hachettespeakersbureau.com or call (866) 376-6591.

The publisher is not responsible for websites (or their content) that are not owned by the publisher.

Print book interior design by Jeff Williams

Library of Congress Control Number: 2020939476

ISBNs: 978-1-5417-4242-0 (hardcover), 978-1-5417-4243-7 (ebook)

LSC-C

10 9 8 7 6 5 4 3 2 1

To our parents: Boris Shcharansky z"l
(1904–1980)

Ida Milgrom Shcharansky z"l
(1908–2002)

Elaine Gerson Troy z"l
(1933–2020)

While wishing long life to Bernard Dov Troy

And to our grandchildren: Those born:

Eitan

Yehuda

David

Avigail

Uri

Daniel

Ariel

and those yet to be born . . .

We are blessed to belong to this chain of transmission,
from generation to generation, always trusting "that a
new light will shine unto Zion, hoping that we all will
be privileged to be enlightened from it."

אור חדש על ציון תאיר ונזכה כולנו מהרה לאורו

FROM THE DAILY PRAYER BOOK

CONTENTS

INTRODUCTION

Living Life Backward

After living my life backward, the usual sequence seems overrated. Whenever I hear of friends separating after decades of marriage, I wonder, "Maybe they did it in the wrong order." My wife, Avital, and I were separated one day after we married. We didn't see each other for twelve years, then lived happily ever after.

I was circumcised when I was twenty-five years old, not eight days old. So, unlike most, I could give my consent. And, two days later, when I joined yet another Refusenik protest, the KGB imprisoned me for fifteen days. Thus, the Soviet secret police enabled me to commune quietly with Abraham, the first Jew, who circumcised himself at the age of ninety-nine, and soon hosted angels in his tent.

Years later, after some other freed Refuseniks and I founded an Israeli political party, we thought up a fitting slogan. Promising that "we are a different type of party, we go to prison first," we won more seats than expected.

Finally, at the age of sixty-five, I had my bar mitzvah—fifty-two years late. The traditional Jewish rite of passage for boys is at thirteen. My belated ceremony was cost-efficient: I now had a squad of grandchildren to pick up the candy the guests would throw at me in celebration, so everything stayed in the family. Most importantly, I could better appreciate my Torah portion's relevance and explain it to everyone without having my rabbi write my speech for me.

A year earlier, when I was sixty-four, one of my sons-in-law had been reminiscing about his bar mitzvah. I asked him what my Torah reading would have been. He looked it up, based on my birth date. I thought he was teasing when he answered a few minutes later: "It's *Parashat Bo*," at the beginning of Exodus.

Parashat Bo? When Moses tells Pharaoh, "Let my people go," uttering those mighty words that became the slogan of our struggle for freedom in the Soviet Union?

"This cannot be a coincidence," I thought. "I will have to have a bar mitzvah." Sixty-five seemed like a perfectly good age—five times thirteen.

On the appointed day, I read the first two parts of the Torah portion, with the proper *trope*, the traditional cantillation. Fortunately, my two sons-in-law stepped in and read the other five parts and the accompanying biblical passage from Jeremiah 43—the Haftorah—which envisions the Jews being redeemed.

Yet the ordeal wasn't over after the candies had been pelted and my young cleanup crew had arrived. I still had to make that speech. I analyzed Exodus 10:1 through Exodus 13:16, which peaks with the tenth plague, killing the firstborn Egyptians.

I asked, "What makes this plague different from all the other plagues the Egyptians endured?"

The first nine plagues seem like a Greek drama starring three protagonists: God, Moses, and Pharaoh. Aaron is a supporting player. The mass of Jewish slaves have no individuality. Their voices merge into one Greek chorus.

But for the big one, the tenth plague, every Israelite must act individually. Every adult in the community has to take a stand. Each Israelite first has to decide to be free, then act free. Each one rejects the Egyptian gods by slaughtering a lamb, an animal Egyptians worshipped. Then the Israelites publicly proclaim they no longer wish to live there, marking their doorposts with the lambs' blood.

I explained that only by defying Egypt publicly could those slaves become free. And only through each individual declaration of independence could they join together in the national exodus. Real change occurs when each person stops being controlled by fear and starts acting independently.

All this paralleled the Refuseniks' struggle against the Soviet system. Like Egyptian slavery, the Communist regime was designed to intimidate, to crush. Every Jew hoping to emigrate had to overcome overwhelming fear by soliciting an invitation from Israel, a Soviet enemy. Applying for a visa required seeking permission from each Soviet school and workplace that defined your life. Essentially, you shouted publicly, "I don't accept your gods. I want to leave this country."

And what was the payoff? In Exodus, God offers the Jewish people ... the Jewish people. The Jews leave Egypt and seven weeks later receive the Ten Commandments on Mount Sinai, accepting identity and freedom as a package deal. This would become one of our people's main missions: balancing our right to belong and to be free.

Thirty-five hundred years later, I got the great payoff by joining that journey. Once I hopped aboard, I was never alone.

THREE PERSPECTIVES

Admittedly, this book reads like an autobiography coauthored with the American historian and Zionist activist Gil Troy. And the book traces my journey from nine years in Soviet prisons to nine years in Israeli politics, then nine years in Jewish communal leadership. But this book is not exactly a memoir. Immediately after my release from the Soviet Gulag in 1986, I wrote my prison memoir, *Fear No Evil.* As for my life in freedom, in Israel, I believe I am still too young to sum it all up. After all, I was only bar mitzvahed seven years ago.

This book tells the story of the most important conversation of my life: the ongoing dialogue between Israel and the Jewish people. I first backed into it on the streets of Moscow, when I joined the movement for Jewish emigration. It is an eternal, global, meaningful, and sometimes shrill conversation that saved my life decades ago. Today, it enriches both authors' lives, as well as many others', by confronting questions about the meaning of faith, community, identity, and freedom. We believe that only through this dialogue can we continue our journey together. And that's why we believe it is a dialogue worth defending.

While wearing different titles during my subsequent journey—Refusenik, Soviet dissident, political prisoner, head of the new immigrants' party in Israel, member of Knesset (Israel's parliament), minister in four Israeli governments, human rights advocate, head of the Jewish Agency for Israel—I always remained comforted by a tremendous feeling of belonging to this ongoing conversation.

My technical drafting teacher in high school taught us that if you view any object from three dimensions—the front, top, and side—you can see its exterior fully and draw it accurately. Zeroing in from each angle highlights specific aspects of the spatial relationship. Having watched the relationship between Israel and other Jewish communities from three perspectives, I hope I can draw it accurately.

I first joined this dialogue from behind the Iron Curtain. I continued it behind prison bars. My contacts were restricted, my involvement sometimes purely imagined, but this dialogue always fortified me. Participating in it, I exercised my newly developed muscles—my newfound commitments to my people specifically and to freedom for all.

Later, as a member of the Israeli cabinet, I represented the Israeli side of the dialogue and saw Diaspora Jews as the Jewish state's cherished partners. While enjoying that bridge-building work, I did find the adjustment from dissident prisoner to party politician frustrating.

Most recently, as the head of the Jewish Agency, the Jewish world's largest nongovernmental organization, I switched perspectives again. I looked to Israel not only as the center of the Jewish world but as a tool for strengthening Jews across the globe.

When things worked well—or when we were under attack—we saw how much we had in common. But I did spend a lot of time defending Israel to Diaspora Jews and defending Diaspora Jewry to Israelis. These days, I often find myself defending the very idea of the need for the dialogue itself.

Dialogue is easy to call for but hard to pull off. To start listening and talking to one another, we don't all need a full-blown, three-dimensional perspective. But we do need to see that the sum of our common concerns is greater than the sum of our many divisions.

MY TOUGHEST CHOICE

During my journey with the Jewish people this past half century, I had to make many difficult decisions. In choosing, again and again, to join a demonstration or organize a press conference, I wasn't just planning my day or our movement's strategy. I spent thirteen years constantly weighing how far to go in my confrontations with the KGB, knowing that my freedom and my life were at stake. I had to decide with my fiancée, Avital, if we should stay together in Moscow, or if I should watch her move to

Israel the day after we married, separating us for who knew how long. I had to decide whether to combine my activism on behalf of Soviet Jews with my involvement in the general human rights movement, defying Israeli objections that the KGB would take revenge on Jews seeking exit visas. I had to decide whether to submit to the Soviet terms for my freedom or to prolong my imprisonment indefinitely.

Decades later, I had to decide whether to enter the harsh world of Israeli politics to serve as an insider helping new Russian immigrants, or to advance their interests as an outside activist staying above party politics. Once in the government, I had to decide many times whether to keep my hard-fought position as a minister serving my voters, or to resign on principle when the government moved in a direction I couldn't accept.

Then, as the head of the Jewish Agency for Israel, I had to decide how to work with Israel's government in strengthening Jewish communities worldwide and when to challenge that same government on behalf of those communities. At a few painful moments, I had to decide just how aggressively to confront my old friend, Prime Minister Benjamin Netanyahu, on behalf of Diaspora Jewry, after he had been my most reliable political partner in building bridges uniting the world Jewish community for thirty years.

Still, none of these decisions terrified me as much as my choice in 1973 to request a simple letter from my friendly boss, certifying where I worked. That was my first public step in applying for a visa to Israel. By taking it, I openly joined the Jewish dialogue.

To understand just how agonizing that act was, we have to return to the distant, chilling world that I was born into, behind the Iron Curtain, in the totalitarian void of Soviet Communism.

PART I

NINE YEARS IN PRISON

1

LIFE WITHOUT FREEDOM, LIFE WITHOUT IDENTITY

My earliest memories are of visiting the countryside for summer vacation when I was three and four years old. I was born in 1948 in Stalino, Ukraine's coal-mining and industrial center. When any of our city's five hundred thousand inhabitants glanced toward the horizon, it looked like we were surrounded by mass-produced mountains. Up close, just blocks from my home and scattered throughout the city, we could see that these hills were mounds of garbage. These *terrikons*—cone-shaped coal waste dumps—looked like they were breathing as they pulsated with noxious gases. They so blended into the landscape that people often climbed the ones near the stadium to watch soccer games for free. Whenever we walked outside, our white shirts blackened with a thin dusting of soot from the pollution piles on the ground and the smoke that so many factories belched into the air.

For me and my older brother, Leonid, our country getaway was magical. This suited the village's Russian name, Neskuchnoye, which means "not boring" or "delightful." We didn't have a dacha, a summer house. Only the elite of the elites enjoyed such luxuries. My parents scratched together a few extra rubles to rent one room in the small house of a peasant, who displaced his family to accommodate us. My parents took back-to-back vacations, with some overlap, so we kids could spend more time breathing freely, away from the city.

I loved every moment of this larger-than-life life. I delighted in waking up early and feeding the squawking chickens. I marveled as the cock started shouting mysteriously, sending the chickens diving under their coop for protection whenever a hawk hovered above, threatening to swoop down and snatch one of the brood. I enjoyed slurping down a cup of hot milk in the mornings, fresh from the cow the old lady had just milked, and, in the evenings, watching the cows return from pasture, wondering how each one knew precisely which stall to lumber into for the night. I loved drifting on a boat with my brother and parents, reaching over to tap the huge lily pads. I was fascinated, as the weeks went by, to see the apple trees bloom, and then, as the delicate flowers faded, to see the hearty, fragrant pieces of fruit appear.

LIFE WITHOUT FREEDOM

Yet, even in this romantic setting, as young as I was, as little as I understood, I sensed some sadness. Gradually, my parents' occasional comments helped me realize what was happening. The peasants we rented from were among the tens of millions of Soviets living on a kolkhoz, one of the massive collective farms the Soviet Union created, violently, starting in 1928. The farmers were desperately poor and hopelessly unfree. When a calf was born, they had to decide whether to slaughter it for meat—and pay steep taxes on it—or give it to the kolkhoz, as each family was allowed only one cow. What looked to us like the lovely, pastoral sight of peasants dragging carts by hand—even when filled with backbreakingly heavy items—reflected the fact that the kolkhoz owned all the horses. Farmers needed special permission to use them. And as soon as those apple trees blossomed, the tax authorities arrived. The taxes reflected the peasants' estimated crop output. Even if nature refused to cooperate and spoiled the harvest, they had to pay.

I vaguely remember a long, hushed conversation one summer, deep into the night, that ended with grim faces. Eventually, my father explained to me that our host had asked if my parents had the right connections to take his daughter to the city to serve as our nanny. It seemed to be her only shot at leaving their life of virtual slavery.

The biggest obstacle the teenager faced was getting access to her identity papers, which the kolkhoz held. Every Soviet citizen above the age of sixteen needed an identity certificate to travel. Without it, you couldn't register once you reached your destination, which we all had to do when-ever we visited anywhere—for business or pleasure, for a few days or a few months—or risk arrest.

In the cities, we always carried our internal passports. We faced other restrictions as well, such as not being able to relocate to a popular lo-cation like Moscow. The Soviet authorities understood that Moscow could not become the Communist showcase to the world—full of special goods—that they wanted it to be if they didn't restrict access to most Soviet citizens. But the Soviet Union was big enough to offer us city folk alternatives. Members of these collective farms, which made up almost half the country, had no such options. Without easy access to their IDs, they were like serfs, bound to the kolkhoz.

My father, sympathetic but powerless, sighed, "Those poor people. We're so much luckier than they are." It's always good to feel you have more freedom than someone else.

REWRITING HISTORY AGAIN AND AGAIN

Although the restrictions on physical movement varied, the restrictions on traveling through time—by learning history—were imposed uni-formly. The Soviets collectivized the past, treating it as state property to be shaped at will.

I was born one hundred years after Karl Marx and Friedrich Engels published the *Communist Manifesto* in 1848, dreaming the socialist dream of mass equality imposed through class struggle, and thirty years after the October Revolution of 1917, when the Bolsheviks started im-plementing this Marxist dream mercilessly. My parents, Ida Milgrom and Boris Shcharansky, were born before the revolution—he in 1904, she in 1908. Married in 1929, they were childless when my father went to fight the Nazis for what ended up being four years of war, from 1941 to 1945. My older brother Leonid was born in 1946. I arrived two years later.

My father had a big library housing a few thousand books. Almost every payday he purchased another volume or two to squeeze into our small two-room apartment, hemming us in more and more. My mother never knew how expensive these books would be. Even with a father working as a journalist and a mother working as a senior economist, we ran out of money most months—as did almost everyone we knew.

Like most of the Russian intelligentsia, and especially the Russian Jewish intelligentsia, we enjoyed escaping into the Russian, French, German, and English classics the censors didn't ban. These books allowed for more intellectual latitude, especially those that were written centuries before the Industrial and the Bolshevik Revolutions. My first favorites were *Robinson Crusoe* and *Gulliver's Travels*.

In addition to the proliferating classics, the beautifully bound, majestically dark-blue volumes of the second edition of *The Great Soviet Encyclopedia* began arriving in our home as early as I can remember.

The authorities touted this achievement loudly. From 1950 to 1958, fifty volumes, with one hundred thousand entries, would be published to "show the superiority of socialist culture over the culture of the capitalist world." These big, thick volumes—our *Encyclopaedia Britannica*, or perhaps, for today's readers, our Wikipedia—impressed me as a boy, brimming as they were with entries explaining history and geography, mathematics and science. I knew that if I was patient enough, eventually the right volumes would arrive and teach me everything I wanted to know. Meanwhile, I learned what I could while appreciating the books themselves. They were very fat and I was very short. I often used one or two volumes to prop myself up in my chair so I could reach our table to do my homework more comfortably.

Alas, the Soviet publishers—aware that the authorities used education to develop "the Communist morality, ideology, and Soviet patriotism" and "inspire unshakable love toward the Soviet fatherland, the Communist Party, and its leaders"—had a problem. In reducing history to propaganda, officials kept changing it to fit the ever-evolving party line. Overnight, leaders could be flipped from progressive socialists to sectarian lackeys of imperialism. People long dead could be boosted or downgraded, depending on the latest twist in some doctrinal debate. Whole branches of knowledge, from cybernetics to genetics, could go from illegal "bourgeois false sciences" to exemplary subjects with the flick of a bureaucrat's pen—or the shift of an autocrat's whim. Living politicians' reputations, of course, were particularly volatile.

As the Communist leaders purged people and shifted tactics, the harried editors kept updating these printed bricks. Especially challenging were people whose last names began with letters early in the alphabet. As the encyclopedia's production slowed, names further down the alphabetical order could have their roles in history changed numerous times without requiring any reprints.

One of the first corrections I remember came after 1953, when Nikita Khrushchev rose to power and purged Lavrentiy Beria, Stalin's brutal head of the NKVD, the secret police. My father soon received a publisher's letter addressed to every subscriber, instructing him to cut out the three-page article praising Beria in the B volume, destroy it, and replace it with some new B entries sent along to fill the space. My father smiled, shrugged, and followed the orders. Subsequently, as politicians rose or fell out of favor, as scientists were exiled or rehabilitated, every reader had to scramble to keep up with the shifting official line.

To those of us living in democracies today, the image of my father sitting at home and razor blading out a page to glue in the newly updated replacement might seem ridiculous. Officials were not going to knock on the door and check. Still, he figured, why take a chance?

Early on, my father taught us that "the walls have ears." The secret police recruited millions of people as informers. Only after Communism fell did we realize just how extensive the network of informants was. During the never-ending winter of the Soviet regime, you never knew who might report you: it could be a neighbor in the cramped communal apartments, a jealous colleague, even a desperate friend. You didn't know who might visit and open a volume mistakenly—or intentionally.

So, not wanting to take chances, my father played the role of true believer, treating history like putty.

LIFE IN SOVIET "PARADISE"

Beyond these fears were the irritations, big and small, of day-to-day life. We were one of three families sharing two rooms apiece in a communal apartment, each room no larger than fifteen square meters. Seventeen of us shared one kitchen uncomfortably. We waited in line endlessly for the one toilet. Each family was assigned one day for bathing. This weekly ritual included boiling water on the stove, then ferrying it quickly to the bathtub.

Squabbling about nonsense, from who cleaned what to who used that, was inevitable. Applying her organizational skills as the Ukrainian coal ministry's senior economist, my mother created a chart distributing the errands proportionally. Then, predictably, arguments erupted over just how her schedule should be followed.

Outside our little home, there was plenty of waiting and frustration. The typical day began with one family member dashing out at 6 a.m. to wait in the first of many lines, this one for milk. Within the first hour, the day's milk supply would vanish. We continued, often securing one consumer item at a time—eggs, cabbage, soap—from one endless line after another. Fashionable clothes or a baby carriage required elite connections. In this world of constant waiting, line management itself became a science.

Yet, despite the cramping, the quibbling, and the waiting, we knew we were in paradise—or at least we acted as if we knew that whenever anyone was watching. We grew up on perpetual official propaganda, in school and on the street. Party slogans, feeding us the lines we were supposed to mouth, were as ever present as the soot. We should "thank Comrade Stalin" for our happy childhoods. We were not just lucky but the luckiest people in history, to be born in the Soviet Union.

Then, under Joseph Stalin's successor, Nikita Khrushchev, the Communist Party Congress introduced fresh slogans boosting its "New Program" to accelerate the revolution. Now we parroted the line that we were the luckiest ever, because "THE CURRENT GENERATION OF SOVIET PEOPLE WILL LIVE UNDER COMMUNISM." Posters proclaiming that slogan followed us everywhere, seemingly as tall as those toxic *terrikons* enveloping our city.

We were approaching the end of history, the party proclaimed, the culmination of humanity's long struggle for justice and proletarian bliss. Communism was now ready to bring us to the final stage of the centuries-long class struggle, guaranteeing "from each according to his means, to each according to his needs."

Communism was a mass-produced dream, a quick ticket to paradise that captured the imaginations of millions of people suffering as their ancestors had. The socialist promise of equality was seductive. But, unavoidably, Communism implemented this utopian idea heavy-handedly, from "the brotherhood of the people" to "the dictatorship of the proletariat"—at KGB gunpoint.

Although a peculiarly godless religion, Communism had its own apostles: Karl Marx, Friedrich Engels, Vladimir Lenin, Joseph Stalin. We fused their sacred names together: MarxEngelsLeninStalin. Their four faces seemed to blur into one another in so many of the supersized propaganda posters surrounding us. It was as if all four were watching, all the time.

The romantic-sounding idea of mass equality and of Communism as the final stage of redemption came wrapped in a package of violence directly from Marx. Contrary to the false nostalgia surrounding him and his socialist ideas today, Marx emphasized that paradise had to be built using all means necessary, no matter how vile or violent. There "is only one way in which the murderous death agonies of the old society and the bloody birth throes of the new society can be shortened, simplified, and concentrated," he wrote in 1848, "and that way is revolutionary terror."

While Marx imagined the proletarian revolution that would create a classless society, Lenin and Stalin brought it to life—by putting people to death. For people to be equal, the state had to remove all differences, be they material, religious, or national. So the state squelched all individualism and creativity. It nationalized all property, controlled the economy, owned everything, and distributed it in a supposedly just way. The party mocked religion as the opiate of the masses as the state destroyed many churches, mosques, and synagogues, all while confiscating their property. The state prohibited any "deviant" nationalist expressions.

People naturally resisted. They wanted their own businesses and their own identities, both religious and national. In response, the machinery of repression blossomed. Lenin initially expected to kill a few hundred capitalists. The death toll escalated quickly to thousands, then millions.

When Stalin rose to power in the mid-1920s, the regime's totalitarian assault on freedom intensified. It stripped some identities particularly brutally. Stalin insisted there could be no diversity, no individuality, no classes. He sought to turn everyone into the "New Soviet Man," cleansed of any loyalties except to the Communist Party. Soviet citizens were expected to echo, with great pride, variations of Stalin's favorite line about "how happy we are to serve as cogs in one big Communist machine."

The town where I was born was abruptly renamed Stalino in the 1920s. In 1961, when I was thirteen, Khrushchev's people purged the town's name, just as abruptly, of any link to that mass murderer. We were told to call our town Donetsk.

By the time I was born, the Soviet dictatorship had asserted its absolute power over us. It had destroyed traditional institutions, having nationalized and collectivized them. It had mass murdered, imprisoned in the Gulag, or exiled to Siberia the bourgeoisie and other "class enemies," along with those belonging to "reactionary nations" like Crimean Tatars or Chechens, by the millions. Industrialists, engineers, clerics, intellectuals, local politicians—anyone suspected of disloyalty or belonging to the wrong class or nation—had disappeared. Historians estimate that under Stalin as many as twenty-five million people were swallowed into the Gulag. This chilling word, the acronym for the Russian phrase "the main administration of camps," described the Soviets' suffocating web of forced-labor camps, prison camps, and prisons.

A repressive regime needs external enemies, not just internal traitors, to justify its control. The Soviet Union had a constantly evolving rationale for war: defending the proletariat from capitalist countries and advancing the worldwide Communist Revolution. Eventually, they called this "the struggle of progressive forces for peace" against the capitalist world, led by the United States of America.

I grew up knowing the United States as a big bad brute. A typical cartoon would show a power-hungry, greedy, grotesque Uncle Sam holding a baton in one hand (for beating African Americans) and grasping a handful of missiles in the other (for targeting progressive nations like North Korea, the People's Republic of China, the East German Democratic Republic, and the Soviet motherland).

In this propagandistic Cold War between the Soviet Union and the United States, the Soviet people living in "Communist paradise" had to be protected from capitalist influence. That's why the authorities closed borders, prohibited immigration, banned contact with foreigners, and electronically jammed foreign radio broadcasts in Russian. The Iron Curtain divided the free world from the Communist world.

Dictators don't need to use terror, purges, and mass murders forever. After seizing power, the regime's main mission became keeping control. It turned life into a permanent loyalty test. You had to express your devotion constantly, loudly, and ostentatiously. Every speech that was scheduled, every parade organized, every class taken, every exam administered, and every conversation initiated provided an opportunity to prove your loyalty. Every state goody, large or small, was at stake. It could be an extra day off from your boss or a resort getaway provided by your union. Or it could be your career, your status, your future, or your freedom.

The KGB—the secret police—maintained control through fear. You feared deviating from the party line. You feared the mysterious network of informers. You feared not demonstrating enough loyalty. You feared something you believed might slip out. You feared hearing someone else's slip of the tongue and being asked about it. You feared not showing up to the right meeting, not saying the right thing, not demonstrating the right amount of loyalty.

Fueling the fear was the unsettling awareness of a parallel world you could fall into instantly. Just say the wrong thing, discuss the wrong topic, make the wrong gesture, break the wrong rule, and you, too, could vanish, as people on our block had, as people in our family had.

We called it casually, even flippantly, *mesta-nyestol-odalyonniye*: "The place that is not too far." You didn't need to see anyone disappear or know victims personally. Like the smog hanging over the city, you just knew that the world of camps and prisons, though actually thousands of kilometers removed, was just one misstep away. You could find yourself there any minute, for any reason, without understanding why.

RAISED IN ANTI-SEMITISM:
LIFE WITHOUT IDENTITY

Growing up Jewish in the Soviet Union offered nothing positive. No Jewish tradition. No Jewish institutions. No Jewish culture. No Jewish history. No Jewish holidays. No Jewish books. No circumcision. No bar mitzvah. No Jewish language. My parents sometimes used Yiddish as a secret code in front of the kids but never tried to teach us. The only real Jewish experience I had was facing anti-Semitism.

I could have had a Jewish name. My grandfather wanted me to be Natan, in memory of his father. But burdening a child with the Hebrew name of a biblical prophet at the height of Stalin's anti-Semitism was too provocative. Instead, my parents gave me the neutral name Anatoly. Still, Grandpa Moshe called me Natanchik.

As good doublethinkers, my parents had made one big gesture to remind us and our relatives that we were Jewish. They possessed a one-and-a-half-foot-tall replica of Hermann Prell's 1899 sculpture of David, standing triumphantly, with his slingshot in hand and one foot on Goliath's severed head. (We recently discovered it's often misnamed "Prometheus.")

This statue was far too large for our small apartment, far fancier than anything else we owned, and far too explicit for us as young boys. I woke up every morning to the sight of David's nakedness.

My mother's somewhat better-off sister had bought the sculpture in a local market and given it to us; we imagined it had been looted somewhere in Europe as World War II ended. In the 1440s, the original Donatello was the first freestanding bronze nude an artist had made since Greco-Roman days.

The embarrassing, lifeless relic represented my first exposure to Jewish history. My father tried. He told us stories of biblical heroes, saying, "You have nothing to be ashamed of—we are not cowards—but be careful, don't talk much about it."

I certainly didn't, especially because the rare reminders that I was Jewish usually made me cringe. At school, when the teachers periodically had a formal roll call, they would read each pupil's name, surname, date of birth, and nationality—that dreaded designation from the fifth line of our identity cards. True, cosmopolitan Communism at its purest dismissed nationality, but during World War II Stalin discovered that national pride was a useful motivator.

Most kids in the class were Russian or Ukrainian. Being Russian meant belonging to the most progressive nation. Russia united us all on the journey toward Communism. Russia's heroic soldiers had defeated Hitler in the Great Patriotic War. Being Ukrainian meant having local pride and being the Russians' closest brothers. In Ukraine, we were constantly toasting what the authorities insisted was a voluntary partnership with Russia, three centuries strong. If someone had told me that in six decades a brutal war would hit my hometown, I would have predicted a clash between Earth and Mars as more likely than one between Russia and Ukraine.

Other nationalities were rarely mentioned and usually overlooked—Armenians, Lithuanians, Kazakhs. But when the word "Jew" was uttered, after my name and that of two or three other students during roll call, it prompted an awkward silence, a grimace from the teacher, and a mean joke about sniveling Jews from the class clown. Occasionally a teacher might intervene, claiming, "We Soviets don't discriminate." But, usually, being outed as Jewish was like being diagnosed with some debilitating disease.

Similarly, we were most frequently the butt of the many ethnic jokes kids lobbed around the schoolyard. Russians might have been naive and drunk, but they were noble. Ukrainians might have been stupid and drunk, but they were sincere. Jews, while sober, were cunning, greedy, cowardly parasites. Even close friends sometimes remarked, "You're such a good guy. It's a pity you're a Jew."

All I got from being Jewish was discomfort and vulnerability, fed by the crude anti-Semitism of the street and the systemic anti-Semitism of the state. The street continued the old Russian prejudice against Jews as Christ killers and money-grubbers. The state superimposed onto that tradition a new Communist hatred of Jews as cosmopolites whose loyalty to the Soviet regime was always in question. We could not discuss the prejudice we faced because, in our worker's paradise, anti-Semitism officially didn't exist.

One of my earliest memories is proudly walking with my father, hand in hand, in the streets of our city. It's Victory Day, celebrating the Soviets' World War II triumph. I'm proud because my father's chest is covered with the medals and decorations he earned during four years of fighting for the Red Army, from the Caucasus to Budapest to Vienna.

"Hey, kike, where did you buy those medals?" some passerby yells. "In Tashkent?" The meaning is clear, even to my five-year-old self: when we Russians were defending you against Hitler, you Jews were cowering behind our backs in safe faraway places like Uzbekistan.

"He's only a drunk hooligan," Dad says, squeezing my hand harder as we hurry away.

Not all the stereotypes about Jews were negative, although we always felt caricatured. Once, the father of a high school friend told me, "I often tell my son, 'Stick to your Jewish classmates and their families.'" He explained, "Their fathers are not drunkards, they don't beat their wives, and their kids study all the time."

There was some truth there. On the evenings after paydays, which came twice a month, you saw many drunken men lying on park benches or snoring away on the sidewalks. Others hurried to drink as much vodka as they could on the way home, before their wives took the remaining cash for household necessities. The police ran extra patrols on those days, gathering many men to sleep it off in the drunk tank.

Of course, not all Jews were sober and not all non-Jews were drunk. But their tendency to exaggerate about us publicly fed our tendency to exaggerate about them privately.

Like most Jewish families we knew, the outside world's pressures bonded us together. In our family we grew up missing many things, but certainly not love. Even the financial tensions, or the outbursts we hadn't specifically expected but always kind of knew were coming, didn't take away from the deep love filling our small apartment.

Although they never talked about it, my parents were grieving. The Nazis had killed many relatives and friends. The years of Stalin's purges—when they went to sleep at night unsure whether they would wake up at home or on the way to prison—left their mark on my parents' faces, although I only comprehended this years later.

All these silent scars only reinforced the central message: work doubly hard to succeed. People hear that today and think we were under pressure to make our parents look good. That wasn't it. Succeeding professionally—especially in science—was the only possible protection against constant uncertainty. Political careers were impossible. Military careers were impossible. The Jewish path to respectability involved more objective subjects, like engineering and medicine.

My parents' love didn't depend on my performance. I was expected to excel, but I knew that love was guaranteed from them, regardless of how well I did.

PLAYING NEAR PROOF OF A HOLOCAUST
THAT NEVER HAPPENED

In stripping away Jewish identity, Jewish history, and Jewish literacy, the state also deprived us of knowledge about the Holocaust, which had occurred only a few years before, precisely where we lived.

I was born two and a half years after the war ended, in the heart of one of the Germans' main killing fields. From 1941 to 1944, Nazi *Einsatzgruppen*, working with their Ukrainian collaborators, murdered nearly one million Jews, usually by spraying them with machine-gun fire. Even though many of my relatives died in Kiev, Odessa, and right in our town, we never heard anything about it.

As children, signs of the Great Patriotic War were all around us. There were constant references at home, at school, on the radio, and on the street to the Soviet Union's long, painful, bloody victory over Adolf Hitler and the Nazis. We often attended ceremonies celebrating Communism's heroic 1945 defeat of fascism. We romped on abandoned, rusting tanks that hung around our town for many years. We constantly played war games, competing for the honor of "belonging" to the noble Red Army, the forces of light who defeated the Nazi forces of darkness. We often compared childish versions of our fathers' war stories, arguing about who faced the greatest danger and who won the most medals.

Yet, while talking incessantly about the war, we couldn't talk about the war against the Jews at all. Official documents mentioned Jews far down the long list of victims, after Soviet soldiers, Soviet partisans, Soviet prisoners of war, innocent Soviet civilians, and Romani. Only decades later did I discover that we were living—and playing—near monstrous proof of the Holocaust that officially never happened. Our playgrounds were some of the bloodiest sites in Jewish history—in human history.

Only a few miles from our apartment building was a shaft in the Rykovskaya mine. After Babi Yar, it is the second largest mass grave in Ukraine of civilians the Nazis murdered. At 365 meters deep and 15 meters wide, it may be the deepest pile of corpses the Nazis left behind.

The Nazis and their local sympathizers often marched people to that pit in groups, then shot them at the edge, so the bodies would fall in without the killers' hands getting dirty. They threw most children into the pit alive—screaming and crying and dying a slow death as other bodies piled on and suffocated them. Many believe the majority of the seventy-five thousand civilians buried there were Jewish.

The Soviet Union, however, didn't recognize the Nazis' systematic slaughter of the Jews. Therefore, it didn't exist, just like anti-Semitism itself. Our parents didn't want to talk about all those friends and relatives who had disappeared. It was too painful to remember the truth, and too ridiculous to participate in the self-censorship the Soviets' new Big Lie demanded.

In the same neighborhood where we played so innocently, seventy-five thousand people—possibly more—had been murdered most brutally. German soldiers had poured in caustic soda to disinfect, seal, and mask this pit of death just outside where we lived. The Nazis had made the corpses disappear, reducing their bodies to biomass. The Soviets furthered the cover-up, making the memories of who the victims were and why they died disappear too.

The cover-up was intentional. When the Red Army first freed territory from Nazi rule in 1943—after two years of cruel occupation—the victorious Soviets arrested Nazi collaborators, collected evidence, and brought several killers to justice. The initial trials were very emotional. Onlookers screamed in agony, and some fainted, as they heard witnesses' incomprehensible tales of the Nazi hell that had incinerated their loved ones. Yet, even while prosecuting Nazis and their collaborators, the So-viets increasingly obscured the Jewish dimension of the Nazi war crimes.

Stalin blocked the publication of *The Black Book of Soviet Jewry*, filled with eyewitness testimonies, which Ilya Ehrenburg and Vasily Grossman compiled in 1944. Their witnesses emphasized the Nazis' anti-Jewish ob-session. The KGB also seized archives detailing the war against the Jews, burying any related documents behind top-secret labels. Special commu-nity memorial books chronicling the Holocaust, town by town, were out-lawed. Like Beria's biography in our Soviet encyclopedia, the Holocaust had to be cut from the pages of history and replaced.

By the time I was frolicking in those killing fields, the totalitarian regime had nearly wiped the Nazi mass murder of Jews from the col-lective memory banks. The Soviet power to shape public opinion—or at least public conversation—was astonishing. Month after month, the government erected war monument after war monument. As a Young Pioneer, I regularly attended solemn ceremonies commemorating a par-tisan's heroism, an officer's sacrifice, this Nazi mass murder, that site of civilian suffering. Such plaques proliferated without mentioning the ap-proximately 1.3 million Jews murdered in those same places throughout the Soviet Union.

What happened?

One day, Stalin decided it was the Jews' turn to become the target. Historians argue about what motivated him. The global solidarity Jews felt as a people clearly infuriated him. Communist ideology belittled any ties beyond its version of intersectionality: that all workers shared similar stories of oppression and an overriding loyalty to the Soviet state.

Still, during the war, Stalin exploited Jews' sense of peoplehood. Shortly after the Nazis invaded Russia in 1941, Stalin launched the Jew-ish Anti-Fascist Committee. He hoped that emphasizing Nazi atroci-ties against Jews would solidify his awkward new alliance with Western democracies. The committee's success in raising more than $30 million, mostly from American and British Jews, ultimately made him suspicious. The committee's chairman, the actor and director Solomon Mikhoels, addressed huge crowds in the West. He claimed the Soviet Union was not anti-Semitic, only to be murdered during Stalin's anti-Semitic purge in 1948.

In October 1948, Stalin seethed when the Jews of Moscow shouted "Am Yisrael Chai"—the Jewish people live—in their euphoric welcome to the first ambassador from the new state of Israel, Golda Meyerson, later Golda Meir. Hostile to particularistic identities, committed to demolishing Jewish pride, and seeking to prove that the Jews were not a nation, Stalin set out to reduce Jewish "influence." He deployed whatever pretexts he could. In a depressingly time-honored tale, he used Nazi propaganda while denazifying liberated areas. As a well-connected journalist, my father saw a Communist Party directive from higher-ups shortly after the war insisting that, because the Nazis had demonized the Soviet regime as Jew dominated, Jews should not return to powerful positions.

Especially after the winter of 1948–1949, Stalin targeted Jewish cultural leaders aggressively. As the government persecuted Jewish actors, writers, intellectuals, and doctors, mention of the Jewish dimension of the Holocaust became inconvenient. Officially, Stalin's propaganda couldn't target the Jews, because the Soviet Union was too progressive to be anti-Semitic. He simply attacked "rootless cosmopolitans" and "bourgeois nationalist Zionists," Communist code for the Jews.

Anti-Semitism is the most plastic hatred—flexible, shapeable, but durable. Just as Jew-haters traditionally attacked Jews as Rothschilds and Marxists, capitalists and Communists, Stalin attacked Jews as universalistic and particularistic.

Stalin was a pioneer in using anti-Zionist rhetoric to spread anti-Semitism. When he and his propagandists attacked "Zionist agents," Soviet citizens understood their Jewish neighbors were targeted, despite most Soviet Jews having no connection to Israel and no idea what Zionism meant. Fifty years later, as anti-Zionism went global, I would develop specific criteria distinguishing legitimate criticism of Israel from the kind of anti-Semitic shorthand Stalin's modern successors used so cleverly.

When Joseph Stalin died in 1953, I was five. The seventy-four-year-old despot was at the peak of his anti-Semitic campaign, torturing Jewish physicians falsely accused of trying to assassinate Soviet leaders in the "Doctor's Plot." The resulting show trial was intended to launch a broader crusade, with some insiders proposing mass firings of Jews and even mass deportations from major cities.

We had no inkling of these plots. Nor did I know that the day Stalin died was already a Jewish holiday, Purim. Like many Jewish festivals, it celebrates our deliverance from an evil politician with mass murder on his mind, in this case Haman. My father would never mention a cosmic coincidence like that to me. Perhaps he didn't know. Even if he had linked the two salvations, it wouldn't have meant anything to me.

On that March day, out of any neighbor's earshot, my father told my older brother and me, "Today is a great day that you should always remember. This is good news for us Jews. This man was very dangerous to us. Remember all your life that this miracle happened when we were endangered. But," he added, "don't tell this to anybody. Do what everybody else does." In kindergarten the next day, as we sang songs honoring Stalin, "the hope of all the people," and mourned his death, I had no idea how many children were crying sincerely, and how many were only following their fathers' instructions.

DOUBLETHINK

The end of Stalin's life, therefore, marked the beginning of my conscious life as a doublethinker. This round-the-clock public charade would define my life for the next fifteen years. That didn't make me special. Most Soviet citizens eventually entered this deceptive order of doublethinkers.

My father's main distraction from this double life was listening to Voice of America in Russian and other free world radio stations. The Soviets responded by trying to jam the frequency. In October 1956, he was listening so intensely to the radio—with his ear to the speaker and the volume high, but not so loud as to attract the neighbors' attention—that he was practically inside the receiver.

He wasn't listening to learn about Israel's Sinai War against Egypt that month. He wanted to hear about Hungarians resisting Soviet power. "Ach," he said, quietly. "If they could only succeed." Later, when our neighbor came by, my father repeated, "Ach, if they could only succeed." But the "they" my father now meant was the Soviet tanks.

In this web of lies, your main job is to fit in. At the age of ten you join the Pioneers, proclaiming your patriotism. Then you join the Komsomol, the All-Union Leninist Young Communist League, proclaiming your patriotism. You mouth their platitudes, you play the good citizen, to get ahead.

KHRUSHCHEV'S THAW

My father guessed correctly that the pressure would lessen after Stalin. By 1956, the new leader, Nikita Khrushchev, denounced the old dictator's "cult of personality." Launching the historical moment known as the Thaw, the new regime released prisoners. It rehabilitated the reputations of many executed innocents. It acknowledged historical "mistakes." The level of fear declined.

Gradually, as the Thaw loosened tongues, some family secrets emerged. Names I had never heard before, pictures I had never seen, resurfaced. A surprising photograph of my grandfather with four sons, not three, introduced me to an uncle my father never mentioned who was living abroad. His older brother Shamai had moved to Palestine during the revolution's early years, fulfilling my grandfather's dream for all his children.

When his brother moved away, my father wasn't buying the Zionist dream. Attracted by the promise of full equality, trusting that Communist universalism would eliminate anti-Semitism, he couldn't imagine escaping from this newly welcoming Eastern European experiment into a Middle Eastern ghetto. Within a few years, however, my father had buried his illusions along with his purged friends. (When, in the late 1970s, my wife, Avital, was traveling the world to free me and finally met my uncle Shamai Sharon, he was proud of his nephew, the Zionist.)

As more memories flowed, things that had never made sense to me suddenly did. I discovered why my father had left his promising screenwriting career in an Odessa studio for an under-the-radar journalism job covering mining in a backwater town. When professional rivals placed an article in his hometown Odessa newspaper denouncing him as a petit-bourgeois intellectual with a Zionist brother, he feared being purged. I discovered that my mother's unnaturally silent brother-in-law, Matvei Isaiahyevich, had spent a year in a KGB prison in 1937 and still couldn't talk about what he had endured. I discovered that another uncle, my mother's brother Munya, who died abruptly in 1953, had killed himself. Serving during the war on a troika (a special military tribunal that signed death sentences without due process) had left this once successful lawyer guilt ridden and despondent. My mother considered her brother yet another victim of Stalin and his purges. I even discovered relatives killed in the Holocaust, and relatives still suffering in the aftermath. The arrested uncle's sister, Paulina, never recovered from seeing most of her family shot to death in front of her, having escaped their fate by sheer luck.

Like my parents telling our family secrets, many citizens started spilling the hidden truths of the Soviet Union. When leaders start speaking more openly about past abuses, it bubbles over. Suddenly, people start speaking more openly about present problems too. As self-censorship weakens, the desire to speak up grows.

The long-suppressed Russian intelligentsia stirred. Artists, poets, playwrights, novelists, journalists, and students tested the new boundaries of debate with particular zeal. Authorities quickly recognized the growing danger. Even if criticizing yesterday's mistakes was OK, the regime could not tolerate public disagreement with the party line.

The most dangerous moment for any totalitarian regime is when the masses lose their fear and individuals cross from doublethinking privately to dissenting publicly. However, the terror lingered, and the authorities had no need to replicate Stalin's mass repression. They simply reminded citizens that dissent would not be tolerated. Red lines remained in a post-Stalin, still-totalitarian Soviet Union.

The end of Stalin's most violent anti-Jewish persecutions had tipped off my family that the Thaw was beginning, and in the same way we saw that the Thaw was ending through a Jewish lens. Had Yevgeny Yevtushenko's 1961 poem, "Babi Yar," stuck to the Nazis' 1941 massacre of the Jews, the Soviet leaders probably would have tolerated his reintegrating Jews into the World War II story. But, emboldened to tell the truth, Yevtushenko condemned Russian anti-Semitism, from the czars to the Soviets. The poem begins bitterly: "No monument stands over Babi Yar."

Only in a regime that could tolerate no criticism could a 311-word poem become so volatile and influential. Its honesty led many Jews to believe that, finally, the truth about anti-Semitism—and other truths—could be told. But its categorical rawness helped doom the Thaw. Within days, state flunkies wrote their own poems and journalistic lackeys wrote their own editorials, all defending Communism absolutely. Who are these cosmopolitan poets to teach us? the party hacks asked indignantly. How dare you accuse the great Soviet state of anti-Semitism? We defeated the anti-Semitic Nazis and saved the world!

So, just as some finally started speaking about the Holocaust in Jewish terms, the authorities panicked and counterattacked. They cracked down on Yevtushenko and other former doublethinkers who were inching down that inevitable highway toward free thought, free speech, and dissent. Honest history was too volatile; exposing the crimes of the past risked exposing the lies of the present.

By the time I was fifteen years old, the fear had returned. We were all doublethinking again. When the Soviets eventually erected a monument at Babi Yar, the word "Jew" still didn't appear. Having tasted some freedom made this step backward especially embittering. We now felt our slavery more keenly. The more imprisoned you feel by totalitarian thought, the more you feel compelled to escape. But some effects of the Thaw lingered. The line had moved. Now to be targeted, you actually had to dissent, and, bit by bit, a dissident movement would emerge.

Even though Stalin's harshest anti-Jewish persecutions had petered out, the regime's baseline anti-Semitism persisted. By high school, I was excruciatingly familiar with the phrase "he has a fifth line problem." It meant you were being discriminated against because that fifth line, defining nationality, on your Soviet identity papers identified you as a Jew—meaning traitorous, incorrigible, unassimilable, disloyal, other. It meant my brother Leonid could pass his written exams but hear in an interview, "Why are you so happy you passed? I won't let Jews into *my* school." Despite being stripped of our freedom and our identity, Jews remained the convenient scapegoats. Every dictatorship needs an enemy, and Jews were a favorite target.

The hatred, however, fostered Jewish solidarity. Many of us trusted one another with our deep secret: we hated the regime privately while loving it publicly. We rarely mentioned such matters outside of our inner circles; informers were everywhere. We would ask "Yid?" or "Nostrum est?" (Is he one of us?), our code for figuring out who was Jewish and possibly trustworthy. We used the Latin phrase so often I thought it was Yiddish.

"YOU ARE A JEW. YOU HAVE TO BE THE BEST": SEEKING ESCAPE

The older I got, the more I confronted the sophisticated anti-Semitism of the system rather than the thuggish anti-Semitism of the street. Family discussions constantly turned to talk about discrimination, restrictions, insults, and unfair burdens. We learned where you could go to study, as well as which institutions never accepted Jews, no matter how qualified. We learned which positions were impossible for a Jew to get and which careers paths were possible. We learned about promotions earned by Jews, yet not granted, or promotions won by non-Jews, yet not deserved. I got the message: You are a Jew, so you have to be the best in physics, or mathematics, or chess, or whatever you do, to have a shot at succeeding in this system. And you will have to twist and turn in all kinds of ways just to survive.

Once a year, the newspaper published the list of laureates for the Stalin Prize, later called the Lenin Prize, for excellence in science, literature, arts, architecture, and technology. The whole family scrutinized the list. Whenever someone recognized a Jewish name, we cheered. It meant that one more Jew had succeeded despite all the discrimination. It encouraged us to work harder, because we, too, might progress. This is how we got used to surviving that disorder we were born with, the one called being Jewish.

When I was five, my mother taught me to play chess. "Here you can think freely," she said. "In chess, you can fly." I tried playing and fell in love immediately: thoughts soar, risks are taken, wits and courage are prized, not punished. Chess became my first passport into the world of free thought, my first great escape.

I loved the game because I could win, even defeating people who were much older or bigger than me. My theory was, the taller the guy, the quicker I beat him. I loved playing blind, without looking at the board. I loved playing simultaneously with many grown-ups. And I loved believing that I could one day be the world champion. In fact, when I understood, after competing on a national level, that I probably wouldn't make it that far, I started looking for another career where I could shine—and that's how I became a political prisoner.

But I'm jumping ahead of the story.

Growing up in the Soviet Union in the 1950s and 1960s, many non-Jewish Jews like me escaped into the chess world. We were stripped of our identities. We didn't know what being Jewish meant, beyond offering another reason to fear the authorities and providing one more set of restrictions in this unfree world.

We had heard estimates that Jews were limited to 5 percent of the student body in a provincial university, no more than 2 percent in a place like Moscow, and barely 1 percent in the best universities. But in a chess club, it seemed the quotas limited non-Jews: 70, 80, 90 percent of the chess players were Jewish.

Only decades later did I realize how deeply programmed Jews were to love these chess clubs. I was already living in Israel when I first visited a yeshiva, a rabbinic seminary, with its massive *bet midrash*, or study hall. The room was filled with hundreds of *chevrutot*, pairs of students learning together, arguing together, trying to outwit one another, and mastering a system of thought, the Talmud and Jewish law.

As I heard the familiar buzzing throughout the *bet midrash*, I realized how similar the two institutions looked, with people paired up, debating back and forth. In competitive chess, there are few openings and end-games, but innumerable ways in between; the arguments never end. In the yeshiva world, there are 613 commandments and a few defining texts, but similarly innumerable interpretations, explanations, ambiguities, and positions, along with endless on-the-one-hands and on-the-other-hands.

In both worlds, as the duos compete against one another intensely, they also work together, seeking a *chidush*, a breakthrough, a new move, an innovative gambit. When the Soviet Union outlawed the traditional dialogue that energized Jews for centuries, we shifted gears. We started on-the-one-handing about chess instead of Halachah, Jewish law.

Alas, while chess could free my mind and sharpen my wits, it was only a game. It lacked Judaism's depth and moral majesty. It offered no wisdom, no ideological worldview, no way of life, nothing greater than myself and my skills. It was a great diversion, freeing me from doublethink for a few hours every day, but it wasn't real. It was an escape into a parallel black-and-white world of thirty-two pieces on an eight-by-eight board.

Science and mathematics seemed to promise a better escape from the smothering Soviet reality. While as objective and creative as chess, the scientific method illuminated the real world. A scientist applied whatever talents he had to understand how the universe worked.

Mastering these fields also seemed to offer the best path to a better life. To pass every exam, no matter how difficult, with the highest marks and to be accepted to one of the best universities, became my great ambition. It was the dream driving every Jewish mother.

When I was accepted to the MFTI, the Moscow Institute of Physics and Technology, the Soviet MIT, in 1966, I felt like I had arrived. I had reached the doublethinker's summit, the greatest success I could hope for. This world represented as far as I could go as a Jew. I was lucky; I was one of the last Jews accepted to study there.

Now, I could start enjoying the great payoff after years of beefing up my portfolio to prove myself academically capable and ideologically pure. In high school, I studied extra hard for test after test, overcompensating for my Jewish handicap. Drowning in problem sets, working around the clock to amass five out of fives in every subject I took during the last three years of high school, I won the Gold Medal in academics. For extracurricular activities, I participated in the math and physics olympics on the city, provincial, and "all-Union" levels, sharpening my skills while showing off to potential recruiters. I mastered chess, winning local and national championships. I also followed the script to get the character reference I needed from the local Komsomol authorities. I spouted the right slogans, participated in the right youth activities, and sang the right songs.

Finally, I was in. I had crossed "the Pale of Settlement." I imagine that I experienced the same joy the rare, lucky Jews felt centuries earlier if they secured permission to live in Moscow, thereby escaping the massive half-million-square-mile western region that czarist Russia had turned into the world's largest ghetto from 1791 to 1917.

Wandering around Moscow, a city of more than five million, I experienced my own personal thaw. By concentrating on science at the institute, I was now an insider on a fast track to success. I expected to be able to think about pure truth more, while playing the doublethinker's demoralizing games less. Sampling life beyond our wunderkind hothouse, some of us students enjoyed exploring the booming metropolis, which was freer and edgier than our sleepy, suffocating hometowns.

Month after month, I ran through most of my living stipend buying tickets to shows in the three Moscow theaters, out of dozens, that gently but stubbornly tested Communism's reimposed cultural and political boundaries. It was two years after Khrushchev's fall, and some in the Soviet intelligentsia were still trying to preserve some hints of the Thaw's short-lived openness. Sometimes the institute hosted great artists, profound poets, and leading intellectuals. Clever but cowed performers resisted subtly, indirectly. Their plays, poems, jokes, and songs often carried "a fig in the pocket"—the Russian equivalent of flipping the middle finger while seeming to salute.

Studying early versions of artificial intelligence, teaching what are now considered to be primitive computers to play endgames in chess, I dived into the republic of science. This world seemed insulated from the doublethink I had mastered at home. My world-famous professors were telling the students what we wanted to hear: With our smarts and our work habits, we could live a full intellectual life. We could succeed. All we had to do was stay focused on our orderly inner world of scientific theories and mathematical theorems. These world-class teachers urged us to ignore the ever-changing pseudo-truths of politics, which was full of ambiguities and deceptions. Stick to science's eternal knowledge, they advised, and ignore the rest. The laws of Newton and Einstein, of Euclid and Galileo, are forever; today's ideological winds are fickle.

We continued paying lip service to the Soviet gods, like everyone else. We kept taking tests on Marxist doctrine every semester, even when studying at the postdoctoral level. Decades later, I would be amused when, during my interrogations, I spied my KGB tormentors studying their Communist handbooks whenever they could, knowing that these never-ending trials kept tormenting them.

Encouraged by our professors, we brushed such annoyances aside. We were the elite, they kept telling us, racing toward a golden future. I felt particularly good, having overcome the extra obstacles of anti-Semitism. Now it was all worth it. I was luxuriating in the sanctuary of science, an asylum protected from the daily insanity the Soviets imposed on nearly everyone else.

It didn't take very long, however, before groundbreaking outside events shook my illusory internal fortress.

2

DISCOVERING IDENTITY, DISCOVERING FREEDOM

The Six Day War broke out during my first round of final exams at the Institute in Moscow. Israel's victory in June 1967—with the small, embattled Jewish state overcoming overwhelming odds—became a turning point for me, although it took time for me to realize it.

In Donetsk, Israel hadn't been central to my life. It was there in the background, one of the conversation topics that bonded us as Jews. As people concerned about our Jewish problem, we were fans of the Jewish state. But demonstrating the solidarity of the suffering, we treated it like an all-Jewish soccer team, something to root for. It remained far less important and engaging than family life, friendships, and career worries. Living in enforced ignorance, we also knew little about this small country born the same year I was, in 1948. We only knew enough to feel burdened by the constant newspaper attacks against it.

Then, boom. Israel's surprising military victory mocked months of Soviet propaganda predicting a historic victory of "progressive Arab nations" over the "lackeys of American imperialism," the "bourgeois nationalist Zionist colonialists." For many doublethinkers watching from afar, we were amused by how easily Israel had defeated these supposedly powerful Arab armies overstuffed with Soviet weapons and trained by Soviet officers. As Jews, we were extra glad. Our team had won.

As the authorities ranted in the media and convened meeting after meeting to condemn American and Zionist imperialism, I could feel strangers, colleagues, and friends looking at me differently. At first, I was taken aback. I was a loyal Soviet citizen just like them. Yet people who knew I had no connection to Israel nevertheless seemed to think I deserved credit for this lightning victory. Rather than asking "How did the Israelis pull it off?" people were asking "How did you guys do it?" Gradually, it dawned on me that friends and foes connected me to Israel far more than I associated myself with the Jewish state.

Even the anti-Semitic jokes changed. Jews were upgraded. We went from greedy, cowardly parasites to greedy, bullying hooligans—dangerous to neighbors and the world too. Ultimately, those who loved and hated us agreed on one thing: Israel was some kind of cowboy superstate.

"One morning," jokesters giggled, "Prime Minister Levi Eshkol and Defense Minister Moshe Dayan woke up bored. 'Let's declare war on China!' Eshkol proposed. 'Then what will we do this evening?' Dayan wondered."

A mixed message was embedded in another joke, about a Jew in the telephone booth, hogging phone time, feeding two-kopek coins repeatedly into the slot, calling relatives all over Moscow. He has heard about Israel's victories from Voice of America or BBC, despite the jamming, and he keeps reporting, "Our tanks have seized the Golan Heights." Then, "Our soldiers are swimming in the Suez Canal!" Loyal citizens behind in line, expecting the Jew to know he should only make one short call because others are waiting, push him aside. The Jew sneers: "We didn't interfere in *your* war. Don't interfere in ours."

There you had it. In one joke, the greedy, self-involved, manipulative Jew as the unassimilable other. The pathetic coward who cowered in Tashkent or elsewhere during the Soviets' Great Patriotic War against Hitler is now boasting about heroics he never achieved, trying to take credit for others fighting the wrong war against the wrong enemy for the wrong reason.

Initially, most Jews didn't know whether to be proud or worried or scared. As the abused victims of this Communist paradise, we wondered if a war 2,400 miles away would hurt our careers. Meanwhile, we wondered about this country, Israel, that, in the eyes of the people around us, was ours. I did what came naturally. I started reading more about the heritage being imposed on me.

It's an old story. Jews often see themselves most clearly through non-Jewish eyes. Noticing how others connected me to Israel linked me to the Jewish state, and the Jewish people. Seeing how the word "Israel" became something that could boost us—not just diminish us—filled me with a pride and dignity I had never experienced. Realizing how little I knew about this country that so many people were now asking about made me hungry to learn more.

LIBERATED BY *EXODUS*

I saw the world through new eyes, like someone falling in love. My father's Bible stories about Jewish heroes like David defeating Goliath, suddenly came alive; Israelis were replicating their feats in the Middle East, right now. Whenever possible, I turned Moscow's art museums into my own Jewish museum or Israel museum. I first learned about the Jewish holiday of Purim by listening to the guide at the Pushkin Museum explain Rembrandt's famous painting *Ahasuerus and Haman at the Feast of Esther*.

Starved by Communism's decades-long cultural fast, I did whatever I could to learn about Israel and my Jewish heritage. Some of the reading was samizdat—outlawed, self-published literature, sometimes photocopied, sometimes printed crudely. These pamphlets were circulated only among trusted friends. Some were now dusty old books written in Russian and still found in libraries. Some were books a friend's father had in his library. I kept visiting him even after he moved six hundred miles away from Moscow. The distance from any possible campus informers justified the trip.

One of the first Jewish-related books I read, in samizdat, was a Russian translation of Leon Uris's historical novel retelling the founding of Israel, *Exodus*. Reading it today, it's hard to believe how such a heavy-handed, sentimental novel could influence so many usually hard-nosed, cynical, Russian Jewish intellectuals. But the book was a revelation. It drew me into Jewish history, and Israel's history, through my Russian roots. It helped me see myself as part of the story.

I hadn't realized that many Russian Jews from my father's generation—like my missing uncle—had shaped the Zionist movement and founded Israel. I was struck that in 1948, heroes my age established the country, making history instead of studying for exams. Looking at that famous picture, of the three soldiers who helped liberate the Western Wall in 1967, I realized they were my age too. It could have been me.

I flipped a switch in my mind. History was no longer distant and alienating. It was now mine. Instead of the short, bloody Soviet history, which began with the October Revolution in 1917 and went nowhere, I joined a story that harkened back to the exodus from Egypt, took me to Leon Uris's *Exodus*, and would soon lead to my own exodus.

Uris's novel was so popular, one family after another would borrow a copy and spend the whole night reading, passing the book around. The next day, they would hand it over to the next family in the long line of people waiting to read it. Then they'd feel embarrassed, breathing a sigh of relief. No one wanted such dangerous material hanging around the house.

A few years later, when I was a dissident spokesman, my friendships with diplomats and journalists made me a clearinghouse of sorts for activists. I distributed books and other material smuggled into Moscow via diplomatic pouch from American Jewish organizations. I sent one message to a New York contact, advising, "Send us one hundred *Exoduses* and we'll have a Zionist Revolution here!"

Jewish tourists starting to visit us smuggled in other books. "Oh, your father is from Odessa. Mine is too," some would say. "We could be in your place," they sighed. "We are one family. How can we help?"

Now, "Nostrum est?" isn't based just on all Jews being persecuted, but on us all being one family, from one global shtetl. Just a few years ago, the borders had been so daunting I hadn't even heard about an uncle who moved away. Now, these travelers, and my allegiances, were crossing borders easily.

I felt a new sense of history, a warm feeling of family, and a tremendous gratitude for this state that, my reading taught me, defined one of its primary aims as helping me and people like me. More and more, I knew that this was the history, these were the people, that was the country, I wanted to belong to.

The more connected to this new parallel universe I became, the more clearly I could see the many ways my fellow Jews and I contorted ourselves to remain enslaved to the Communist world. The more I realized this, the less faith I had in the shelter I had long sought in the ivory tower of science, which kept me trapped in exhausting, demoralizing doublethink.

I was not only exposed to Jewish books. Samizdat and friendly smuggling introduced me to many classics that would shape my new worldview.

My favorites included Boris Pasternak's soaring homage to individualism and romance, *Doctor Zhivago*; Arthur Koestler's sobering exposé of Stalin's purges, *Darkness at Noon*; and, most especially, George Orwell's suffocating evocations of Big Brother's power, *Animal Farm* and *1984*.

I remember being thunderstruck by *Animal Farm*. "My God," I thought, "we understood the newspeak imposed on us. But how can this British writer from decades ago understand so well what we're living through right here, right now, in Russia?" Orwell's literary achievement in reducing the Communist revolutionaries to a series of farm animals was just the added bonus. Years later, I discovered that Orwell got a full taste of Communism when Stalin's Soviet masterminds hijacked the Spanish Civil War, for which he and other idealists had naively volunteered.

It was getting harder to play the good Soviet citizen. After 1967, the Soviet Union broke diplomatic relations with Israel, and cracked down on Jews. For a Jew to be accepted into my institute became almost impossible. Even those of us discovering these exciting new links to Israel and our extended Jewish family still held on to the familiar: our ambitions to succeed.

A joke from those confusing days, probably improvised by a Jewish cynic, has Rabinowitch coming home depressed. The Communist Party has expelled him for not condemning Zionism and Israel. Falling asleep, he dreams that a superstrong Israel conquers the Soviet Union. Israel's victorious one-eyed general, Moshe Dayan, and the legendary former Israeli ambassador to Moscow (on her way to becoming prime minister), Golda Meir, enter Red Square on white horses. They stand atop Lenin's mausoleum as Jews from all over the Soviet Union gather below to celebrate.

"Jews of the Soviet Union," Meir proclaims, "after years of persecution, here's your opportunity to take revenge. What do you want as spoils of war? Should we send Russians to the Pale of Settlement, where they imprisoned us for so many years?" she asks. "No," the Jews respond. "Should we put quotas on the Russians, limiting their university acceptances and jobs as they did to us?" General Dayan asks. "No," the Jews yell.

"So what *do* you want?" Golda demands, surprised. All the Jews shout as one: "We want Rabinowitch back in the Communist Party!"

The growing government pressure kept testing Jews' loyalty. In Donetsk, my favorite high school teacher, Yisrael Yaakovolevitch, a local legend who for decades prepared talented physics students to get accepted to the best institutions, received a petty, insulting command. The principal, a half-literate Communist career apparatchik, whose assignment to run our school probably represented a major demotion, targeted the teacher, whose name meant "Israel, son of Jacob." "If you want to continue teaching, change your first name," he was ordered. Apparently, it was disturbing for the principal to hear his students saying that word "Israel" with love and respect. Yisrael became Ilya.

My teacher's surrender angered me at first. But hearing from mutual friends how he agonized about what to do, I softened. "It's not worth the battle," most advised. I understood. I, too, was Anatoly, not Natan.

"This illustrates our fate," I thought. I was increasingly fed up with the accommodations he made, we made—the humiliations we absorbed. "He at least does it to continue teaching young students," I sighed. "I'm just doing it for myself, for my precious career."

Looking at him forced me to reexamine the adjustments I had made to stay afloat in this world without identity. I was realizing, intrusion by intrusion, that even as the authorities indulged us as wunderkinds, we students still felt scrutinized. It's natural, in an advanced academic institute, to worry "Am I good enough?" and "Will I get thrown out for not keeping up?" It was unnatural, however, to also worry "Am I good enough at hiding my true thoughts?" and "Will I get thrown out for not staying loyal enough?"

Gradually, you realize that science cannot save you from your portable, permanent chamber of fear. You worry the authorities might doubt your loyalty or decide you sympathize with a dissident, or catch you reading something they deem political. Even if you aren't arrested, you can be bounced from the institute or blocked in your career path—no doctorate, no postdoc, no job. Instead of a brilliant future, you could end up languishing. Living in fear, enslaved to your ambitions—and thus beholden to the masters who control your career—you remain mired in doublethink.

ANDREI SAKHAROV BURSTS MY SCIENTIFIC BUBBLE

Israel's heroics in the June 1967 war helped me discover how much I was missing by living in a world without identity. A year later, one scientist's bravery helped me realize how little freedom I would have, even if

I excelled in the artificial bubble of superstar Soviet science I had fought so hard to enter.

My fellow students and I revered Andrei Sakharov. He was our role model, sitting at the peak of the pyramid each of us was trying to climb so single-mindedly. At thirty-two, he became the youngest person elected to the Soviet Academy of Sciences. A brilliant physicist, he helped develop the Soviets' hydrogen bomb. He won numerous awards, including being named a "hero of socialist labor" three times—the state's highest honor.

In May 1968, this celebrity scientist circulated a ten-thousand-word manifesto with a mild title that unleashed the second wrecking ball to smash my complacent life. "Reflections on Progress, Peaceful Coexistence, and Intellectual Freedom" warned from the very top that systemic Soviet repression threatened the state's scientific advancement and the world's survival. Essentially, he exposed the world I had built my life around as an illusion.

"Intellectual freedom is essential to human society," Sakharov declared, demanding the "freedom to obtain and distribute information, freedom for open-minded and fearless debate, and freedom from pressure by officialdom and prejudices." Exercising those freedoms, he bravely denounced official Soviet thought control, mocking "the ossified dogmatism of a bureaucratic oligarchy and its favorite weapon, ideological censorship."

Some of my professors might have dismissed this political critique as another frivolous distraction from the pursuit of eternal scientific truths. But Sakharov warned that Soviet science was imperiled without "the search for truth." Imaginie "two skiers racing through deep snow," Sakharov suggested. While the Soviet skier had started catching up to the American one—who first "broke the snow"—our suffocating lack of freedom kept us "not only lagging behind but . . . also growing more slowly." At the time, there were few who could understand the depths of this critique. The Soviet Union wasn't just relying on its scientific wizards to develop nuclear weapons; we now know that the research ran in tandem with an elaborate spying operation that stole as many of America's atomic secrets as it could.

The subversive essay started circulating in samizdat typewritten copies. Duplicated secretly, spread informally, read hungrily, Sakharov's words skipped from house to house, from trusted skeptic to trusted skeptic, interrupted sporadically but fruitlessly, cat-and-mouse-like, by repeated KGB raids.

Before our eyes, the Soviet Union's most decorated scientist was becoming its most prominent dissident. I read his unsettling yet liberating message as if it were addressed directly to me. "You want to run away from your life of doublethink and fear by making a scientific career," I imagined him telling me, "but that's impossible. It didn't work for me, it won't work for you. There's no scientific breakthrough you can make that will free you, as long as you're enslaved to this immoral doublethink. Knowing the truth while collaborating with the regime's lies only produces bad science and broken souls. You will be handicapped as a scientist, forever following behind, like a second skier in the tracks of the trailblazer."

Risking everything he had with no chance of success, Sakharov inspired and confused me with his bravery. He exposed my hopes of losing myself in science as naive. I realized that if even he, at his altitude, wasn't settled, I was sunk. Just starting out, with no chance of reaching his heights, I could spend decades forever chasing the next advancement, the next summit. Then, after a lifetime of toil, I would discover that what he was saying and I was sensing was true: I would never be free. Sakharov was warning that life in a dictatorship offers two choices: either you overcome your fear and stand for truth, or you remain a slave to fear, no matter how fancy your titles, no matter how big your dacha. Ultimately, I couldn't escape myself or my conscience.

Sakharov's heroic manifesto spurred the growth of a dissident movement that was just budding in a post-Stalinist world, where speaking truth to power no longer all but guaranteed being shot down. Reading Sakharov taught me that obsessing about my career was a coping mechanism, a survival skill, but no way to live. Living in the moment, for myself, made it hard to believe there was anything bigger than my daily concerns, anything more lasting than my latest success, anything meaningful in this void. When getting ahead professionally is the most important thing in life, you become too willing to go along with everything. Why take any risks? Why buck the system?

Just as chess couldn't give me the depth science was supposed to provide, science couldn't give me the anchor I needed. To become free, to transcend doublethink, you must first overcome the fear that is always with you. There must be something more important than your career. But in a world without identity, such higher values hadn't existed for me.

Book by book, revelation by revelation, encountering my identity, my history, my people, and my country, Israel, I scrutinized my psychological prison of Soviet survivalism. The more I learned about Israel, Judaism, and Jewish history, the more I realized I could be part of something bigger than myself, pursuing missions more important than getting the right grade or the great job.

Coinciding with Czechoslovakia's rebellious Prague Spring, Sakharov's words had some of us who longed for reform hoping that change was in the air. The leader of Czechoslovakia's Communist Party, Alexander Dubček, was trying to reform from within, gradually and peacefully. His lighter vision of "socialism with a human face" paralleled Sakharov's naive hopes at the time. But Dubček's pluckiness triggered yet another shock. The violent Soviet-led invasion of Czechoslovakia in August 1968 crushed our hopes, along with Dubček's reforms. Now I felt ashamed to be a Soviet citizen.

Eight Soviet citizens who felt similarly ashamed went to Red Square to denounce the invasion and ended up in jail. Although I didn't know them, I envied them. They had something even the privileged scientific superachievers lacked: the freedom to follow their conscience.

Nevertheless, I remained imprisoned by my fear. One MFTI student sympathized with the protesters publicly. Facing expulsion, he first had to endure being denounced at a Komsomol meeting. The Komsomol apparatchik pointedly invited me, even though I belonged to a different faculty. Clearly, he wanted to test my loyalty. Rather than taking a stand, and pointlessly giving them someone else to expel, I ducked, saying, "I'm ill."

That act of cowardice made me feel truly sick. My doubts were growing. But I wasn't yet ready to abandon my—and my parents'—dream of finding refuge in science. The longer I stayed paralyzed, the more self-respect I lost.

Every day, you wake up and you trudge along to the institute, but like an actor following an elaborate script, you always have to concentrate. You don't want to violate the rules, but you don't want to embrace the regime. Timing is critical. You feel constant internal pressure not to say the wrong thing—especially not to the wrong person at the wrong time. Luck helps too. You don't want to be near someone who bashes the regime, because you might have to disagree more than you want to, or you might accidentally agree more than you should. You're just never sure. Someone who agrees with you might nevertheless bristle at something you say, uncertain if you're testing him, leaving you suspicious. After all, maybe he's testing you.

TESTING THE BOUNDARIES

Despite all this pressure, I couldn't help pushing the boundaries more and more, just like the singers, poets, and playwrights who were being similarly subversive during those performances I practically bankrupted myself attending. Night after night, I waited for the easily decoded lines mocking today's regime in some French drawing-room comedy from yesteryear. In laughing together at these gibes, we in the audience exercised our critical thoughts secretly, safely, and spinelessly.

Sakharov kept crossing the lines. On November 4, 1970, he and two other dissidents established the Committee on Human Rights in the USSR. I heard about it on Voice of America, past the jamming. I knew that most students, fellow doublethinkers, heard the news too. But nobody dared discuss it at the institute. It would be like waking up one day and publicly confessing, "I secretly listen to bourgeois lies—and believe them," which is what most of us did.

One morning that autumn, I was practicing my English as usual, this time by reading the *Morning Star*, the only British newspaper allowed in the Soviet Union. This Communist Party propaganda organ criticized Sakharov's efforts. The condemnation broke the official silence. In the West, Communists had to denounce Sakharov; behind the Iron Curtain, they tried ignoring him.

Here was my chance to be mischievous. I could break the taboo gingerly. While staying within the law, I would publicize Sakharov's next step in his flight from doublethink. I could admit we knew what we all knew, and discuss what we all wanted to discuss, without being accused of listening to what we all listened to. After painstakingly translating the article word for word, I posted it on our dormitory's bulletin board and awaited the reaction.

Unable to tolerate such defiance or such subtleties, the system pushed back. The institute's KGB representative summoned me to his office. Our encounter became my first interrogation. The legal niceties justifying my action did not interest him. He kept asking about my ties to Sakharov, how this subversive idea came to me, who helped me translate the article, who conspired with me in posting it. I didn't know Sakharov then. I had nothing to admit. But the KGB never overlooked an opportunity to flip yet another Soviet citizen, using careerist worries and threats of professional humiliation to recruit informers.

Still, I was terrified. Looking back, my attempts to reassure the KGB officer of my loyalty leave me feeling ashamed. I was trying to assert my freedom and dignity while avoiding confrontation. I still wanted to study, still wanted to succeed.

Both the KGB department head and I achieved a certain clarity that day. After rounds of back and forth, the officer understood he couldn't get any useful information from me. I had no future as an informer. But I also understood that I wasn't going to get any further in my scientific career. I had no future in the scientific ivory tower the Soviets controlled.

During my rare visits home, every six months or so, my family discussed the new Zionist rumblings among Soviet Jews. The conversations usually focused around the age-old question, "Is this good for the Jews or bad for the Jews?" In this exciting, unnerving new phase, this meant, "Will it bring more restrictions or fewer, more pressure or less, more obstacles to escape through careerism or fewer?"

As I confessed my deepening fascination with the Jewish question, my parents seemed caught at the intersection of pride and fear. I sensed that they appreciated this twist in our lives. Home was one of the rare places where I could talk about my new discoveries: our history, our identity, our nation. I was connecting to the life from which they had been forced to disengage. They had run away from identity and pushed us toward professionalism, for our sakes. Now I was running away from professionalism, back to an identity they had never rejected voluntarily.

Ultimately, their fear spoke loudest. As I spoke about Jewish history, they asked if I was making it harder to advance at the institute. When I shared my dream of moving to Israel, they warned against new purges.

It escalated. The more involved in the movement I became, the more my parents worried. "You don't remember Stalin," my father would say. "You were too young. You have to be very careful. It's so easy for them to make you disappear from this life." Over the years, as I started thinking of emigrating to Israel, the negotiations became more practical and incremental. "We can't give you permission to apply for a visa while we are still working," they would say. "Wait till we both retire." "Maybe not this season. Can you wait a bit longer?"

My father often warned me about the impact my activities would have on my mother's health. But his heart reacted worse. He had a heart attack immediately after my arrest in 1977 and never recovered. I never saw him after that; he passed away in 1980. My mother would live to fight much longer: first with the KGB until the day of my release, then with me and my wife over the right way to educate her granddaughters. She lived with us happily until the age of ninety-four.

My first KGB interview was humiliating but liberating. I started feeling the Soviets no longer had the control, and I slowly freed myself from the leverage careerism had over me. I was wriggling out of the regime's grip, tired of being handcuffed by fear. For nearly three years, I had been tasting a different reality and enjoying my new identity in that parallel world beyond the authorities' reach. Totalitarians could dictate Soviet history, changing it as easily as switching encyclopedia pages. But the Jewish history I discovered was independent of them, making it—and soon me—no longer subject to their whims.

THE MOST DIFFICULT CHOICE I EVER MADE

Breaking the shackles is the hardest thing to do as a doublethinker. Once you do that, the released energy gives you a rush you've never experienced before. Step by liberating step, I was running toward freedom.

In 1973, I became a Refusenik, one who applied to emigrate to Israel and was refused. Two years later, I was an activist and the informal international spokesman for both the Refusenik movement and the human rights movement. By then, I was working closely with my new friend and mentor, Andrei Sakharov. We met during one of the many courthouse vigils he attended to attract the world's attention to Soviet repression.

In 1976, I was one of the activists who launched the Moscow Helsinki Group, trying to mold various dissident organizations into one big battering ram against the Soviet empire. A year later, I was arrested for high treason and espionage—capital crimes—and was on my way to what ended up being nine years in prison. By then, I had learned that living a life of belonging and freedom involved constantly confronting dilemmas and forever making my own choices, rather than having Big Brother push me around.

No choice I made—or would make in the future—was anywhere near as difficult as my decision in 1973 to request a letter acknowledging my employment. It should have been nothing, something procedural that I, as a good careerist, had done many times in my life. All I had to do was walk down the very familiar hallway in the Institute of Oil and Gas, where I worked as a computer specialist, to speak to my boss, with whom I got along. But that move was so nerve-racking that I had to take a tranquilizer that morning, for the first and only time in my life.

Taking this minor bureaucratic step was so earth-shattering because I needed the letter to start the long, torturous process of applying for aliyah, that special Hebrew word that means "ascent," to designate that emigrating to Israel is a spiritual step up. I was now saying I no longer belonged in the Soviets' world, and committing career suicide within the Soviet system.

The bureaucracy forced me to get all kinds of signed documents from my workplace, residence, and family. That drip-by-drip process compelled me to keep admitting publicly I no longer wanted to be a loyal Soviet citizen, thereby subjecting me to the reactions of friends, colleagues, relatives, and bosses. I knew that, by doing this, my future employment would be limited to serving as a janitor here, a tutor there, or a hall monitor in an apartment building somewhere else.

That morning, I was so nervous that I didn't go to work. I didn't know which friends I was about to lose, what interrogations I was about to experience, what price I would have to pay, how long I would have to wait, or if I would ever make it out.

I had requested the meeting. My boss probably assumed it would be another routine conversation about our work. It was clear to me he was a doublethinker like me, and he rarely was assigned such well-trained scientists. We never spoke about it, but it seemed he understood that I had been stuck with a lesser job because of that fifth line on my identity card: *Evrey*, Jew.

My hands were shaking. My stomach was rumbling. I may have been a bit light-headed from the sedative my aunt had provided me the night before. "I know this will be unpleasant news for you, Maxim Maximovich," I began, surprised by how hoarse my voice sounded. "But I wish to join my relatives in Israel. To apply for the exit visa, I need your letter certifying my employment."

My boss's hands started trembling like mine. He was so flummoxed, his voice grew hoarse too. My problem was his problem now. He didn't know what to say. He didn't know how the authorities would react. Neither did I.

At that moment, my life as a loyal Soviet citizen ended. My life as a doublethinker, which I had consciously begun at age five the day Stalin died, was over. The professional world I had built for myself, my castle of science, collapsed instantly. Now, I could say what I thought, do what I said, and say what I did. Finally—thirteen years before my release from prison and my move to a free, democratic Israel—I was liberated. Having made the most difficult choice, all the others that followed would feel easier.

TO BELONG AND TO BE FREE

I was lucky. In the Soviet Union, I grew up deprived of freedom and identity. Then, after 1967, I discovered them both. In embracing my Jewishness, I inherited a 3,900-year-old identity—the history, values, ideas, and country that would shape me. That breakthrough propelled me to end a life of doublethink—the constant juggling of maneuvers and lies just to survive, the push to get ahead without really going anywhere. Only by ending that sterile life could I speak freely. Once I was no longer afraid, I realized how enjoyable it was to be free.

Encountering these two deep human desires, to belong and to be free, taught me that they are interconnected. Having one would give me strength to fight for the other. In my prehistoric life, the highest value was physical survival, and the best tool for that was a successful professional career. I had no identity, no values, nothing to live for, nothing to die for. In joining the Jewish people, I discovered that when you have an identity, when you are part of something bigger than yourself, fear for your well-being no longer imprisons you. Putting myself back into my people's history, into our community, freed me to fight for my rights, for the rights of my fellow Jews, and for the rights of all the people around me.

Subsequently, I was challenged again and again to choose between these two impulses: Is my first loyalty to my people or to my universal ideals of freedom? Today, the whole world seems divided between those who choose their identity first and those who choose their freedom first. That's a false choice. Enjoying a free, meaningful life in accordance with our identities, while letting others do the same, should be our shared aim in the common pursuit of happiness.

3

BECOMING A REFUSENIK

After I broke out of the ivory tower of doublethink, I became a free person living in an unfree land. I knew I was joining a struggle with no guarantee of a happy ending. I was sure, however, that my life would be filled with a sense of purpose, a feeling of belonging, and the blessings of freedom—even if I never reached the free world. What I didn't know was that I would get a special bonus. Very quickly, I found myself in the center of one of the most exciting—and challenging—movements in Jewish history.

I grew up in a world where Jewish solidarity was only expressed through coded hints and secret nods. I went to a school where I could not even acknowledge I was considering moving to Israel with the select group of roommates who huddled around the radio with me at night, secretly listening to Voice of America. Then, suddenly, within a few weeks, I found myself openly, overly connected to Jews. In joining the struggle, I entered an exhilarating, exhausting world that attached me to my fellow Soviet Jews, Israelis, and Jews from communities across the globe in the least secretive, most exposed way.

The struggle to save Soviet Jewry was unique. It was global, involving Jewish communities on both sides of the Iron Curtain. It was pluralistic, mobilizing French Communists and British aristocrats, pious rabbis and assimilating lawyers, American patriots and Zionist activists, countercultural hippies and Establishment leaders. And it was focused. Everyone wanted to rip a hole in the Iron Curtain to free millions of Jews. The shared mission came down to three Hebrew words: *shlach et ami*, let my people go.

A HISTORY OF THE STRUGGLE FOR
SOVIET JEWRY: ABRIDGED EDITION

As with every totalitarian regime, the Soviet Union's rigidity caused great instability. It was as vulnerable as a big man highly allergic to a small bee. Trying to control everything ultimately meant that any deviation, no matter how small, could threaten everything. Ever fearful that its obedient armies of doublethinkers were about to turn into dissidents, the regime could not permit its citizens to decide what to read or what to say. Recognizing the mass desertions open borders could cause, it also couldn't allow its citizens to choose where to live. That's why this command-and-control society had no official procedure for emigration.

There was only one legal way out: pleading family reunification. Most people, however, feared admitting they had relatives abroad. Beyond that, applying for a visa set you on a bureaucratic obstacle course with little chance of success. The conditions were so daunting that the authorities assumed few would dare to start the process.

That is why the Jews' post–Six Day War identity awakening surprised the Soviets. Suddenly, dozens, hundreds, then thousands of once-quiescent Jews proclaimed they wanted to leave. Exploiting the family reunification loophole, Israeli officials helped every Jew interested in immigrating find Israeli "relatives" to certify their relationship and their pressing desire to reunite.

Feeling threatened, the regime pushed back, cautiously. In the 1950s, it would have been simple: anyone suspected of such criminal thinking would have faced immediate arrest and possible execution. But by the 1970s, the Communist elites didn't want a Stalinist bloodbath. Looking inward, they learned that all this purging and mass murdering was too risky for them; today's killer became tomorrow's kill too easily. Looking outward, the Soviet Union, desperate for the West to help its failing economy, was now pretending to respect international norms. As the regime tried, in Andrei Sakharov's words, to follow in the Western ski tracks economically, it became vulnerable to Western pressure politically.

The counterattack against Soviet Jewry, approved at the highest level, followed a two-part strategy. By letting a limited number of Jews reunite with their families, the Communist system pretended to be humanitarian to impress the West. At the same time, the regime prosecuted some Jewish activists in show trials while refusing the visa requests en masse. Soviet Jews understood the thuggish message: anyone starting this emigration process could lose everything for no clear gain.

Today, the word Refusenik describes young Israelis who refuse to serve in the army, babies whose birth mothers refused to take them home from the hospital, and even teenagers refused service at a bar despite their fake IDs. Half a century ago, a modest Russian language teacher from London, Michael Sherbourne, coined the term to describe the class of people in the purgatory these new Soviet tactics created. Michael's single word describing those refused permission to emigrate by the Soviet authorities became a global brand. Eventually, tens of thousands of Refuseniks were denied their right to emigrate.

The label took on a deeper meaning for a tiny subset, who resisted the regime's diktats twice: first, by applying for visas and then by refusing to accept the refusal silently. Particularly inspired by the events of August 6, 1969, when members of eighteen Georgian Jewish families appealed to the United Nations for help to leave the Soviet Union, Refuseniks protested in the streets, circulated petitions worldwide, and became the voice of Soviet Jewry. The number of activists ready to confront the authorities rarely exceeded two hundred. In all my years of organizing petitions, I don't recall ever collecting more than 130 signatures.

Deprived of serious Jewish educations, most of us Refuseniks were just discovering our roots. In breaking through from doublethink to dissent, we also broke into the storehouse of Jewish history. We developed a sweeping narrative that reflected our activist passion more than any scholarly erudition. Our appeals often connected our cause with the chain of Jewish freedom fighters we knew: from the exodus from Egypt, to the Maccabees in ancient Judea, to the founders of Zionism and the pioneers of modern Israel.

The Soviets tried jamming the Refusenik message systematically. The authorities staged press conferences starring Jewish mathematicians, scientists, writers, chess players, and ballerinas—some of whom were world-famous. All issued carefully rehearsed statements affirming how happy they were in the Soviet paradise. But the world wasn't fooled. These official Jews were obviously doublethinkers mouthing Soviet propaganda. By contrast, the words of a few Jews, far less famous, were more sincere. The world took the small band of Refuseniks—who had the chutzpah to speak in the name of three million silenced Jews—very seriously. Having abandoned the life of Soviet lies, Refuseniks said what they—and most Soviet Jews—really thought.

Moscow's show trials in 1970 and 1971 against Jewish activists also backfired. They catalyzed global protests. The burgeoning international movement earned one of its first big victories when the regime commuted two death sentences imposed in December 1970, following the first Leningrad trial. The Soviet retreat demonstrated a new sensitivity to world public opinion and a vulnerability to the movement, encouraging even more activism.

But, no matter how loud, the small group of Soviet Jewish Refuseniks could never have survived alone. From day to day, even minute to minute, our struggle only worked because we joined a broader struggle for Jewish freedom. While Jews and non-Jews from all over the world eventually helped, Israel's contribution to the cause was unparalleled, symbolically and practically.

The state's founding in 1948—and its fight to survive in 1967— triggered the Soviet Jewry movement. Israel was determined to reach out to Jews behind the Iron Curtain. After all, this is why Zionists founded the Jewish State. Saving them was such a priority that, starting in 1951, a secretive organization to advance these goals operated out of the Israeli prime minister's office.

Officially given a misleadingly bland name—Lishkat Hakesher, the Liaison Office—Nativ was headed from 1970 to 1980 by Nehemiah Levanon. Levanon was so formidable that we activists whispered his name in awe. A devoted Zionist and kibbutznik, a character straight out of a Zionist novel, Levanon led his colleagues in harnessing Israel's state power to assist the Soviet Jewish campaign. They collected whatever information they could about Soviet Jews, even in the 1950s, when the Iron Curtain seemed impenetrable. They sent thousands of tourists over the years to encourage Refuseniks, executed complicated diplomatic maneuvers, and choreographed the emigration process, finding "relatives" whenever necessary.

Golda Meir's devotion to Soviet Jewry made her the "mother of the movement." By 1969, this Ukrainian-born, American-educated Labor Party leader (and Israel's first ambassador to the Soviet Union) was Israel's prime minister. No matter how busy she was, she regularly met planes landing in Israel with Soviet immigrants. "I'm not just welcoming these newcomers," she said. "I'm doing it for them," meaning those of us still stuck in the USSR. "I want Soviet Jews to know they are important to us."

Zionism meant that a country thousands of miles away, which most Soviet Jews had never visited, would never stop fighting for us; Israel made that far-fetched idea appear normal. The best example of how far Israel would go to save Jews occurred on July 4, 1976. That night, one hundred Israeli commandos secretly flew over 2,500 miles to Entebbe, Uganda, refueling in the air, to rescue twelve Air France crew members and ninety-four Jewish passengers—mostly Israeli—whose plane had been hijacked by pro-Palestinian terrorists.

Soviet Jews considered this successful operation a personal message from Israel. As soon as I could find a photo of the martyred commander of Entebbe, Yoni Netanyahu, I hung it on my wall. Later, throughout my years in prison, whenever I heard a plane flying overhead, my pulse quickened, reminding me that Israel and the Jewish people would never, ever abandon me, or us.

The global network of the Jewish people amplified the Refusenik voice, and our power. A new generation of Jews arose. Most felt comfortable as free, increasingly prosperous citizens in the West. They were often empowered by the courageous New Jew in the Middle East. But their defiant cry of "never again" was tinged with guilt. They were vowing to avoid another mass failure, of free Jews not doing everything possible to save endangered Jews.

Elie Wiesel became the living link connecting the horrors of the Holocaust, the bounty of America, and the biggest Jewish community still in distress, Soviet Jewry. Wiesel first traveled to the Soviet Union in 1965 as a journalist from the Israeli newspaper *Haaretz*. The Jewish despair he encountered shocked him, twenty years after his liberation from the Buchenwald concentration camp. His 1966 book *The Jews of Silence* challenged the world to speak up about our isolation. This modern prophet shamed many American Jews into action. Later, for all his achievements as a novelist, Holocaust memoirist, human rights activist, entrancing lecturer, and Nobel Peace Prize winner, Wiesel told me he hoped to be most remembered for giving voice to the millions of Jews living behind the Iron Curtain.

Thanks to Wiesel and others, news about the Soviet "Jews of silence" spread throughout the Jewish world in the 1960s. Committees formed. Organizations developed. In 1971, organizations from across the ideological spectrum gathered in Belgium. Overcoming many deep differences, the eight hundred delegates at the first Brussels conference agreed on one central idea: let my people go. This Jewish human rights movement became an international cause célèbre, one of history's most successful human rights campaigns.

Jews of the free world lobbied their leaders as concerned outsiders and, occasionally, as political insiders. Tourists to Russia—who didn't tour much—became the living bridges between Refuseniks and the outside world. They kept coming, no matter how many KGB informers masquerading as Intourist guides menaced them. They kept calling, no matter how many telephone lines the KGB cut. They created a global communications network, updating Soviet Jews and others by dialing the phone and handing off mail, person-to-person, decades before the Internet's invention.

Characteristically, Jews followed many different paths to visit us in Moscow or fight Moscow with us. Some activists, vowing "never again," were Jews born on American soil, embarrassed that their *sha-shtil*, don't-rock-the-boat immigrant parents and grandparents did nothing while six million died during the Holocaust. Some, shouting "Freedom now," were civil rights activists applying the skills they had mastered in Alabama and Mississippi to help their people in a human rights struggle. Some, singing "Am Yisrael Chai" and proclaiming, "We are one," were Orthodox Jews or Zionists acting on their values as Jewish nationalists.

But, above all, the Soviet legal demands framed it nicely: it was a worldwide family-reunification project. One branch of my family, the Lantsevitskys, had arrived in Canada decades earlier, before World War I. All contact was cut off for years. When my case was in the news, the family patriarch, Noah, said, "This guy must be related to us. We used to be Shcharanskys too." When they contacted Avital, it turned out to be true. The family, now the Landises, plunged in, helping the struggle in so many ways, from hosting Avital to recruiting others to fight. Irwin Cotler, my Canada-based attorney, used my newfound Canadian connection to convince Prime Minister Pierre Trudeau that Canada had a real stake in freeing me, beyond the broader human rights fight. In the grand sweep of the struggle, this was just one more relatively minor episode. But for me, the symbolism was very significant. After decades of distance, Soviet and Western Jews were rediscovering that we were all part of one big extended family.

Some tourists came well briefed by Israelis or Jewish organizations. Others were acting independently. Whatever their motives, whatever their level of involvement, we in Moscow were often surprised by how committed these strangers were to our cause.

Once, I gave a young woman from Philadelphia a copy of a letter one hundred Refuseniks had signed. She was going to smuggle it in her underwear out of Moscow's Sheremetyevo International Airport. She would deliver it to a Jewish organization, which would then pass it on to one of our champions, Henry Jackson, a non-Jewish Democratic senator from Washington, a state with few Jews. Watching her fold up the letter, noticing how hard she was trying to mask her nervousness, I felt badly for her. "Don't do it, if it makes you feel uncomfortable," I said. "We can always find other ways, by telephone or diplomatic pouch."

Echoing something hundreds of tourists said over the years, she explained, "No, you don't understand. I'm not doing you a favor. You're doing me a favor. You're changing our lives. You're letting us make Jewish history together with you."

The free, cushy lives of American Jewish baby boomers couldn't have been more different than our unfree, severe existence. Many of them were drifting away from the Jewish identity we were running toward. Suddenly, we shared the common thrill of rejoining Jewish history and changing it together. Decades later, one American Jewish leader told me, "You Refuseniks saved my generation from assimilation."

The Soviet authorities dismissed the movement as a fly-by-night annoyance. KGB officers mocked this "bunch of hooligans," who would soon get distracted by some newer, sexier headline-making cause. Indeed, more Diaspora Jewish activists were bankers than bomb throwers. Few in power expected that these commonplace crusaders, leading a global grassroots movement, would be so persistent—fighting for decades, sometimes passing the responsibility like a family heirloom from activist parents to activist children.

The authorities couldn't control the problem. Like water leaking into a basement, it threatened their very foundation. As mass refusals and show trials failed to discourage Jewish visa applicants, the Soviets experimented with more sweeping restrictions. In August 1972, they imposed an "education tax." Anyone who benefited from the Soviet Union's free higher education had to pay retroactive tuition before emigrating. This is the kind of Soviet Trojan horse that would have tricked earlier generations of Western dupes, especially because, in this case, Americans were used to paying big money to send their kids to college. But by now, most Westerners had learned to look for the ugly reality behind the decorative Communist façade, thanks to the Refuseniks' coaching. The fees the Soviets assessed were almost one hundred times the average monthly salary, in a world where few people had any savings.

The charade and the repression backfired again. The free world was proving equally inventive and responsive. The outrage over the education tax helped build support for the Jackson-Vanik amendment to the Trade Act of 1974 in the US Congress. Just as the Soviet Union was about to reap the fruits of its new policy of détente toward the West and gain economically beneficial most-favored-nation trade status from the United States, Senator Henry Jackson and Congressman Charles Vanik stepped in, making these economic benefits contingent on the regime granting freedom of emigration.

Henry Jackson's linkage of American foreign relations to human rights concerns was controversial. Secretary of State Henry Kissinger wanted to advance détente with no strings attached. The debate intensified during negotiations over the Helsinki Accords in 1975. Few realized that, by signing the seventh clause promising "respect for human rights and fundamental freedoms," the Soviet Union had settled the debate and signed its ideological death warrant. The Soviet Jewish movement's grand coalition, cooperating with other dissident groups, had pressured diplomats into injecting human rights considerations into all dimensions of the Soviet Union's relationship with the West. From lonely demonstrations in New York and London during the mid-1960s to the December 1987 march on Washington, mobilizing a quarter of a million people, there was one clear message: Jews throughout the world—with cherished allies—would not stop demanding that the Soviets "let my people go."

This global coalition, spearheaded by Israel, continued demanding our freedom into the 1990s. In December 1991, the Soviet Union collapsed. By then, more than two million Jews were on the move. More than one million ultimately arrived in Israel.

JOINING THE MOVEMENT MID-ARGUMENT

A movement that big could not be as simple as its message. In early 1973, I started visiting Archipova Street regularly, across from Moscow's central synagogue. The Jewish activists met there every Saturday. Before I knew it, the most radical activists recruited me. But even this motley group was splintering. Younger activists willing to risk arrest—or worse—by demonstrating publicly without others' approval challenged the more cautious veterans, among other frictions. The Establishment Jews dismissed the young Turks as *hong weibing*, Red Guards, a snide reference to the homicidal zealots of Mao Zedong's Cultural Revolution in the People's Republic of China.

"Of course we don't trust them," the rebels snorted, equally dismissive of the older *bonze*—Russian slang for rigid, self-important bureaucrats. While watching KGB agents riling up both sides, intensifying the split, I appreciated our shift from totalitarian rigidity to democratic chaos. When we disagreed, we didn't hide behind doublethink. We expressed ourselves freely. As in most families, whatever tensions we had didn't prevent us from uniting when necessary, especially when attacked.

Sharing this new feeling of freedom, flourishing after decades of stifling restrictions, we activists often felt like we had joined a small, select club. We usually could pick out our fellow freedom finders in a crowd. In fact, watching another young Soviet Jew blossom as she discovered her identity and freedom is what first drew me to Avital.

I quickly became swept up in many activities that took me beyond Archipova Street. I drafted petitions and planned demonstrations. I traveled with other young Refuseniks to various cities, collecting information about the anti-Semitic and anti-Zionist harassment Jews suffered all over the country. We issued semiannual reports tracking the official repression of Jews and the Jews' response. I helped compile lists of Refuseniks. Increasingly, my main job became connecting Refuseniks to the outside world.

I watched myself crossing one line after another: my first petition, my first public protest, my first roughing up, my first KGB tail, my first interrogation, my first arrest. Naturally, I felt dread whenever I nudged the edge of the envelope ever further. But each time, overcoming the fear triggered a surge of liberation. And, whenever possible, I sought any victory, no matter how small, that boosted my self-confidence. I was proud the first time I heard my name on BBC radio, or frustrated an interrogator, or figured out how to ridicule the KGB rather than letting them abuse me.

As KGB agents started following me everywhere, I tried conquering my initial skittishness. I teased them. I called KGB headquarters to report one tail for disgracing the state by being too drunk to follow me properly. I engaged another agent in conversation on a bus, detailing how happy a now-freed Refusenik he had followed is in Israel, until an eavesdropping passenger accused the KGB agent of spreading Zionist propaganda. I made two others pay half the fare when they pushed their way into my taxi because they feared losing track of me. I graciously thanked them for unwittingly protecting me from hooligans when I wandered through a seedy apartment block. And, as my involvement grew, I kept repeating that Indian proverb I had read in a chess primer long ago: "When you're riding on a tiger, the most dangerous thing is to stop."

AVITAL

I also learned that if I played my cards right, my KGB escorts could help set the stage for romance. I met Avital, then Natasha Stieglitz, during a moment of great tension and intense KGB scrutiny: the Yom Kippur War in October 1973. The war began when the Egyptian and Syrian armies surprised Israel on the Jews' holiest day.

I was at the standard Refusenik hangout, in front of Moscow's main synagogue, on a Saturday, Shabbat. I kept asking people to sign a pledge offering to donate blood to the Israeli army. After an hour or two, we planned to ask representatives of the Red Cross a few blocks away to respect our pledges by taking our blood and sending it to Israel. We were being mischievous. The Soviets would inevitably veto our request. During these challenging weeks, we just wanted to keep demonstrating our solidarity with Israel.

Natasha came to our outdoor Refusenik headquarters, wondering what had happened to her brother Michael "Misha" Stieglitz. Unbeknownst to us, he and I had met a week earlier, on Yom Kippur, when the war had started. He had wanted to join our demonstrations. Within three days of our meeting, he was protesting. He ended up jailed for fifteen days.

This tall, shy, tender young woman's quiet strength and beauty almost blinded me. Natasha looked vulnerable, exotic, out of place, like a beautiful southern flower lost in this northern land. I found myself terribly distracted as I delivered the bad news: Misha was in jail. But there was good news too. Trying to stop our movement's growth, the KGB was making it easy for new troublemakers like him to get exit visas rather quickly. (And that's what happened. Misha moved to Israel at the end of November.)

Hoping to impress Natasha, I walked away from her and toward one of the KGB agents surrounding us. "You see, this is my tail," I proudly told her. Then I approached him. Thrusting the list of volunteers in his face, I asked, "Are you ready to donate your blood to the Israeli army?" He didn't respond to my provocation, but I wasn't really trying to get his attention.

I soon realized I wasn't the only one interested. I asked Natasha if she was studying Hebrew and offered to help her find a group at her level. Suggesting she join our class, I asked, "What level are you?"

She answered my question with a question: "And you?"

"I know about a thousand words," I replied. She claimed that was exactly her level. When we studied together a few days later, I saw she was off by about 990 words. I was thrilled. I realized she wanted to learn Hebrew with me.

By the time Misha left prison, Natasha and I were connected for life. Whenever people ask me if I have regrets about what I did, about what happened to me, I look at them quizzically. I know I never could have met her in my previous life. From the moment we met, I could see in her eyes that Natasha was a free person. She never could have existed in the world I was raised to live in.

Within a month of meeting, we had decided to live together, fight together, and reach Israel together. But how would it work practically? I was already a Refusenik. Should she join me in a joint application, so we could go to Israel together? Or should she try her luck at getting there before me? We could not bear thinking about being apart at that moment, so we pushed aside this burning question.

One day, a few months after Natasha and I met, the activist Refuseniks planned a publicity stunt. We would deliver an open letter to the Central Committee of the Communist Party, signed by as many of us as possible, demanding our freedom. We invited foreign journalists, knowing the

KGB would arrest us as soon as we entered the office. We distributed copies of the letter to the reporters and left the original with Natasha. She was not yet on the KGB's radar, so we figured that if she arrived half an hour later, she could deliver the formal letter without being hassled.

Natasha followed the plan, but the KGB waited patiently and grabbed her too. They took us to Moscow's drunk tank. During my activist years, I visited Moscow's Sobering Station Number 8 regularly. Usually, the police would escort us there after demonstrations, while moving the regulars elsewhere. They put us in cells for preliminary interrogation, then released us a few hours later.

They interrogated us one by one. I hadn't expected Natasha to be arrested so I hadn't prepared her. As a rookie, she refused to say anything, including her name. Infuriated, the cops kept her all night. I waited outside for her, hour after hour. When that interminable night ended, I knew what my vote was. If there was a shot to get her out, she needed to go for it. When she walked out, I said, "I decided you should apply for a visa immediately."

We started planning our wedding, but a prominent guest interfered. On June 27, 1974, President Richard Nixon arrived in Moscow for a summit with the Soviet leader Leonid Brezhnev. On June 19, two men accosted me just as I arrived at work. They drove me in a black Volga for two hours to a jail in Volokolamsk. I was caught in a preventive sweep of potential troublemakers to ensure a smooth presidential visit, even though Soviet law deemed preventive arrests illegal.

While I languished, caught on the Nixon-related list of agitators to contain, Natasha ended up on the Nixon-related list of goodwill gestures to make. On the seventh day of my imprisonment, Natasha received an exit visa to join her brother Misha in Israel. The Soviets wanted to appear generous with the president in town.

Natasha considered refusing the visa but knew she might not get another chance for years. On the evening of July 3, a few hours after Nixon left Moscow, I was released. I had spent fifteen days in prison, without any trial or sentence. When I arrived home, my mother told me that Natasha was leaving in thirty-six hours.

Scrambling, Natasha arranged a wedding to be held in our apartment on July 4. It would be the first Jewish wedding either of us had ever attended. A Jewish wedding ends with the breaking of a glass, symbolizing the destruction of our Holy Temple in Jerusalem two thousand years ago.

It leaves most Jewish couples mingling the sadness of the past with the joy of the future. Starting off in reverse, we mingled the joy of our past eight months with the looming sadness of our future separation.

It was a wedding with no honeymoon. Like many newlyweds, we went to the airport. But only one of us took off. I dropped off a shy, quiet young woman who spoke no language other than Russian. With everything else going on, she hadn't added many words to her Hebrew vocabulary. As I said, "See you soon in Jerusalem," I had no idea that "soon" meant twelve years. But I had no doubt that we would stay together, no matter how long the separation.

Holding my new wife's hand, I tried reassuring her. "I'll be there within six months at the latest," I said. When I returned home, I plunged into despair. I feared we were no longer climbing our way to freedom. After all the excitement of the wedding, I was left alone and filled with dread.

The next morning, I woke up nursing a different kind of hangover than most newlyweds. I had a growing sense of alarm, wondering how we would stay in touch. I went to our usual place near the synagogue. There, I bumped into a family of New Yorkers on their way to Israel, Jerry and Jane Stern, with their two kids. I mentioned that I had gotten married two days before and my wife had already left me—to go to Israel. They seemed skeptical at first.

These tourist-Refusenik interactions had a peculiar power to them. In just a few minutes—feeling tense, rushed, and watched—you often shared more and bonded more intensely with strangers than you normally would. When the Sterns arrived in Israel, they tracked down Natasha. They found her in Tiberias, took photos, and encouraged her to write a letter to me. Then they returned to New York, networked, and found some other Jewish tourists to deliver the care package to me.

That started a cross-continent relay, involving hundreds of tourists, athletes, journalists, even US senators, who all kept me and Natasha in regular contact. Photos, letters, and cassette tapes flowed back and forth flawlessly, without any interruption, for the next three years until my arrest. These Jews were our own living bridge, connecting me and Natasha, who soon changed her name to Avital. This vast network of carrier pigeons from the free world is why, despite all their attempts at jamming, the KGB never truly isolated us.

By 1975, my Refusenik career had peaked. We didn't have any official positions, but my comrades started calling me, half-jokingly, "the

Spokesman." I earned the nickname by being in touch with a mind-boggling range of Jewish organizations. I learned how to respect turf considerations and ideological sensitivities. I met regularly with foreign journalists and diplomats, usually under KGB surveillance.

Even as I got used to being followed wherever I went, I received regular reminders of how much the KGB terrified others. When I visited my parents, who had moved to the Moscow suburbs, my mother looked distressed. My father quietly asked me to avoid visiting in the future with my "entourage." Eventually, my arrest ended the cat-and-mouse games, and began new ones.

OUR DIASPORA JEWISH PARTNERS
FIGHT AMONG THEMSELVES

Still, while Diaspora Jews seemed united in their adulation of Soviet Jews, they were deeply divided too, especially the Americans. There were so many organizations, it was hard to keep track of all their names: the Student Struggle for Soviet Jewry (SSSJ), the Union of Councils for Soviet Jews, the National Conference on Soviet Jewry, the Coalition of Soviet Jewry, and so many others.

Once, we hosted two charming young couples from New York who started comparing notes with one another. It had been a long afternoon, and I had no interest in doing two more briefings back-to-back. "How about I brief all of you together?" I suggested. All four looked offended. "Our organization needs its own briefing," each couple insisted in a huff.

Most Refuseniks had no idea what distinguished one organization from another or the distrust that often pitted them against each other. To pass information to the world with maximum publicity, however, I had to know who was who. The bickering sometimes threatened our work. It often forced us to double our risk of exposure, and theirs, by smuggling two sets of documents to two rival organizations—even when they were only blocks apart in midtown Manhattan.

It took a long time to realize that the chaos benefitted us. The range of organizations helped us reach a wide swath of American Jews. Underlying the competition was a classic division between activist and Establishment groups. Although they could not stand one another, they needed each other. The struggle for Soviet Jewry needed the activists' insistence to start and the Establishment's muscle to succeed.

This bristling alliance between insiders and outsiders originated with the movement in the 1960s and continued through the Soviet Union's collapse. The arc of our dialogue focused on how all this colliding energy could ramp up our power instead of dissipating it. There's nothing like sharing an enemy when you need to bond.

Many baby boomers thanked the Soviet Jewry movement for rooting them in Jewish history and Jewish causes. Fighting the good fight against KGB bad guys was significant. But there was something else. The smorgasbord of Jewish ideologies, tactics, and organizations welcomed many people. They didn't have to leave other values at the door, because having so many differences proved useful.

The KGB's seal of disapproval drove away all the doubts and divisions. Every warring, supposedly ego-driven organization earned its place on the same list of anti-Soviet organizations in my KGB files. They were all honorable accomplices in the crime of defeating the Soviet Union.

WE PROTEST!

I still remember the electric jolt—that exciting, overwhelming, thrilling feeling of Jewish unity—that filled us with power when a dozen Refuseniks stood for a full five minutes in front of the Kremlin, waving crude, homemade placards, demanding GIVE US VISAS TO ISRAEL and LET MY PEOPLE GO.

We limited the protest to a dozen, fearing that too many people knowing would give the KGB too many chances to find out. We lasted no more than five minutes before being arrested. Even if the authorities weren't tipped off in advance, how long could we have stood in the center of Moscow exercising our rights of free speech in a regime that constantly robbed us of those rights?

But those delicious, triumphant, boundless five minutes were all mine. I watched the scared, or perplexed, I-see-nothing passersby. Every now and then, I spied a surprised smile, a raised eyebrow, or one of the dozens of little signs people use to telegraph encouragement in totalitarian societies.

I stood there, looking like I was all alone. I knew I was standing in front of the headquarters of an empire that killed tens of millions of its own citizens to control the lives and the minds of two hundred million others. But I didn't feel alone; they didn't control me anymore. I felt exhilarated. The adrenaline was pumping, but so, too, was an amazing, almost physical, sensation: the Jewish people were behind me. The overwhelming feeling was one of empowering unity.

I saw a lonely foreign journalist lurking in the crowd. It had been quite a task to make sure he knew about the demonstration without the KGB finding out. His presence meant that, within hours of my arrest, the BBC, Voice of America, and Kol Yisrael would inform the world about it. As a result, the next day, our group's brief protest would unleash an avalanche of activity: Jews I had never met in North America, Europe, and Australia would take to the streets in the world's greatest cities, waving similar signs, shouting the same slogans, lobbying their senators and their members of parliament, their presidents and prime ministers, to force their governments to act.

LAUGHING TOGETHER AT OUR DIFFERENCES

Though many of us were strangers, we were all on this Jewish journey together. The ride was thrilling, even when it got bumpy. We discovered how we could fight together as comrades, despite being so different.

One evening in the mid-1970s, yet another most welcome young American couple entered our headquarters in the center of Moscow, the apartment of the famous veteran Refusenik Vladimir Slepak. I asked what our guests did professionally.

"I am a rabbi," the man replied.

Although I knew little about Judaism then, I knew enough to ask, "So why no kippah, no head covering?"

"We are Reconstructionists," his wife explained.

I looked at them quizzically. "As a mathematician, I love logic and I love these mathematical terms. What are you Reconstructionists deconstructing?"

"Well, we understand there is no God," the rabbi explained after some hesitation. "But 'God' is nevertheless a great moral idea, and we build on it while developing a sense of community through Jewish people power and the greatness of Jewish civilization."

Another leading Refusenik, Sasha Lunts, my mentor in the world of Zionism, chuckled. "Only America produces rabbis who know there is no God."

We all burst out laughing, but nobody was insulted. We were amusing ourselves, delighted by the many different paths each of us took to rally together in this struggle. As long as we were united as comrades on our journey, why should I care how my new partners found their way to this apartment in central Moscow? Did it matter to me if God chose them or they chose "god"? All it took was to look out the window and see my KGB tails to remember just how unimportant those disagreements were for our mutual venture.

That sense of Jewish unity was a real force, like the current that helps you swim downriver. But Jews don't swim alone. We're not even supposed to pray alone, seeking nine others for a quorum, a minyan. When you belong to the Jewish people, you don't just get an identity, with all the ideas and values and stories. You get a family, with all these people and personalities too.

4

JOINING THE DIALOGUE

"Why did two Jews survive the sinking of the *Titanic*?"

"Because they were talking."

When telling the joke, you have to gesticulate wildly but rhythmically, as if you're swimming. This was one of many Soviet anti-Semitic jokes I grew up with that mocked "dandruffy kikes." We supposedly "smelled of garlic." We spit when we talked. And we spoke too intensely, aggressively, violently. "How did your shirt get ripped? I walked between two Jews while they were talking." "When are Jews dangerous? When they talk." And on and on.

I confess, of the hundreds of anti-Semitic jokes I heard in my youth, the *Titanic* one is my favorite. Whatever the joke's originator had intended or known about Jews, it captured something deeply Jewish. Here's one of our eternal survival skills: we have been passionately arguing with each other, in good times and bad, for better and worse, for 3,900 years.

Sometimes, those arguments kept us blessedly distracted. At one of our lowest moments, in 70 CE, when the Romans destroyed our Temple, our holy city Jerusalem, and our independence, Rabbi Yohanan ben Zakkai wrangled one small concession from the victorious Emperor Vespasian: opening a yeshiva in Yavneh, forty miles from Jerusalem. Blocked from governing our homeland, we stayed alive as a stateless people by arguing about texts.

Throughout 1,900 years of exile, we would be martyred by Christians, humiliated by Muslims, menaced by Cossacks, hunted by Nazis, and tormented by the KGB—and yet we kept arguing. Sometimes we fought about big philosophical questions. Sometimes we quibbled, equally passionately, about picayune rituals.

These arguments not only kept us alive; they helped us thrive. One of our greatest collective accomplishments, the Talmud, is a sixty-six-volume transcript of what? Arguments. Our rabbis then built an elaborate system of specific laws based on those intense, sweeping debates, even though many of the philosophical questions remained unresolved.

One key to modern Israel's start-up success is the rich, contentious culture of questioning anyone, anywhere, anytime, regardless of rank or stature. The shouting starts in the Israeli army—up and down the chain of command—and continues, feeding Israelis' aggressive, out-of-the-box creativity in high tech and pharma.

The classic Jewish argument is a particular kind of clash. It's over issues that people take personally and will shout about vehemently. It respects few boundaries. It has zero tolerance for the hypocrisy of double-think or the sensitivities of political correctness. And it pivots on the dialectic, the clash between opposing views that requires each person to understand the other side—to annihilate the counterarguments while partially absorbing them.

The classic joke has a rabbi mediating between combatants. He says, "You're right" and "you're right." Then he admits that the outsider's cry—"They can't both be right!"—is "right too." The punchline captures the Jewish argument's freewheeling, open, yet ultimately constructive nature.

The modern Zionist idea, and eventually the state of Israel, emerged from a deep, decades-long Talmudic debate, starting in the late 1700s, about the Jewish people's future in the modern world. Over the years, as various movements formed in response to this crisis, Reformers yelled at Orthodox Jews who yelled at Conservative Jews who yelled at socialists who yelled at Bundists who yelled at Zionists. Even as Zionism developed, the clashes between Theodor Herzl's Political Zionists, Ahad Ha'am's Cultural Zionists, Abraham Isaac Kook's Religious Zionists, Ze'ev Jabotinsky's Revisionist Zionists, and David Ben-Gurion and Golda Meir's Labor Zionists were often bitter and nearly paralyzing but ultimately productive.

"IT WAS SUCH A GREAT TIME
WHEN YOU WERE IN PRISON"

A few years after I arrived in Israel, a neighbor who moved to Jerusalem from New York saw me playing with my children in the backyard. Looking wistful, she said, "You know, Natan, it was such a great time when you were in prison. Back then, we were all united. We all protested together. Those rallies were great places for dating too—I know many marriages that resulted. There was such a loving atmosphere between us and Israel." Sighing, she asked, "Where is it now?"

Despite having no intention to return to the Gulag, I almost shared her nostalgia. In the '70s and '80s, that feeling of joining our people in a historic struggle was so overwhelming, it outshone our many differences. Soviet Jewish Refuseniks, Diaspora Jews, and Israelis all felt like one big fighting family.

Our movement represented a remarkable alliance. Zionism and liberalism, the fight for Jewish identity and for human freedom, united easily under one banner. Zionists and Orthodox Jews and civil rights crusaders and anti-Communist cold warriors all cooperated. Only the most marginal players in the Jewish world—harsh anti-Zionists and uncompromising Communists—could not fit themselves into this broad communal coalition.

Like my neighbor, people tend to feel nostalgic about our moment of unity, focus, and effectiveness. But back then, it rarely felt so orderly. The dialogues were sometimes charming and sometimes enlightening, but usually irritating.

At first, the competing worldviews and sensibilities struck me as ego-driven or turf-oriented distractions. Eventually, I realized we were hashing out the enduring questions of the Jewish and Zionist world, which continue to shape today's Israel-Diaspora tensions. We updated the struggle between Ahad Ha'am's Cultural Zionism and Herzl's Political Zionism, asking: Do we focus on renewing Judaism or on building a Jewish state? We continued exploring the mystery that started with the Enlightenment in the 1700s and intensified after 1948, wondering: Is total assimilation inevitable in the Diaspora, or can one adapt just enough to be accepted yet stay Jewish? We addressed an even older question, debating: What's the Jewish mission, to better the Jewish people's lot or better the world?

Our movement ended in the 1990s. These arguments—and my involvement with them—continue.

VISITING SENATORS GET CAUGHT UP IN
OUR POLITICAL-CULTURAL SPLIT

Although the KGB targeted us Refuseniks as members of an underground organization seeking to undermine the Soviet regime, we insisted that our movement was legal, even under Soviet law. Our methods and goals remained clear. Our statements, press conferences, and demonstrations had one major aim: to publicize our case and contrast the declared Soviet policy on human rights with our unfortunate reality as Soviet citizens. Admittedly, planning public protests, collecting signatures, and transmitting messages to the free world required secrecy until the last minute. Otherwise, the demonstrations would never have occurred, the petitions would have remained unsigned, and the letters would have been intercepted.

Dodging the KGB bugs in our apartments and the listening devices eavesdropping on our conversations in the streets, we often used "magic slates" for any sensitive exchanges. Every Refusenik's apartment was overstuffed with these children's toys, brought in by our Jewish friends from abroad along with Hebrew manuals, Jewish books, and Star of David souvenirs. It was easy to scratch letters with a stylus onto these flimsy, colorful wax boards covered by a sheet of acetate. Then—poof!—it was just as easy to erase them by raising the acetate sheet. Often decorated with Disney cartoon characters like Mickey, Minnie, Pluto, and Goofy, these magic slates were essential weapons in our war with the KGB. Anytime someone brandished this little children's plaything, we knew the conversation was turning serious.

One day in the summer of 1975, the American embassy's diplomatic attaché, Joe Presel, told me that the largest delegation of US senators to visit the Soviet Union would arrive in two weeks. The red-carpet treatment would include meeting with the Soviet leader, Leonid Brezhnev, at the Kremlin. The timing was significant. Congress's passage of the Jackson-Vanik amendment in January 1975 infuriated the Soviet Union. The summertime delegation suggested that both countries hoped to rebuild relations.

Joe then reached for the ever-present magic slate, signaling there was more to the story. He scribbled that two senators, Jacob Javits, a Republican, and Abe Ribicoff, a Democrat, wanted the delegation to meet with Refusenik leaders before meeting Brezhnev.

I was thrilled. Our movement was constantly trying to mobilize members of Congress. Usually, the best we could do was write a letter, get a tourist to smuggle it out, and trust one Jewish organization or another to deliver it. Face-to-face meetings with senators or representatives were rare and risky. Even when a prominent senator like Ted Kennedy bravely broke the taboo, he visited Refusenik scientist Alexander Lerner at midnight, only after completing all of the scheduled talks. This deprived the Soviets of the opportunity to cancel any meetings in protest if they objected.

Usually, when such distinguished visitors arrived, I introduced them to leading Refuseniks, then arranged for them to meet Andrei Sakharov too, in support of the broader human rights movement. Although these meetings buoyed us psychologically, they remained off the dignitaries' official itineraries to avoid a confrontation with Soviet authorities.

Now, for the first time, a leading delegation of fourteen American senators would incorporate a meeting with Refuseniks into the schedule. They would then take our concerns to the top Soviet leaders. The senators were telling the regime clearly: you can't improve relations with the United States if you oppress Soviet Jews.

Joe asked, "Can you get five or six key activists to Senator Jacob Javits's hotel suite without the KGB finding out in advance and disrupting the plan?" Even most of the senators would only get last-minute invitations to the briefing, which was planned during their few hours off on the Sunday before meeting Brezhnev.

Knowing how many factions and personalities I had to satisfy, I needed more seats at the table. I insisted, "You have fourteen senators. Give me fourteen Refuseniks." Joe agreed.

Over the next two weeks, I tried to be as discreet as possible as I made the arrangements. I worried that the KGB would stop us at any moment.

The day before the Refuseniks met the senators, we gathered in our spot on Archipova Street across from the Moscow synagogue. Those of us in the know were excited but a bit nervous too. We all remembered how the KGB celebrated President Nixon's 1974 visit by arresting a dozen of us potential troublemakers.

Our biggest challenge came from an unexpected source. Vladimir "Volodia" Prestin—a leading Refusenik and a decent, elegant man, known respectfully as "the Count"—approached me that Saturday. Volodia was a Hebrew teacher passionate about resurrecting Jewish culture in the Soviet Union. Ideologically, our small movement was finding itself increasingly split between the *kulturniki*, activists like him who were committed to a Jewish cultural revival within the Soviet Union, and the *politiki*, the Refuseniks focused on the political fight for freedom, centered on the right to emigrate to Israel.

I was instinctively a *politiki* but didn't take the debate seriously. We all signed the same petitions. We all attended the same protests. We all tried learning Hebrew, and some of us taught the language too. And we all shared whatever texts we could find about Jewish history, Jewish heritage, Jewish culture, Zionism, and Israel. I assumed the split was mostly about fragile egos and silly turf wars, yet another reflection of our people's long, loud history.

"Natan, I want you to know it's great that this meeting is taking place," Volodia said that tense Saturday. "And I don't want to disappoint you. But we are not attending this meeting. Our group will request another, separate meeting with the senators."

"You're kidding me," I exclaimed. We weren't planning on meeting a bunch of congregational rabbis happy to bop around the city indulging our little tiffs. These were fourteen of America's most powerful politicians, here for a heavily monitored, high-profile visit. We were about to enjoy an extraordinary moment of recognition. Now, we risked senatorial outrage, international embarrassment, and KGB mockery as the gang that couldn't even meet properly. I couldn't imagine how to explain this to my friend Joe the diplomat, let alone to the senators I didn't know.

At the same time, Volodia was the last person I would expect to be petty. He explained himself fairly. "Natan, you know yourself. You guys will dominate the meeting, talking about the Jackson amendment, the Jackson amendment, the Jackson amendment—then about emigration quotas, which will get you back to the Jackson amendment."

I claimed we would also speak about freeing prisoners of Zion—Jews imprisoned for their Zionist activity—boosting emigration, ending the arbitrary visa rejections, and stopping illegal harassment. "I understand," Volodia replied. "But who will speak about the most important problem, that it's almost impossible to get access to Jewish education and culture? The future of Soviet Jewry depends on this. We're trying to revive a rich

Jewish culture the Soviets decimated. We don't want our cultural agenda hijacked by your passing political concerns."

Still, I warned, the KGB could exploit our split to fragment the movement. I added that I had no idea how to ask for separate meetings. "I also lack the authority," I told him.

He reassured me. He would make the request through his journalist contacts. I started working the back channels. I tried calming emotions on both sides while keeping the meeting secret.

Senator Jacob Javits's sense of humor saved us. When a reporter conveyed Volodia's request for a separate meeting, Javits didn't sweat it. Well practiced in our people's quarrelsome, quibbling ways, the veteran Jewish senator from New York said, "We don't have time for two meetings, but my suite has two adjoining rooms. Let each group choose its own salon."

The next day, ten senators joined Javits and Ribicoff for a comprehensive discussion with the fourteen Refuseniks. We were thrilled that twelve of the fourteen-member delegation participated. Although Javits's suite had two rooms, no one noticed any divisions among the Refuseniks. We had enough time to air all our concerns, to the frustration of the many KGB tails, who stood outside the hotel or in front of Javits's suite, unable to interfere as we prepped the senators to meet Brezhnev.

The KGB agreed that this meeting was momentous. Two years later, it won the KGB's version of a gold medal. Beating hundreds of other gatherings, protests, and petitions, it ranked as one of the key finalists the KGB chose to include in my indictment. The KGB singled out my role in organizing the meeting as one of the nineteen episodes to be classified as "high treason" in "aiding the capitalist countries in their struggle against the Soviet Union."

OUR SPLIT GOES PUBLIC

All the squabbling before the meeting risked exposing the conflicts among the Refuseniks. Days later, one of my closest and most helpful reporter friends, Robert Toth of the *Los Angeles Times*, told me, "I am going to write an article about the split."

"Don't do it, Bob," I pleaded. "The article will harm us, and you're our friend." We believed we had to keep our disagreements far below the public radar to avoid aiding the KGB.

He replied, "If I don't, somebody else will. The other reporters know about this and are talking. Why should I stand by while they get the scoop? Besides," he added, "trust me, your movement will survive this—and might even learn from it."

I refused to cooperate. Bob interviewed others. His subsequent article was headlined "Split Among Activist Soviet Jews Breaks into Open over Talks with U.S. Senators." It emphasized the growing division between "emigration" and "culture" among Refuseniks.

"You don't understand," he later explained. "It's good for this discussion to go public. If it's a serious split, articles like these can help you argue it out—and sort it out."

Bob was right. Opening the debate emphasized the ideological differences, not the personal fights. And this focus on *tachlis*, Yiddish for substance, sharpened both sides' arguments.

Volodia and his *kulturniki* allies rooted their argument in math and poetry. Thinking statistically, they argued that the Six Day War only transformed, at most, a few thousand Jews into activists. None of us had any idea if or when we would be free. Volodia would languish for eighteen years in total. "Today, there are maybe thirty prisoners of Zion and barely three thousand Refuseniks. Rather than focus on a small minority's political fight, let's remember the millions," Volodia and his allies insisted. "There are three million Soviet Jews deprived of Jewish education, knowledge, and identity." And, they often added, "if we can inspire them with the Jewish education and culture they deserve, the masses will keep the Jewish flame alive for decades, no matter how long the fight takes."

We *politiki* agreed the numbers were small. But if the price of emigration wasn't so high, and the chances of emigrating weren't so low, the floodgates would open. So we, too, were mathematicians and poets. We were fighting for the masses at a historic moment. We could tap the Jewish world's post-1967 energy while exploiting the Soviets' increasingly desperate attempts to woo the West.

Tactically, we also feared that shifting our movement to emphasize Jewish education would make it easier for the Soviets to fool the world. The authorities could claim that Jews had the same freedom that Christians did. They could open some Jewish school to parallel the official Christian church, make a big splash, invite journalists, con the Americans, and rob our movement of its potency. It was harder to fake emigration statistics or pretend to free prisoners who remained imprisoned.

We were really squabbling over priorities and timing, not core values or mission. Everyone in our small, overextended movement was doing double duty. We were all cultivating our newly discovered Jewish souls while asserting our newly activated Zionist pride.

POLITICS VERSUS CULTURE

We didn't know it at the time, but we were replaying a classic argument about how to best strengthen the Jewish people. When the formal Zionist movement began in the late 1800s, the Cultural Zionist Ahad Ha'am dismissed Theodor Herzl's Political Zionist dreams of a state as a grandiose delusion distracting from the national cultural revival the Jews needed.

Both thinkers agreed that, after centuries of persecution, Jews were in crisis. But they disagreed, as we did in the 1970s, regarding how best to mobilize the Jewish masses. Herzl's Political Zionists wanted a Jewish state as soon as possible to save as many Jewish lives as possible. Examining the fundamental cause of Jewish misery, Herzl articulated his "chief tenet": "Whoever wishes to change people must change the conditions under which they live." Moreover, "All human beings ought to have a home."

The notion of Jews moving to Palestine en masse is "a fantasy bordering on madness," Ahad Ha'am scoffed. He also doubted that "the land will afford them adequate sustenance." The "truth is bitter," he warned, "but with all its bitterness it is better than illusion."

Ahad Ha'am's Cultural Zionists emphasized Jewish education. More worried about the "problem of Judaism" than the "problem of the Jews," he wanted to save Jewish souls.

As with the *politiki* and the *kulturniki*, both Herzl and Ahad Ha'am were correct, and in many ways overlapped. In both cases, as usual, while the bickering over priorities continued, the Jews' biggest problem— Jew-hatred—became the great leveler. By the 1940s, the Holocaust, then the expulsion of Jews from Arab lands, proved we needed a state. The cultural renaissance followed.

In the case of Soviet Jews, the KGB targeted both factions. The persecution against political activists that intensified in the 1970s broadened in the 1980s, as the KGB harassed Hebrew teachers and other *kulturniki* too. The debate about saving Jewish bodies by getting them to Israel or saving Jewish souls by educating them wherever they are continues today.

Nearly thirty-five years after my conversation with Volodia on Archipova Street, I became the head of the Jewish Agency for Israel. Since 1948, the organization has brought nearly 3.5 million Jews on aliyah to Israel from dozens of countries. By the time I became chairman, fewer Jews needed an "aliyah of rescue." After the Soviet Union fell, most Jews lived in freedom. Moving to Israel, therefore, became less a matter of fleeing persecution and more a matter of choosing freely.

In this new era of an "aliyah of choice," I believed that strengthening Jewish identity had to become the Jewish Agency's central mission. "Let's focus on reconnecting young Jews to their history, culture, heritage, community, and Israel," I declared. "Deciding to make aliyah is now a consequence of this connection."

When traditionalists resisted this reform, my old friend Volodia called. "Congratulations," he needled me. "Welcome to the club. Finally, you understand that Jewish education comes first."

I didn't want to argue with him about timing and priorities. Instead, I described a recent experience: my first attempt at the Jewish Agency to mediate between two groups of emissaries from Israel we had sent to the former Soviet Union. Although both groups worked for us, the *chinuch shlichim*, the educators, and the *aliyah shlichim*, the emigration recruiters, wouldn't work together.

I gathered them in one room. Playing peacemaker, I said, "We're from the same organization. We have the same aim. Let's see how we can unite our efforts."

They all started shouting.

"What Jewish culture? Bah," the immigration types scoffed. "It's an indulgence, like painting the toenails of a corpse. Bring 'em to Israel: that's how they'll learn about Judaism and Jewish culture."

"Enough!" the educator types responded. "You care about bodies, not souls. You don't care whether they're Jews or not—you only want volume."

"Sound familiar?" I asked Volodia.

We both laughed. Volodia added, "At least the KGB isn't lurking behind their backs. Let them argue."

"And two million Jews have already left the Soviet Union," I said.

INGATHERING EXILES OR
FREEDOM OF EMIGRATION?

In the beginning, everything looked simple. Israel helped Soviet Jews rediscover our identity. Israel sent us invitations to join our relatives. Even if these relatives were fictitious, the possibility of reunification with our Jewish family was very real.

Through the words of a song written by a young Jew from Belarus, Israel Reshel, we celebrated Israel's colors. We sang, "Kachol v'lavan, ein tzeva acher."

> *The blue and the white*
> *I have no other colors*
> *The blue and the white*
> *I'm merely returning home.*

This simple song, with barely a dozen words, captured our sense of rebirth. We were beginning our way back to our people, our language, our country. It became our anthem.

Those lucky enough to receive permission to emigrate quickly collected their things and parted with friends at Sheremetyevo International Airport. These goodbyes were always dramatic. Nobody knew if they would see each other again. No one knew who was next in line to get a visa—or go to prison.

With no direct flights to Tel Aviv possible—because the Soviet Union had broken diplomatic relations with Israel following the 1967 war—the lucky person traveled to Vienna. There, a Jewish Agency representative greeted every Soviet Jew. After a day or two of processing, the Soviet émigré made aliyah to Israel, gaining automatic citizenship. One more person, one more family, reached the homeland.

The Jews arriving in Vienna by train or air soon realized they were now free people. They could choose: continue on to Israel or "drop out" and move elsewhere. Once they informed the Jewish Agency that they wanted to go to the United States, the Hebrew Immigrant Aid Society (HIAS) stepped in.

Founded in New York City after the anti-Semitic Russian pogroms in 1881, the legendary HIAS helped resettle many of the two million Eastern European Jews who arrived in America until the 1920s. The organization rescued more than three hundred thousand displaced Jews in the chaotic years following World War II. Subsequently, by helping Jews expelled from Communist Europe, Muslim Arab countries, and Ethiopia, HIAS remained the American Jewish immigrant's best friend.

By the 1970s, HIAS was considering closing its Vienna office. There were few Jews left in Europe to emigrate anywhere. Then, as the number of *noshrim* (Hebrew for dropouts) started to grow, HIAS developed a new mission: to bring Soviet Jews to America.

HIAS searched for American relatives or representatives of American Jewish communities who were willing to sponsor these Soviet Jews. If successful, the émigrés could get refugee status from the American government. HIAS now generously funded offices in Vienna and Rome, and started helping Soviet Jews find their way to the *goldene medina*, America.

The number grew every month. By 1976, at least half the Soviet Jews escaping Russia with Israeli visas were dropping out of the aliyah process in Vienna. These dropouts disappointed most of us activists. Sometimes, friends who had fought to return to "our historical motherland" only admitted at the airport that they had decided not to go to Israel. I could not help feeling let down.

However frustrated we in Moscow were with the dropouts, Israelis felt even more betrayed. They believed these "ingrates" were abandoning the Zionist mission and mocking all the resources invested in getting them to Israel. Moreover, the dropouts were endangering the entire struggle. How, the Israelis reasoned, could the Soviets tolerate citizens using this family reunification fig leaf to join the Union of Soviet Socialist Republics' greatest enemy, the United States of America?

Israel's leaders resented American Jewish organizations for "stealing Jews from us" and wasting a precious visa that could have gone to a future Israeli. They demanded that their American Jewish allies close HIAS's European offices and quit luring Soviet Jews to America. They asked the American government to stop giving dropouts refugee status. "With a Jewish state open to every Jew," the Israelis reasoned, "there can be no Jewish refugees."

Most American Jews' grandparents and great-grandparents had left Russia for America, not Palestine. "We can't close our gates to our cousins," they explained. "We cannot shut down the organizations that helped us. And we certainly can't ask the American government to stop welcoming these oppressed fellow Jews as refugees."

Having failed to convince American Jews directly, Israeli officials asked Refuseniks to join their campaign. Even before Israel's Liaison Office intervened, many Jewish activists had criticized the dropout phenomenon. Dozens of Refuseniks—including some prisoners of Zion—signed emotional appeals asking their fellow Jews to feel a broader sense of responsibility for this struggle to "let my people go—to Israel." They saw immigration as a communal responsibility, not just a vehicle for indulging émigrés' individual ambitions.

I sympathized with the Israelis emotionally and ideologically. Still, as hard as it was to say no to their request to denounce the dropouts, I couldn't say yes. A small group of us *politiki*—including Vladimir Slepak, Dina Beilin, Sasha Lunts, Alexander Lerner, and Vitaly Rubin—sent a letter disagreeing with the Israeli government's official position. We wrote it as unapologetic Zionists fighting for our right to go to Israel. We affirmed that Israel was the only place for us. Still, we believed that Israel's role was to welcome Jews home, not block them from going elsewhere.

We believed in the Zionist project enough to stick by our commitment to free emigration and free choice. It would hurt our movement if Soviet Jews compared the commissars of Communism, forcing Jews to stay, with some imagined commissars of Zionism, forcing Jews to go to the homeland.

We also doubted the Israeli claim that the Soviets cared whether emigrants moved to America or Israel. Today, historians who have researched the Soviet archives confirm that we were correct. The Kremlin fury centered on Jewish emigration *from* the Soviet "paradise," not *to* America instead of Israel.

During this tense dialogue, the head of the Jewish Agency, Arye Dulzin, demanded that American Jews stop helping the dropouts. When he claimed to be speaking in the name of Soviet Jews, not just Israel, American Jewish activists waved around our letter, abruptly ending the debate.

The telephone calls and tourists' messages from Israel reprimanding us dissidents included some unofficial warnings: "After such disloyalty, don't expect to get a place in the preferred absorption centers in Tel Aviv or the Jerusalem hills. We will send you to the edge of the universe, in the newly started development town of Arad."

So, before being threatened with exile in Siberia, I was threatened with exile to the Negev.

THE SPECTER OF ASSIMILATION

The tensions over dropouts continued until the early 1990s, when the decaying Soviet Union permitted emigration to all countries and direct flights to Israel. But in 1986, when I arrived in Israel, the fight was at its height. As I prepared for my first visit to America to thank many of our freedom-fighting allies, including President Ronald Reagan and the congressional leadership, Israeli officials and Jewish activists briefed me. We were all wondering how to keep building the movement's momentum.

I received two off-the-record requests. Prime Minister Shimon Peres asked me to cool my critiques of Soviet authorities; irritating them too much might endanger future emigration. Foreign Minister Yitzhak Shamir requested that I ask America's leaders to stop granting refugee status to Soviet Jewish dropouts. I was a new immigrant, appreciative of everything Israel had done for me. I felt particularly grateful for Peres's and Shamir's efforts. But I refused both requests.

Moshe Arens, the cabinet minister responsible for Soviet Jewry, also approached me. "I get it," he said. "I understand your position respects free choice. I made aliyah from America. I, too, cherish human rights. But, remember," he added, "we are responsible for the Jewish people's future. Watch what's already happening. Those who go to America assimilate quickly. They will disappear as Jews. You fought so hard for Soviet Jews to join the Jewish people. Don't you feel some responsibility to help keep them Jewish?"

Arens's words were particularly convincing and sobering. This threat was real. In the future, I would watch survey after survey show how the number of Jews in America abandoning Judaism galloped ahead. Increasingly, the children of Jews who had left the Soviet Union led the way.

Why? The defining American Jewish institutions didn't speak to them. Soviet Jewish identity was wired differently and took other forms. Synagogues were too religious for these mostly nonreligious, proudly nationalist Jews. American Jewry's many fundraising organizations were too giving oriented for the Soviet Jews, who arrived with nothing from an economy of privation dependent on state, not private, funding. While the American Jewish community helped them most generously, few of the arriving Soviet Jews joined any existing organizations.

Even today, when I address audiences in the big Russian Jewish émigré communities in Brooklyn, San Francisco, and Chicago, young people often ask me if it is true that Israel didn't want their parents coming to America. I describe the dropout battle and quote Arens. I then say, "So, it's your obligation, and mine, to prove him wrong. You Jews are going to build a Jewish future."

I still believe there are no shortcuts when ingathering exiles. You cannot separate Zionism from freedom of choice. Jews will only move to Israel, let alone stay there, if they want to, not because they're forced.

But I wonder, could we have done better? Couldn't the leaders in Israel and the rest of the Jewish world have conferred, thinking one step ahead? While helping the immigrants resettle, couldn't they have created programs to help the newcomers integrate into their new Jewish worlds, on their terms? We might have developed a Birthright or some other game-changing innovation thirty years earlier.

Unfortunately, the charged atmosphere around the dropout issue made it impossible to have the constructive dialogue we needed. Israelis would have had to accept reality, debating how to help the Soviet Jews, not stop them. American Jews would have had to accept that their US-born ways of "doing Jewish" were not universal and didn't suit these immigrants. The Jewish organizations would have had to understand that their responsibilities didn't stop with delivering subsidies and job-seeking advice. They should have developed identity-building programs tailored to this new phenomenon of Russian American Jewry.

Instead, Israelis were too busy mourning the émigrés as bad Jews, and Americans were too busy welcoming them as good Americans. It took decades before a constructive dialogue about new kinds of Russian Jewish identities began.

In 2015, when French Jews felt menaced by terrorism and anti-Semitism, I spoke to Prime Minister Benjamin Netanyahu about the factors discouraging them from making aliyah. As head of the Jewish Agency, I mentioned the high apartment prices, the nonrecognition of French diplomas, and other issues facing them in Israel. Many, therefore, were choosing other destinations, including Canada and Australia.

"We have great relationships these days with the Canadians and Australians," Netanyahu said. "We can ask each government not to let the Jews in—and tell them to try Israel first."

Clearly, neither the Canadians nor Australians would restrict French citizens' freedom of choice. Moreover, I was disappointed that this proprietary attitude persisted. Bibi was not some heavy-handed socialist Ben-Gurionite, but one of the most sophisticated westernized Zionists, who had lived in America for years. Yet he, too, like most Likud liberals I knew, was deeply committed to democratic individualism but still believed that if Israel belongs to the Jews, the Jews, in many ways, belong to Israel.

A STRUGGLE FOR JEWISH RIGHTS OR HUMAN RIGHTS?

Although relations with the Israelis turned testy at times, the dropout battles didn't cloud our day-to-day cooperation. My relations with our Israeli "bosses" only became strained when I linked the Jewish struggle for free emigration with the democratic dissidents' broader struggle for human rights in the Soviet Union.

Among Soviet Jewish activists, my connection with democratic dissidents made me a maverick. To Israelis, it made me suspect. It's too easy to oversimplify this fight in retrospect. It wasn't a conflict between the white-hat, altruistic crusaders for civil rights versus the black-hat, selfish Jewish nationalists. It wasn't a struggle between naive democratic dreamers and hard-nosed Zionist realists. Instead, it was the sort of tactical debate every movement faces about focus, alliances, and mission creep. In our case, it played out against a long-standing Jewish debate about how best to save ourselves, while also trying to save the world.

Most Soviet Jewish activists sympathized with the democratic dissidents. We all despised Soviet totalitarianism and anti-Semitism. We cheered anyone who defied these modern-day pharaohs. Many of us revered Andrei Sakharov, whether we knew him or not. He showed us all, Jews and non-Jews, how to stand for what we believed in, even if it meant sacrificing a position at the top of the Soviet pyramid.

Nevertheless, most Jewish activists believed that our movement should keep its distance from the dissidents. Many reasoned that, having announced that we wanted to leave the Soviet Union, it would be dishonest to tell the Russians how to live.

For many activists, the distance from dissidents and the Soviet Union's problems often went hand in hand with the Jewish awakening.

Zionism created a new stage in Jewish history. Finally, we were work-ing for ourselves. We were solving our problems in our homeland, or struggling to get there. "Let's not distract ourselves with other causes that might muddy the focus on building our nation," many Zionists warned.

The Jewish activists in the USSR felt this keenly, because so many Jews over the centuries had been so involved in so many nationalist and cosmopolitan causes. We were czarists and Ukrainian nationalists. We were Bolsheviks and Mensheviks. We were Leninists, Trotskyites, and Stalinists. In the end, what did it accomplish? Nothing, or worse.

Since the rise of modernity, these causes often served as escape hatches for Jews from Judaism and the Jewish people. When trouble erupted, the prominence of so many Jews in these movements often backfired. Rather than earning any goodwill, the Jews were often blamed, intensifying the anti-Semitism. Jews were overrepresented among revolutionaries and among victims of revolution. Jews led many KGB departments during the bloodiest years of Stalin's purges, and Jews led the long list of the many victims.

Israelis shared this historic wariness. They saw how many idealistic Jews invoked their favorite universal causes to justify abandoning the Jewish people. For Israelis, recent history—the anguish of the Holocaust and the emergence of Israel—dictated the agenda. The Jewish people shouldn't deviate from the most pressing priorities: building the state and ingathering exiles.

More practically, the leaders of Israel's Liaison Office feared that the KGB viewed the human rights cause as threatening the entire Soviet enterprise. As shadowy government operatives themselves, they believed they had an informal understanding with the KGB. Zionists should focus on rescuing Jews while distancing themselves from subversive activities. The Russians might then tolerate occasional spurts of emigration from this small marginal minority, especially if pressured by the West. Allying with the democratic dissidents, however, would be declaring war against the entire Soviet system.

I believed the Israelis were being naive. There was no playing nice with the KGB, especially on emigration. Letting Soviet citizens feel they had the freedom to choose anything, let alone where to live, was too threaten-ing to the stability of the regime. The Communist system was too rigid for such autonomy: it had to control the lives of millions of doublethinkers.

Besides, we activists didn't want a few thousand Jews out today and a few thousand more out tomorrow. We wanted a mass exodus of Jewish people from the land of oppression. We wanted to rip a hole in the Iron Curtain and free millions.

Having said we want to leave, I agreed it didn't make sense for us Refuseniks to fight for a different way of life in the Soviet Union. But I befriended dissidents for a different reason. Dissidents became a part of my life as a free person as soon as I abandoned the world of doublethink.

I gained the strength to be a free person by discovering my people. Essential to this new freedom was speaking my mind. The new person I was becoming would no longer simply be inspired by the moral example of Andrei Sakharov's essay or the Prague Spring supporters' Red Square protests. I would speak on their behalf.

For me, it was a gradual process. As you free yourself from doublethink, you fight for your own freedom. Eventually, naturally, you sympathize with others, you say what you feel, you start fighting for their rights, because you are no longer afraid to say what you think.

Beyond your own individual liberation, you understand that you now belong to the free world. You want it to be strong. The more people who join you in freedom, fleeing the world of doublethink, the more you all strengthen your new world, this free world.

Still, I never expected that supporting the dissidents would risk getting me excommunicated from my national struggle, which had freed me in the first place.

I also made a more tactical calculation. I saw how important supporters like Sakharov were for us. No one else attracted as many cameras and journalists as he did, and his activism would earn him the 1975 Nobel Peace Prize. After I became close to Sakharov, American Jewish leaders frequently asked me for Sakharov's signature on this, his involvement with that. As so often happens, the right thing to do was also the shrewd thing to do.

In 1975, I started volunteering to help Sakharov in his relations with foreign correspondents and other important visitors. He and his wife, Yelena Bonner, appreciated my fluency in English and my comfort with journalists. Having worked as the spokesman for our movement, I had learned how to translate our message. Journalists had particular ways that worked for them, and their editors, when reporting stories.

Over the years, I have met many supposedly great people. They often shrink in your estimation when you see them up close. Sakharov was the opposite. My admiration for him only grew. His humility, his sincerity, and his generosity made him even greater in private than he appeared in public.

Another Refusenik, Vitaly Rubin, was also close to the dissidents. Thanks to him, I met other legendary figures. They included Yuri Orlov, a physicist who would also serve nine years in prison; Andrei Amalrik, the brave writer who published an essay in 1970 asking the unthinkable, *Will the Soviet Union Survive Until 1984?*; Alexander Ginzburg, the poet who helped Alexander Solzhenitsyn distribute the royalty revenues from *The Gulag Archipelago* and some of Solzhenitsyn's Nobel Prize funds to political prisoners; and Lyudmila Alexeyeva, a prominent Russian historian who was expelled from the Communist Party back in 1968 and fought for Russian human rights into her nineties, until the day she died, December 8, 2018.

Initially, our Israeli partners tolerated my connection with the dissidents as my little hobby. Occasionally, some Israelis warned me not to go too far with this distraction. Then came Helsinki.

When the Soviet Union and thirty-four other nations signed the Helsinki Accords in 1975, Soviet officials celebrated it as a victory. Many dissidents mourned it as a loss. Since it first seized control of Eastern Europe and the Baltic states after World War II, the Soviet Union had sought to legitimize its newly expanded borders. The "first basket" of the accords, formally called the Conference on Security and Cooperation in Europe, delivered that international approval. The Soviet Union also wanted greater economic cooperation with the West. The "second basket" promised that payoff. In return, the Soviets had to accept the "third basket," which included promises to respect basic human rights, facilitate family reunification, and allow cultural exchanges. But all the liberal, democratic commitments were nonbinding. Soviet officials were masterful at paying lip service to these rights, at the United Nations and elsewhere. By 1975, the West had a long record of stomaching Soviet lies.

Dissidents feared the Soviet Union would fool the West yet again. Yuri Orlov, Andrei Amalrik, Lyudmila Alexeyeva, and I had many heated debates, wondering how we could hold the Soviet Union to these new commitments. I proposed that we write letters inviting Western politicians, media organizations, and human rights organizations into a dialogue about how to fulfill the "spirit of Helsinki." By showcasing how various countries honored the agreements, I hoped to create a public atmosphere that would discourage the Soviets from trampling our rights.

Orlov feared that letters would just be more chatter. Cleverly and courageously, he proposed establishing a monitoring group. He figured that such an ongoing body would trigger the kind of Soviet backlash against us that would force the West to notice the constant Soviet violations of this freshly signed agreement.

Led by Orlov, eleven of us established the Public Group for Monitoring the Fulfillment of the Humanitarian Articles of the Helsinki Final Act by the Soviet Union, dedicated to updating the West about Soviet compliance. It would become famous as the Helsinki Monitoring Group or the Moscow Helsinki Group. Vitaly Rubin and I were the two Jewish activists involved. When the Soviets rushed Vitaly's emigration along and he left for Israel, Vladimir Slepak replaced him. I also became this group's unofficial spokesman, responsible for sharing the reports we produced and the evidence we found with Western journalists and politicians.

Being in this group introduced me to the struggle of different groups throughout the Soviet Union. Suddenly, I found myself speaking on behalf of Tatars exiled from Crimea, Pentecostalists persecuted for teaching their religion to their children, Lithuanian priests, Armenian nationalists, and so many others. From my vantage point, it was clear that all these struggles were interconnected. Ultimately, each of their successes contributed to our mutual aim of tearing a bigger and bigger hole in the Iron Curtain separating Soviet totalitarianism from the free world.

Within ten months, each of the founding monitors would be arrested or exiled. By then, we had changed the conversation about Helsinki and human rights. Our group published more than twenty documents. The reports detailed the Soviet empire's constant assaults on human rights. We highlighted the oppression of dissidents, the suppression of Jewish emigration, the suffering of political prisoners, and the persecution of Catholic priests in Lithuania, Pentecostalists in Siberia, Crimean Tatars in Kazakhstan, and many other targeted groups.

Public groups dedicated to monitoring the Helsinki agreements started popping up in many countries on both sides of the Iron Curtain. On Capitol Hill, Congress established the Commission on Security and Cooperation in Europe, originally involving eight members of the House of Representatives and eight senators, along with three administration representatives. This unique bipartisan initiative scrutinized our documents, amplifying the voices of the victims of Communist cruelty.

Soviet violations of Helsinki's nonbinding third basket clouded every future negotiation between the USSR and the West. This ongoing scrutiny put the Soviet Union under unprecedented, and unanticipated, pressure. Demands that it respect these commitments hounded the regime until it collapsed a decade and a half later.

It turned out that, in 1975, the Soviet Union had signed its own death warrant.

MY SITUATION TURNS TENSE
WITH THE SOVIETS AND THE ISRAELIS

But in 1976, the situation looked different. I was sure that I was doing exactly what needed to be done, not only for the broader struggle for human rights but to advance our Jewish agenda. This growing coalition of freedom forces could only benefit the cause of Jewish emigration.

Israel's Liaison Office disagreed. Zionist activities and anti-Soviet initiatives seemed to be overlapping for the first time. Leading Zionists and dissidents were both signing anti-Soviet documents, and the Israelis genuinely feared the Soviet reaction. "How can we say to our Russian counterparts that we don't interfere in your internal affairs?" they snapped. They concluded that the danger to the Zionist movement was so great that they had to cut me off.

When the KGB started targeting the members of the Moscow Helsinki Group, one of the leaders of the Liaison Office invited Avital for a frank, off-the-record conversation.

"Your husband has crossed all the red lines," he said. "He's become a dissident. He is no longer part of our Zionist movement and his behavior endangers it. Soon he will be arrested. And we, the state of Israel, won't defend him."

He then offered some fatherly advice for Avital: "Forget about him. He's ruining his life and will eventually ruin yours too. You're still young. We will help you start a new life."

This conversation triggered two urgent telephone calls between me and Avital. Our discussions were strained. We knew the KGB was taping every word. She could not tell me with whom she had spoken and what she was told exactly. And I couldn't tell her what my next steps would be. Still, Avital conveyed the message the Israelis wanted me to hear: "You have gone too far. Your involvement with the Moscow Helsinki Group and the dissident movement is dangerous for you and for our Refusenik cause. Stop."

Many tourists had delivered similar warnings numerous times before. But this time, I couldn't ignore the message, because the messenger was Avital. Is she simply passing the message on, or does she believe it? I kept asking myself. If she did, we had a problem.

Luckily, I got the clarification I needed very quickly. Somehow, Avital arranged another call to Moscow the next day. And somehow, she conveyed the message about where to be when her call came through. That second call was simple. "Forget yesterday. It was a moment of weakness. I believe in what you are doing," she said. "I am with you."

Shortly thereafter, on March 4, 1977, a full-page article in the Soviet newspaper *Izvestia* appeared. It accused me and other leading Jewish activists of spying for the United States. As usual, it was a lie. But this time, the authorities were raising the bar, from anti-Soviet activities to high treason, which is punishable by death.

Immediately, eight KGB men surrounded me. Their walking cage encased me wherever I went. The message was clear: "There's nowhere to go, and arrest is imminent."

Avital knew it was senseless to ask Israel's Liaison Office for help. Instead, she turned to her close friends and spiritual mentors, Rabbi Tzvi Tau and Hannah Tau. Since moving to Israel, Avital had discovered the world of Judaism in their home. With their teaching and coaching, she became a devout Jew.

Although it was late at night, Rabbi Tau rushed Avital and her brother Misha to his teacher, Rabbi Tzvi Yehuda Kook. The son of Palestine's legendary chief rabbi, Abraham Isaac Kook, the younger Rabbi Kook was already eighty-five years old, and ailing. When they translated the *Izvestia* article and he heard the accusations of espionage being bandied about, Rabbi Kook immediately understood the threat. Despite the late hour, he called disciples to his house. "Again, the Soviet Jews are in big danger," he explained. "If one Jew is accused of espionage, every Jew is endangered. Remember. We are our brothers' keepers. Now is the time to close the books and fight."

The next day, Rabbi Kook's followers established what became the headquarters of a global solidarity network, called I Am My Brother's Keeper. Hundreds of Rabbi Kook's students started organizing, lecturing, and writing to promote solidarity with the endangered Soviet Jews. Thanks to them and to hundreds of thousands of people, both religious and nonreligious, all over the world, Avital was never alone in her travels. She was always accompanied by some of Rabbi Kook's followers, who often mobilized local support wherever she campaigned, during the nine years I was in prison.

Long before our world went digital, there was a Jewish Internet. All the different subnetworks of the Jewish world used all kinds of "routers" to get Avital the phone numbers, influential contacts, strategic advice, financial assistance, hospitality, and moral support she needed. In the years to come, this worldwide web of relationships would help her reach nearly every important leader in the free world.

Even after my arrest, Israel's Liaison Office didn't stop its attempts to "save the purity of the Zionist movement." One leader of the Brother's Keeper organization, Rabbi Oded Wolanski, was broadly respected for the sophisticated religious lessons he taught in all kinds of venues, from yeshivas to the army.

Rabbi Wolanski was summoned to meet with the number-two man in the Liaison Office at one of the off-the-beaten-path places the administrators, with their spy training, liked. "Sharansky is not Zionist," the grizzled government representative told the young rabbi. "You should stop working on his behalf. It is dangerous for our movement." Rabbi Wolanski disagreed. He said he knew this Sharansky quite well through Avital. Moreover, many students were reading his letters, to learn about Zionism in action.

The conversation turned ugly. "You think you are the state," the officer said. "We are the state. You think you know whom you are defending. You know nothing. What you are doing now is endangering Soviet Jews. You better stop. Immediately. Or *anachnu nashmeed etchem*" (we will destroy you).

During this time, the Liaison Office sent letters to Israeli diplomats and leaders of Establishment Jewish organizations in key cities, advising them to abstain from supporting Avital. The letters had a "we know something you don't know" tone and emphasized that no one quite knew why the KGB had arrested her husband.

The Liaison Office also stepped in as two young lawyers, rising stars in the international human rights world, started building a case to defend me. Both Irwin Cotler, at McGill University, and Alan Dershowitz, at Harvard University, received direct messages to stay away from me. They didn't.

It quickly became obvious that Israel was much bigger than a few bureaucrats. No government body could limit Jewish solidarity, not in the Jewish state and not in any other Jewish community around the world.

The protests against my arrest gained strength, day by day, month by month. Inevitably, the Liaison Office had to join the struggle. Once involved, the Israeli government proved essential during every stage of the effort that eventually freed me.

THE FIGHT IN RETROSPECT

I first met Nehemiah Levanon when we appeared together at a conference in New York on the Soviet Jewish struggle, two years after my release. Levanon had retired in 1982, after working at the Liaison Office for three decades and heading it for twelve years.

Levanon was a true Zionist pioneer. For all his heroics, he had retired to the kibbutz he helped found in 1943, Kfar Blum. He did chores there like everyone else, working in the cultural center and at the communal dining room.

After we spoke, I invited him to breakfast the next morning. He was friendly but reserved. I asked him, "Yesterday, it was clear to the audience that we are comrades in arms in the same war on the same side, fighting on different fronts. So I wonder. Back in the first, most difficult days after my arrest, the KGB was debating whether to make a case against our entire Zionist movement. It was obvious that their decision depended on the world's reaction. When all kinds of people, including President Jimmy Carter, mocked the espionage charges against me as an obvious lie, why did you send letters to Jewish organizations discouraging them from working with Avital and hinting I might be a spy?"

Levanon was taken aback. After thinking for a long, awkward moment, he answered carefully. "I didn't send the letters. It was Tzvi Netzer," Levanon's number-two man, who was no longer alive. Netzer was famous for his brusque, take-no-prisoners approach. "But we never suspected you personally," Levanon added. "We feared some of the journalists and diplomats around you might be CIA agents. We also worried about Avital's brother, Misha. His English was too perfect. Only Russians who graduated from the KGB spy school spoke English so well."

Indeed, Misha spoke the Queen's English. Whatever Avital's brother did, he mastered it: archaeology, history, military service, establishing a network of activists for our struggle, or learning languages. At the time, my extraordinary brother-in-law was enjoying a successful army career and would soon be Israel's first military attaché to Moscow. In 1996, after a day of escorting Russian generals around the Golan Heights, he would die of a heart attack at the age of forty-eight.

During our breakfast, Levanon offered up lame excuses. It was obvious that, if history repeated itself, he would do it again. He believed that keeping the line of separation between the Jewish emigration movement and the dissident movement was in Israel's best interests. If that meant sacrificing any pawns from the Jewish side, then so be it.

Nevertheless, by 1988, it was the big picture that counted. The Soviet empire was collapsing. All the prisoners of Zion were being released. Many Refuseniks were finally free, some after decades of waiting. The smell of victory was in the air, and Levanon and I both had reason to celebrate our mutual victory.

5

LIVING FREE IN PRISON

I left the center of our struggle for Soviet Jewry as quickly as I entered it. In 1973, I gave up being a lonely doublethinker and closeted dissident and plunged into the heart of the movement. Four years later, my exit was even more abrupt.

One minute, you're in the middle of your press conferences, telephone calls, and Hebrew lessons. The next minute, a sea of hands pulls you out of an elevator and four KGB agents push you straight into a car.

They squeeze you into the middle of the back seat, packing enough men in so that you cannot make final, fleeting eye contact with friends and reporters, who were kidding around with you just moments ago.

The two iron doors of Lefortovo Prison close on you. First, one clangs shut, then the other. You look up and see the muzzle on every window, a wire mesh cage that traps you here. It is March 15, 1977. From now on, even a lonely ray of sun will be a rare visitor in your life.

They strip you. They search you in every orifice, up and down. It's senseless. They know you have nothing hidden. Eight of them have been hounding you, tailing you around the clock for weeks. But as you stand there, naked, in front of three sergeants and an elderly female paramedic, involuntarily wincing with each poke or prod, you know the message they're giving you: "From now on, nothing at all belongs to you. Even your body doesn't belong to you."

You will now live in front of their eyes full-time. You have no privacy. You cannot hide from them, not even for a moment.

They can come and search you at any time. The light is on in your cell day and night. And if at night you try to pull a blanket over your head to block out the light, they will demand you take off the blanket, or they will enter and pull it off themselves.

The moment they bring you to prison, just before they strip you, they read the accusation aloud. They're accusing you of treason under Article 64A: high treason. This is a capital crime, they tell you immediately, although you already know that. The punishment: R-A-S-S-T-R-E-L. Death by shooting.

TRYING TO BULLY ME BACK INTO DOUBLETHINK

"There will be no more press conferences." The colonel reading the accusation smiled. "Now everything depends on you."

I knew what they wanted. I knew very well what they wanted. They wanted to send me back to the world where I say what they want me to say. To the world of doublethink.

They wanted me to stand in front of the journalists and say the Soviets were right and I was wrong. That was how they kept control in a country filled with hundreds of millions of doublethinkers. They didn't need to kill more dissidents. They only had to show everybody that there was no way to be independent from the authorities in the Communist world.

But this kind of surrender was no longer an option for me. I could not return to that world; I had already lived there. I knew what living as a doublethinker was like. So I found myself standing there, naked, trying not to show my nervousness. I told myself, "They cannot humiliate me. Only I can humiliate myself."

In the first weeks, the interrogation team grew to seventeen officers, as they set their sights on the Refusenik movement throughout the Soviet Union. The chief interrogator, a colonel, liked to say, "We are not bloodthirsty." They all kept insisting, "You can save yourself by cooperating with us."

The colonel reminded me that he had freed two famous dissidents a few years ago. Viktor Krasin and Pyotr Yakir had disavowed their "anti-Soviet activities" in a press conference in 1973, betraying their comrades. "I promised them they would be released," he said, "and, you see, we kept our word."

Well, that was a mistake. Reminding me of these two people, fallen heroes of the dissident movement, backfired. Yes, they were released, and some of their comrades were then imprisoned as a consequence. I remember hearing rumors about how miserable Krasin and Yakir were after they confessed. It was too difficult to return to living a life of lies as a doublethinker while burdened by the guilt of being a traitor. I had already heard that Yakir was drinking, and by 1982 he would drink himself to death. In 1975, the KGB helped Krasin and his wife emigrate. The authorities were worried about their mental states; broken men can't be trusted to keep to their confessions. Arriving in Paris, Krasin gave a second press conference to recant the recanting he made in his first, forced press conference.

In 1984, Krasin would write about his confession: "What did I feel during those hours? Nothing. My soul was empty. . . . How I would live after everything I had done was not something I wanted to think about." Everyone said that, when he left prison, you could see the emptiness in his eyes.

I answered the colonel, who was surprised I knew about Krasin's backpedaling: "You want me to have two press conferences. I prefer to have none."

Just as they could not take my freedom, they could not take away that feeling of being part of a historic struggle. By connecting me with the past and the future, that struggle gave my life meaning and depth. The Soviets isolated me physically. They wrenched me from my home, my friends, my routines, and my little comforts. But did they take me away from the struggle?

I kept going back to what ended up being my last telephone call to Israel. I was anxious to get through because I feared it might be my final opportunity to hear Avital's voice. When that *Izvestia* article accusing me of treason appeared, and Avital started mobilizing allies in Jerusalem, things turned tense in Moscow too. The days after the article appeared felt like a death watch. Every telephone call felt like the final one, and every meeting felt like a farewell, with forced smiles and false assurances. I wrote my "goodbye" letter to Avital and gave it to a trusted American journalist to pass to her.

Amid all this activity, I received a message. Avital would try to reach me by telephone at a certain time, at one of the homes of a fresh Refusenik.

Most veteran Refuseniks' telephones had been disconnected long ago, so we always relied on a new crop, whose lives hadn't been fully shut down yet.

The phone rang on time. But, after all that anticipation, instead of hearing Avital, I heard a young male voice on the line. A twenty-nine-year-old rabbi in Jerusalem, who introduced himself as Eli Sadan, reported that Avital and her brother Misha had already left for Geneva to launch the struggle against my imminent arrest. The article had alarmed them too. "And we have opened our headquarters: *Shomer Achi Anochi*, I Am My Brother's Keeper," he said, briefly describing the group's round-the-clock efforts to support Avital and prick the world's conscience.

"We're all fighting for you," Sadan said. "You are our hero."

Sadan's teacher, Rabbi Tzvi Tau, then got on the line. "The whole world is watching what is happening with the Jews in Moscow," he said. "What happens to you affects all of us. You are now in the center, influencing the entire Jewish world. All the struggle depends on you." Tau added, "Chazak v'ematz," the traditional Jewish blessing, be strong and courageous.

At the time, I barely heard the words, that's how upset I was that the rabbis weren't Avital. But in the prison vacuum, I replayed every interaction. I thought through their words, which sprouted a new meaning: "You are now in the center, influencing the entire Jewish world." The rabbis' once-frustrating distraction now gave me a new sense of responsibility.

I started reasoning with myself. "What really changed?" I wondered. I had been in the middle of the struggle, connected to so many people around the world. I had moved just two miles away: from Slepak's Moscow apartment to the KGB's Lefortovo Prison. But now I was even more in the center. The world was watching me. Every word I said, every action I took, would be more important than before.

But it's not enough to feel important. It was also good to know that I had troops behind me.

BREAKING THE KGB ISOLATION

Day after day, interrogation after interrogation, the KGB tries to make you feel that you are alone in the world. Beyond isolating you, muzzling you, and violating you, they try to demoralize you. In the first interrogation after my arrest, they shouted, "Enough! No more slander! Nobody can hear you here except us."

In the hundred-plus interrogations over the next year, they would be much more subtle. They stopped shouting. Instead, they tried reasoning with me. They offered all kinds of explanations, in all kinds of different ways, to show me how lonely I was, how disconnected. They said that everybody had abandoned me, and that the Refusenik movement was falling apart.

They thought they could convince me because they controlled all the information. There was no radio. No meeting with relatives. No letters. The interrogators tried to be logical and specific. They used every bit of information they had collected during the years of monitoring the lives of Refuseniks: about petty quarrels, power struggles, ego trips. "You know how A dismissed B," they would say. "How envious is C and greedy is D. They have enough problems among themselves without you."

They continued, "You know these so-called Soviet Jewish organizations, how they cannot stand one another. How long do you think all these spoiled brats abroad can stay with this cause? They have their own lives to live. But we, we have all the time in the world."

I said to myself, "I have no choice. I have to break the isolation, and I can rely only on my memory."

I tried hard not to listen to my interrogators, not to hear them. Instead, I went back to the world in which I had lived, which I knew well. I reminded myself of every meeting, every conversation I had ever had with my fellow Refuseniks in Moscow. I tried to think about what each person might be doing today. I remembered arguments, accusations, and suspicions. But what did all that mean now? It seemed so trivial.

From my jail cell, the community had never looked more united. The KGB kept emphasizing our internal chaos. But if a fellow prisoner had asked me, "Who are you closer to, the *politiki* or *kulturniki*? The Right or the Left? Likud or Labor? Reform or Orthodox? Union of Councils for Soviet Jews or National Conference on Soviet Jewry?" I would have scoffed. The disagreement-scarred dialogue had vanished. In its place was my dialogue of one. True, it was only in my mind, but it was also one dialogue of one people, united in one struggle.

Every squabbling Jewish organization was now on the same page, listed as anti-Soviet in my KGB file. It proved how meaningless the disagreements were. So I relived, again and again, the excitement of every demonstration, the power of every press conference, the determination of every signature on every petition. I resurrected those joyful feelings of solidarity, freedom, and mutual responsibility we felt for one another.

I thought about all the Jews from abroad I had met during the struggle. What was each one doing right now? I wondered about that housewife from Miami, that lawyer from San Francisco, that student from Toronto, and that Russian language teacher from London.

I thought of every living bridge who had connected me with Avital. All those who hid our letters in their underwear before crossing the border. All those who worked so hard to avoid having our communication cut. I tried to imagine their surroundings, their daily lives, their political activism. They would not forget. They would not abandon me. They would not stop fighting. I trusted them now as I had trusted them then. I believed—I knew—that they were continuing the struggle. And our struggle was my main weapon.

My imagined, ideal picture clashed daily with the miserable reality the KGB tried to impose. All the arguments, jealousies, and petty emotions that filled our days and the KGB files became irrelevant.

Then, there was Avital.

ONE FIXED POINT

While studying game theory, I learned that there always exists an optimal strategy to minimize losses. Proof of its existence is based on the fact that, when you move from one system of coordinates to the other on the globe, there will always be one fixed point. The KGB specialized in shifting coordinates, trying to demoralize you by changing perspectives and contexts, making you feel powerless, and sowing doubt. Until my release, my one fixed point was Avital. She kept me centered, sane, and focused on the community that was behind me, not the unknown looming ahead.

To stay anchored, I composed a prayer in my primitive Hebrew. Before and after each interrogation, I said, "Blessed are You, Adonai, Ruler of the Universe. Grant me the good fortune to live with my wife, my beloved Avital, in the Land of Israel. Grant my parents, my wife, and my whole family the strength to endure all hardships until we meet. Grant me the strength, the power, the intelligence, the good fortune, and the patience to leave this jail and to reach the Land of Israel in an honest and worthy way."

That's how I tried to reestablish myself as a free person in prison: as a participant in the imagined struggle of an imagined global Jewish community. It restored my self-confidence and my optimism.

WHO IS TRULY FREE?

Just as I once teased my KGB minders as they shadowed me all over Moscow, I realized I could toy with my interrogators too. It reminded them and me who is really free and who is a scared doublethinker.

It was easy. All I had to do was tell some joke about the Soviet leader, Leonid Brezhnev. Thank God, there were plenty of yarns about his arrogance, his crudeness, his senility. Of course, they were all underground jokes. One played on Russian words about him mistaking the British ambassador for the French one. Another kidded about him forcing Soviet cosmonauts to outdo the American astronauts who landed on the moon by rocketing to the sun, then reassuring them they wouldn't be incinerated because they'd be launched during the night.

I'd tell my interrogators a joke. I'd laugh. And they would want to laugh, but they couldn't, especially if there were two of them together. That would end their careers. They'd cover up with a tantrum. They'd pound the table, shouting, "HOW DARE YOU!!!"

"Look," I'd say to them calmly, "you can't even smile when you want to smile. And you claim that I'm in prison and you're free?" I did this to irritate them, because they spent so much time trying to irritate me. But, mainly, I was reminding myself that I was free, as long as I could laugh or cry as I felt.

I also contrasted their picture of what was happening beyond the barbed wire against my vision of the current struggle, and I challenged them. I pretended to know what was going on, usually by reading into something they had said or didn't say. "Hmm, it's good to know that you didn't succeed in breaking even one Refusenik, since you have no one to bring for cross-interrogation against me." Or, "Wow, I hear that, despite what you said, and all your efforts, those Jewish organizations keep fighting for us."

Then I gauged how confused they seemed. They didn't want to deny or confirm what I said, but they wanted to know how I had gotten that information. They searched me again. They interrogated my cellmates more aggressively. All their nervousness proved one thing: that the imagined world I was projecting forward from my past was far more real than the world they were trying to impose on me in the present.

Frustrated, they kept returning to their only weapon, their fixed point, R-A-S-S-T-R-E-L, death. "You are playing all your games," they sneered. "They have nothing to do with reality. Are you ready to give up your life as a talented scientist, with a young beautiful wife waiting for you, to keep playing your jokes and your games? You will be brought to trial. You will face the death penalty. That is what you have to think about, Anatoly Borisovich," the interrogators said.

I had never fielded so many KGB compliments praising my scientific skills and my wonderful spouse. But the life they wanted to send me back to would not be the life I wanted or needed. Their aim was to convince me that nothing was more important than physical survival. But I knew I could not control that. "If physical survival is my aim, I am finished," I reasoned to myself. "Because physical survival depends fully on their goodwill. My aim should be different: to live as a free person until my last day."

This aim was realistic. Because it depended only on me.

WHAT AVITAL AND I KNEW THAT OTHERS DIDN'T

A few years ago, when Michael Oren was Israel's ambassador to the United States, he called me. "You're not going to believe what Max Kampelman is saying," Michael said. Ambassador Kampelman had represented President Ronald Reagan during many negotiations with the Soviet Union in the 1980s. "Kampelman told me that your wife was such a right-wing, religious fanatic, she prevented you from being released for health reasons in 1983, three years before you finally were freed."

I chuckled. Even thirty years after our victory, some of our most committed allies could not comprehend how total our struggle was or what really drove us. Confused, they resorted to primitive clichés. It was easier to believe in religious or political bogeymen than in the effectiveness of our idealism.

Avital didn't try to prevent my release. On the contrary, she fought persistently for my freedom every day during my nine years in prison, never losing hope that the next day would be the day of my release.

In mid 1983, Max Kampelman and Lawrence Eagleburger, two leading American diplomats, invited Avital to the White House. By this
point, administration officials, State Department diplomats, and many
congressional leaders were frustrated. Despite all their efforts, Russia
wasn't budging, and my situation was worsening. One internal White
House assessment from October 1982, which I read when it was released
decades later, warned, "The chances of freeing Anatoly are bleak indeed."

Nine months later, however, Kampelman and Eagleburger were jubilant. They believed they had made the impossible possible. They proudly
informed Avital that the Reagan administration's intense pressure had
finally forced a Russian retreat. The Soviets were ready to release me. They
dropped their demand that I acknowledge my "crimes" or request a par-
don. I merely had to sign a one-line statement requesting that the regime
free me for humanitarian reasons, "on the grounds of poor health."

I had just completed a 110-day hunger strike. Prison guards had force-
fed me thirty-four times. I weighed thirty-five kilos, down from sixty-five
kilos just before my arrest. The health considerations were justified. Still,
Avital answered Kampelman and Eagleburger immediately. "He won't
do it."

She left. Both diplomats walked away stewing and bewildered. What
did she understand that they did not? She and I knew that ours was not
just a struggle for my physical survival. It was a struggle to open the gates
of the Soviet Union. My release, if it was to come, could not be at the cost
of the struggle. It could only be thanks to our struggle.

How could I contribute to the struggle in prison? By reminding the
world that the regime was evil and hypocritical. By showing that the accusations of high treason against me were based only on open meetings
and public statements as a Jewish activist and democratic dissident. And
by explaining that this sinister accusation of espionage stemmed only
from my sharing a widely circulated list of Refuseniks, sent to Jewish
organizations and public figures.

How could I weaken the struggle? By recognizing the regime's moral
authority and legitimacy.

On the first day after my arrest, preparing for what I expected would
be round after round of KGB grilling, I settled on the approach that
guided me for nine years. My aims would be to refuse to cooperate, to use
every interrogation to learn something about them and their methods,
and to unmask their lies and charades whenever possible.

That is why, after a year of interrogations, I prepared for my trial by studying the fifteen thousand pages in my case file so thoroughly. That is why I rejected the lawyer they chose to represent me, so I could use every opportunity to prove the accusations false. That is why my first words to the court were "I am innocent, and all the accusations against me and our movement are absurd." And that is why my last words to the court before they sentenced me to thirteen years in the Gulag, that dark network of prisons and camps, were "And to the court, which has only to read a sentence that was prepared long ago, to you I have nothing to say."

I wasn't really addressing the court. I was advancing my mission of exposing the real nature of this trial to the world. After the trial, I refused to talk to any KGB officers again, treating it like the illegal organization that it was. Their response was predictable: they imposed tougher and tougher physical conditions, sent me to punishment cells, canceled meetings with my family, and confiscated letters I wrote.

During nine years in the Gulag, I would be in a camp for less than one year in total. At camps, you could interact with a dozen or so people and get some sunshine. During the other eight years, I spent half the time in a cell with one or two cellmates, half the time in solitary confinement.

Solitary sounds worse than it was, when the alternative was cellmates who might be KGB informers. I always found solitary comfortable, if I could read or write there, if it was warm, and if there was food to eat. If I wasn't going to be with fellow dissidents, what else did I need?

The punishment cell, however, was barbaric. This sensory deprivation chamber, where I spent 405 days in total, was small, cold, and dark. There was little stimulation—no light, no furniture, nothing to read, no one to talk to, and barely anything to eat.

Then there were the hunger strikes.

While confiscating the letters I wrote, the authorities would occasionally deliver letters to me from my seventy-four-year-old mother, who asked with alarm, "Are you alive?" and "What happened to you?" The bits of information my tormentors most enjoyed conveying had to do with her spiking blood pressure and periodic hospitalizations. "You see what you are doing to your mother," they said. "Talk to us. Accept the rules of our dialogue. Then, you can send her a letter."

HUNGER STRIKE

I had no choice. I had to use the most powerful weapon available to me: an unlimited, open-ended hunger strike demanding my right to send letters. But for it to contribute to the struggle, my family and the world had to know about it.

One thing I had in prison was time. I waited patiently for half a year, looking for an opportunity to send the message. Finally, one of my fellow political prisoners was about to be released. By misbehaving, I arranged to be sent to a punishment cell below his cell. I tapped a message to him in Morse code. Then I waited another two months for a signal that my family had received the message.

I started the hunger strike on Yom Kippur 1982. My timing was deliberate. It meant that, as I began, millions of Jews would be fasting with me. I would need this feeling of unity in the days to come, as I languished on the border of life and death, living from one forced-feeding to another.

It's a three-day cycle. At the start, I would drift away slowly, until I was lying there, barely conscious, unsure if I was awake or asleep. Then, they would violently swoop down on me with their clamps and rubber hoses. Before I knew it, the blood was knocking forcefully around my head. My heart felt like it was jumping out of my chest. My stomach felt bloated. Then, whoosh, my body was no longer in overdrive but had started that slow deterioration into the next cycle.

Minute by minute, as I downshifted again, as everything vital ebbed out of my body, I only had enough strength to hold on to one feeling: the confidence that I was never alone. Avital and my family and my people were with me. As I got woozier and woozier, yet again, I felt I had done whatever I could; I'd passed the baton in this existential relay. Now, it was their turn.

On the forty-fifth day of my hunger strike, it wasn't my heart that failed, but Brezhnev's. "Avital is doing a good job. Brezhnev couldn't take it anymore," I joked to myself. The new supreme leader was Yuri Andropov, the head of the KGB who had sent me to prison by signing the first documents initiating my criminal case.

The pessimist in me knew how cruel he could be. The optimist hoped that he might feel pressured to show a different face to the West as he assumed his new position. Soon, he let the West know that he was open to reviewing my case.

On the 110th day of my hunger strike, I was allowed to send a letter to my mother. Actually, I gave the letter to the prison warden, who cursed me for treating him like a mere mailman. But I insisted on proof of delivery by receiving a letter back. That demand triggered more shouting and cursing about my disrespect.

A reply arrived an hour later. My mother was in another part of the prison, negotiating desperately with the authorities. They still forbade any visiting. But they allowed us, finally, to exchange letters, as was my right under Soviet law. That is why, on January 14, 1983, I ended my hunger strike.

Meanwhile, another round of negotiations monitoring compliance with the Helsinki Accords began, this time in Madrid. President Reagan, who had become emotionally involved in our story after meeting Avital, kept encouraging her campaign. He instructed his negotiators not to sign a joint communiqué unless I was released. That's when the Soviets proposed their noble health compromise. And that's when the Americans fell into the Communist trap.

THE INTERCONNECTION OF SOULS

I learned about the diplomatic maneuvers and public campaigns in July 1983, five months after my hunger strike ended, when the KGB allowed my mother and brother to meet me in prison. After being so stubborn about banning visitors, the authorities had approved the visit so my family could deliver the American proposal Kampelman and Eagleburger had negotiated.

"No," I answered immediately. "I committed no crimes. The crimes were committed by the people who arrested me and are keeping me in prison. Therefore, the only appeal I can address to the Presidium is a demand for my immediate release and the punishment of those who are truly guilty. Asking the authorities to show humanity means acknowledging that they represent a legitimate force that administers justice."

I saw how difficult it was for my mother to give up hope. I decided to use my hard-won privilege, after weeks of starving, to explain my logic. I sent long letters to my family in Moscow and Jerusalem. My handwritten letter to Avital was twelve pages, single-spaced. I recalled how one of my

first cellmates, clearly cooperating with the KGB when they were inter-
rogating me, mentioned Galileo Galilei. The Inquisition in 1633 forced
this great scientist to recant his true theory that the Earth orbits around
the sun. Nevertheless, at the end of his life, he proclaimed, "Yet, it moves,"
restoring the truth.

"Now there was a smart man," my cellmate, Timofeev, told me.
"He recanted to the Inquisition and was able to continue his scientific
research with so much benefit to humanity." That was the KGB's constant message: "Just say that we are right. Get released, then do whatever
you want."

What I took from this conversation was that, nearly four hundred
years after Galileo's moment of weakness, this legendary scientist's stature could still be used to pressure me. That proved that what we do really
does matter, that we all are interconnected. I certainly didn't want any
secret police ever using my name to weaken anyone else.

In my letter to Avital, I wrote, "In addition to Newton's law of the
universal gravitational pull of objects, there is also a universal gravitational pull of souls, of the bond between them and the influence of one
soul on the other. With each word we speak and each step we take, we
touch other souls and have an impact on them. Why should I put a sin
on my soul now?"

Connecting this moment to the moment when I crossed the line from
loyal Soviet citizen to dissident, I continued, "I have already succeeded
once in tearing the spider's web, breaking with the difficult life of doublethink and closing the gap between thought and word. How is it now
possible to take even one step backward toward the previous state?"

That's how I felt in those days. I was interconnected with thousands of
my people. I had full confidence in their determination. And I knew they
had full confidence in mine. I was not going to weaken them.

6

MY DIALOGUE WITH THE JEWISH COMMUNITY

Imagined Reality?

On February 11, 1990, four years to the day after my release, the South African government freed Nelson Mandela. He had served twenty-seven years in prison. Over the nearly three decades, some in the West had honored him, others denounced him. Now, it seemed the whole world greeted him enthusiastically.

A few weeks later, I received a phone call from Abe Foxman, the head of the Anti-Defamation League. Since we had met in Moscow during Hanukkah 1974, Abe had been my trusted accomplice. "Mandela knows who you are," he said excitedly. "He read your book in prison and wants to meet you when he visits America."

I was curious to meet Mandela too, wondering how he coped during his prison ordeal. I was planning to be in the United States. Abe, who hoped I would help make the case for Israel to Mandela, arranged for me to fly to Los Angeles on Friday, June 29.

When I arrived at the downtown Biltmore Hotel, where Mandela was staying, his wife Winnie told me that her seventy-one-year-old husband, who was being rushed from celebration to celebration and interview to interview, was sleeping. I sympathized, remembering my own exhausting, exhilarating freedom tour. But it was a Friday. With Sabbath approaching, I considered rescheduling. Everything in Los Angeles is too far away from everything else; if Mandela rested too long, I would not make it to my hosts in the suburbs on time. But the wait was worth it. Eventually, I met Mandela, refreshed and expansive, after his nap.

He told me that, in 1988, Helen Suzman, the only South African parliamentarian who had fought stubbornly for the right to visit him in prison, gave him a copy of *Fear No Evil*. Mandela was in his twenty-fifth year of imprisonment. Glancing at my four-hundred-page prison memoir, he told her, "It's too thick. I won't have time to read it all."

Once he started, though, Mandela said he read the book from cover to cover. "The interrogations were familiar to me," Mandela told me, "but boy, you really suffered."

"I suffered?" I asked, surprised. "You suffered three times worse. Twenty-seven years!"

"But," Mandela replied proudly, "my people were with me. And you were alone."

I was surprised how agitated his words made me. It felt like he was insulting my partners in crime, the Jewish people. "But my people were with me too," I proclaimed, equally proudly.

Mandela smiled. "I read your book. It was all in your imagination. My people were with me in real life, all the time."

We compared notes. While both of us had been stuck in a place called a prison, we were in vastly different institutions. Mandela explained that, during his long stretch on Robben Island, he met regularly with his comrades. They ran their revolutionary struggle from their cells. They received frontline reports, set strategy, made tactical decisions, and sent instructions to the field. He didn't have to play chess in his head.

Was the world of my struggle only imagined? Was I really that alone? For me, my dialogue with my people in prison was no less real than Mandela's.

MY PRISON DIALOGUES

In prison, dreams offer a welcome escape from the depressing reality. Imagination usually helps keep hope alive. But, for political prisoners, these fantasies are risky. If you become too dependent on your dreams, it gives your captors another advantage over you. They know how to smash your delusions. When they undermine you by highlighting how far your imagination is from reality, the inevitable disappointment weakens your resistance even more.

In my mind, I was fiddling on the roof. I wanted to build my own world, with my own visions, that they couldn't control. But I could not let my dreams or hopes propel me too far from reality.

Once you build an inner world where you control everything, you try to prop it up with whatever scraps of information you can hoard. You replay the interrogations in your mind, analyzing each word and gesture to see if your captors know something you want to know, if they let something significant slip. You find yourself analyzing every interaction you have for hints, for signs of what's happening, and not, in the outside world.

It was significant, for example, that aside from two informers outed before my arrest, not one of the hundreds of Jewish activists I knew had betrayed me. If anyone had, the KGB would have pitted us against each other in a cross-interrogation, or used inside information gleaned from the informant to trip me up. The absence of any traitors proved to me that what I imagined was true: the movement remained robust and united.

Similarly, I was reassured when they kept pulling back at the last minute, lessening the physical pressures they imposed just enough, whenever my health deteriorated so much that my life was endangered. Their concern about keeping me alive showed that people far beyond my small cell were looking out for me.

When I was not in a punishment cell—where they deprived me of all conversations and reading material—I read the official Communist Party newspaper, *Pravda*, religiously. I read every line and between the lines. I wanted to see if the movement had attracted any attention or disrupted the dictatorship in any way.

That was why President Reagan's words condemning the Soviet Union as an "evil empire" were so meaningful for all of us in the Gulag. Here was a Western leader who wasn't fooled by the Soviet propaganda machine. I later discovered that his American critics condemned his speech as "the worst speech by a president, ever." They claimed he had escalated world tensions by threatening a fellow superpower. For us prisoners, though, it was a great relief. It proved that the real world was catching on and standing up to the Soviet liars.

Month after month, my mail privileges were violated and no visitors were allowed. Whenever I served in a camp instead of a prison, I was entitled under Soviet law to one three-day meeting with relatives each year. Due to what the authorities called my "bad influence on the others," I only had two such meetings, limited to one day each time, in my nine years. None were with Avital, of course, but my mother and brother visited. These rare interactions delivered buckets of information I could stockpile and use to feed my imagination for years thereafter.

For decades, my parents, my brother Leonid, and his wife, Raya, lived the life of loyal Soviet citizens. But my arrest turned them into real fighters. Despite being in her seventies, my mother made the long trek to the prison, sometimes in temperatures approaching forty below zero. One time, she had to walk the final miles, crossing a frozen river, only to leave disappointed when, once again, they would not let her see me.

After my mother's second visit, Major Osin, the head of the camp Perm 35, approached her menacingly. As usual, the prison administration had listened in on our visit. "Be careful not to discuss what you heard from your son," he said, unashamed at how obvious it was that he had eavesdropped. "It will not improve his situation."

My short, peppery mother looked up at this tall, mean major towering over her and said quietly, "You have nothing to be afraid of. I will only tell the truth." At that moment, he shrank and she grew. As soon as she returned to Moscow, she spoke to the reporters waiting for her train.

MY ARMY OF STUDENTS AND HOUSEWIVES

Did I know about the demonstrations and vigils and lobbying efforts for my release during those nine years? Obviously not. But I saw one protest on videotape, which was enough to fuel my imagination.

Before my trial, as I waded through the fifteen thousand pages the KGB had collected to use against me, I stumbled across some quotations from a film proving my "criminal activity." It was a 1977 television documentary made by the British network Granada after my arrest, *The Man Who Went Too Far.*

I demanded to see the film. "Denying me the right to choose my own lawyer forced me to serve as my own defense attorney," I explained. "I therefore have to understand everything being used against me."

The KGB refused. I persisted. I refused to sign a statement acknowledging I had reviewed all the evidence. Shortly thereafter, I saw my first VCR when a Japanese machine rolled into the chief interrogator's office.

First, they showed another Granada film they were using against me, *A Calculated Risk.* That took me back to 1976, when I told the Refuseniks' story by sneaking around Moscow with a friendly British camera crew.

Then they inserted the second tape. The film focused on a demonstration demanding my release in front of the Soviet embassy in London. Scanning the crowd, I recognized some of my comrades in arms and some tourists I had met in Moscow. There were also many unfamiliar young people, waving signs with my face on them, shouting slogans demanding my freedom.

My heart started racing. There was Avital, leading the demonstration. She spoke perfect Hebrew and good English. She was determined, resolute, as she marched straight from the heart of London into my prison hell. The film's twenty or so minutes passed too quickly.

I demanded to see it again.

"What, you liked it?" a KGB investigator sneered. "Once is enough. A prisoner under investigation may not watch television."

I insisted, "I have the right to understand every word you are using against me." I kept inventing more reasons: I missed this. I didn't understand that. What was that English word?

After we had watched it three times, the head of my interrogation team, Colonel Viktor Ivanovich Volodin, exploded. "That's enough! What do you think, that your fate is in the hands of those people, and not ours? They're nothing more than students and housewives!"

Thank you, Colonel Volodin. I think you should go down in history with these words. You gave the best possible definition of our army.

The modest London protest of students and housewives, led by Avital, became for me the mother of all demonstrations. It typified the thousands of protests that would take place in my imagined world in the years to come.

Students and housewives. These were the good soldiers who had accompanied me before I entered prison. These were the comrades who continued to be with me in my imagined world. These were the people who never abandoned me in the real world I couldn't see. I was thinking about them, and so many others, when I used every scrap of evidence

I received to convince myself that this imagined world was real. And I was right.

Students and housewives. Well, technically, some were teachers, like Michael Sherbourne, a Russian language instructor. When he estimated in the film that he and I had had thousands of telephone conversations about the human rights situation in the Soviet Union over the years, the KGB quoted him to further prove my criminal activity.

One day, just as the movement was beginning, Michael started calling Refuseniks in Moscow from London. He never stopped until we were freed. He became a human switchboard, connecting us Refuseniks with world Jewry. When I was most involved in the movement, he and I spoke two, three, four times a week.

Michael spent most of his evenings speaking to Refuseniks, taping the calls, transcribing them, and then distributing the transcripts. The more phone calls he made, the more he had to use assumed names and borrowed phones. He reassured us. He put us in touch with one another, playing London matchmaker. He shared our stories with the world.

In my imagined world, Michael continued dialing and chatting and updating. He refused to let any of us feel forgotten and never stopped pressuring the Soviets, who discovered that he wouldn't let any Refusenik fall between the cracks.

Meanwhile, in the real world I couldn't see, at the start of my trial in 1978 a British student arrived in Moscow and leased a room in one of the city's most luxurious—and KGB-protected and watched—hotels, the Metropol. Every night, the one relative allowed to attend my trial, my brother, Leonid, would visit the young student. Using the KGB's protected phone lines, Michael, in London, would call his young friend at the Metropol. Leonid would then get on the phone and describe the day's proceedings in detail so Michael could spread news of the trial globally.

Another educator, Rabbi Haskel Lookstein of New York, had starred in the KGB's list of my accomplices. We had met in Moscow in 1975 and became friends when we marched together for miles all over the city one Saturday—Shabbat. It was the first time I had discovered this particular price to being Jewish, the prohibition against driving one day a week. We walked and walked and walked so he could deliver his lecture on Jewish heroism, both spiritual and physical, to different groups of warring Refuseniks.

In my imagination, this popular principal continued leading generations of students from Ramaz, the school at his synagogue, to demonstrations at Dag Hammarskjöld Plaza, urging the United Nations to act.

In the real world, Rabbi Lookstein had mobilized the students and housewives and lawyers and real estate moguls at his magnificent synagogue, Kehilath Jeshurun, on New York's Upper East Side. Having calculated the number of Sabbaths in my thirteen-year sentence, every week he publicly posted on East 85th Street how many of the 679 Saturdays I had served and how many I had left. He placed an empty chair on the bimah, the podium, during the High Holidays "to remind the worshipers that as they prayed comfortably Soviet Jews had no such opportunity."

Like hundreds of other rabbis, he became a fashion plate and a matchmaker. He encouraged congregants to sport cheap metal bracelets engraved with the names of "prisoners of conscience." And he twinned younger congregants with twelve- and thirteen-year-old Soviet Jewish pen pals who weren't free to have similar bar or bat mitzvah coming-of-age ceremonies.

Lookstein's synagogue became a center of braceleting, twinning, lobbying, let-my-people-going, and never-againing. He and his educational staff raised generations of Ramaz students to understand that "saving Soviet Jewry" was as central to their education as math, science, and Bible studies. Reaching out to Jews through the Iron Curtain was as important as getting into the Ivy League.

As for housewives, there were many of them too: Irene Manikovsky from Washington, DC, Lynn Singer from New York, Connie Smukler and Enid Wurtman from Philadelphia, and June Daniels from Des Moines. I had met them when they visited Moscow with their spouses, and they became the Refuseniks' living phone lines to the world.

In my imagination, they kept visiting and connecting and pressing their representatives in Congress, earning respectable places on the list of my accomplices within my KGB file.

In the real world, some of them so abused the regime's hospitality that they were banned for life from the Soviet Union. Connie Smukler was detained for twenty-four hours and threatened with a one-way ticket to Siberia. Back home, she and her comrades created an international network of hospitality, hosting the families of prisoners of Zion, who crisscrossed the world, like Avital, going from home to home, town to town, and country to country, advocating for their loved ones' freedom.

Then there were the students. In 1964, four students from Columbia University initiated the first demonstration for Soviet Jews. From there, they created the Student Struggle for Soviet Jewry and continued to be enthusiastic partners.

In my imagination, they continued mobilizing at key moments and interrupting Soviet business and cultural delegations who arrived in the United States, refusing to leave Soviet officials alone until the regime let our people go.

In the real world, the leader of the SSSJ from 1982 on, Rabbi Avi Weiss, went on a hunger strike in front of the Soviet consulate in New York, just as I started my hunger strike in Chistopol prison. For years, Rabbi Weiss traveled with Avital all over America, mobilizing support for our cause.

My imagined world came impressively close to the real world. Sometimes these parallel worlds met. During my prison years, whenever I read newspaper attacks mocking my wife, I was thrilled. Articles satirizing the "travels of that adventurer" or condemning meddlesome Americans for meeting with the wife of a spy electrified me. The blood would rush to my head. My heart would start pounding. Here was one more clue that, maybe, instead of my dreams misleading me and unfairly raising my hopes, they were too cautious and constrained. I started wondering if what was going on in the outside world was even bigger and better than I imagined.

AVITAL'S ARMY

The art student I had married, and then saw whisked off to Israel a few hours later, was quiet and shy. People mistakenly thought that meant she was fragile too. Still, neither Avital nor I imagined that she would spend years leading marches, inspiring hundreds of thousands of people at rallies, and lobbying presidents and prime ministers.

Avital's first circle of supporters consisted of Rabbi Kook's followers. Through the I Am My Brother's Keeper organization, they accompanied her as she traveled. Her second circle was the students and housewives: the growing global network of tourists, phone friends, letter writers and protesters. Beyond that, she learned to work with the Soviet Jewish organizations, despite their turf wars, and with the Israeli government, despite its initial ambivalence.

From the moment of my arrest, Avital rushed into battle with a spirited determination. Every day felt critical to her. Initially, when she encountered people who didn't share her sense of urgency, it could bring her to tears. On one of her first trips to Washington, DC, she met some of the members of Congress I had met in Moscow. She expected them to understand the imminent danger I faced and act immediately.

Instead, they reacted cautiously. "We don't know the real circumstances of the arrest," said one. "We must be careful," said another. "Let's take it slow," said a third.

Frustrated that legislators were so plodding when the danger was so pressing, Avital went into the next room and burst into tears. "There, there, *maidele*," Jacob Javits, New York's senior senator, said as he consoled her, using the endearing Yiddish term for "sweet child." "I understand. You have such a big job on your shoulders. You will have to grow with the case. But remember this: Don't just do one hit. Think big."

Early in the global campaign to keep me alive, we scored a big success. Two months after my arrest, when rumors were flying about me, President Carter pronounced in a press conference that he had "inquired deeply within the State Department and within the CIA as to whether or not Mr. Sharansky has ever had any known relationship in a subversive way or otherwise with the CIA. . . . The answer," he declared, "is no."

This statement marked a major departure for American policy. Presidents usually kept silent about Soviet spying allegations. Denying any one accusation risked implying that others might be guilty.

But the chain of influence had passed the message to Carter that this was a matter of life and death. It started on the street, with Avital supported by students and housewives. Through the legal network of professors Irwin Cotler and Alan Dershowitz, it reached Dershowitz's former student Stuart Eizenstat, Carter's chief domestic policy adviser. Eizenstat convinced the president.

This unprecedented statement, distancing our movement from allegations of spying, wasn't news to the Soviets. They knew the truth. But Carter's statement helped neutralize the official Soviet propaganda and the unofficial rumors against me that had been disseminated in the West and in the Jewish community.

Though I was convinced that the Jewish world would not abandon me, I never imagined such a massive global coalition would emerge. I do not believe it would have grown or persisted as it did without Avital's energy, idealism, and deep faith that all would end well.

Years later, when I met French president François Mitterrand, he said, "You know, over the years, your wife sat in that same chair you're sitting in many times. She always asked for help and I always did whatever I could. I couldn't say no to her." He recalled Avital's pure faith, how she told everyone that tomorrow might just be the day I would be free and we could start our family. "Frankly, I didn't believe her," he admitted. "It was the Soviet Union. We knew what they did to their enemies."

Mitterrand, like most of the others, had essentially thought, "Whatever gets you through the day." If this woman needed to believe her delusions to keep mobilized, why not indulge her? "I have to say now," he confessed, "she was right. She proved it to those of us who had doubts. She never stopped and always believed. I helped, but I didn't believe." Mitterrand had belonged to a broad army of good-hearted skeptics, who often found themselves helping more than their rational selves calculated they should.

An American friend in Washington went even further. He said that Avital often claimed that releasing me and other prisoners would be like uncorking a bottle; the system would never survive it. But everyone knew back then that the world was divided into two stable, unshakeable superpowers: the Soviet Union and the United States. Few took her delusion seriously.

One of the first telephone calls Avital made after my arrest was to Israel's opposition leader, Menachem Begin. Rather than chiding her for the late hour, he thanked her for calling and asked, "How can I help?" Two months later, in May 1977, Begin was elected prime minister after nearly three decades in opposition. He helped however he could.

Yehiel Kadishai, Begin's personal assistant, once approached the prime minister with an unusual request. Bezeq, Israel's phone company, had complained that Avital's international phone bill was too big, and growing. International calls were incredibly expensive then, especially in socialist Israel, which had a phone monopoly. Kadishai asked Begin if the government could pay the bill, which ran into the thousands of shekels.

"No, the government cannot pay the bill," Begin said. "But I can." He pulled out his personal checkbook.

Leaders from the opposing party helped as well. Avital met Mitterrand through Shimon Peres, who introduced her to his network of leaders through the Socialist International.

When Prime Minister Begin, President Carter, and President Anwar Sadat signed the Egypt-Israel Peace Treaty in March 1979, Begin invited Avital to join the Israeli delegation to Washington. At the formal celebration on the White House lawn, Avital was seated far away from the center, where the three leaders sat surrounded by security guards. Never willing to miss an opportunity, Avital marched toward them and started speaking.

Fortunately, Begin's Israeli guards recognized her and let her approach. "Menachem, what about my husband's case?" she asked. There was an awkward pause as everyone looked down, unsure of what to do about this breach of protocol. Sadat, the ever-charming Egyptian, was the first to pop up and welcome her with open arms. He said, "Oh, Mrs. Sharansky, your husband is a real hero in Egypt."

Naturally, Avital used the Jewish network as much as possible, even though she sometimes encountered resistance there too. During my hunger strike, knowing little and imagining a lot, Avital was desperate. She spent a lot of time abroad, mostly in America. One day, she heard that a top Soviet official would be meeting Margaret Thatcher. In 1980, Thatcher, the British prime minister, had offered to help, telling Avital, "Your predicament exemplifies the great suffering inflicted on those in the Soviet Union who dare to speak their minds."

Provided with another key phone number from another supporter, Avital called Thatcher's chief of staff, David Wolfson. When he answered, she started chatting away. "You know," she said, "my husband is in serious danger. I am flying to London immediately. I want to speak to Mrs. Thatcher tomorrow."

There was a cold silence on the other end. "My lady, did you look at your watch? Do you know what the time is?" Wolfson asked haughtily. It was after midnight London time.

"I'm sorry. I got confused," Avital admitted. "But tomorrow I will be in London."

"Who do you think you are?" Wolfson started shouting. "Appointments are made months in advance. Leaders of countries wait that long and don't make these kinds of last-minute requests. Do you think the world revolves around you and your husband? You cannot wake people up in the middle of the night just because you have a cause!"

It was the wrong thing to say, in the wrong way. Avital, who is usually so soft-spoken, stopped feeling guilty about disturbing Wolfson. Calmly but firmly, she said, "Yes, in fact the whole world does revolve around this. There are Jews in the Soviet Union who are being held in prison simply for their desire to be Jewish and to come to the Jewish homeland, only a few decades after the Holocaust. We have no choice but to work day and night to fight this."

Pausing for effect and returning to her more spiritual self, she added, "Who knows. Perhaps this is your role in history right now, to make sure I meet Margaret Thatcher and hasten the end of this tragedy."

The phone call ended badly. Avital flew to London anyway. When she landed in Heathrow Airport the next day, a limousine Wolfson had sent was waiting to take her to five o'clock tea with Prime Minister Thatcher. Avital and Wolfson apologized to one another. The next day, the Iron Lady, as Thatcher was known, had the Soviet ambassador to Great Britain called in to the Foreign Office and told that the British government objected to the USSR's treatment of dissidents, including me.

A nine-year emergency runs the risk of becoming routine. Reporters yawn in the face of persistent injustice. Journalists would shrug off Avital's pleas for yet another "my husband's unfairly imprisoned" story, snorting, "Is he dead? Is he released? If not, sorry, there's no story." That only forced Avital to get more creative.

On International Human Rights Day, December 10, 1984, Avital and eleven other human rights activists were invited to meet President Reagan at the White House. Reagan's handlers instructed them to shake the president's hand briefly and move on. By this time, Avital followed Orthodox Judaism's modesty guidelines, which prohibit men and women who aren't married to one another from touching.

Ignoring the handlers, and relying on the Jewish permission to break religious law when lives are at stake, Avital grasped Reagan's hand and wouldn't release it, saying, "I have to speak to you." The next day, a moving photograph of the concerned president looking tenderly at the determined wife dominated the front page of the *New York Times* and many other papers. Reagan's gesture telegraphed an essential message to the Russians: the president was extremely sympathetic to this cause. And the Russians were noticing.

Just a few weeks later, in January 1985, American officials tried to ban Avital from a tense diplomatic summit between US secretary of state George Shultz and Soviet foreign minister Andrei Gromyko. A friend had helped her enter the pressroom about ten minutes before members of the American delegation gave their regular briefing. Journalists seeking a story about tensions during the peace talks pounced. Avital ended up addressing the world about our cause. The Soviet diplomats were furious.

At a meeting that afternoon, the American diplomats were tut-tutting about her disruption. They worried their Soviet colleagues would blame them and view Avital's plea as an American provocation. Her intrusion particularly offended a representative of the Joint Chiefs of Staff. The officials started suggesting ways to send Avital away as a public punishment that might mollify the Soviets.

Secretary of State Shultz shut down his subordinates. "Hey, wait," he said. "Don't touch her. I'd like to think that if my wife were out and I were in the Gulag, she would be commandeering a room to demonstrate for me."

The US-Soviet negotiations finally resulted in the first summit between the two countries since 1979, also held in Geneva. In November 1985, President Reagan met the new young Soviet leader, whose openness Westerners were praising, Mikhail Gorbachev. Dressed in a prison uniform, Avital tried delivering a letter to Gorbachev's popular wife, Raisa Gorbachev, taking advantage of all the fanfare surrounding the charismatic couple.

Pressed by the Soviets, the Swiss police detained Avital for two hours. According to other arrested protesters, the officers spent the time yelling at her "abusively." The letter, which she distributed widely to the press, read, "Dear Mrs. Gorbachev: You are a wife and mother. Permit me to be a wife and mother. Release my husband, my Anatoly." It added, "Whenever he travels, you want to see your husband when he comes home—so do I."

At the summit, the president of the United States told the general secretary of the Communist Party of the Soviet Union, "You can keep saying that Sharansky is an American spy, but my people trust that woman. And as long as you keep him and other political prisoners locked up, we will not be able to establish a relationship of trust."

Three months later, without any of the previous preconditions, I became the first political prisoner Gorbachev released.

ZIGZAGGING TO FREEDOM

It was a long way from the Geneva summit's fairy-tale mansions where President Reagan demanded my freedom to the nightmarish Ural Mountains labor camp where the Soviet regime had imprisoned me. In the Gulag system, the different penal institutions build a pyramid of deprivations. From the labor camps, to the prisons, to the labor camps' prisons, to the punishment cells, you get more isolation, less mail, fewer visits from loved ones, increasingly limited exposure to fresh air, and reduced nutrition. There were eighteen so-called diets. These were the levels of rations, from 1a down to 9b, which was the punishment-cell special: three pieces of bread and three cups of hot water a day. In November 1985, when Reagan and Gorbachev finally met for the first US-Soviet summit in eight years, I was once again on the lowest level, the punishment cell.

A few weeks later, I started experiencing unprecedented disruptions in the Gulag's never-ending prison routine. My captors took me straight out of the punishment cell to the hospital, yanking me from the 9b diet to 1a overnight, skipping the sixteen levels in between. They were suddenly generous in their portions, serving me foods I had almost forgotten about, like eggs. They started injecting me with vitamins and glucose, as if I were a racehorse, clearly trying to strengthen me. They let me walk outside for two hours a day so I could rediscover fresh air, snow, and sunshine after being deprived of nature for so long.

Even the smallest deviations from totalitarian monotony trigger a prisoner's imagination, usually raising false hopes. But these dramatic violations of the rules cried out for explanation.

Nine years of confinement train you to limit your mental meanderings, or risk depression when your hopes are dashed yet again. So I told myself, "They must be preparing me for some meeting with higher-ups."

The clearest sign that something was up came when the barber skipped me. The barbers came regularly to shave our heads so we would look like walking skeletons. They never missed any of us. Obviously, the powers that be didn't want me looking like a prisoner anymore. That was the most convincing proof that they wanted to parade me before someone, somewhere.

The miracles accumulate. Events that exceed my wildest dreams start coming true. A three-car convoy with sirens blaring drives me away from the labor camp. We whiz through the villages and forests until we arrive at the nearest airport. We board a passenger jet large enough to carry more than one hundred passengers, but it's only for me and four KGB escorts. We land in Moscow. We then return to my alma mater, Lefortovo prison.

I spend a few days in the KGB's Moscow jail, with no explanation of course. Then, one morning they replace my prison garb with civilian clothes, many sizes too large for my still-underweight body. The only non-civilian touch is a drawstring to keep my pants up. Prisoners aren't permitted belts or shoelaces.

It's all happening abruptly and harshly, steeped in the usual KGB silence. All I have to do is watch the dream unfold and remember to protest now and then, so I don't passively accept the KGB's script. As usual, the Soviets' brutishness makes it easy. I keep protesting whenever they insist I leave everything behind, including my book of Psalms, a special gift from Avital I had received a few days before my arrest. I had spent weeks in hunger strikes and punishment cells because I insisted on keeping this gift, which she managed to send to me via Jewish tourist airmail from Jerusalem. Since then, my regular meetings with King David, the psalm writer, had entertained me, soothed me, and improved my Hebrew. This was no time for us to break up.

So I throw myself down in the snow and shout loudly, wherever I am, to make sure my one made-in-Israel possession keeps traveling with me. I note how quick they are to cave in, to smooth things along.

Like the locks in a canal that lift passing boats from lower water levels to higher ones, I climb to freedom in stages. A second, even larger airplane takes off, again with just five of us. I still refuse to believe that it's happening, really happening. Yet, judging by the sun, I see we are flying west. I start calculating just when we might fly across the border.

As we cross, the leader of the four KGB men comes from behind the curtain at the front of the airplane. He informs me stiffly that, by special decision of the Soviet government, due to misbehavior, I am being stripped of my Soviet citizenship and exiled from the Soviet Union.

Now I cannot deceive myself anymore. I surrender to the realization: I am free.

He had made a statement, so I make one too, even though he tries to cut me off, saying, "We don't need your statement." Still, I insist on saying our truth, expressing the hope that freedom will soon come to the many others I am leaving behind.

Finally, after nine years, I can turn to King David for praise, not just comfort. I read the psalm that I had chosen years ago, back when my release was still an impossible dream. It's Psalm 30, a song of thanksgiving at the *chanukkat habayit*, the dedication of the house of David: "O Lord, you have brought up my soul from the grave. You have kept me alive, that I should not go down to the pit."

We land in East Berlin, the capital of the German Democratic Republic, a city of bridges and that infamous wall dividing East from West. Berlin strikes me as an odd place for a Jew to get his freedom.

"You see that car, Anatoly Borisovich? Go straight to it and don't make any turns," one escort says calmly, expecting to stay out of camera view and in the warm cabin of the plane as I walk out into the February freeze. "Is it agreed?"

"Agreed?" I am still in KGB world, and therefore cannot agree. "Since when do I make agreements with the KGB?" I ask. "You know that I never agree with the KGB about anything. If you tell me to go straight, I will go crooked."

"You see, you are not serious. We cannot deal with you," he snaps, as the minders mumbled among themselves. As a result, two of them get out of the plane first and flank me on either side. As promised, I zigzag across the tarmac, from the Russian airplane to an East German car. As I lurch left, then right, the TV cameras are rolling and the KGB agents are yelling at me to straighten out. One flustered cameraman ends up banging into the window of the waiting car as he films.

The next day, in the final stage of my release, I am driven onto the subzero, snow-covered Glienicke bridge. I am then escorted to freedom by the tall American ambassador to the Federal Republic of Germany, Richard Burt.

I don't need to zigzag here. I am no longer in KGB hands. Besides, I have a more pressing worry: those big pants and that flimsy drawstring. I ask Ambassador Burt, "Where is the border, exactly?" He points to a four-inch line the Germans had kindly cleared of snow. As I mark my entry to freedom, I jump with joy—and the string pops. I enter the free world just barely catching my pants before they fall down.

THE END OF ONE LONG DAY

Somewhere in the Frankfurt Airport, I enter some godforsaken room. There, I see the same girl I had taken to the Moscow airport twelve years ago, a few hours after our wedding. I had promised my new wife we would reunite soon. Now, trying to control my tears, I say to her in Hebrew, "Silchi li she'icharti kzat"—sorry I'm a little late. I am living inside my dream, and not resisting it. I just keep clutching Avital because I fear the dream will stop. Holding her hand will prevent me from waking up back in the punishment cell.

The small airplane Israel sent lands at Ben-Gurion Airport, just outside Tel Aviv. The door opens. "Here's our prime minister, Shimon Peres," Avital says, making introductions. "And here's our foreign minister, Yitzhak Shamir. And here are the two chief rabbis. . ."

Soon I would talk to President Ronald Reagan by telephone, and after that his secretary of state, George Shultz. I thank them for all they did, and remind them the struggle continues.

"How could you have been so calm?" people ask me today after watching videos of those conversations. By then, nothing could ruffle me. I was living my dreams. If, at the moment, I had been told that the next phone call was coming from King David himself, it would have made as much sense as everything else. After all, wouldn't it have been natural for me to compare notes with my comrade in arms, after we spent all that time together?

I had run out of the ability to be surprised. I had moved straight from hell to paradise in a flash. A day that had started in the hands of my captors ended at the Western Wall in the hands of thousands of dancing, cheering, singing Jews celebrating our reunion. "It was just one long day," Avital sighed later that night, in our new home in Jerusalem. "I arrived in Israel in the morning. You arrived in the evening. It was just one very, very long day in between."

EVERYDAY LIFE IN PARADISE

From a life of a few daily macro decisions—yes or no, surrender or resist—my life became filled with micro decisions. I found myself having to make thousands of the most mundane choices, big and small: Tea or coffee? A white shirt or a blue one? In the beginning, it irritated me. "Why do I have to think about all this?" I grumbled. I pawned off as many of these little choices as I could onto my wife. Gradually, freedom spoiled me enough to enjoy these options, to choose my morning coffee, my afternoon tea, a favorite shirt.

The landscape of Israel, the light of Israel, became part of my life very naturally. In one of her first letters from Israel, Avital, with her artist's eye, said the light there was different, so bright while Moscow was so gray. She was not giving a weather report. She was bathing in the light of old-new Jerusalem—and the lightness of freedom.

After a week of nonstop meetings, interviews, and hugging and high-fiving on the streets of Jerusalem whenever we walked out of our new home, Avital and I escaped up north to Safed.

The morning after we arrived in this mystical city and looked out from our balcony and heard birds chirping, I felt like we had arrived in the Garden of Eden, paradise itself. The almond trees were blooming, and the canopies of white and pink flowers looked like our own personal escort—custom-made signs of my homecoming. Today, whenever I hear the classic Zionist children's song "Hashkediya Porachat" (the almond tree is blooming) for the Tu B'shvat Arbor Day holiday, and every winter when those trees bloom, Avital and I delight in this symbol of our reunion.

In February 1986, the history I had desperately wanted to join since 1967 became a part of my everyday life. I was steeped in it wherever I wandered. King David had had to work hard, overcoming a gap of thousands of years, to reach me through his psalms. Now, by choosing to live in Jerusalem, the City of David, I had made my former companion an old neighbor. I visited the Valley of Elah, where a young David fought Goliath, and remembered the looming, unclothed statue in my apartment growing up.

Given a chance to touch Jewish history at its most intimate, I got a special tour of the vast, two-thousand-year-old tunnels beside the Western Wall. I stopped at the spot closest to where the holy of holies, the center of the Temple, once stood. This was not only where so many Jews for so long wished they could be. This was where Avital had prayed for me occasionally, having been given special access by the Western Wall rabbi at the height of my hunger strike and during other dark moments of that four-thousand-day-long day.

Shortly after arriving in Israel, Avital had started living a fully traditional Jewish life. Her faith gave her great strength over the years. My movement toward traditional observance was slower. This gap in our outward observance began to fuel much speculation. Many couldn't imagine how we would overcome our differences. The silly debate started in the newspapers: What will happen first? the gossips snickered. Will Natan put on a kippah, or will Avital take off her head covering—and will they divorce? Of course, this was ridiculous to us. We didn't feel endangered by our differences. How could variations in religious ritual prevent us from staying together when the KGB couldn't tear us apart?

But, like crazed soccer fans, people were rooting for me to join their team and wear their uniform: stay bareheaded with the seculars, accept the simple black kippah of the ultra-Orthodox, or find the right mix of color, material, and size that would ally me with one slice or another of the Religious Zionist community.

Irritated by all the leering at my bald head, I put on the green Israeli military cap, which had a flimsy brim in front. I got my first one from an American visiting Moscow, who gave it to me along with the thrilling compliment that we young Jewish activists seemed as brave as Israeli soldiers. That hat stuck to my head. It remains affixed to this day. The Israel Defense Forces (IDF) stopped producing such caps long ago. So the latest hats that look closest to the original say on the lining, "Made in China."

On my first Saturday together with Avital, I was invited for a special VIP sightseeing tour in Jerusalem. Avital said nothing, but clearly preferred that I not violate the Sabbath. I skipped the tour without hesitation. The most important thing to me was *shalom bayit*, a happy, tranquil home. I would defer to Avital when it came to choosing our future children's schools and educational paths.

I soon understood what a treasure the Sabbath was in our life, and I started complaining that we didn't have two every week. Adjusting to the sheer volume of Jewish prayers took a bit more work. Here, too, it was easy in prison: knowing no prayers, I could invent them for myself and say whatever I wanted, keeping it short. Now, I had no excuse; I had to follow the lengthy text.

But the most profound change was that this new freedom truly liberated me to live comfortably with my identity. Suddenly, in Israel, I wasn't a Jewish doublethinker anymore. In my past life, being Jewish had always been an effort. Whether it was a burden, a birthright, or a passport to pride, it made me stand out. I was often self-conscious that, as a Jew, I represented the Jewish people, even when doing the most trivial things in public.

I discovered that many of my friends in America shared this Jewish doublethinking burden, but it was different in Israel. There, I didn't represent the Jews. I didn't speak for them. I simply lived like one of them, with my family. Now I could relax and be myself.

Like all immigrants, I was uprooted. I had left part of myself in Russia. While becoming accustomed to technological surprises—such as record players in most people's cars, called CD players, and telephones in diplomats' and politicians' vehicles—there were cultural adjustments too. As I listened to the news in Hebrew, I understood more day by day, but I also understood that I would never express myself in Hebrew as I did in Russian.

To this day, whenever I open a new book or go to the theater, I feel a pang. I miss that excitement, that sense of anticipation, that comes from encountering a work of art that flirts with dissent, that's passing on a hidden message or subtly trying to defy the authorities. By contrast, everything in Israel is open, direct, and often lacking sophistication. And whenever I lick an ice-cream cone, I miss the tastes and smells of my childhood.

Within minutes of my liberation, the Americans told me that their agreement with the Soviets included granting exit visas to my closest relatives. But by the summer, the Soviets were procrastinating, refusing to release my mother; my brother, Leonid; his wife, Raya; and their two sons: Boris, who was one, and Aleksandr, who was fifteen. The authorities hoped to use my concern for my family to bully me into silence. But I knew I couldn't bargain with gangsters.

In July, I called David Shipler of the *New York Times*. David had stood by my mother and brother during the difficult days of my trial, and subsequently, as a reporter and a sympathetic ear. I told him the Soviets were breaking their commitment. "They could play with me; I have years ahead of me," I said. "But my mother is of such an age that I cannot permit them to play this game too long."

David published my words, and within weeks my seventy-seven-year-old mother was on her way, along with Leonid and his family. Leonid lived in Israel for a few years, then found work in the United States. Today, he and Raya split their time between Des Moines and Pasadena (where their children and grandchildren live) and Eilat (where they prefer to live).

My mother settled in Jerusalem and lived near us as a proud mother and grandmother for another sixteen years. Both our daughters blossomed in her lap until they outgrew it.

Yet, with all this excitement, with all these adjustments to paradise, we didn't forget for a moment that the struggle had to continue for those left behind.

THE MARCH OF 250,000
FROM IMAGINATION TO REALITY

It was time to end this chapter of my life, when the borders between my imagination and reality kept blurring. For some time, that imagined world of Jewish unity continued to shape my real life. The best example of this was the historic march on Washington to free Soviet Jewry on December 6, 1987. That mass demonstration would be the last big public act of our global struggle to tear down the Iron Curtain.

Avital and I were slowly comparing notes about our experiences during our "minus twelve," the long years apart. We didn't need to do it all at once; we had our whole lives ahead. We continue to uncover new stories to this day.

Just a few weeks after my liberation, the doctors delivered great news: Avital was pregnant. We were overjoyed, and quite relieved. We had feared that by the time I was free it would be too late for us to have a family. But the news came with a health warning. Avital was bedridden for most of the pregnancy. The doctor's demands at least fulfilled one of Avital's desires. She was retiring. She was no longer interested in playing the public role our fate had imposed on her. "Now you are my spokesman," she told me.

Passing the baton to me, she happily vanished from the TV screens and newspaper headlines. But she kept sharing the key lessons she had learned as a reluctant activist. We both knew the fight had to continue. Avital and her allies had long refused to limit their cause to saving her husband, a few dozen prisoners of Zion, or even a few thousand Refuseniks. Seeking the exodus of an entire people, they started speaking about four hundred thousand Jews impatiently waiting for visas to go to Israel. That number represented all the Jews who had requested that the Israeli government send invitations to emigrate, minus those who had already left. That number proved that the fight for Soviet Jewry was a grand historical struggle for freedom. Only a big, broad, and ambitious campaign would work.

That sweeping vision, she informed me, had become the latest wedge issue separating her activist friends from the leaders of the organized Jewish community and the representatives of the Israeli government. We called them the Establishment.

Instinctively cautious and fearful of making the problem seem too daunting, the Establishment leaders opposed this "irresponsible" inflation of the numbers. They preferred to speak at most about thirty thousand Jews they believed had already applied to go to Israel. Israel's diplomats stuck to that number too.

Avital reported that one insider had dissented: Israel's ambassador to the United Nations since 1984, Benjamin Netanyahu. At his previous posting in Washington, Bibi had become Avital's main strategic adviser in dealing with the American government. He was the only Israeli official in the United States ready to ignore the Liaison Office's marching orders.

"Wow," I interrupted her. "Does he have any connection to Yoni Netanyahu?"—the hero of Entebbe whose portrait was hanging in my room when I was arrested. Working with Yoni's brother felt like yet another miracle, magically closing the circle between my old world and my new one.

Many like to forget this now, but back when he was Israel's ambassador to the United Nations, Netanyahu was the toast of New York—and of American Jewry. The *New York Times* praised him in 1985 "for his ability to speak spontaneously" with great "passion," while hailing "his effective use of sarcasm to make a point." Beyond his eloquence was real cleverness. Avital explained to me that shortly after President Reagan launched the Strategic Defense Initiative—popularly known as Star Wars—in 1983, Bibi figured out how to use it for our cause. Star Wars unnerved the Soviets. They feared it threw off their strategic standoff with America.

Bibi advised Avital that she had an opportunity to help the Soviets realize that the way they were treating the Refuseniks only fed American distrust of the Soviet Union, which then strengthened support for Star Wars. This argument truly made it in the Soviets' best interest to treat Soviet Jews more humanely. Supplementing Avital's already extensive contact list, Bibi helped her use whatever levers in Washington and New York were possible to deliver that message clearly.

Avital also recalled complaining to Bibi in 1985 about the Establishment's resistance to any discussion regarding the four hundred thousand
Jews.

"But what do you believe is true?" Bibi asked.

"We are sure that four hundred thousand is the minimum number of
Jews who want to leave. It's probably higher," she replied.

"Then go with your truth," he encouraged her. "Let's put this figure
into circulation. Don't give up!"

Bibi introduced Avital to influential lobbyists, especially Marvin
Josephson and his National PAC. Together, Josephson and Avital met
with key congressional leaders, speaking about the four hundred thousand Jews who needed help. They urged legislators to pass a resolution
affirming that what President Reagan called "real friendship" and "real
peace" with the Soviet Union depended on our people being freed.

The result was S. J. Res. 161 of the Ninety-Ninth Congress. This joint
resolution, which became law on August 6, 1985, called for my release,
along with the release of Yosef Begun and all "prisoners of conscience."
It singled out long-term Refuseniks, including Vladimir Slepak and Ida
Nudel, both in their fifteenth year of waiting. The original resolution also
called for releasing the heart-tugging, epoch-making number of four
hundred thousand Soviet Jews seeking to emigrate.

Yet, somehow, when the resolution passed both the House of Representatives and the Senate and insiders reconciled the two texts, our magic
number vanished. Instead, there was a vague call for "thousands of Jews
who wish to emigrate." The Establishment had intervened.

Now, it was my turn to lead the fight for the four hundred thousand.
Before I flew to the United States, Avital detailed the constant tensions
between the different Jewish organizations. "Everybody is going to want
you to join their organization," she warned. "But don't join anyone. Stay
independent. And understand, our first allies are the students"—best
represented by the Student Struggle for Soviet Jewry—"and the housewives"—best represented by the Union of Councils for Soviet Jews (UCSJ)
and the Thirty-Five, a women's organization in England and Canada.

"You need these grassroots activists to get things started," Avital explained. "Still, the Establishment"—best represented by the National
Conference on Soviet Jewry—"wields the real power. The Establishment
will be the last to join. But when they finally step in and take the credit,
then you will know you have won."

That's exactly what happened—eventually.

Before my trip, I spoke to David Makovsky, the head of the World Union of Jewish Students (WUJS), who had organized many demonstrations supporting Avital. David told me that people were feeling confused, unsure whether to continue pressing the increasingly popular Mikhail Gorbachev. Elie Wiesel had advised the students: Take matters in your own hands. Don't wait for the Establishment. Go to Washington. March, lobby, protest. No one will do it for you.

I arrived in New York in May 1986 to thank and to spur. In every meeting—with the president, other politicians, journalists, professors, students, Jewish leaders, and thousands of Americans—I expressed my gratitude, then called for renewed efforts to save the four hundred thousand.

During a reception New York mayor Ed Koch hosted for dozens of Jewish leaders, I had my eureka moment. Thinking about the four hundred thousand, and anticipating that Gorbachev would eventually visit Washington as US-Soviet relations continued to improve, I just blurted it out. "Four hundred thousand Soviet Jews are waiting for us to act," I said. "When Mikhail Gorbachev visits the White House, let's have four hundred thousand American Jews march on Washington shouting 'Let my people go.'"

I didn't mean four hundred thousand protesters literally. And there was no summit planned yet. I was trying to illustrate the magnitude of the Soviet Jewish problem. But the minute I said it, I liked it. The picture of hundreds of thousands of Jews, marching on Washington, demanding that the Soviet leaders free hundreds of thousands of Jews, came straight from my prison memory bank, from the imagined world that had sustained me for nine years. That's how a quick quip became an action plan.

"Natan, the Establishment organizations will do nothing," Wiesel warned me when we conferred the next day. "Don't waste your energy on them. Go to the students."

The Establishment's first reaction confirmed Wiesel and Avital's warnings. The leaders lectured me. They insisted it was irresponsible to speak about four hundred thousand Soviet Jews without proof. And it was irresponsible to speak about four hundred thousand American Jews. "How many Jews live in Washington?" they asked. "It's not New York."

What if the leaders' summit fell during the winter? Experts from the National Conference on Soviet Jewry estimated a maximum of eighteen thousand marchers. We would all look foolish. Besides, it was irresponsi ble to endanger American Jews by having them sound like warmongers. Gorbachev had dazzled Americans as an agent of change. Even Democrats were starting to applaud Reagan, the Republican right-winger, for giving peace a chance.

Some sneered, "With all due respect"—that killer American phrase that always means an attack is imminent—"what do you understand about American politics, the Jewish community, or organizing protests here?" Nevertheless, I persisted, month after month, meeting after meeting.

Trying to save me, Morris Abram offered a compromise. This exemplary community leader, who chaired the National Conference on Soviet Jewry and the Conference of Presidents of Major American Jewish Organizations, promised to get all one hundred senators standing on the Capitol steps, demanding freedom for Soviet Jewry.

Another invaluable ally and new close friend, Rabbi Avi Weiss, stepped in. As leader of the Student Struggle for Soviet Jewry, he warned me, "Don't expect anything from the Establishment. Even if they say they will do it, they cannot do it." Instead, he offered to find one hundred rabbis to chain themselves to the Russian embassy whenever Gorbachev visited, ready to be arrested for the cause. But I didn't want one hundred of anything. I envisioned a mass rally echoing my prison dreams.

In the middle of the summer of 1987, I once again checked in with David Makovsky about our progress. "Nothing's happening," he reported. The Establishment still opposed a mass march. The US-Soviet summit remained unscheduled. Students were distracted, with many working at Jewish summer camps. "Nobody's talking about it," he said. "If you want this to happen, you have to come to America and speak constantly about it here."

That August, Avital, our ten-month-old daughter Rachel, and I moved to New York. By October, they had returned home. I stayed through early December, when Gorbachev finally visited Washington.

I traveled from one place to another, visiting thirty-two Jewish communities in total. In each city, I would brief the leaders, give interviews to reporters, meet with the editorial boards of newspapers, address two or three synagogues, and recruit as many students as possible.

To avoid the organizational trap Avital warned against, we had an independent operation. Two former top policy aides to Speaker of the House Tip O'Neill, Ari Weiss and Jack Lew, who had both helped Avital, volunteered. Using their Washington network, we found a base: Van Ness Feldman, the new law firm founded by some of Senator Henry Jackson's former aides. For months, a rotation of high-powered chaperones accompanied me: Ari, Jack, David Makovsky, and his brother, Michael Makovsky, a student at the time.

My message to the Jewish communities was simple: now is your moment to change history. "We've come so far," I said. I listed Americans' many shared achievements in championing Soviet Jewry. "This march is the last push," I pleaded.

Wherever I spoke, the rank-and-file Jews were excited about a mass demonstration in Washington. Nobody echoed the leaders' objections. I knew the Jewish people's strength, their enthusiasm, their determination. Now I experienced it as I traveled from community to community, campus to campus. Everyone seemed as committed and mobilized as I had dreamed them to be.

RONALD REAGAN LIVES UP TO MY IMAGINATION

As "Gorby fever" started building in America that fall, the skeptics became even more skittish. "We cannot appear to oppose this new détente with the Soviets. It's too popular," they said. "And we cannot cross Ronald Reagan after he has been so helpful."

Ronald Reagan? The Reagan who had made my day in prison in 1983, when he called the Soviet Union "the evil empire"? The Reagan whose precious words we had passed from one prisoner to another by tapping it in Morse code or whispering it through our "toilet telephones," sticking our heads deep into the bowls so neighbors could hear us through the pipes? Impossible. The Reagan who presided over my imagined prison world could not oppose this march for freedom.

In Avital and my absolutist world of struggle, there were no barriers, walls, protocols, or niceties that could stop us. So we went straight to the president of the United States in late September. We thanked him jointly for his help and asked him what he thought of a march, whenever a summit materialized. Trying to ease into the conversation, because so many had warned that he would be offended, we reassured him that any protests against Gorbachev would not be opposing American policy but Soviet oppression.

"Why would someone think I want to be friends with a person who keeps his own people in prison?" Reagan asked. "You do whatever you have to do, and I will do what I have to do."

"Reagan wants this demonstration." I told the Jewish leaders. But Morris Abram remained skeptical. In October, when the president announced Gorbachev's visit, Abram turned to Secretary of State George Shultz.

"Do you really want this rally?" Abram asked, as Shultz later told me.

"Not only do we want it," Shultz replied, "I want it to be the first thing that Gorbachev sees on every TV screen in America when he arrives for the summit!"

Finally, I got the call. In late October, as the Americans and Soviets were finalizing the December date, I heard that the Establishment was in. The head of the American Jewish Committee's Washington office, and longtime advocate for Soviet Jewry, David Harris, would run the operation.

As Avital had predicted, the impact was immediate. When I spoke at a university the next day, everything had changed. I was no longer a lonely prophet but a recruiting sergeant. Representatives of the Jewish Federations and the Hillels—the Jewish student centers—appeared. There were buses to sign up for and tasks to volunteer for. Overnight, I had been integrated into an extraordinary logistical operation. And, yes, as Avital had warned, they mobilized, strategized, advertised, fundraised, spent generously—and took the credit.

But it worked. They chartered planes, rented buses, and secured parking lots. On the day of the demonstration, airplanes landed from Los Angeles, Miami, and Toronto. Trains pulled in from Boston, Philadelphia, and Chicago. Overnight buses arrived from Buffalo, Pittsburgh, and Cincinnati. Thousands of private cars scrambled for parking.

The marchers came from different organizations, different synagogues, different corners of North America, and different political perspectives. Our cause continued to be a rare issue uniting Republicans and Democrats in Reagan's polarized Washington.

In all, 250,000 Americans, in an operation of military precision throbbing with hippie happiness, braved the Washington cold to shout "Let my people go." The protest matched the size of Martin Luther King's legendary 1963 civil rights march on Washington. Once again, my prison-shaped delusions had come true.

To be honest, there were too many speakers. Most spoke far longer than was necessary. But it didn't matter. Standing on the podium, looking into this sea of solidarity, I felt like I could touch those sweet feelings of Jewish unity and sense the impending victory.

The skeptics were wrong about the weather. Rain threatened but never came, until the rally ended and people started dispersing. As the freezing rain started pouring down, three of us remained on the huge makeshift podium on Washington's vast, rapidly emptying Mall. It could have been an awkward moment. I watched Morris Abram, the head of the Establishment, look hesitantly at one of his rivals, Pamela Cohen, the head of the Union of Councils for Soviet Jews.

Suddenly, all three of us shouted, "We did it!" We started slapping each other on the back. Hugging, we danced a little hora. We had made it, together.

It was still one year before the last prisoners of Zion and Refuseniks were released. It was still two years before the Berlin Wall fell. It was still four years before the Soviet Union collapsed. But we knew that the war was won. Finally, in December 1987, I faced a new challenge: to start real life again. It was time to become Israeli.

PART II

NINE YEARS IN ISRAELI POLITICS

7

BECOMING ISRAELI

There I was, in April 1993, marching for Soviet Jews, again. This demonstration was neither as dangerous nor as dramatic as ten Jews confronting the Kremlin. It was neither as overwhelming nor as global as 250,000 Jews marching in Washington. Still, it was as exciting and empowering as the other protests—and more fun.

This time, instead of marching on Capitol Hill and targeting the Soviet government, we marched on our own parliament in Jerusalem. Instead of waving placards and shouting slogans, we wielded brooms.

Fifteen thousand of us demanded that the Knesset pass *chok tkufat nikayon*, the cleaning internship law. It paralleled *chok tkufat nisayon*, the professional internship law, which imposed a *stazh*, an apprenticeship, on professionals before they could recertify in Israel. Our "law" added an obligatory internship period of *nikayon*, sweeping floors or tidying apartments. The more advanced your degree, the longer your cleaning assignment. For young engineers, three years. For academics, five years. For professors of medicine, ten years.

Actually, no such proposal reached the Knesset. We were waving our brooms with our tongues firmly in our cheeks. We were echoing the Soviet law that said the more advanced your degree, the more your exit visa cost. Some actors, freshly arrived from Moscow's greatest theaters, impersonated harsh bureaucrats, barking out each profession and its proposed length of cleaning services.

This demonstration was one of many dramatic moments as hundreds of immigrants came to Israel by the planeload, week after week. By 1993, the four hundred thousand Soviet immigrants we expected had already arrived. The total soon exceeded one million.

With the number of professionals arriving daily, it wasn't surprising to see so many unemployed or underemployed. Who could reasonably expect an appropriate job right when you land in a foreign country?

Most of the Russian immigrants—as they were called, regardless of where they came from in the Soviet Union—had been raised as I was. Absolutely assimilated, they had followed one guideline: "You are a Jew. To succeed in this anti-Semitic environment, you must be number one in physics, mathematics, chess, music, doesn't matter what. But that's how we Jews survive."

Their drive became their identity. After reaching the professional elite in a country of more than two hundred million, they moved to a country of five million. Almost overnight, the number of Israel's doctors, engineers, musicians, and chess players doubled.

"What do you call a Russian Jew who walks off the plane without carrying a violin?" Israelis joked. "A pianist!"

It became a stereotype: the night watchman with the PhD, the orderly with the MD, the maid with the concert gold medal. The reality was more subtle: the professor teaching high school, the engineer fixing televisions, the classical violinist giving music lessons.

More irritating than the employment problem was how dismissive Israelis were about it. Israeli society downplayed how many people felt crushed by the mass displacement. The Russian Jews of the First and Second Aliyah, around the turn of the century, had sweated away in the fields, draining the swamps. The 850,000 Jews expelled from Arab and Muslim countries in the 1950s and '60s, the Mizrahim, languished in *ma'abarot* (makeshift absorption camps), then helped make the Negev desert bloom. "Look at the country we created when we came and paid our dues," we were told. "Why should your immigration be different?"

The Israelis' Zionist logic was clear: The suffering parents are like the Bible's lost generation of Jews, who wandered the desert for forty years. Their children will grow up in Israel and go through the melting pot of the army. Then, they'll become real Israelis, just like us!

Soviet immigrants resisted this life sentence. Our street sweeper demonstration was another expression of our refusal. The minister of absorption, Yair Tzaban, a social activist from the Meretz Party, rose to speak. But, feeling empowered by the brooms, the demonstrators shouted, "NO! WE WANT THE CLEANING LAW. WE WANT THE CLEANING LAW." A key lesson of Moscow theater: to make your protest memorable, push life's absurdities to the grotesque extreme.

CREATING THE ZIONIST FORUM

The demonstration didn't happen in a vacuum. There was an organization behind it all. Shortly after we returned to Israel from Washington in December 1987, my friends and I shifted our focus. On May 1, 1988, over one hundred representatives of our aliyah convened. Former prisoners of Zion, ex-Refuseniks, and long-established immigrants founded the Soviet Jewry Zionist Forum to push our concerns onto Israel's agenda. I was elected chairman, and Yuli Edelstein, the future Speaker of the Knesset, became the deputy. The demonstration in Washington had brought the number four hundred thousand into American Jewish consciousness. But was Israel prepared for such a massive aliyah?

Our first meetings with Israel's leaders answered the question: no, they weren't. Foreign Minister Shimon Peres was friendly but skeptical. "Of course I'd like them to come," Peres began, "but only a few will actually arrive. We'll get ten to fifteen thousand at most. Why should they leave? Now that Mikhail Gorbachev's perestroika and glasnost are bringing freedom there, they can enjoy life. Why would they come to a war-torn country? First, we have to make peace."

Peres led Israel's Labor Party. Peres and other Labor Zionist romantics believed that, with Gorbachev's reforms, the Soviet Union was finally moving in the right direction, toward the socialism of their youth. Meanwhile, they worried about Israel's future, with no peace in sight.

Israel's right-wing prime minister Yitzhak Shamir had no illusions about a human face to socialism or an expressway to Middle East peace. He offered the same estimate but a different rationale. "We'll get ten to fifteen thousand at most. We have our intelligence sources," he said when we met. "They report that most Jews in Moscow are studying English, not Hebrew. They want to go to America." Shamir was still grumbling about the dropouts.

Both Israeli leaders, however, offered similar assurances. If Russian Jews arrived in such large numbers, the more the better. Each insisted, "Israel will be ready. You'll see how the whole country will mobilize."

When the gates of the Soviet Union started opening in 1989, Israel really did mobilize. As the Iron Curtain fell, Jewish Agency representatives fanned out throughout the vast, teetering Soviet empire. They assisted impressively, from filling out visa requests to arranging flights to expediting processing at Ben-Gurion Airport. Not enough housing for so many people? "No problem, have some *savlanoot*," patience. Soon, tens of thousands of caravan towns started popping up, from Beersheba to Haifa.

Not enough absorption centers? "No problem, *smoch alai*," trust me. Soon, the government started a more individualized approach, direct absorption. Every immigrant received a *sal klita*—an absorption basket, thousands of dollars in subsidies to get settled. American Jewry raised more than $1 billion to help, thanks to the Federations' massive campaign, Operation Exodus.

Tough conditions? "No problem, *yihyeh beseder*," it'll be OK, they said, hitting you on the shoulder. "You think you have it bad, we had it worse! We had to drain swamps, resist malaria, fight Arabs, dodge the British!"

We joked that Russian immigrants were limping around lopsided, with their right shoulders pounded down by every Israeli shouting "*Savlanoot-smoch-alai-yihyeh-beseder*," as if it were one word.

The Israeli government's no-nonsense, one-size-fits-all approach to newcomers worked. After Israel's establishment in 1948, waves of immigration, starting with the European Holocaust survivors, soon doubled the population. In the 1950s and '60s, 850,000 immigrants expelled from the Arab countries and North Africa arrived: the Sephardim, today known as Mizrahim. Each time, Israel met the challenge. Refugees from over one hundred countries who spoke dozens of languages became Hebrew-speaking Israelis.

Now, in the 1990s, Israel had to absorb an aliyah one-fifth the size of its current population. But Israel's melting-pot approach was paternalistic. Sabras (native-born Israelis) and early immigrants believed they knew what newcomers needed. They had already proved they were on the right side of history by becoming Israeli before Hitler's rise.

The Israelis' embrace of Holocaust survivors had been heroic. The small, poor, struggling country, surrounded by enemies, had doubled its population, welcoming home strangers with strange customs and strange languages. But Israelis saw these people as passive victims. The nickname young Israelis threw around in the street at these European survivors was chilling: *sabonim*, soap bars, because that's what Nazis had made out of some dead Jews' skin.

By contrast, Israelis were proud to be making history in their country. So, before joining their fellow Jews as actors in the new Jewish drama, these newcomers had to have the deference, oppression, and weakness of the exile—Galut—drained out of them, like the swamps themselves.

As planeloads of Jews expelled from Arab countries arrived in the 1950s, the paternalism became more problematic. The Socialist Zionist leaders—Russian Jews who had arrived at the beginning of the 1900s with the Second and Third Aliyah—decided for the new immigrants, not with them. Ben-Gurion Zionists, leading the government and the Jewish Agency, wanted to turn these people into New Jews—proud, strong Israelis.

Suddenly, these secular Ashkenazim were deciding what kind of identity the newcomers from Morocco, Yemen, and Iraq should have, how much of their culture they could keep, which Jewish traditions they should maintain, where they would live, what jobs they would have, and what their new names would be.

This process left psychological and social scars. In 1977, Menachem Begin of the Likud Party—himself Ashkenazi like all of us Russians, Poles, and Western Europeans—rose to power as the first mainstream Israeli politician responsive to Mizrahi anger.

Their new name reflected their trauma. Before moving to Israel, they were Moroccan, Algerian, Syrian, or Libyan Jews. While they shared Sephardi (from Spain) liturgy and rituals, no collective identity linked them politically as Mizrahim, meaning Easterners. The Jewish state had bestowed that identity on them. Eventually, Mizrahim started expressing their anger politically. Seven years after Begin's election, the ultrareligious party Shas emerged, promising to use Mizrahi political power to revitalize Sephardic culture and pride.

In Russia, we never appreciated the depth of the Mizrahi fury. When I arrived, I heard constant complaints about Ashkenazi domination and discrimination, insults and arrogance. As usual, the cabbies nailed it. One driver in 1986 told me how exciting my release was for Israelis. "We were all crying," he said. Then, he added, "But you understand that if you weren't Ashkenazi, if you were Moroccan like me, they never would have organized such a reception for you."

"Even if someone spent nine years in prison?" I asked.

"Of course," he snorted, listing Mizrahi Jews he claimed the state neglected.

A few years later, when Soviet immigration was at its peak, another taxi driver told me, "I'm so happy to see how you Russians are coming in big numbers to Israel. Together, you Russians and we Sephardim will show those Ashkenazi Jews who's the boss now."

EMBRACING HERZL'S ROMANTIC VISION OF THE "MOSAIC MOSAIC" OVER BEN-GURION'S

Israel was a unique laboratory. Usually, a nation-state produces a Diaspora as people leave. Here, the far-flung Diaspora was producing a new nation-state. It came with no instruction manual, except its founders' imaginations.

Reading history, I learned that the contemporary debate about how to handle immigrants reflected the founders' clash regarding the legacy of the Diaspora. Modern Zionism's founder, Theodor Herzl, was a proud Jewish nationalist who loved European culture. He respected the deep connections that immigrants brought from their first homes to their old-new homeland. He wanted to welcome Jews from all over to transplant their individual characters and skills, not abandon them. Then, they would evolve together to be transformed. A mosaic requires stones and cement. The resulting "Mosaic mosaic," a Jewish patchwork, would be fused together by the tradition of Moses while dazzling everyone with its worldly diversity.

Israel's first prime minister, David Ben-Gurion, envisioned an all-new Israeli melting pot, not a Diaspora-tinged mosaic. Ben-Gurion considered that sacred Zionist task, what was formally called the "ingathering of the exiles," part of "a wholesale revolution in a Jew's image and his way of life."

Hoping to make two thousand years of weakness vanish, Ben-Gurion wrote, "With their arrival in their homeland, this Jewish dust (*avak adam*), living among strangers, dependent on vagrancy and serfdom, coalesces into an independent, national brigade, attached to and rooted in its great history." Israelis were saving newcomers, not do-meaning them. Redemption would be achieved when each immigrant exorcised the broken, exiled Jew from within and became a proud, assertive Israeli: the New Jew.

Ben-Gurion's homogenizing vision long dominated Israeli society, guiding the government agencies responsible for absorption. Then, in the 1990s, the Russian immigrants resisted. They didn't consider themselves "dust." They were fleeing the Soviet system, not Russian culture. Many were proud of their Russian identity. Refusing to see their past as wholly negative, they demanded another approach.

This conflict played out for me in 1990, when some famous Moscow actors and directors contacted me. They were considering aliyah. They wondered if Israel would consider establishing a Russian-language theater. I thought, "Wow, here's Israel's chance to show potential immigrants that it's not a cultural backwater." This old-new land could absorb customs Russian Jews cherished in the old country, especially theater. I rushed to the Ministry of Education and Culture with the good news.

But few Israelis shared my enthusiasm. "What you want is against Zionism," I was told. "We won't promote Russian-language theater. We never approved of theater in German, Romanian, or Bulgarian, not even Yiddish." They added, "Don't you as a Zionist recognize the miracle of bringing a dead language back to life? We must strengthen the connection between Hebrew and the Jewish people. All immigrants should learn our language. Your approach will prevent newcomers from becoming part of Israel."

Perhaps such rigidity made sense during the first years of state building. The reviver of the Hebrew language, Eliezer Ben-Yehuda, only spoke to his wife and children in Hebrew, despite missing many words necessary for everyday life. Ben-Yehuda's first son didn't speak until he was four. A century later, we didn't need to be so unyielding.

I went to the other Zionist capital, New York. Our friends from the New York Federation, America's most generous Jewish philanthropy, gave the Forum the first $24,000 to produce a few Russian-language performances. Our Soviet Jewry Zionist Forum found more money for the start-up, which we called the Gesher Theatre. *Gesher* means bridge. Over the years, performing in two languages, the theater has won many prizes. It's hard to believe that hard-core Zionists first considered this successful Zionist project antithetical to their cause.

Immigrant organizations often aligned with political parties. We founded the Zionist Forum to give immigrants an independent voice. We would be partners and fellow citizens. We had lots of experience fighting for ourselves—including confronting the Zionist Establishment— and had friendships in the Diaspora to finance our independence.

REUNITING WITH AMERICAN JEWRY

With everyone now recognizing that we were on the eve of a massive aliyah, the Zionist Forum spoke out publicly and sharply, criticizing the Jewish Agency and the government for not being prepared. Once, after I made some peppery comments in the *Jerusalem Post*, the head of the Jewish Agency, Simcha Dinitz, invited me for a chat. Dinitz and his wife, Tamar, had welcomed Avital warmly when he was Israel's ambassador in Washington. "Natan," he said sincerely, "you and your friends from the Zionist Forum are heroes. We love you. We respect you guys. You fought the Soviet Union."

I knew what was coming next.

"But," he said, "you don't understand how democracy works, or what works in Israel. Watch the other immigrant organizations. If you want to criticize, go ahead," he waved me on. "It's a free country. You'll be popular. Journalists will interview you happily. But you won't help even one new immigrant, because you won't get a shekel from us. Instead," he proposed, "stop criticizing. Work with us, and you'll have money, influence, whatever you need."

As a Labor Party veteran, Dinitz understood how Labor's version of Israeli democracy, revolving around strict party discipline, operated. The Association of Soviet Immigrants, organized by Labor in the 1970s, remained fully dependent on the party.

The same article that had annoyed Dinitz prompted a phone call from New York. It was a man whom I had never met named Joseph Gruss. "You write that the support the government gives to new immigrants for buying apartments is not enough," the retired Wall Street financier said. "You proposed a special fund to help them. How much additional money do you think will be needed to settle those who come in the next year?"

We were at the beginning of an aliyah whose size even we insiders hadn't yet grasped. My understanding of business and real estate was minimal then. I threw out what sounded like a big number: $20 million. Actually, it was a drop in the bucket.

"OK," Gruss said, "I will give you $1 million. Find another nineteen donors to match me."

He called two weeks later, asking, "Did you find the next nineteen?" I had started running the numbers, looking around, but had not found any additional donors. I started mumbling about needing more time.

Gruss cut me off. "I am old," he said. He was eighty-six. "I don't have time to wait. I will give you the $20 million." Thanks to the creative approach of David Blumberg, the CEO of Israel's largest mortgage bank, Bank Tefahot, Gruss's gift grew to $80 million worth of second-mortgage credit, which helped 7,500 families purchase apartments, often with me or other members of our presidium signing as guarantors. Many Israelis who knew about guaranteeing mortgages warned us not to sign personally. Nevertheless, everyone paid up on time. Other banks, seeing the mortgage business booming, soon rushed to compete.

That became our approach. We came up with ideas, from Russian TV to a system offering legal advice to new ways to teach math and physics. Representatives of the Establishment would usually say, "No, you don't need it. We know better than you how to absorb immigrants." We would then raise some money from old friends in the Diaspora to start the project. We were nonpartisan, attracting support from across the political spectrum.

We wanted Russian-language summer camps for new immigrants. This idea also offended the melting-pot sensibility, so we were told, "We speak Hebrew, not Russian." I approached Charles Bronfman, the Canadian philanthropist whose wife, Andrea Bronfman, had been a leader in the struggle for Soviet Jewry. That summer, we ran a camp. The next summer, the Israeli government took it over.

We thought of seeding entrepreneurs with small-business loans. This time, the bureaucrats lacked the funds and the faith in the project. I approached Ludwig Jesselson and George Klein, two New York businessmen who had embraced Avital like a daughter. Again, we set a precedent.

The Zionist Forum became a trade union, a civil rights organization, and a laboratory for different social initiatives, all wrapped in one. And through the growing partnership between immigrants and the Israeli government, the Forum reframed the dialogue between the Diaspora and Israel.

On my first trip to America, I met Mort Zuckerman, the scrappy Montreal-born real estate mogul who used his money to buy *U.S. News & World Report*. When he interviewed me, we started comparing experiences: his as a prisoner in New York's high society, and mine as a free man in the Gulag. We became close friends.

Mort's company, Boston Properties, developed and managed more than thirty million square feet of buildings, and he had many homes. Eventually, I said to him, "With all the houses you have and build, we found a good one for you in Jerusalem. Isn't it time for you to have a house in Israel too?" He agreed. That is how we got our headquarters.

Mort came to Jerusalem with an entourage of celebrities to dedicate Zuckerman House. As we nailed the mezuzah on the doorpost, this crusty billionaire choked up. Remembering how his grandparents had come to Montreal from the Ukraine, Mort said, "This is the first time I feel that, finally, I did something for them."

"This made the trip," the TV broadcaster Barbara Walters exclaimed. "I never imagined I'd see Mort so sentimental."

These kinds of friends made our work possible and preserved our independence.

PARTNERING WITH THE ESTABLISHMENT— WHILE CRITICIZING IT

Soon, even the resistance in the Jewish Agency melted. Mendel Kaplan, a leader of the South African Jewish community who became the first non-American chairman of the board of the Jewish Agency, was impressively open-minded. "You can criticize the process all you want," he told me. "It's healthy for us. But we have to raise tons of money to absorb your people, and we need you. As long as you also help us raise money for absorption, we will finance your Zionist Forum."

This informal agreement kept me traveling to America, fundraising for the United Jewish Appeal's billion-dollar Operation Exodus campaign. In return, we proved Simcha Dinitz wrong. Our independent Zionist Forum gained a substantial $2 million budget, half from the Jewish Agency, half from private donors.

Israelis had never seen such an influential organization for immigrants. Our budget was larger than all the dozens of new immigrant organizations combined. Continuing our tradition as Soviet Jewish activists, we partnered with the Establishment while criticizing it. Sometimes, it got touchy. Often, after our loud protests, some ministers grumbled, "Why are we giving them public money? So they can embarrass us with their protests?" But we were careful. Jewish Agency dollars went exclusively to absorbing immigrants. Donor dollars bankrolled the protests.

When gossips started speculating that the Forum might become a political party, the knives sharpened. The head of the Knesset's aliyah and absorption committee talked about "slaughtering the sacred cows around us, starting with Sharansky." Soon, the leading Hebrew daily *Maariv* recycled the complaints the Liaison Office had about Avital and me never following the Zionist line.

It was not the first critical article about me in my new home, but it was the first one attacking Avital for her stubborn independence during the struggle. I was furious. I stopped speaking to *Maariv*'s editor, Dan Margalit. Years later, he cornered me and asked what was wrong. I mentioned the article. He was surprised, saying he and his readers knew not to take that grumbling seriously. By then, I had entered politics, and had learned the hard way to be less sensitive to press attacks.

The Zionist Forum's activities kept me busy. Recalling my Moscow years, when my friends and I were so eager to become Israelis, I now often wondered: What are we fighting for? In 1967, when I discovered my identity, it seemed simpler. Feeling like I had no identity because it had been stripped by Communism, I just wanted to embrace a new one. I wanted to belong immediately, to join a different history, a different people, a different country.

My friends and I did not know about Herzl's mosaic or Ben-Gurion's melting pot, but we were instinctively Ben-Gurionites. Fleeing from slavery, we hoped to fit into a new, free, Israeli life. After arriving in Israel with the other Russians, I realized that identity is not a one-dimensional either-or. It's not a battery you can replace. It's more like fuel: when you add more into your tank, the new mixes with what was there before. Herzl's vision captured this contradiction. I now understood how I could feel so tied to Israel, yet still feel most comfortable speaking Russian.

In the Zionist Forum, we kept weighing how to offer the newcomers an identity while accepting their Russian accents. Seeking a balance, we broke the melting pot's paternalistic paradigm. That's why we resurrected Herzl's "Mosaic mosaic."

FOUNDING YISRAEL B'ALIYAH:
DEFENDING AN ALIYAH OF "MAFIA AND PROSTITUTES"

Even with the melting pot shattered, even with all the Diaspora's gener-osity, our impact was limited. A historic migration on this scale required billions of dollars, not millions. Ministries would have to change their priorities, and the Knesset would have to pass new laws.

Only a party representing the immigrants' interests could deliver so much. Still, I resisted the idea of a Russian immigrant party for years. I feared this would build a Russian ghetto, just like Shas was further ghet-toizing the Mizrahim. It seemed to violate the Zionist ideal that had long motivated me, of one people returning and building one state together. Wasn't it better to defend the immigrants' interests by making our case nationally and cultivating influence within each major party?

I was also personally reluctant. I fell naturally into championing the Soviet immigrants. It maintained my dissident spirit, even though I was now a patriot, supporting my democratic country rather than trying to escape my oppressive birthplace. But as I became controversial, as Labor and Likud insiders stopped bickering just long enough to grumble about me, I felt uneasy.

As soon as I became involved in politics, friends warned, "You're going to lose your standing with Israelis. Everything's so factionalized." I had tried not to let the adulation go to my head. I knew I couldn't be everybody's hero. Still, I wanted to preserve that unique feeling I had in the Gulag of being connected to all my people. I knew that, by becoming a politician, this imaginary connection risked being broken.

Ultimately, the pressing social challenges the immigrants faced changed my opinion about the need for a separate political party—and about my future. It was impossible for so many educated, ambitious, en-ergetic people to move to the Jewish state, in such a dizzyingly short time, without causing tension. Some Israelis who now faced unexpected job pressure wondered, "How did all these people get all these degrees from all these places we never heard of in Siberia?" Some Israeli professional associations spread rumors about doctors and engineers buying degrees on the Russian black market, like everything else in the Soviet Union.

As the immigrants blamed the government for its failures, some government ministers blamed the immigrants. Ora Namir, the minis-ter of labor and social welfare in the Labor government, called Russian immigrants a social burden. She said Israel should be more "selective" in accepting future immigrants. She claimed that younger, productive Russian Jews sent their elderly relatives to Israel, "to relieve themselves of their care, as they go to the United States." The Iraqi-born minister of police dismissed the aliyah as a "Mafia immigration." Newspaper headlines screamed about Russian prostitutes and white slavery scandals.

In the years after the Communist economies collapsed, hundreds of thousands of Eastern European women were swept into sex trafficking. First, they moved into Western Europe, but it soon hit Israel. Because this spike in prostitution coincided with the big Russian wave of immigration, some people linked the two. It became too easy to caricature the Russian aliyah as one of whores and mafiosi.

The shift in the image of Soviet Jews was dizzying. One friend was hired for a computing job. On her first day in the office, her boss, pleased with himself for hiring a Russian immigrant, asked, "Why are there so many prostitutes among you?"

Smiling mischievously, she answered, "There are many of us Russians all around. If you go to the theater, you'll see us. If you go to the philharmonic, you'll see us. If you go to the chess club, you'll see us. Where one goes determines what one sees."

With every defensive interview, with every press conference, with every lovely new initiative encouraging dialogue between Russian newcomers and veteran Israelis, we felt more and more helpless. It's hard to break popular stereotypes. Eventually, after years of squirming and defending, we decided there had been enough explaining, enough apologizing. It was time to change tactics. We wanted to place representatives of new immigrants in all those places where the decisions about the future of our community and our country were being made. The best way to fight prejudice was to sit on municipal councils and in parliament.

There, we would argue together, decide together. We would share responsibility on housing, education, and jobs. As a common language emerged, stereotypes would fade and friendships would form. By arguing together, we'd start swimming together.

The Russian rookies had to join the internal Israeli dialogue. To do this, we needed a political party. So we—a band of former dissidents who excelled at street demonstrations, public spectacles, and sweeping statements—would have to become politicians. We would even have to learn the art of compromise.

THE PARTY WHOSE AIM IS TO DISAPPEAR

In early press interviews, I said a successful immigrant party should not be a lobby in perpetuity. Once the process of integration started working as it should, our party, uniting new immigrants from different ideological camps, would no longer be needed. If we succeeded, our party and its agenda would become irrelevant. To make my point, I kept saying, even in front of reporters, that our party hoped to commit suicide as quickly as possible.

My colleagues were not amused. "What kind of a leader are you?" they asked. "How can you kill us off before we've been fully born?" I learned that party founders have to believe their new party will last forever and constantly contribute to the public good. I was also learning that politics and my ironic sense of humor didn't match.

Launching a new party is expensive. The existing parties received government funds, a certain amount for each seat won in the previous election. We had no money, and our base was penniless immigrants. Once again, old friends helped. The $1 million we needed to establish ourselves as an electoral force came from a Bank Hapoalim loan, guaranteed by Mort Zuckerman and the Jewish philanthropist Ambassador Ronald Lauder.

Unlike other newly created parties, we were committed to democratic procedures from the start. Our list of candidates for every Knesset election was determined by a secret ballot, involving hundreds of our activists.

Before going public, I felt I should inform one politician privately. Benjamin Netanyahu had been instrumental in helping Avital navigate New York and Washington. As the leader of the opposition Likud Party for the upcoming 1996 election, he was probably counting on my support. I expected him to be disappointed that I would be running my own party, which would remain neutral in the prime ministerial contest to keep focused on our agenda.

When I informed him of our plans, Bibi was extremely gracious. "If that's what you decide, I wish you much success, and I hope we will work together in the government," he said. "But I want to offer you one piece of advice. Launching a party is difficult and expensive. There are many financial and legal questions. And the mix of politics and money is always explosive. Never touch money, at all. Don't touch financial questions, don't sign papers. Hire professionals to handle it all, to do all the

In our family we grew up missing many things, but certainly not love. Here I am in 1951 with my parents, Ida and Boris, and my older brother Leonid.

There was nothing Jewish in my childhood except for anti-Semitism and this one-and-a-half-foot-tall statue of David and Goliath, which was too big for our small apartment.

Chess became my first passport into the world of free thought, my first great escape. This photo was taken in 1961 when I was 13.

Five years later, I graduated high school, having worked doubly hard to pursue my second escape, success in the academic worlds of math and science.

Ultimately, I only discovered my real freedom and identity when I joined the world of Jewish activists. Here I am in 1974.

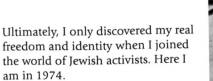

In 1975, we Jewish Refuseniks celebrated the Jewish holiday of Sukkot in a birch forest just outside Moscow with Israeli athletes who had come to Russia for an international competition. Shortly after this photograph was taken, as we were singing and dancing, police summoned by the KGB tried breaking up the festivities. *Courtesy of Sasha Luntz*

Michael Sherbourne, a modest Russian-language teacher in London, helped share our stories with the world, making thousands of phone calls to us, night after night, for years.

Courtesy of Michael Sherbourne

Here, in Moscow, in May, 1974, one of many "American tourists" over the years, Louis Rosenblum, founding president of the Union of Councils for Soviet Jews, poses with some of us young Turks, dismissed by the older Refuseniks, as hong weibing, zealous "Red Guards."

At one of many press conferences I organized for Refuseniks and for democratic dissidents, a group of Kulturniks and scientists launched an international symposium on Jewish Culture in the Soviet Union. But before the conference began, the authorities arrested most of the organizers—while barring any foreign visitors invited from arriving.

Below, my mentor, the leading Soviet scientist Andrei Sakharov, his wife Yelena Bonner, and I edit yet another human rights appeal to the West, which two "housewives" from Philadelphia, Enid Wurtman and Connie Smuckler, will smuggle out for us.

Courtesy of Connie Smuckler and Enid Wurtman

My father took this photograph of Avital (then Natalia), in June, 1974, days before we married and she left for Israel.

Nearly three years later, shortly before I was arrested, some Jewish tourists passed me this book of Psalms from Avital. I spent a lot of time fighting to keep both of these in my possession during my nine years in the Gulag.

All told, I spent about a year in this "strict regimen colony" labor camp Perm 35, pictured here in a flattering light, without guards, police dogs, or the mounds of snow you'll find there eight months of the year.

Pierre Perrin

I spent about half of my 405 days in punishment cells in this actual cell, inside Perm 35's prison camp.

Pierre Perrin

Shortly after Avital met Ronald Reagan for the first time on May 28, 1981, he wrote in his daily diary: "D - - n those inhuman monsters," meaning the Soviet Communists. "I promised I'd do everything I could to obtain his release & I will."

Courtesy Ronald Reagan Library

At one of many vigils of "housewives and students" for Soviet Jewry that various Jewish groups organized, Avital, dressed in prison garb, sits next to Rabbi Avi Weiss, the chairman of Students Struggle for Soviet Jewry, who is standing to her right.

Getty Images

The happy ending: reunited with Avital to start our honeymoon – twelve years late.

Henrik Nati Israel Government Press Office (hereafter referred to as GPO)

But first, a warm greeting in Jerusalem, at the Kotel, the Western Wall.

Saar Yaacov GPO

finances and the accounting. If you don't stay completely clean, they will blacken your name before you know it. You will be a target for police, reporters, and gossips."

It was generous and timely advice. Today, so many scandals later, I understand that many people will hear it as ironic. But the Bibi I know has always cared about power, not money. I have seen politicians calculate how much more money they could be making as lawyers and use that gap to justify their financial finagling. That's not Bibi.

When I first met him, Bibi was Israel's thirty-eight-year-old ambassador to the United Nations, and he told me he would be prime minister one day. Less than ten years later, he became Israel's youngest prime minister ever. Since then, I have watched him study power, build power, obsess about power, and sometimes sacrifice friendships for power. But I never saw him try to turn his power into a source of income. I also remember how careful he was about insulating financial matters from party affairs.

As for our party, quite predictably, after we won our first election, false rumors claimed that Russian Mafia money was funding us. Police investigations followed. Because our party of amateurs relied on professionals to manage our finances from A to Z, we were protected from many sloppy mistakes that could have been used against us unfairly. "You got out of this unblemished," the police interrogator pronounced with surprise and respect.

From the beginning, we had a good name for the party: Yisrael B'Aliyah, a play on words that emphasized Israel with immigration and Israel ascending. We also had two perfect slogans. Trying to smash the melting-pot paternalism, we proclaimed, "There is no integration without representation!" And, thanks to one of our young American volunteers, Ron Dermer, a second slogan emerged: "We are a different political party, we go to prison . . . first."

After the May 1996 elections, seven representatives of our new party joined the Knesset, including two of us in the cabinet. Within two years of our party's founding, a series of municipal elections brought dozens of new immigrants into government, some of whom barely spoke Hebrew. We had deputy mayors in cities from Beersheba to Haifa.

The great Russian migration became part of the solution, not just part of the problem. We were finally swimming together with our fellow Israelis. The idea of members of a lost generation passively watching what was happening to them was buried, at least for this aliyah.

8

IMPRISONED BY POLITICS

More Power, Less Freedom

Early in the morning of June 18, 1996, I entered a hulking, decaying building in the heart of Jerusalem. It had been built in 1928 as the grand mufti's Palace Hotel. Now, it housed the offices of Israel's Ministry of Industry and Trade. I arrived by bus as a private citizen. I returned home that evening in a chauffeur-driven Volvo, as minister of industry and trade, already overprogrammed with a long list of leading industrialists, bankers, mayors, and ambassadors from Israel's top trading partners asking to meet me.

For three weeks, since the elections on May 29, Israel had been stuck in yet another unprecedented political crisis. Benjamin Netanyahu of Likud had beaten Prime Minister Shimon Peres of Labor by 29,457 votes of the over three million cast. That election began a three-time, quickly ended experiment of Israelis directly electing the prime minister, then voting for a party to represent them in parliament, the Knesset.

Everyone had assumed Peres would win. They remembered how the nation had united in mourning Prime Minister Yitzhak Rabin's assassination in November 1995, and Peres was Rabin's successor. The polls kept showing Peres ahead—and polls are never wrong, of course. The experts were so fooled that the American embassy didn't prepare briefing materials about Netanyahu, who kept telling me that his nearly hourly polling showed him inching up day by day.

Election Day was thrilling. I traveled the country by car and helicopter—from the center to the north, from north to south, and from the south back to the center—to reach as many polling places as possible. Everywhere, immigrants voted in droves and greeted me enthusiastically. We started the morning assuming that if we won three or four Knesset seats (of 120) we would have pulled off a miracle. When reporters announced the first results on TV at 10 p.m., we had seven seats, nearly 6 percent of the vote. We celebrated until one o'clock in the morning.

Throughout the night, Shimon Peres had the lead, as did his Labor Party. I went to sleep assuming Labor would court our party to join its coalition. The finance minister and Labor Party fixer Avraham Shochat had invited us to meet him the next morning at seven o'clock to start the preliminary bargaining about joining his coalition.

We met. But the tone was less celebratory than Shochat expected. By morning, Bibi had won. Shochat kindly offered some useful bargaining tips.

Netanyahu's Likud Party and its allies ended up with thirty-two Knesset seats, two fewer than their Labor rivals. Netanyahu formed a governing coalition in the 120-seat Knesset, with three religious parties, the National Religious Party (NRP), Shas, and United Torah Judaism; a new, centrist, ultimately one-term party, the Third Way; and our party, Yisrael B'Aliyah. The other parties together added up to fifty-nine seats. Our seven gave Netanyahu and Likud the majority of sixty-six.

The Israeli political Establishment was stunned—and furious. Many reporters were particularly annoyed because their predictions were so wrong. They couldn't accept Netanyahu as a legitimate winner. Given the harsh right-wing demagoguery before Rabin's assassination, many Bibi critics treated him as if he had killed the prime minister then stolen the election, in an evil attempt to deprive Israel of peace. When I joined Bibi's government, that anger often made it difficult to govern—and for rivals and reporters to maintain civil relationships with the new ministers.

It was as if we were back in the world of opposing totalitarian regimes, where good genuinely fights evil. Having suffered under a dictatorship, I still find it hard to see how easily citizens living in a democracy forget that most of their political rivals have legitimate demands, expectations, and reservations.

After intensive negotiations, our party received two ministries in the eighteen-person cabinet and some key Knesset posts. As newcomers, we couldn't believe our luck. In retrospect, we could have demanded more.

Before the campaign, when friends asked me which ministry I wanted, I gave what they thought was a cagey answer. "I am not sure I want to be a minister. I would like to be the prime minister's chief adviser on aliyah, absorption, and world Jewry," I said. Conscious of my thin résumé as an administrator or policy expert, I believed professionals should run complicated ministries like defense, treasury, and trade.

Eventually, insiders explained to me the basic laws of Israeli political gravity. "Your power comes from two main sources," they told me. "Having a seat at the cabinet table with a vote. And having a ministry with actual budgets and real appointments. Otherwise you're irrelevant."

So advised, I became the minister of industry and trade, with membership in the security cabinet, the inner cabinet committee that made Israel's most pressing life-and-death decisions. I would also head the Interministerial Committee on Aliyah and Absorption. Foreshadowing future battles, and approaching my initial vision, Netanyahu agreed to rename it the Interministerial Committee on Aliyah, Absorption, and Diaspora Affairs. Such committees functioned independently. Their decisions automatically became government policy unless other ministers objected within a short window of opportunity. Yuli Edelstein, my fellow Prisoner of Zion and the former vice president of the Zionist Forum, became minister of absorption.

DAY ONE

The Volvo was nice, but the job was daunting. I walked into the depressing but intimidating offices with a small team of assistants who had worked with me in the Zionist Forum or during the campaign. All had been born in Russia, except for one Israeli-born Sabra. Avi Maoz was a young, Yeshiva-trained, sandal-wearing Israeli with long, swaying tzitzit, ritual garment fringes. He had traveled around the world with Avital for the last two years of her campaign. Although many in the Establishment usually disdained such a type, he would become a highly respected director general in various ministries during the next decade. Eli Kazhdan, born in Moscow, made aliyah from Boston at twenty-one. He had had only one job during his time in Israel, working for me in the Zionist Forum. He would become my chief of staff. Roman Polonsky, a musician and theater director in the Soviet Union and a Hebrew teacher in Russia and later in Israel, had become a journalist for the Russian Israeli press. He was my campaign spokesperson and media relations expert. Luiza Walitsky had only been in Israel for a few years. Her first Israeli job was working for the campaign. She would coordinate our relations with other ministers and Knesset members. Sonja Shebalan, a veteran Refusenik, counseled new immigrants in the Zionist Forum. She would be our liaison with the Russian immigrants and the broader Israeli public. Cumulatively, the number of days all of us had worked in Israeli government, or any government, added up to zero.

I was briefed by the now ex–minister of industry and trade, Micha Harish. Years ago, as general secretary of the Labor Party, he had offered the party's help to the Zionist Forum as long as we sent the Russian immigrants to their health services, Kupat Holim Clalit, and other institutions. We said, "No, thank you." Now, he was showing me the diagram of the ministry, with the names of the key departments and central functions. Acronyms like BaSaSaCh and RaShPaT and new phrases like *chok idud hashkaot hahon*, jumped off the page at me.

I was overwhelmed by all these incomprehensible Hebrew terms: the insurance for Israeli businesses abroad (BaSaSaCh), the industrial development authority (RaShPaT), the laws for supporting business in Israel. Eventually, I broke. Each bit of jargon made me imagine one dangerous long-tailed monster after another, all chasing me. Once that started, I couldn't stop. BaSaSaCh sounds like Babai, the demon who starred in many of my mother's favorite ghost stories, which terrified us as kids.

Trying to concentrate, I glanced at Eli and Roman. Both looked as shell-shocked as I was. "I feel like that gypsy from the anecdote, who became king," I joked when the meeting finally ended. Roman laughed. Having grown up in a Russian-speaking household in America, Eli didn't get the old-country cultural reference.

We explained that it was a bigoted Soviet joke. When the gypsy is asked, "What will you do if you become a king?" He answers, "I will steal a horse and run away."

I looked around dramatically at our cavernous office in this once-majestic building and asked, "What will be our horse?"

At that moment, Avi Maoz entered and informed us that hundreds of employees were in the ministry's auditorium, waiting for direction from their new leader. My calendar was filling up. My call list was already too long for any one person to manage. Avi suggested, however, that before going downstairs I speak to a woman who had been begging to see me and was near tears.

"*Kvod hasar*," she began. This was the first time I had been called "the honorable minister." I squelched my instinct to say, "Just call me Natan," although I spent much of the next nine years saying that. She introduced herself as a custodian in the building. "I need this job," she said. "I am a single mother, and I must feed my children."

Confused, I looked at her silently. "Please don't fire me," she pleaded. "I already started learning Russian."

My God, I realized, she was scared to death of me because she expected some Russian purge. At first, I was indignant. "Who told her such nonsense?" I asked.

Watching her tremble, I recalled a fellow prisoner telling me, "To be a good KGB interrogator, you have to enjoy watching people be scared of you." That's how I knew I couldn't be a good interrogator. Now, in my first minutes as a minister, I felt terrible. Without saying a word, I had terrified this poor woman.

When I greeted the department heads, I tried defusing the tension by emphasizing my own linguistic shortcomings. Admitting I had a lot to learn about the ministry, I added with a smile, "I will work on improving my Hebrew too. I hope it will be good enough, so you won't have to learn Russian." Their laughter was forced. My joke had backfired. They were so nervous, the new boss's wisecrack sounded threatening.

These mutual fears didn't last. My new colleagues soon saw that we planned no big shake-ups and that we hired based on merit, not ethnicity or connections. And though my personal aides lacked professional experience, they made up for it with intelligence, curiosity, and goodwill.

Through my years in the government, many colleagues appreciated the friendly, even lighthearted atmosphere in our central office suite. These good feelings usually radiated throughout the ministry, unlike the tension that usually resounds through the corridors of power.

IT'S HARD GETTING USED TO BEING A POLITICIAN

Overcoming the fears of imaginary purges was easy. Getting along with other politicians was also easier than I expected. But getting used to being a politician was really hard.

In the beginning, I found myself oddly nostalgic for the simplicity and clarity of prison life. In prison, you remind yourself every day why you are there, and convince yourself that you've made the right decision. You have a lot of time to do that. In the end, you have few choices to make. All of them connect logically to your central aim: to stay free and keep to your strategic goals—to resist, to learn, to unmask. You control your life and your decisions. That which you cannot control, including your physical survival, you put aside. With everything so clear, every move you make becomes meaningful and understandable.

Governing sometimes makes you feel surprisingly helpless: the more power you have, the less control you have over your time and even over your decisions. Serving in the government and the Knesset, in the heart of the political struggle, you are a prisoner to everyone else's agendas, demands, and timetables. Long before the Internet, Instagram, and Twitter, a politician's life was dictated by demands, hour by hour, sometimes minute by minute.

As a minister, as head of a party, as a Knesset member, as a committee member, I had to respond to accusations, make my own declarations, decide where I stood on hundreds of issues simultaneously, and figure out what I was going to say and whom I was going to see and not see.

To succeed, I had to be responsive to others' needs and concerns. My old life had few tactical decisions, all easily in line with the overall goal. Now, my whole life had become tactical: how to respond to this, how to solve that. I was always reacting, often automatically, with minimal time to think about strategy—or why I was doing whatever I was doing.

I joined the governing coalition. That made it easier to triage. I chose which questions to delve into in-depth, which to assess more superficially, and which I'd rely on other colleagues to decide. But I knew I would share responsibility for each decision. It meant I needed a crackerjack team of experts, advisers, and assistants. But even with them, I could rarely take a breath—and even more rarely think big. I often felt like I was in the middle of the flood, being swept away, having to double-check that I was at least being swept in the right direction.

I was fortunate. I could avoid many party-related headaches. Yuli Edelstein, who was so central in implementing our immigrant-oriented agenda as minister of absorption, also ran the party's operations, before and during elections. I often teased him that he could not be number one in our party, as he had only spent three years in prison. He continued his life in politics, becoming Speaker of the Knesset and a powerful force demanding civility in the parliament while protecting its independence.

In adjusting to this frenetic activity, with everyone treating you as if you are so powerful, you also sometimes feel your freedom is under attack—your freedom to speak your mind, to move at your whim, and to act as you wish.

With power, you can do a world of good, but the world around you also assumes it can decide what's good for you. You have to control your language, your gestures, your reactions, and especially your jokes.

During the Soviet Jewry struggle, we were very good at emphasizing the big picture that united the movement. We laughed off the differences among friends while dismissing the enemy with irony and sarcasm. In politics, that once-useful sense of humor kept getting me in trouble.

One day, I took my two daughters to Tel Aviv to see the visiting Moscow circus. It was fun sharing a cherished piece of my childhood with them, thanks to the improvement in Russian-Israeli relations. Immediately after our outing, a reporter interviewed me. I joked that it didn't feel like much of a day off, because my new life in the government struck me as one big circus: You must learn a high-wire act, constantly walking a tightrope. You must be a contortionist, twisting yourself into all kinds of compromising positions. You must tame some fierce lions, and find yourself occasionally putting your head in their mouths. And everyone always looks to the ringmaster for direction.

I thought my riff was funny, until Saturday night after the Sabbath, when Bibi called me, furious. "How dare you say my government is a circus," he said, genuinely hurt.

"What are you talking about?" I asked, unaware that the reporter had turned my quip into a story claiming that even Netanyahu's closest allies saw his coalition as a circus. My insisting that "it's only a joke" didn't placate the prime minister. "Be careful with your jokes," he fumed. "Nobody gets them here."

Much more damaging was another throwaway line in 1997. The government was managing an ugly scandal, the Bar-On Hebron affair.

Reporters and rivals were accusing Netanyahu of having appointed an unqualified lackey, Roni Bar-On, as attorney general for political purposes. They claimed the appointment was part of an elaborate deal securing the Shas Party's approval to withdraw from the ancient holy city of Hebron, in exchange for a weak attorney general who would go easy in prosecuting Shas's corrupt leader Aryeh Deri. Essentially, they were accusing Israel's prime minister of auctioning off Israel's security to one of his coalition partners to keep a suspected criminal out of jail.

This conspiracy theory—pushed on television and linking Bibi, Deri, Hebron, and Bar-On—struck me as groundless. Nevertheless, the outcry was so intense that Bar-On resigned within forty-eight hours of his appointment.

Later, the new attorney general, Elyakim Rubinstein, found no evidence of any deal. Rubenstein's investigators used what at the time struck me as a novel approach. They reviewed all the principals' cell phone calls. I had no idea our private mobile phone records could be tracked so easily.

Nevertheless, I was angry with Bibi and his justice minister. We had trusted our leading coalition partners regarding this appointment, exactly as they had trusted us with top appointments in our ministries, but they let us down. They rushed through the appointment without informing us of the doubts surrounding Bar-On's credentials. Feeling burned, I, along with the minister of finance, Dan Meridor, gave an ultimatum, demanding the formation of a special committee of professionals that would assess every top appointment and report its recommendation to the cabinet. Our demand was accepted. That procedure is still followed today.

"Minister Sharansky, what do you think of the charges?" reporters asked me at the height of the scandal. To illustrate how ridiculous even a hint of such corruption was, I said, "If there is even 10 percent of truth in Israel TV's story, this government has no place in continuing to govern." Oops.

Another morning, another phone call from Bibi. "Do you realize what you said?" he asked. "If you plan on bringing down the government, I have the right to know about it. But if not," he added knowingly, "you have no idea what a mess you're bringing upon yourself. And you're going to have to clean that up by yourself."

He was right. Reporters didn't hear me saying the charges were absurd, they heard me saying I'd resign. My "if, then" construction was a gift to the Bibi haters. They interpreted my line as an ironclad promise. Certain that Bar-On, Bibi, and Deri were 100 percent guilty, the government's opponents considered my 10 percent promise a low bar. My words fed their fantasy that Yitzhak Rabin's death was going to be avenged, corruption would be revealed, and the government would collapse in disgrace.

In their minds, I was the perfect weapon. The fallen hero, now redeeming himself, had viewed things from the inside and realized how evil Bibi was. They didn't hear my "if," which I had thought was my oh-so-clever way of showing doubt.

When I didn't resign, some reporters decided I had betrayed them. One journalist had given me my first job in Israel as a contributing editor to the *Jerusalem Report*. We became close over the years, enjoying hundreds of conversations about many subjects. Nevertheless, he was so blinded by Bibi hatred that he blasted me in an article titled "Mr. Ten Percent," without bothering to question me about what I said or what I was thinking.

The lack of logic, the contempt for evidence, the refusal to compromise, the harsh judgments—in short, the black-and-white approach to politics—was stunning.

Beyond missing my ability to speak and joke freely, I missed my freedom of movement and spontaneity. At the time, ministers didn't always have permanent bodyguards. That started after three Palestinian terrorists murdered Tourism Minister Rehavam Ze'evi at his Jerusalem hotel in 2001. But, beginning in 1996, my family knew when tensions were high, even before reading about it in the newspaper, because the bodyguards would arrive.

I was used to living with guards. Back in Moscow, I had figured out how to get my KGB tails to work with me, forcing them to pay their share of the taxis they jumped into and using them as a private security detail when necessary.

"At least this time," I thought, "they're working for me." I was mistaken. I quickly learned that, despite my fancy title, I wasn't in charge of my bodyguards, the Security Service was.

Avital and I tried welcoming these young men into our family, which also pleased our daughters, Rachel and Hanna. But it wasn't up to us. During one particularly stormy Friday night, Avital insisted that the hulking security agent, who was standing outside our door in the rain and looking particularly pale, join us inside. He radioed for permission to enter the house and was ordered to stay outside, even as it started to hail.

That night, as we were sleeping, we heard a big thud outside. We scrambled downstairs, opened the door, and saw that the Hulk had fainted. Avital and I struggled to drag him into the house. There we were, outside, in our pajamas, in a hail storm—a perfect target for terrorists. I had a special phone for Sabbath-observing ministers. I called in the emergency. "What are you trying to do, kill him?" Avital shouted when the supervisor arrived. "How will that keep us safe?"

The Security Service soon built a little guardhouse outside our home. This attempt to make our guards more comfortable cost us our small ping-pong arena. These days, as I wander around Israel, I often encounter our security alumni, now much older and much less fit men. They light up, speak nostalgically, and send regards to my family.

When you enter a room surrounded by bodyguards, people, especially reporters, enjoy drawing various conclusions about you. Some journalists accuse you of using the guards to prop yourself up; others say you're wasting state funds. That's the cost of being in the public eye. Much as I wanted to pull some of my Moscow tricks to restore my freedom of movement, I understood that bodyguards were as unavoidable as reporters in a modern democracy.

WHO'S THE BOSS? REPORTERS BLACKMAIL MINISTERS

During my time as a spokesperson for the Refusenik and human rights movements in the Soviet Union, the Russian word *Korrespondent* inspired me. "Natan will connect us to the Kors," my comrades often said. The Kors—reporters—were a lifeline for us. They lived in three special apartment buildings guarded by the KGB, for the KGB's sake of course. By visiting the compound you were defying the state. The KGB noted it, taking your information laboriously after the reporter signed you in. It felt like crossing the border. But the payoff, once you entered a journalist's home, was your first taste of life in a sanctuary of liberty.

Some journalists became close friends. A select few helped me smuggle in "anti-Soviet" materials by diplomatic post—books on Jewish history, novels like *Exodus*, samizdat publications of Alexander Solzhenitsyn's banned writings, and, sometimes, personal letters.

In return for helping feed our vast below-the-radar distribution net-work—among other favors—I thanked helpful reporters with inside tips, quotes, and other journalistic goodies that helped them write their stories while telling our story too.

Despite always emphasizing in both movements' public statements that we activists had nothing to hide, we kept this dimension of our rela-tionship with the press secret. I had no regrets. We were circumventing a totalitarian regime's illegal restrictions on our free thought. I was grateful to those journalists, some of whom remain dear friends.

Once in Israel, I had to learn to tolerate harsh articles about me as the cost of freedom. Nevertheless, I was friendly with most reporters, some of whom became my colleagues when I worked for the *Jerusalem Report* from 1990 to 1995.

Once elected to government, I was reminded of my previous double life in an unexpected way. All cabinet deliberations were supposed to be confidential. I took my vow of secrecy seriously. After my first cabinet meeting, one of my favorite TV reporters, Dan Semama, called, seeking my comments. Tunisian born, Dan spoke Hebrew slowly and clearly, al-lowing me to understand every word. Most Israeli reporters' idiomatic Hebrew came out in bursts that sounded like machine-gun fire, especially to my immigrant ear.

"*Nu*, Natan what was that conflict between Bibi and Dan Meridor about?" he asked.

The question surprised, even offended, me. "Dan, are you serious? Go ask the press secretary of the PMO," the Prime Minister's Office, "don't ask me. We just got this briefing emphasizing that when government meetings are off-the-record, they're off-the-record."

"C'mon, Natan. I'm not soliciting state secrets. People have the right to know. And I know about this exchange because others told me. I won't use your name. I just want your take," he explained.

"Natan, I want to tell you as a friend—we are friends, right?" he con-tinued. "You are a politician now. You want to succeed. You have to be heard. You will not exist as a politician if you don't talk to us, publicly and privately."

"You know, Dan," I said. "I'm willing to repeat what I said in the cab-inet meetings regarding topics that aren't secret. But what the others said, you will have to find from others." That was as far as I could go. Clearly, it was not what he wanted.

After a few weeks, it was obvious that Semama was right. My press people could read any article and explain why one person was mentioned here instead of there, why another was ignored, why one received good coverage and another didn't. They guessed pretty accurately as to who provided the information. I often witnessed leading politicians rushing to be the first to connect with journalists as soon as meetings ended, even after some of the most sensitive cabinet deliberations.

I saw that, when your people issue a press release about some achievement in your ministry, if you're lucky it's buried in the back of the business pages. Otherwise, unless you're hit by scandal or pay off reporters with the information they demand, you suffer a politician's worst fate: invisibility.

I value the free press as a guardian of democracy. But this behind-the-scenes back-scratching between journalists and politicians has become too entrenched in most Western democracies. It's insidious.

A FREE MAN ENSLAVED TO EVERYONE'S AGENDA

The moment you're elected to public office, you go from being a free man to communal property. Suddenly, it seems that everyone is looking for leverage and waving whatever they have on you in your face.

Soon after I joined Netanyahu's government, I received a joint letter from some friends in the New York Federation. They reminded me of our long history together: how they fought for me when I was in the Soviet Union and how they helped me launch the Zionist Forum. Worried that the new government was too right-wing, they insisted I repay their loyalty by pushing Bibi to "make peace in the Middle East."

The "you owe me because we helped you" demand was a leftover from my earlier life. The "you owe me because we voted for you" plea was more typical. Anyone who opposed anything I did seemed to enjoy mobilizing Russian-speaking workers against me. Each time I finalized a free trade agreement, the industrialists who felt threatened organized their immigrant employees to cosign attack ads in the Russian-language press. Their accusations often turned personal, essentially saying, "We didn't give you our votes so you could take away our jobs."

In the final rounds of a long-negotiated agreement with Turkey, the owners of Israel's leading glass manufacturer, Phoenicia, feared competition from cheap Turkish labor. After taking out the usual advertisements, they brought Russian-speaking employees from Phoenicia to protest outside my house.

I invited the demonstrators in for a cup of tea. In this friendlier atmosphere, I joked that everything seemed much easier in the Soviet Union. "There, everyone had jobs, with no worries about competition." Most smiled. One person, frowning, spit out a Russian proverb: the man with a full belly can never be friendly to the hungry. It meant: You're no longer one of us. You cannot understand us.

Phoenicia survived, as did Israel's free trade deal with Turkey, despite the two countries' tense geopolitical relationship. In twenty years, Israel's trade with Turkey increased tenfold, making Turkey Israel's fifth-largest trading partner for years. Today, it remains in the top twenty.

THE 1999 CAMPAIGN:
WINNING VOTES AT WHAT COST?

In my new life, press relations and public opinion were not my biggest problems. Even moving from the breathless "you're such an inspiration have a nice day" to the equally breathless "you're such a disappointment have a nice day" was not that big a blow. The worst part for me about being a politician was managing a problem built into multiparty democracies: how to reconcile your obligation to your party and your voters with your desire to feel connected to the entire citizenry and, in my case, the Jewish people.

I now realized that living in my imagined world of Jewish unity had been easy in prison. I didn't have the luxury to choose among factions. As an Israeli politician, I was constantly torn. Usually party interests came first, which meant prioritizing immigrants' rights.

This constant headache overshadowed the 1999 elections. We approached our second campaign ambivalently. Our party had succeeded, pushing immigrant issues to the top of Israel's agenda. We had many achievements we were proud of in housing, employment, education, and in promoting some new immigrants into important positions. At the same time, as I expected, the more this aliyah integrated into Israeli society, the more our voters felt ready to make ideological choices. Increasingly less willing to ignore the peace-process controversy and secular-versus-religious differences, many now wanted to vote based on more nationally oriented issues.

This time, we were insiders, bankrolled with public funding to run a costlier, more sophisticated campaign. We hired a young political consultant with a particularly good ear, Moti Morel. After extensive surveys to hear what fired up the Russian base, he targeted the Interior Ministry. In addition to being dominated by Shas, the ministry was easily caricatured as a suffocating, Soviet-style bureaucracy run by religious fanatics.

Most Russian immigrants were secular, deprived of any religious identity by our Soviet upbringing. By contrast, even non-Orthodox Mizrahim respected their rabbis. Shas supporters claimed we wanted to overwhelm Israel with non-Jewish Russians who would sell pork on the streets. In one campaign ad, Eli Suissa, a Shas leader, called Russian immigrants "counterfeiters, con men, and call girls."

Shas's stranglehold on the Interior Ministry since the 1980s became the flash point. It may have looked like religious tension, but our leaders ranged from kippah-wearing religious Jews to pork-eating secular Jews. None, however, could tolerate the Interior Ministry's rigid, slow-motion, often dismissive bureaucrats.

Moti grasped this. While brainstorming with some Russian party insiders, including our spokesperson David Shechter, Moti, who didn't speak a word of Russian, came up with the perfect slogan.

Israeli elections are public spectacles. Back when television dominated, in the final weeks of the campaign most of the country would stop every evening to watch a marathon of colorful, often sarcastic commercials. Each party's TV time was proportional to its number of members in parliament. We ran ads highlighting the heartbreaking story of, say, a Russian mother not welcomed into Israel, blocked by the Shas-dominated Interior Ministry from reuniting with her wounded soldier son, because she wasn't Jewish. Each ad ended with the lyrical jingle: "MVD pod Shas kontrol? Nyet, MVD pod nash kontrol." This slogan meant: "This foreboding, heavy-handed Interior Ministry under Shas control? No way, under OUR control."

The moment our first ad appeared on Israel's television ad-athon, our campaign took off. The slogan electrified the Russian street, and amused most Israelis. Within a few days, Israelis had learned some Russian. They kept echoing the slogan, which took on a life of its own. Our campaign started getting so much attention, I joked that I felt like a tall, handsome man with curly hair.

Unfortunately, the messaging pitted Russians directly against Mizrahim and ultra-Orthodox Jews. The commercials stereotyped them as threatening religious fanatics, making our reelection campaign look anti-religious. I could see how effective the ads were. I knew my job as party leader was to win as many seats as possible. But I felt sick. I felt like I was running against the Jewish people and undoing all the unity I believed in.

I started scrambling, looking for ways to lower the tensions, to re-cage the beasts.

"Natan," Moti and members of my team kept saying, "this is the time to gain votes. After the election, you'll have enough time to make peace with Shas, like every other Israeli politician."

As politicos, they were right. But for me, it was yet another moment when I realized I was a bad politician. Whenever someone on the street greeted me exuberantly, asking "Shas kontrol?" then shouting, "Nyet, nash kontrol," I cringed. The passersby were complimenting us. But I heard their echo as an accusation; it felt like I was betraying my life's mission.

After dreaming so long of Jewish unity, I couldn't tolerate feeding intra-communal hatred. As Election Day approached, I defied most of my advisers. I had our commercials reshot. The new ads called for "nash kontrol" without the key setup line about "Shas kontrol." Now, the consultants cringed. They warned that my antics would cost us precious Knesset seats.

I could feel the despair in party headquarters about all the trouble I was making, but I persisted. On one of the last broadcasting nights before Election Day, amid the other parties' funny, slick, us-versus-them TV advertisements, I seized some of our precious TV time. Speaking directly into the camera, I called for unity. I insisted that we did not oppose anyone who worked for Shas. I wanted votes for us, not votes against them.

"I'm glad you feel good about what you did," Moti Morel said, "but you're no politician. By cooling down the temperature you lost votes today."

We won six mandates. We were down one seat from last time, but far ahead of what the earliest polls had predicted. I became minister of interior in Ehud Barak's short-lived government. I am still greeted occasionally by older Israelis exclaiming "nash kontrol!" It was our party's biggest public moment, our great PR breakout. Few people realize how that success still makes me squirm.

FOUR MINISTRIES IN FOUR GOVERNMENTS

Four missions kept demanding my attention during my years in government. First, remembering our party's voting base, I kept seeking ways to integrate new immigrants into Israeli society. Second, I served as an informal emissary of Diaspora Jews. Although Jews worldwide didn't vote, the Soviet Jewish exodus had proved how intertwined we all were. It was fitting that Jerry Stern threw our biggest Yisrael B'Aliyah victory party, with hundreds of activists, in his Jerusalem home. This was the Jerry Stern who had started the international lifeline linking me and Avital during our years of forced separation. Third, as a member of the cabinet who had only served for three weeks in civil defense training, I had to think what contribution my particular experiences could make to the questions around Israel's security and foreign relations. Fourth, and most time consuming, as a minister I ran three bureaucracies with thousands of employees, making decisions that could affect quality of life for millions.

From 1996 to 2005, I served in four ministerial roles. After our party won seven seats in 1996, I was minister of industry and trade for three years. In 1999, I became minister of internal affairs for one year, until I resigned to protest Prime Minister Ehud Barak's one-sided concessions to Yasir Arafat, the terrorist. A few months later, after Ariel Sharon's election, I returned to the government. I was deputy prime minister and minister of housing and construction from 2001 to 2003. In Sharon's second government, I was minister of Jerusalem and Diaspora affairs. I left the cabinet a second and final time in the spring of 2005, to protest Sharon's unilateral disengagement from Gaza.

Surrounded by chaos, facing tactical decisions and daily headaches, I needed to arrive with a big-picture vision and a few key goals the first day, especially when leading a big ministry. I identified two big, equally important strategic goals. One was to continue freeing the economy from centralization, removing as many obstacles to competition as possible. Another was to try bridging the gaps between the haves and the have-nots through economic development, especially targeting the Arab-Jewish and immigrant-Sabra divides.

With these and other goals in mind, I negotiated many new free trade agreements in Europe, Asia, and the Americas; launched some long-stalled housing projects; and modernized the Interior Ministry, developing more user-friendly application processes for identity papers, naturalizations, and passports. I pioneered professional training courses for ultra-Orthodox Jews and Arabs and redrew some municipal borders that unfairly prevented Israeli Arab towns from flourishing. Moreover, when my team and I developed industrial zones, we insisted they offer equal access to every population sector and pushed development nationwide. Putting politics aside, I strongly believed in building the infrastructure for the prosperity of Arabs and Jews throughout the Land of Israel, be it in a Jewish settlement in the ancient heartland of our country or an Arab village in the Galilee.

The negotiations in the cabinet, the Knesset, and the ministries to launch each initiative were often exhausting. Opposition could be vicious. But, when things turned controversial, I realized that being from a new party with no experience and no connections could be an advantage.

Israel is a small, clubby country. Businesspeople often advance their interests by lobbying their friends and longtime contacts, who still sit on the leading parties' central committees. As a leader of a new party, I was under less pressure. After all, what kind of connections did the members of my party's central committee have? A Jewish Agency emissary here, an Absorption Ministry clerk there?

I felt particularly nimble, for example, during the long, complicated battle we waged for a simple, fair reform: requiring price labels on every grocery product. Without labels, sellers raised prices arbitrarily. The powerful lobbies representing the food monopolies and the supermarkets fought hard to keep consumers in the dark. The industry pushback had silenced two ministers before me via their party central committees. Because we weren't an insider-dominated party, we could give Israeli consumers the Transparent Pricing Law.

Similarly, for years party central committees had blocked the necessary reallocation of undeveloped lands from the Jewish city of Rosh HaAyin to the Arab town of Kfar Kassem for industrial development. When I asked a Labor Party representative why successive Labor ministers did nothing to help, despite their policies of supporting Arabs, the answer was logical: Labor Party politicos from Rosh HaAyin, who wanted to keep the land, used their insider influence.

We implemented the plan. Furious, Rosh HaAyin's mayor accused me of anti-Zionist activity. He said I was stealing his land, as if I had FedExed it to Saudi Arabia rather than simply redrawn municipal boundaries within Israel's borders.

Perhaps most significant, I could defy the business elite in a budgetary tug-of-war over the Law to Encourage Investment. A leftover from Israel's socialist past that delighted some Israeli industrialists, this law promised state subsidies reimbursing up to 32 percent of new investments, to encourage business initiatives that generated exports. Having some incentives to lure corporations into helping the economy makes sense. Too many, and it becomes corrupting.

For years, finance ministers had tried shrinking these funds to help balance the budget, while industrialists resisted because it would make them more risk averse. Here, too, without a central committee of elites, I had more latitude than ministers from bigger parties. We halved the maximum to 16 percent, without insiders blocking us.

Still, with all these achievements, was there a need to create a party for this? Definitely not. I understood that if it had not been me in the seat, it would have been somebody else who was similarly inclined to support the reforms.

ADVANCING IMMIGRANTS' INTERESTS

Nevertheless, Yisrael B'Aliyah made history and a unique contribution by giving immigrants a voice and a seat at the table. Our efforts turned passive clients into active citizens. We helped settle the million-person Russian aliyah and implemented programs tailored to their particular needs. We placed new immigrants on dozens of boards, committees, and councils to decide their own futures, not have others decide for them, no matter how well-meaning.

The shift from being an activist and lobbyist to wielding power is abrupt. You see why power is addictive. Before entering office, you and your comrades had to shout yourselves hoarse at demonstrations demanding that doctors be given licensing examinations in their native language; suddenly, as a minister, you are the one setting the criteria. Before, you had to beg for every scientist who needed a special stipend; suddenly, you could fund scientific incubators to employ dozens of immigrant scientists. Before, you had to lobby others whenever you heard of some homeless senior citizen; suddenly, you could launch an initiative to house thousands. Before, you had to fight for cost-of-living increases to the aliyah basket immigrants received, each time inflation hit; suddenly, you could link the *sal klita* to the cost-of-living index.

The bigger the problem, the more allies you need to wield power effectively. Finding public housing for the elderly proved to be particularly challenging. Beyond the sheer volume of immigrants who arrived unable to make down payments on apartments, so many older Russian Jews arrived penniless, without savings and stripped of the pensions they had earned but couldn't take out of Russia.

A special task force addressing this issue involved four ministers. I worked with Absorption Minister Yuli Edelstein, Finance Minister Dan Meridor, and Deputy Housing Minister Meir Porush. Porush was a deputy minister with no boss. He and others in the ultra-Orthodox Agudat Yisrael faction of United Torah Judaism were too ambivalent about Israel's existence as a Zionist state to serve as full cabinet members.

We launched a massive, and expensive, public-housing initiative from north to south, building and renovating buildings to serve as special hostels for the elderly. With financing from the Israeli government and the Jewish Agency, we united the efforts of Israel with the Jewish people worldwide.

Porush and I developed a warm relationship. When I showed him my prison Psalms book, he held it reverently before kissing it. After that, he loved calling me out whenever he saw me, as "the man with the Psalm book in his pocket." I, in turn, enjoyed the colorful family stories this eighth-generation Jerusalemite told.

When we all toasted our housing initiative, Porush grabbed my army hat. I grabbed his big fur hat. The resulting picture of our task force, with me wearing an ultra-Orthodox *shtreimel* and Porush with my khaki green cap perched uncomfortably on his head, was a big hit. I liked it too. For me, it symbolized how easily we can cooperate for the benefit of all people.

Alas, the next "who is a Jew" battle, which soon erupted, reminded us that sharing hats is easier than sharing a common political agenda. Both Porush and I resisted compromising on core principles. Beyond this housing success and so many others—in fact, from this success and all the others—I remained well aware of the high price of politics, personally and nationally.

9

ENCOUNTERING ONE PEOPLE DIVIDED BY ONE RELIGION

In mid-September 1997, I arrived in Mexico City to launch another laborious free trade negotiation. I felt good about our strategy in the Ministry of Industry and Trade to open Israel economically through such agreements. I had picked up my predecessors' negotiating pace and scale. Eventually, I launched and signed free trade agreements with Canada, the Czech Republic, Slovakia, Turkey, Poland, and Hungary. In November 1997, we would announce a three-way agreement with the United States for a free trade industrial zone in Jordan. Two decades later, it remains one of the rare surviving Israeli economic projects with the Arab world.

Whenever I traveled abroad, after the political meetings and business forums, I scheduled local Jewish community meetings, visiting Jewish day schools, Jewish community centers, and other Jewish institutions. Remembering how important Israel was to us in the Soviet Union, I was particularly proud to represent Israel to the world Jewish community. That was why I insisted in the coalition agreement that we add "Diaspora Affairs" to the title of the Interministerial Committee on Aliyah and Absorption I now chaired.

Israeli ministers usually travel with high-profile delegations, including many business leaders. While the Israelis who accompanied me often competed to join the more intimate political and economic meetings with officials, which might help open economic doors for them, most happily skipped the meetings with fellow Jews. When I visited the community centers and schools, they went to shop.

Whenever I invited them along, most waved off me with Israeli brashness: "Bah, what will I learn from these Jewish schools where they pretend to speak Hebrew? Why do I need to see nostalgic photos of Israel with camels and Jaffa oranges? If they really love us, let them make aliyah, and we'll talk there."

On this trip, some of my fellow travelers broke the usual Israeli boycott. Mexico City's Jewish community is famous for being particularly colorful, blending a diverse mix of different Jewish ethnic groups.

This time, the boycott came from the other side. At our first event, a big community breakfast, my host reported that the leaders of Mexico's Reform Jewish community would not be showing up, now or at any other time. Looking embarrassed, he delivered a letter from them. They explained that their movement was boycotting all ministers who voted for *chok ha'amara*, the conversion bill. This proposed law would guarantee the Chief Rabbinate's monopoly on conversions in Israel.

What? Boycotting me? Their voice in the Israeli government? Really? After all those demonstrations together? Didn't they know where I stood on this issue? Why couldn't they appreciate how hard I had fought to find a way to defend their institutions? At first stuck in this defensive reaction, I tried being dismissive, thinking sarcastically, "Well, there are so few Reform Jews in Mexico, maybe that's their way of trying to be noticed."

On second thought, my protective irony collapsed. In recent months, whether I was dealing with ministry, cabinet, Knesset, or party issues, the religion-state problem haunted us. On a deeper level, I kept wondering, "Is it possible for Israeli politicians to represent the interests of Diaspora Jews who don't vote in Israel without betraying their obligation to the Israelis who do?"

THE RELIGIOUS STATUS QUO
UNITES ISRAELIS AND DIVIDES JEWS

As it worked out, just weeks before this Mexico trip, the conversion bill the Reform movement disliked had passed its first reading in the Knesset. The intense controversy surrounding the bill represented the latest round of the "who is a Jew" crisis, which continues to complicate Israel-Diaspora relations today.

The problem began even before the state of Israel's creation. On June 19, 1947, eleven months before Israel became a state, David Ben-Gurion sent what became known as the "status quo letter" to representatives of the ultra-Orthodox Agudat Yisrael movement. Ben-Gurion made certain defining promises, which he implemented as Israel's first prime minister. Shabbat would be the national day of rest. All state institutions, including the army, would keep strictly kosher. Religious schools would be state funded but independent. And—perhaps the most restrictive commitment—Halachah, Jewish law, would dominate in personal realms such as marriage, divorce, and conversion.

Why did this secular Jew, this Socialist Zionist leader, make such sweeping, long-term concessions to ultra-Orthodox rabbis? Didn't he realize it would handcuff the state? Ben-Gurion was a pragmatist. In June 1947, just two years after the Holocaust ended, he sought to unite the deeply scarred Jewish people behind the pressing need to establish a Jewish state.

Ben-Gurion chaired the Jewish Agency, the Jewish people's proxy government in Palestine. A delegation from the United Nations Special Committee on Palestine (UNSCOP) was arriving to explore options for the territory as it slid into civil war between Jews and Arabs, with the British mandatory authorities looking on helplessly.

Ben-Gurion was worried. If anti-Zionist, ultra-Orthodox Jews told UNSCOP they opposed a Jewish state, it could derail the momentum building for Jewish statehood. With their black hats and long beards, the ultra-Orthodox looked like what most non-Jews imagined all Jews looked like. These "real Jews" seemed more representative of "the Jews" than Ben-Gurion and his clean-shaven, work-clothes-wearing, modern Zionists.

Approval from ultra-Orthodox Jews in Palestine would also convince the many skeptical Jews outside Palestine that there was a pro-Zionist consensus that recognized the pressing need for a Jewish state. So, ironically, one of the issues that divides Diaspora Jews from Israelis today started as an attempt to unite them!

Ben-Gurion cut a deal. He wrote a letter, which he never formalized into law. The ultra-Orthodox support helped in the United Nations, which on November 29, 1947, authorized creating a Jewish state in Palestine. This exchange created the precedent: to secure ultra-Orthodox support for the State's existence, Israel's leaders made concessions on issues they considered less important.

Ben-Gurion was no mere tactician. This arrangement also advanced his strategic vision. Beyond creating and defending the state, he was building the New Jew, forging one identity out of many. Just as Israelis would speak one language, Hebrew, they would have one religious baseline, Orthodoxy. The "status quo letter" made the Orthodox shul the synagogue secular Israelis didn't pray in.

Ben-Gurion also feared continuing the denominational fights he saw in America and Europe in his new Jewish state. "I see danger in a war against religion and in a war for religion," Ben-Gurion admitted. His job was cultivating Israeliness, not creative forms of Jewishness.

As a politician, Ben-Gurion needed to satisfy his Orthodox minority, not America's liberal majority. He noticed how few Reform Jews lived in Israel. There wasn't a Reform temple in Israel until 1958. In 1970, when some young American Jews asked Ben-Gurion how Reform Judaism could establish itself in Israel, he offered a realpolitik answer: if Reform Judaism wanted recognition, three hundred thousand Reform Jews should move to Israel.

Ben-Gurion also assumed, incorrectly, that this bargain was temporary. He assumed Orthodox Jewry would melt away in the Jewish state, and even religious kids born in Israel would grow up to become New Jews—secularized pioneers like him.

In May 1948, the state was established, with Ben-Gurion as its first prime minister. The old-new Jewish state quickly justified itself by ingathering exiles, offering Jews a long-needed refuge from persecution. Continuing that mission, a foundational law passed in 1950, the Law of Return, proclaimed, "Every Jew has the right to come to this country as an immigrant."

Initially, the law did not define who a Jew was. It welcomed all Jews as citizens unless the immigration minister deemed the applicant to be "engaged in an activity directed against the Jewish people" or "likely to endanger public health or the security of the State." Having been persecuted, exiled, wandering, homeless, Jews now had a home.

But determining who exactly is and is not a Jew became a bureaucratic question for immigration authorities. And while the Law of Return was vague, Ben-Gurion's status quo letter was specific: follow Halachah. So, given the historic overlap between Jewish religious and national identities, separation between synagogue and state became impossible. A political, legal, and religious collision was inevitable.

In 1958, Ben-Gurion's coalition teetered when he and his minister of the interior, Israel Bar-Yehuda, showed their true feelings about the "who is a Jew" question. Under orders of the former minister, Moshe Chaim Shapiro of the National Religious Party, Interior Ministry functionaries were demanding that immigrants prove they were Halachically Jewish. This offended Bar-Yehuda and Ben-Gurion. These secular, socialist revolutionaries wanted Israel to be as welcoming as possible to build the state.

The Bureau of the Registration of Inhabitants started issuing Israeli identity cards defining immigrants as Jews based on individuals' "good faith" declarations that they were Jewish. Theoretically, if you called yourself Jewish, you could get citizenship.

This sweeping improvisation violated the status quo agreement. It weakened the Chief Rabbinate's hold on the Interior Ministry in assessing an immigrant's Jewishness. Two cabinet ministers from the NRP objected. They resigned, threatening Ben-Gurion's coalition.

Ben-Gurion now faced a dilemma: risk losing religious support and his power, or risk alienating non-Orthodox Diaspora Jews. Seeking some cover, Ben-Gurion took an unprecedented step, which has never been repeated. Seeing himself as the leader of the Jewish people, he sent letters to forty-seven leading Jewish thinkers from around the world, asking how the state of Israel should define who is a Jew. The novelist S. Y. Agnon advised the prime minister to drop the question, because religion and state are like two neighbors who cannot move away from each other but make one another uncomfortable. Any attempt to mediate between the two would only cause trouble.

But there was no way to avoid this question. Even before the majority of the sages advised him to follow the one shared standard, Halachah, as the only way to unite Israelis, Ben-Gurion, the practical politician, had made up his mind. To continue the Zionist enterprise, he caved to the religious parties' demands, granting them a monopoly on personal status issues. The NRP's man, Moshe Chaim Shapiro, returned to the Ministry of Interior and restored his stricter definition of Jewishness. Every prime minister since has replicated Ben-Gurion's bargain.

In this defining moment, Orthodox politicians showed they were ready to bring down the government over religious issues. And most non-Orthodox leaders showed they were equally ready to surrender.

The Knesset eventually updated the Law of Return twice because it was so vague. Amendments in 1970 fine-tuned the original rationale, which was that every Jew Hitler persecuted needed a home. The law defined Jews by the traditional standard: you had to be born to a Jewish mother or to have converted to Judaism. But it added that immigration would be open to anyone with a Jewish grandparent or their spouses—Hitler's standard for targeting Jews in Germany.

By not specifying Orthodox conversions, the 1970 amendment infuriated the ultra-Orthodox. While the status quo only allowed Orthodox conversions in Israel, liberal conversions done in the Diaspora were now acceptable for Israeli citizenship.

Although Ben-Gurion's commitment to uniting Israel divided the Jewish people, he kept much of this under the legal radar. Except for the constructively ambiguous Law of Return, these agreements emerged during coalition negotiations, at cabinet meetings, or within the ministry, not as laws passed in the Knesset.

Critics say Ben-Gurion created a built-in Jewish identity time bomb. I believe he understood the power of ambiguity. The Knesset never passed a law formally treating Orthodox and Reform as equal. That would have been unacceptable to some extremely influential Israelis. But the Knesset also never passed a law formally declaring the non-Orthodox unequal either. That would have alienated most Diaspora Jews.

Naturally, combatants turned to the Supreme Court. And the judges left no doubts: if the Knesset would not pass clear laws, the court would respond, making decisions unlikely to please the ultra-Orthodox parties.

THE CONVERSION BILL
HAUNTS BIBI'S GOVERNMENT

The religious parties started to panic. To stop the court-driven drift toward more liberal standards, they demanded a law guaranteeing that in Israel only Orthodox conversions would be considered legitimate for citizenship. That is why it was called the conversion bill.

As Netanyahu formed his government in 1996, the religion and state fight had already hit a critical crossroads. The Supreme Court looked to the new government for clarity. The religious parties joined Bibi's co-alition only after he promised to pass a conversion bill. The bill would formalize a key aspect of the Ben-Gurion understanding by giving the Orthodox Chief Rabbinate a monopoly on conversion.

The anger was growing on both sides. The ultra-Orthodox parties considered any steps toward recognizing non-Orthodox conversions in Israel as a get, a bill of divorce, proof that the state no longer respected the status quo agreement. Many liberal Diaspora leaders considered any steps to delegitimize liberal conversions equally insulting, proof the state no longer respected them.

As the chairman of the Interministerial Committee on Aliyah, Absorption, and Diaspora Affairs, as the chairman of my party, and as a member of the cabinet, I needed a clear position. But, Agnon, the novelist, was right: the status quo worked best amid clouds of ambiguity. I concluded that if one side won, we would all lose—as one people united around Israel. I believed we had to keep this fight out of the Knesset and out of the Supreme Court. For this, we needed a compromise.

I hoped, naively, that my experience mediating among so many different players during the Soviet Jewry struggle would come in handy as a government minister. I kept remembering how easily we had overcome religious differences while marching on Washington.

I had visited Cleveland on one of the last weekends before the march. The chosen location for the communal dinner on Saturday night was the Reform temple, whose rabbis invited me to speak there Saturday morning. We faced two problems. Without a microphone, no one would hear me in the vast sanctuary, but I wouldn't use a microphone on the Sabbath. And the temple's kitchen was not kosher, but there were no other available halls big enough to hold the large crowd we expected.

Urged by an Orthodox friend, Morry Weiss, who mediated, I spoke standing beside the microphone, far away enough that I wasn't quite using it, but close enough that people could hear. And, for the first time in its history, the temple koshered its kitchen to host the community. If we could make such compromises for the march in Washington, I wondered, what kinds of compromises would we make to continue our march through history together?

To compromise, one first has to talk to the other side. Not to agree, but at least to hear the other's arguments and to try understanding your rival's logic. I wanted to try out some of the less inflammatory Orthodox arguments in front of my hometown crowd, at a meeting with liberal Jewish leaders hosted by my friends at the New York Federation. Addressing the "Orthodox monopoly," I said, "Obviously, there's a problem here. But when they say that Halachah, Jewish law, kept our people together for thousands of years, and non-Orthodox movements don't have such a long track record, aren't they right at least in historical terms? The liberal movements have barely been around for two hundred years. When it comes to questions of keeping the Jewish people alive, even if we strongly disagree with some Orthodox policies, shouldn't we give them the benefit of the doubt?"

The atmosphere in the room turned frosty. People looked agitated. They all seemed to be asking one question with their eyes: Et tu, Brute?

One Federation friend snapped, "Are you also with our enemies? This is the thanks we get for all our support for you? Now, as soon as you join the government, you betray us."

I ended my attempt at diplomacy abruptly. I saw their pain. We were no longer joking about Russian atheists and American Reconstructionists, cooperating as KGB agents glared at us. People who had devoted their lives to Israel, and had been told that it represented them, now felt rejected by it. In such a fight, most people were too upset to start understanding the other side or see anything amusing in the situation.

This "you owe us" loyalty argument was always a nonstarter with me. The first people who tried it, shortly after I arrived in Israel, were Meir Kahane's followers. In the late 1960s, the charismatic, fiery Kahane was one of the first American Jews to draw attention to Soviet Jews' suffering, through his militant group the Jewish Defense League (JDL). Despite appreciating his foresight, I signed a letter, with a few other Refuseniks, at the height of our struggle, condemning his use of violence in New York against Soviet targets. The JDL's tactics undermined our nonviolent moral struggle. Once we were both in Israel, I kept a disdainful distance from Kahane, his Kach Party, and his anti-Arab bigotry.

The Soviet Jewry movement included everybody from Kahanists on the right to French Communists on the left. How could I stand for anything as a politician, if I had to make all of them happy, all of the time?

By contrast, the followers of Rabbi Kook, led by Rabbi Tzvi Tau, never tried leveraging their unique role at the heart of Avital's struggle to press me. They remained restrained despite the fact that they strongly supported the conversion bill. They fervently opposed Reform Judaism entering Israel and were very critical of my stance on this issue.

After my failed attempt with my liberal New York friends, I tried starting a dialogue from the other end. I invited ultra-Orthodox Knesset members to listen to non-Orthodox American Jews.

My party, Yisrael B'Aliyah, had cooperated with ultra-Orthodox parties on other issues. Together, we started breaking down some prejudices. The first success was in resolving the heartbreaking problem of mixed Russian Jewish families separated after death, because the Chevra Kadisha burial societies refused to bury those who were Halachically non-Jewish in Jewish cemeteries. This included some IDF veterans who had risked their lives defending the state. It had been a hot issue in our campaign.

When we joined the government, we insisted that the chief rabbis address this issue urgently. The chief Ashkenazi rabbi lectured us, claiming that the purity of cemeteries had kept the Jewish people alive for millennia. "Look at Europe," he said. "It's all cemeteries now, but everyone knows those cemeteries are Jewish because we kept them Jewish. You can't start twisting Jewish law because of one person's needs," he concluded.

We kept pushing. Fortunately, Israel has two chief rabbis who rotate responsibilities. When the Sephardi chief rabbi Eliyahu Bakshi-Doron took charge, he embraced a different approach. Troubled by the families' misery, he found a solution in the rabbinic concept of *darchei shalom*, paths to peace in society. Slight, not-very-noticeable barriers could hive off an area in each cemetery, he explained. That would create a section where anyone could be buried, ever so subtly.

Rabbi Bakshi-Doron directed the burial societies to respect each family's wishes, accommodating anyone who wanted the Kaddish, the traditional mourning prayer, said or any other rituals followed. The rabbi's expansiveness solved this emotionally charged problem.

"Can I convert to Sephardi?" I asked. "They seem to have more fun." They eat *kitniyot*—legumes like corn and peanuts—on Passover, making the holiday's food restrictions more manageable, and their rabbis are more understanding. More seriously, I wondered if the flexibility in Sephardic communities explained why no Reform movement emerged there. The rabbis' openness might have prevented the rebellions that Ashkenazi rigidity fueled.

Similarly, we defied the conventional wisdom that claimed ultra-Orthodox Jews had no interest in regular jobs. A leading Agudat politician, Rabbi Avraham Ravitz, approached me with a proposal to create special professional courses for ultra-Orthodox Jews, concentrating on skills such as accounting and computing. Our ministry, together with the Jerusalem College of Technology, piloted a series of such programs, understanding that Israel needed more yeshiva students to become productive citizens. Today, more than ten thousand ultra-Orthodox Jews are graduating from vocational or academic programs annually, and the numbers keep growing.

At the same time, ultra-Orthodox politicians helped us secure mass budgetary commitments for housing initiatives for new immigrants. Overall, I found the ultra-Orthodox much more flexible than I expected, even on religious matters.

I started wondering, could we leverage this goodwill and encourage a dialogue between these ultra-Orthodox politicians and representatives of the liberal movements? I was hosting a delegation of American Jewish leaders at the Knesset. Two of the leaders represented the Reform movement. I invited a number of members from various parties to discuss the conversion bill.

The ultra-Orthodox politicians' first reaction was, "No, we cannot meet with them." Trying to speak their language, knowing that the way I framed it would have insulted the Reform Jews if leaked to reporters, I told the ultra-Orthodox parliamentarians, "They're Jews like us. They are part of our people by the most Orthodox standards. If you don't consider them rabbis, can't you see them as community leaders? And if you don't see their temple as a synagogue, can't you see it as a Jewish community center? Don't we in Israel have to speak to all the Jews of the world?"

Two ultra-Orthodox politicians grudgingly agreed to participate. They were ready to listen as long as there would be no direct interaction with the delegation. The session was off-the-record, with no photographers or stenographers allowed. These ultra-Orthodox politicians couldn't be seen meeting "the Reformim."

We started smoothly. But after ten minutes, one visitor made some political calculations. Noting that the Israelis I invited included clean-shaven secular members of the Knesset as well as bearded Orthodox ones, and confident he would have a pro-liberal majority, one American

Jew proposed, informally, American style, "Hey, let's just start by taking a quick vote on this conversion question."

I thought, mistakenly, "Why not?"

That ended it. The ultra-Orthodox politicians walked out. They accused me of violating our agreement. Politely showing up was one thing. But they could not afford to have the ultra-Orthodox newspapers exposing their active involvement in such meetings.

The Reformers wouldn't listen to arguments. The ultra-Orthodox wouldn't sit with Reformers. But what about the silent Israeli majority? All the religious parties combined averaged between 15 and 20 percent of the vote. Nevertheless, most non-Orthodox Israeli politicians stood on the same ideological quicksand. These kinds of issues were not important enough to them or their voters to bring down the coalition whenever they were in power.

Only when they were on the outs did they suddenly start caring about their Diaspora brethren. As a result, we all sank into this strange position of passively allowing the conflict to grow.

SHARON'S POLITICAL ADVICE

Being a part of this impasse frustrated me. I felt torn between what my constituents expected me to do—stay in the government—and what my Diaspora friends expected me to do—walk, or at least threaten to leave. Ariel Sharon, who had been in the Knesset since 1977, felt badly for me.

I had the best seat at my first cabinet table. On one side was Yuli Edelstein: my old comrade in arms, a fellow prisoner of Zion, and one of my Yisrael B'Aliyah Party cofounders. Sitting on my other side was the former major general Ariel Sharon, serving as minister of national infrastructure.

For us Soviet Jews, Sharon was the 1973 Yom Kippur War's great hero. His counterattack in the Sinai turned Israel's certain defeat into a historic victory, humiliating the Soviets along with their Arab clients. This turnabout shut down the taunts of all those who were tailing us young Moscow activists. That made Sharon the man who made the KGB cringe, right when I was starting to learn about Israel.

My perceptions of Sharon soured during Israel's first Lebanon War in 1982. At the time I was in the middle of my hunger strike, so I only heard bits of propaganda. Still, the Soviets kept calling Sharon the "butcher." They blamed him for the massacres Christian Phalangists had committed against Palestinians in camps Israeli troops controlled, Sabra and Shatila. While I knew how distorted Soviet news was, Sharon's moral failure embarrassed me. Israel's internal Kahan Commission would conclude that Sharon, while not guilty of murder, bore responsibility for "not taking appropriate measures to prevent bloodshed."

When I landed in Israel in 1986, Sharon welcomed me along with Shimon Peres and Yitzhak Shamir. Even on that euphoric day, I had mixed feelings about him as he hugged me. When Sharon invited me to visit his massive ranch in the Negev, I hesitated.

Over the years, I learned about Arik's efforts to help free me and other Soviet Jews. Then, when the big aliyah came, he lived up to his loving nickname, the Bulldozer. As the head of the Zionist Forum for Soviet Jewry, I discovered that what could take months of political wrangling with other ministries, Arik often solved in one meeting, sometimes in five minutes. He plowed through bureaucratic obstacles to get thousands of caravans for immigrants and provide essential discounts for contractors to start building permanent houses. It seemed that nothing could stop him.

After Yisrael B'Aliyah's electoral victory, Sharon greeted us warmly, saying he appreciated that Russian immigrants finally had a voice. Arik won us over the first time Yuli and I started strategizing at the cabinet table, in what we thought was secret, speaking Russian. "Um, guys," he warned us. "I just want you to know that I understand Russian." It was his parents' mother tongue.

This master politician proved to be a generous mentor. He spent a day with Yisrael B'Aliyah's activists, shepherding us around the territories past the Green Line, Israel's 1949 borders. He knew the history of every community, the geography, industry, and agronomy of every region, the military dynamics of every sector. He kept waving maps around as props. We found them helpful, but we noticed that he never needed to glance at them. It was all in his head.

Arik was committed to helping the immigrants integrate. He attended our interministerial committee meetings regularly. He often was the only other minister who showed up, besides Yuli and me. He offered us advice, ranging from how to manage the government bureaucracy to how to maneuver in the Knesset. Seeing how troubled I was by the "who is a Jew" and conversion bill questions, Sharon invited me out for a coffee. Today, we would call it coaching.

"Natan, you know I want you to succeed," he said. "I think I am even more liberal than you are on the question of who is a Jew. Any individual who wants to be with us, who could be a good soldier, or who suffers for being connected to us is a Jew and should be welcomed here. But," he added, "if you want to be a successful politician, first, you have to deliver to the people who sent you here, your voters. You also have to broaden your outreach to voters who didn't vote for you this time—but might next time. Don't forget, even the best of the Diaspora Jews are not voting here. They won't help you."

Then, Arik added the kicker: "I was with you on every meeting about housing. You and Yuli just pulled off a great coup by getting that big housing initiative, which is so important for immigrants. But you couldn't have done it without Meir Porush," the minister from the ultra-Orthodox Agudat Yisrael. "These people also cooperated when you needed to solve the cemetery problem. They helped you on an issue important to you and your electorate. Now these people are asking you about something important to them and their electorate, the conversion issue. If you let them down on this issue key to their constituents, you won't get their support on issues important to your constituents. Besides," Arik finished, "you have to understand. We aren't compromising with the KGB here. We are making compromises among Israelis to build Israel together."

WHY DISSIDENTS DON'T SURVIVE IN POLITICS

There it was: the instruction manual to every political souk. I no longer had the dissident's purity. I had to be a politician.

Arik often mentioned the KGB in our conversations, just as Ehud Barak would often mention the *tsinok*, my punishment cell, when I served in his government. These references usually were the Israeli warriors' way of looking past our out-of-shape bodies and pale faces, hailing us as fellow fighters, Zionist heroes who were not just mere party hacks.

This time, in mentioning the KGB, Arik meant something different: It's time to leave your idealistic utopia, the fight between good and evil. You're not a Refusenik in Israel; you're a leader. Become a politician.

Successful politicians—David Ben-Gurion, Ariel Sharon, Benjamin Netanyahu—never felt they were betraying anyone or anything, as long as they were broadening their base and gaining power. They defined the politician's mission as using power to build the country. To succeed in politics, you have to see compromising in a messy, even morally fraught, situation as a necessary step in solidifying your standing, so you can wield power for the common good more effectively.

Dissidents, however, think about their activity in terms of struggle and betrayal. A moral campaign is zero-sum. Compromise is the tool of the regime to seduce and divide. When a dissident's struggle ends in victory, this contempt for compromisers often continues. Some dissidents, still stuck in their black-and-white world, end up seeing every opponent as wicked. My fellow dissidents usually ended up hating politics.

In my dissident activity and in my years in prison, I became friendly with a number of people who, after the Soviet Union collapsed, would serve in the parliaments of Russia, Ukraine, Lithuania, and Armenia. Like me, many went to prison first. None of them lasted more than one term in parliament. All of them quickly became miserable—and made their colleagues miserable too. They had been such valuable political assets during the first election, representing the fresh start. But it all quickly soured: everyone soon realized that politicians require the talent of compromise, which they lacked.

The most successful dissident turned politician I knew was Václav Havel. But his extraordinary popularity made him president of Czechoslovakia, then of the Czech Republic, both honorary positions. Havel confessed to me that he could never be a prime minister. He had no appetite for political messiness; the daily political battles and cease-fires were not for him.

Sharon's statement was axiomatic for every politician. These are the rules of the democratic political game: your voters grant you the power. But his advice only reminded me that I was not a good politician. I could not divorce my political career from my struggle in the Soviet Union and the commitments I had happily made there. I entered the Knesset because so many people back then felt connected to our cause, our people, and our homeland.

I survived in the Gulag by feeling this grand sense of unity. As a politician, I couldn't pretend that preserving those connections was not my responsibility. When responding to some specific demands of

Diaspora Jews, I could answer, "Thanks for your input, but you are not citizens of Israel." But when it came to nurturing their fundamental connection to the place and the state, I represented them as well. Israel belongs to all the Jews, wherever they live. That was Israel's founding mission. That's the idea behind the Law of Return. And I felt that was my mission too.

Resignation was always an option. But after winning the voters' trust, resigning and removing my party from the coalition would be serious acts. I would only take that plunge if my conscience no longer allowed me to serve or if my resignation could create new political realities. My understanding in 1997, that the conversion bill question wasn't black and white, kept me negotiating within the government. At the same time, I wondered, "Would a different government have a better chance of reaching compromise?"

The answer was no. Taking down our Likud-led coalition would have had no impact on this religion-state issue. To the contrary, the Labor Party's history suggested they would cut the same deals with the ultra-Orthodox.

David Ben-Gurion's tradition continued. In 1993, Yitzhak Rabin had given the ultra-Orthodox more power than before. He needed their backing to advance his negotiations with Syria's dictator Hafez al-Assad about possibly returning the Golan and to pass the Oslo Accords. Both leading secular parties were always ready to sacrifice what they considered to be secondary worries about state and religion to mobilize support for their primary concern. For Labor, it became guaranteeing Israel's security by advancing the peace process; for Likud, it became achieving peace by resisting pressure for one-sided concessions while keeping Israel's historic and biblical lands.

Facing such a deadlock, I could do little except rely on a classic parliamentary maneuver. Proposals only become laws if they pass three readings in the Knesset. A standard political tool for buying time was to agree to vote for a bill on its first reading, thereby fulfilling your obligation to the coalition agreement you signed. But then you insist the proposed law go to a special committee for revision, because you will not vote in subsequent readings to pass the law without an acceptable compromise.

As a result, shortly before my Mexico City trip, when the conversion bill had its first reading in the Knesset, my party colleagues and I voted aye. Following this Israeli political tradition, we let it be known we would not vote for the bill a second time, or allow it to pass, without the compromises we sought.

This strategy was too sophisticated for most Israeli voters to grasp, let alone Diaspora Jews. The pre-vote shouting continued after the vote too. That was how I found myself in Mexico City, facing the ultimately short-lived Reform boycott.

THE NE'EMAN COMMITTEE'S
HISTORIC COMPROMISE

Of course, as soon as you finish the first reading, the clock starts ticking toward the second one. How could we possibly achieve a compromise? Despite the hullabaloo around the conversion bill, only a handful of us in government cared about the issue enough to try finding a compromise. In addition to Yuli and me, the only politicians really engaged were Attorney General Elyakim Rubinstein, Michael Eitan of the Likud, and Alexander Lubotsky of the Third Way.

After the bill passed its first reading, the prime minister formed a committee of experts to seek a compromise. It would not be easy mediating between two sides that could barely sit in the same room together.

On June 27, 1997, Bibi turned to his finance minister, Ya'akov Ne'eman, to chair the committee. One of Israel's first superlawyers, Ne'eman had already served as justice minister—and, on another level, as my first lawyer in Israel. The well-respected Ne'eman was skilled at finding Maimonides's golden path of moderation toward compromise.

The commission held fifty meetings, hearing the testimony of nearly eighty witnesses. After most committee sessions, we politicians would meet to brainstorm, seeking "a consensual solution." But we kept hitting the same ideological deadlock. Trying to solve this problem in the abstract, it became zero-sum. Either the ultra-Orthodox would win by cementing their monopoly over religious practices, or the liberal denominations would win by gaining some legitimacy.

My friend Irina "Ira" Dashevsky's testimony broke the logjam. Ira and her father, Dr. Zeev Dashevsky, led Machanaim, an organization founded in Moscow in 1979 for *kiruv*, to bring Soviet Jews closer to Judaism. By the 1990s, Machanaim was in Israel, helping the many Russian immigrants who arrived without proper documents proving they were Jewish.

Machanaim also offered conversion classes for Russian immigrants who were not Halachically Jewish, yet wished to convert.

Ignoring the legal technicalities, Dashevsky gave the big-picture sociological realities with her characteristically human touch. She asked, "What do you do with so many immigrants from the Soviet Union, accepted under the Law of Return, studying, fighting, working in Israel but ultimately rejected by the society, unable to marry, blocked from burial in a Jewish cemetery?" She wondered how creating so many second-class citizens would affect Israel's future. She pointed out how unfair it was that, after they decided to join the Jewish family, after the Jewish state admitted them, the Jewish religion rejected them.

Dashevsky emphasized another anomaly that surprised many liberal Jews. Most Russian immigrants who wanted to convert wanted an Orthodox conversion. They didn't care about Jewish theology. But only the Orthodox could provide what these immigrants sought: a conversion all of Israeli society accepted.

She proposed more generous readings of immigrants' documents to welcome them as Jews. She also suggested a more liberalized conversion process, especially for minors, whom the rabbis might accept more easily.

I don't know whether Ira's sweeping picture of the problem was as eye-opening for Ne'eman as he claimed. Perhaps, as a good lawyer, he knew how to convince his clients to replace unrealistic expectations with more practical ones. But Ne'eman seized the moment. He redefined the committee's aim as solving the "difficult humanitarian problem" of integrating masses of non-Halachic Russian Jews. Rising to this historic challenge, and not wanting to be blamed for abandoning the immigrants Israel had fought so hard to free, most hard-liners softened.

In January 1998, the Ne'eman Committee recommended a more open, multidenominational approach. The commission proposed creating an institute for Jewish studies to help the immigrants "integrate totally into Israeli-Jewish society." Classes for conversion would be available and taught by teachers from all the streams, including Reform and Conservative Jewry.

Echoing Ben-Gurion, the commission also endorsed a "unified governmental conversion procedure—according to the Law of Torah—that will be recognized by all of Israel" and would "ensure the unity of the Jewish people." Quoting the Jewish scholar Maimonides, the final report advised that the rabbis should "not be strict" with the convert. Use only "soft and acceptable words."

The compromise was intended to end the battles in the Knesset and the Supreme Court, at least temporarily. Each side won some concessions. Orthodox conversion practices continued to dominate. But the non-Orthodox denominations gained legitimacy as part of the educational process, and a formal law granting the Orthodox rabbis a monopoly on conversion was avoided. The representatives of both the Chief Rabbinate and the liberal streams were unenthusiastic yet willing to cooperate, in their way. Eighty members endorsed the compromise in the Knesset.

When he announced the compromise in the Knesset, Ne'eman generously said two "best men" were walking "this bride"—the compromise—down the aisle, Likud's Michael Eitan and me. The agreement suggested there was hope for compromise and some grand resolution to these ongoing headaches. But the Chief Rabbinate would continue trying to undermine the compromise and disrespecting the liberal streams, while Reform and Conservative Jews would continue campaigning for equality.

This conversion crisis showcased the depth of the growing tension between Israel and the Diaspora. The sides were not ready to listen to one another, let alone talk to one another. The *Titanic* joke no longer worked: we had stopped arguing strenuously with one another, which had long been our best guarantee to survive future catastrophes.

The Ne'eman Committee's compromise bought us some time. The great clash ended up being postponed about twelve years. It was essential that, by the inevitable next crisis, we had improved our communication channels. But when the crisis returned, the channels of communication were still dysfunctional. By then, I would confront the question from a different perspective, representing the Diaspora while chairing the Jewish Agency for Israel.

10

A MINORITY OF ONE
ON DEMOCRACY AND PEACE
IN THE MIDDLE EAST

Every day in politics, you feel forced to be an instant expert. Serving as a minister, sitting on government committees, voting in the Knesset, you have to make far-ranging governmental decisions on endlessly complicated issues far beyond your knowledge base. You usually rely on particular experts, staffers, and your instincts. Nevertheless, facing so many aspects of my still-new home I had never encountered before, I often played catch-up on budgetary matters or improvised on urban affairs, education, culture, or sports questions.

There was, however, one area where I felt I was an expert: how to deal with dictatorships. In the Soviet Union, every political question shrank before the biggest existential question: How can we be free from the dictatorship's grip? In Israel, every domestic issue shrinks before the biggest international one: How do we survive amid so many hostile dictatorships and terrorist groups seeking our destruction, without controlling the lives of millions of Palestinians? Whatever political party you belong to, whatever your political philosophy, you keep returning to this mystery.

Having been a dissident in the Soviet Union, I knew why dictatorships look so strong from the outside and why they are so weak and unstable from the inside. I recognized the quiet, invisible, but irreversible process of turning the army of true believers into doublethinkers. I understood how desperate dictatorships are to keep controlling their citizens. I saw how much they need external enemies to justify their own internal power. I realized how easily democratic leaders were fooled by the dictatorship's compulsory military parades and the people's forced displays of solidarity, not realizing that totalitarian regimes are muscle-bound, while democracies are surprisingly resilient. I recalled how much these economically dysfunctional regimes depend on cooperation with the free world.

DISSIDENTS' UNDERSTANDINGS OF DICTATORSHIPS ARE OFTEN IGNORED

In the Soviet Union, we dissidents spent a lot of time debating dictatorships' vulnerabilities and speculating how to undermine them peacefully. We then spent even more time testing our theories with our lives. We kept publicizing Andrei Sakharov's warning: "Never trust a government more than the government trusts its own people." We tried explaining to Western leaders why linkage provides leverage, meaning that raising human rights questions when dealing with dictatorships provides Western leaders with both a strong moral position and a clever hold on their natural enemies.

Ultimately, Soviet dissidents' assessments and predictions of Soviet collapse—which Western experts often ridiculed—practically mapped out the history that unfolded. By contrast, the illusion of Soviet power blinded most Western Sovietologists. Feeling vindicated, we dissidents assumed democracies would rely on our experiences and expertise in navigating the post–Cold War world.

That's where we were naive. I cannot complain that I wasn't heard. Everybody seemed happy to keep learning about the Soviet Union's fall from the inside. I shared my views with many national leaders, in Israel and worldwide. I gave many interviews on this topic and wrote many articles. The book I wrote with Ron Dermer, *The Case for Democracy: The Power of Freedom to Overcome Tyranny and Terror*, became a best seller in 2005, especially after President George W. Bush's kind words endorsing our vision.

But most politicians treated these stories as history, irrelevant to the world's fresh challenges. As Ariel Sharon once said, "Your theories are good for the dungeons of the KGB, not the sands of the Middle East." Less colorfully, in different accents, and using all sorts of reasons, most Western leaders echoed him.

OSLO'S MORAL FAILURE

I have always recognized that controlling the lives of millions of Palestinians is very bad for Israel. The sooner we can let go, the better. But Israel cannot commit suicide. I regret every act of violence, every human rights violation, every day Palestinians lack full democratic rights, and every day our young people are forced as soldiers to protect us by imposing on our neighbors.

Checkpoints are heartbreaking. I don't want soldiers searching or Palestinians being searched. But I don't want locks on doors, burglar alarms, and police in my neighborhood either. Our job as leaders and as human rights advocates is to cope with reality, no matter how ugly, while searching for just and lasting solutions.

From my first weeks in Israel in 1986, I kept saying I wanted the Palestinians to have all the rights I had, individually and collectively, as long as they could not use those rights to destroy us. We Israelis can find security in two ways. Our army can continue guaranteeing our safety from our enemies. Or Palestinians, by developing civil society, can diminish the threat coming from their side. That's why I believe that the real peace process, the true path to peace, requires the emergence of a democratic society, and that is why I criticized the Oslo Accords of the 1990s from the time they were first announced.

The Israeli motivation at Oslo—to give as many Palestinians as possible as much control over their daily lives as possible, as quickly as possible— was admirable. But the method that Israel chose was reckless, shortsighted, and stupid. Imposing Yasir Arafat on Palestinians meant installing a terrorist as dictator. Supplying Arafat with twenty thousand guns and more so he could be strong, and paying him tens of millions of dollars monthly so he could be our dictator, with the hope that he would bring us peace, contradicted everything I had learned about the nature of dictatorships.

My fears that Israel was trusting a corrupt, ruthless dictator to provide us with the security we needed was confirmed when Yitzhak Rabin admitted, shortly after the September 13, 1993, signing ceremony, "When the Palestinians ... are responsible for taking care of their own internal problems, they'll handle them without a Supreme Court, without [the Israeli human-rights organization] B'Tselem, and without all kinds of bleeding-heart liberals."

Responding to Rabin's words, I published a *Jerusalem Report* column that October, rejecting his main illusion. Called "The Kind of Neighbors We Need," the article warned that we can't have it both ways. Empowering Arafat as "our dictator" to crush Hamas and other enemies of peace would come back to haunt us. I was particularly alarmed by Foreign Minister Shimon Peres's claim that terrorism "won't be our problem. . . . The PLO [Palestine Liberation Organization] will handle it far better than we ever could." That was as delusional as it was dangerous.

The "society which would emerge as a result will have nothing in common with the rosy picture of a Switzerland in the Middle East," I insisted. "Arafat, after all, isn't a mercenary who will come and then go; the society which will emerge from fighting 'without a Supreme Court, B'Tselem, and bleeding-heart liberals' will inevitably be based on fear, and on unlimited totalitarian authority." As a dictator, Arafat would need us as an enemy and would guarantee that the next generation of Palestinians would hate us more.

Underlying my fears of what was emerging was a different vision of what true peace would look like. "We must try to ensure the building of real democratic institutions in the fledgling Palestinian society, no matter how tempting a 'solution'" without such institutions might be, I wrote.

The peace-now Left was euphoric about Oslo. The security-first Right was despondent. But neither side accepted my logic. To the Oslo believers, any linkage with democracy sounded like a pretext, a delaying tactic to avoid making peace. To the Oslo deniers, making substantial ideological, political, or territorial concessions for such abstract principles seemed absurd.

That's why, in each of the four governments in which I served, I felt alone when it came to Palestinian issues. The conflict wasn't about political ideology or party politics. This question of what kind of society we should make peace with entered a dimension far beyond squabbles over specific clauses of any peace treaty. Nevertheless, in Israel's political universe, I was branded a right-winger.

I admit, I had excellent credentials to fit the stereotype of a typical, even extreme, right-winger:

- I criticized the Oslo peace process as soon as it was announced in 1993, protesting that the Palestinians were put at the mercy of a corrupt dictator, Yasir Arafat.

- I resigned from Ehud Barak's government in 2000 to oppose his sweeping concessions to the dictators Yasir Arafat and Hafez al-Assad in Syria, which included sacrificing Jerusalem for a peace that was not going to come.

- I resigned from Ariel Sharon's government in 2005 to challenge the unilateral disengagement from Gaza, which was destined to bring rocket fire to our homes.

These seemingly right-wing positions made me unpopular with many Israeli and American opinion makers, including many of my natural allies, the liberals who had fought with me against Soviet totalitarianism.

I didn't take the attacks personally, not the false accusations, the personal insults, or the occasional lost friendships. Nor the media hit jobs: "Betrayer of Peace! . . . Obstructionist . . . intellectually and politically dishonest. . . . Something happened on the way from Anatoly to Natan"—all that just in one *New York Times* article. As long as I followed my principles, it was easy to laugh off most attacks. After years as a dissident, I felt comfortable becoming the democracy outlaw, especially on the peace-and-freedom issue.

It sometimes seemed as if Westerners just enjoyed being duped by certain magic words: "equality," "social justice," and especially "peace." The Soviet Union was particularly skilled at cynically using peace as a club to bully Western democracies into silence, despite Communist repression and aggression. "You speak of human rights," Soviet propagandists would say. "Isn't the right to live in peace the highest human right?" Their World Peace Councils and other Communist fronts against the supposedly warmongering West essentially said, "Don't rock the boat, don't you dare challenge our regime, or it will threaten the peace."

The appeal of peace talks grew during the 1960s, despite Soviet aggression. The Vietnam War era taught baby boomers to make love not war. Chanting, "All we are saying, is give peace a chance," they considered "peace now" the highest value, to be achieved as soon as possible, at almost any price.

We dissidents tried exposing the Soviet ploy, insisting that the free world did not value peace at any price, but a free life under peaceful conditions. That was history's lesson from the American Revolution and World War II. By contrast, in the Middle East, dictators and terrorists were replaying the Soviet swindle. They called for peace to get concessions to help dictators wage war against democracies.

Shifts sometimes take time. I trust that, eventually, the world will realize that cultivating civil society is the necessary condition for a lasting peace. But it was upsetting to see how hard it was to cut through the slurs and engage politicians in any discussions about my vision for peace and its underlying principles.

In all my articles criticizing Oslo and in my two letters of resignation, I kept expressing my faith in liberalism and human rights for Arabs and Jews. Most of my dark warnings, which I desperately hoped would not turn out to be true, proved to be accurate. I said these steps would hurt us as well as the Palestinians, and we saw a loss of life on both sides and a loss of rights on theirs, thanks to their own leaders' power grab. That nightmare became their reality—and our reality—sometimes within a few years, sometimes with a few months, sometimes within days.

I was trained in the world of physics to check your theories by experimentation. If your prediction proved true, your theory was confirmed, at least partially. You then identified what aspect of reality your idea captured. But if the experiment yielded results contradicting your theory, it was time to find a new theory. The true believers in peace above all never seemed ready to accept that the theory was flawed from the beginning.

Ten years after the Oslo agreement, I showed my new spokesperson, Iris Goldman, the first article I wrote objecting to the accords. "This is exactly what happened, and this is still what you're saying now," Iris said, surprised. A seasoned radio journalist, she had joined our staff despite her skepticism about my approach. Iris now regretted the missed opportunities for a real democratic peace. At the time, we were at the height of what the Palestinians called the Second Intifada. Cries to kill Jews were ringing in Palestinian ears daily, as Palestinian suicide bombers blew up Israeli buses and cafés regularly. With a mischievous look in her eye, Iris proposed, "Let's send it to some journalists who were pro-Oslo then and get their reactions today." She also had my old article republished in the *Jerusalem Post*.

Most of the reporters ignored her. In today's quickly changing world, no one cares what happened ten weeks ago, let alone about something written ten years ago.

When Nahum Barnea, the veteran columnist of Israel's popular daily, *Yedioth Ahronoth*, came to interview me shortly thereafter, Iris asked him about the article. "OK, OK, I get it," Barnea said. "You want me to say you were right. But your way keeps the occupation going. I prefer to be wrong but to oppose this awful inhuman occupation committing war crimes."

What was Barnea saying? What did his answer imply? Essentially, he was saying, "I feel good for being against 'occupation,' regardless of the facts." This pie-in-the-sky approach to Oslo reflected a self-righteous surrender. Rather than testing if the moral pose fit the facts, it dismissed any evidence that might undermine the moral stand.

Barnea was right. It feels good to applaud Oslo's noble intentions. But what about its consequences? Who pleaded guilty for imposing Arafat's corrupt dictatorship on Palestinians, as he crushed any early stirrings of Palestinian civil society? Who took responsibility for Israel's kicking back as much as $30 million every month of Palestinian tax funds into Arafat's personal bank accounts, dictated by formal international agreement, as his payoff for being our dictator?

The whole scheme backfired. Palestinians hated Arafat's repressive kleptocracy. A beleaguered majority started hoping Hamas might be better. So not only did Arafat fail to confront Hamas, his abuses strengthened it. Most Palestinians also started hating us more and more, with more incitement and more alienation between Israelis and their neighbors post-Oslo. Tragically, one thousand Israelis and three thousand Palestinians died post-Oslo.

Rereading the article I wrote when Oslo was signed, I realized I had pulled my punches because I was predicting the future. If I had been writing ten years later, I would have used harsher language.

If there is one real crime the Israeli government has committed against the Palestinians, it's the Oslo Accords. Those agreements imposed Arafat's terrorist dictatorship on the Palestinians, instead of cultivating the more grassroots democratic leadership that was sprouting in the 1990s—and it was done with the free world's enthusiastic endorsement.

JIMMY CARTER'S PIE-IN-THE-SKY PEACEMAKING

I first saw this unrealistic style of peacemaking during my first meeting with President Jimmy Carter, a few years after my release. I began by thanking him for speaking up so quickly after my arrest. He had broken the presidential tradition of never commenting on Soviet allegations to confirm that I was not an American spy.

Before I knew it, Carter started lecturing me about the importance of making peace in the Middle East by withdrawing from all the "occupied territories" immediately.

I replied that it was hard to trust the dictators surrounding us. I reminded him that he put human rights in the center of American foreign policy. "These dictators don't believe in human rights," I said.

"You know, you're right," the Arab world needs democracy, Carter acknowledged, "but don't try to be too rational about these things. The moment you see people suffering, you should feel solidarity with them and try to help them without thinking too much about the reasons."

To convince me, Carter mentioned "one of the few close personal friends" he had made among all the world leaders he had met, Syria's Hafez al-Assad. "It's true, Assad is a dictator," he admitted. "But you can rely on him. He never lied to me. If you sign an agreement, he'll keep it."

Carter recalled visiting Syria as president and confronting Assad about violating "one of his obligations on a security-related issue." Assad denied it. Carter complained to his aides about how "disappointed" he was, "because Assad never lied to me before. But on the way to the airport," Carter told me with great satisfaction, "Assad called to apologize. He told me he had checked the point I raised and that he had been mistaken. He promised to correct the problem. So you see, he never lies. If he signs an agreement with Israel, he'll keep it."

What I saw was something different: like the good dictator he was, Assad had probably bugged Carter's rooms. After eavesdropping on the president's anger, Assad rushed to undo the damage. He assumed Carter would be easily manipulated. He was right.

Carter's advice to "go with your heart, just give back the territory" backfired with me. A seemingly moral position that obviously strengthens evil only *feels* moral. It's not. Similarly, when leaders go with their hearts so much that it overrides their brains, they are acting irresponsibly. Carter was saying that once you decide what the moral position should be, you're not responsible for what happens. I call that dodging responsibility, which is an immoral position, especially for a leader.

Had Israel trusted Assad—or trusted Carter's faith in Assad—we would now face an enemy with no qualms about using chemical weapons against his own people looming over our Sea of Galilee, our citizens in the north, from the strategic Golan Heights.

THE DISSIDENTS' THREE BASIC QUESTIONS

Admittedly, my constant nagging "I told you so" about the peace process's failure doesn't prove that my KGB dungeon experience applies to the Middle East. I understand that many people are skeptical, doubting that Palestinians need to develop civil society for Middle East peace to take root. Over the years, people keep asking three basic questions about my claim:

- Why do you think that Palestinians are interested in democracy? Who says they want a new kind of politics? Different civilizations and different cultures have differing attitudes toward human rights.

- Even if Palestinians develop civil society, how could it contribute to Israelis' security?

- Finally, how can outsiders like Israel and the West influence this process? You cannot impose democracy from the outside.

In *The Case for Democracy*, Ron Dermer and I distinguished between free societies and fear societies. The dividing line was the town square test: Can you express your individual views loudly, in public, without fear of being punished in any way? If yes, you live in a free society; if not, you're in a fear society. This is a rough distinction. There are different levels of freedom and fear. In some societies, you might be punished at work. Others might jail you. In the worst dictatorships, you could be shot.

Every fear society produces three distinct groups: true believers, doublethinkers, and dissidents. True believers embrace the official ideology. Doublethinkers lose faith in their beliefs but fear the consequences of speaking out in the town square. Dissidents reject the ideology, overcome their fear, and express their views publicly.

There is an inevitable, invisible process as natural as entropy: people drift constantly and chaotically from true belief to doublethink, from buying in to turning off. The ranks of the doublethinkers swell as the regime's restrictions irritate, intimidate, and alienate. At the loud, colorful parades expressing solidarity with the great leader, true believers and doublethinkers are twins: they look alike but no longer think alike.

THE FIRST QUESTION:
DOES EVERYONE WANT FREEDOM FROM FEAR?

Year after year, Israelis see Palestinians celebrating one vicious terrorist attack after another. This offers dramatic proof that they are our enemies who want our destruction. At the same time, year after year, Israelis see long lines of Palestinians slowly going through checkpoints. This offers equally dramatic proof that they are victims suffering under the burdens of occupation.

Like many others, I see both realities. In addition, I see on their faces and hear in their voices something else that goes beyond enemies or victims: fear and doublethink.

During my involvement with the Moscow Helsinki Group, I met all kinds of people fighting for different national and religious causes. But, for all their differing agendas, they shared one thing in common. The first barrier facing them was overcoming fear and freeing themselves from the shackles of doublethink.

I believe everyone, including Palestinians, wants to live without that fear. If there is one law of human nature I have learned over the years, it's this: the phenomenon of doublethink is universal, and the fear that prevents a doublethinker from crossing over into dissent, and the desire to be free of that fear, is cross-cultural. No one wants to live with the sick feeling in the doublethinker's stomach day after day, the fear of exposure as someone who is no longer a true believer. These conclusions are not only from my experience and from my dissident friends' experiences behind the Iron Curtain. Dozens of dissidents I have met from around the world underwent similar processes. Nearly every testimony I have ever read about life under a dictatorship describes coping with fear, doublethinking, and weighing whether to dissent.

Take any of these books off the bookshelf. It could be Nien Cheng describing the Chinese Communist Cultural Revolution of the 1960s in *Life and Death in Shanghai*. It could be Jacobo Timerman describing the Argentinian military dictatorship of the 1970s in *Prisoner Without a Name, Cell Without a Number*. It could be Azar Nafisi describing today's Iranian mullahocracy in *Reading Lolita in Tehran*.

The leaders of the Arab Spring also spoke about the fear they all lived with and were fed up with. In *Voices of the Arab Spring: Personal Stories from the Arab Revolutions* (edited by Asaad Alsaleh), a forty-five-year-old hematologist from Benghazi, Aisha A. Nasef, writes, "It is an indescribable feeling to be free from fear, to be able to express yourself openly against Qaddafi and his regime, in daylight, and in front of everyone!" Abduljalil Yousef, a twenty-eight-year-old teacher from Sanaa, writes, "Now life is not what it used to be—there is no fear, no despair, no submission or surrender. It seems as if the people of Yemen suddenly were resurrected and saw the truth."

Perhaps most movingly, Adel Abdel Ghafar, a thirty-two-year-old activist from Cairo, explains that "revolutions are not hatched in smoke-filled rooms or by activists armed with Twitter and Facebook accounts; rather, revolutions are made by everyday people who are no longer afraid." Recalling a confrontation with riot police, who then turned and ran from protesters, he writes, "We all knew that something profound had just taken place. There was a raised collective consciousness among us. A realization. An epiphany. Simply that we will no longer be afraid. . . . In that moment, the Mubarak regime had lost its most significant weapon: fear. Eighteen days later, the tyrant stepped down." This was the precise "moment the barrier of fear broke down."

It's eerie. Abdel Ghafar's minute-by-minute description of how the gathering of Egyptian doublethinkers at Tahrir Square turned into a revolution echoes many descriptions and video clips of similar pivots in East Germany, Hungary, Romania, the Soviet Union. The freedom tsunami hit Hong Kong in 2019. "People are injured by rubber bullets, tear gas, pepper spray. It happens a lot," Chan, a twenty-one-year-old student, told *Vox*. "But I would say that people are getting braver and braver." The protesters' boldness was making Chan and other organizers "more worried about the situation, because they're not scared anymore. . . . People are doing stuff that's actually changing the whole situation, because they're not scared."

The wave of fearlessness starts with individuals, then spreads to dozens, then thousands of people crossing that line from doublethinker to dissident. Once it starts cascading, it becomes a revolution. At the same time, a great transfer of dread occurs. As citizens get bolder and lose their fear, police and security officials turn timid and inherit it.

Piling up various memoirs and photographs and eyewitness testimonials from different countries and cultures reveals something profoundly human. All the differences in mentalities, traditions, and social structures cannot stop this universal process. If Leo Tolstoy in *Anna Karenina* said, "All happy families are alike; each unhappy family is unhappy in its own way," we can flip it around for freedom's sake: "Oppressive dictatorships all look different, but each dies in the same way."

True, the Arab Spring didn't bring democracy—yet. Democratic revolutions, whether in the Middle East or Eastern Europe or anywhere else, even if followed by elections, don't guarantee democracy. If you don't hold free elections in a free society, you don't have democracy. And building a free society often takes time. Even the mother of modern liberal European revolutions, the French Revolution, was followed by decades of dictatorship and bloodshed until a free, stable France emerged.

The Arab Spring proved that Middle East dictatorships are as unpopular with their people as Latin American and Eastern European dictatorships were with theirs. History repeated itself in late 2010. The rebellions throughout the Arab world essentially proved what should have been learned from Communism's collapse: trust the democratic dissidents, not the Western don't-rock-the-boaters. Brave voices in Egypt and Syria—who should be listened to more carefully—declared their respective state regimes doomed, even as Western leaders continued describing dictators like Hosni Mubarak and Bashar al-Assad as stable and reliable peace partners.

The Palestinians living under the Palestinian Authority (PA) hated their oppressive regime too. When I served in Ehud Barak's cabinet, Shimon Peres asked me to stop calling Yasir Arafat a corrupt dictator.

"Isn't he?" I asked.

"Of course he is," Peres replied. "But he is the Palestinians' leader. When you try negotiating for peace, it doesn't make sense to insult the party on the other side. And you are insulting them because they love their leader."

"They love Arafat no more than the Russians liked Stalin at the height of the purges," I replied. Our conversation ended abruptly.

Democratic leaders in Europe and America constantly talk about how merciless dictators are loved by their people. We all heard how Saddam Hussein of Iraq, Hosni Mubarak of Egypt, and Hafez and Bashar al-Assad of Syria were loved by their people. Most recently, President Donald Trump declared that the brutal Kim Jong Un of North Korea "loves his country very much," and that North Koreans love him in return, supporting him with "great fervor." When democratic leaders try making peace with dictatorships, they try to feel less guilty by convincing themselves that at least the people love their dictator.

THE SECOND QUESTION:
WHY DOES IT MATTER WHO OUR NEIGHBORS ARE?

Even if emotional scenes from Tahrir Square or Hong Kong inspire skeptics, next they say: "OK, it's lovely. These people deserve to live in freedom. But how does it advance our security and stability? Do you really believe that we're better off with freer regimes that hate us than with dictators who might love us?"

Dissidents usually constitute a small minority. But the authorities understand that if conditions shift, and it becomes easy for the masses to move from doublethinking to dissent, revolution follows. That's why dictatorships are obsessed with constantly stoking an atmosphere of suppression. Autocrats must keep intimidating the doublethinkers they cannot see but know are there, to stop them from becoming dissidents.

Totalitarian regimes have two main weapons for suppressing their subjects and maintaining their grip on power. A security apparatus, unleashed against the people, hunts down independent thinking. And a well-chosen enemy, real or imagined, keeps the country permanently mobilized.

The dictator's dual weapons of repression and aggression are like the scissors' two blades: sharpening one another and cutting down anyone in the way. Like all bullies, dictators are aggressive because of their inner weakness. But that's what makes it so hard for doublethinkers to cross the line to dissent. When your society is on red alert against enemies, dissenting not only jeopardizes the life you know, it forces you to defy an inflamed public opinion. You risk being called a traitor to the nation, not just the regime.

From the October Revolution onward, the Soviet Union tried making all its people completely dependent on the regime. By confiscating all property, becoming the only way for people to get paid, and liquidating the independence of all organizations and institutions from factories to trade unions, the Soviets reduced almost everyone economically to serfs. By crushing any political independence and wiping out opposition, they reduced everyone politically to pawns.

Soviet society was permanently mobilized for a never-ending ideological class war, a global Communist revolution. Whether there would be a full military conflict depended on changing interests and calculations of strengths. But in such a red-alert world, anyone could switch into total war mode immediately.

From the moment Israelis and the West propped up Arafat as the Palestinian Authority's leader, he used whatever tools he had to control his people. He couldn't hermetically seal Palestinian borders, as the Soviets did, but he did his best. He declared war on the Palestinian civil society that had started developing before he arrived. He closed down or harassed any independent newspapers, turning the Palestinian media into his mouthpiece and a constant source of incitement against Israel. He squeezed any businesspeople who tried operating outside his orbit. Rather than improve living conditions, he kept many Palestinians living in misery in refugee camps, stoking their resentment of Israel.

Arafat centralized control over Palestinian lives, economically, culturally, and politically. He kept his people mobilized for war, just like the Soviets. And he lied like the Soviets too. While speaking in English to Bill Clinton and the rest of the West, he talked peace. But when he spoke in Arabic to his people, he talked about total war against the Zionist enemy.

Arafat created an educational system that taught three-year-olds to kill Jews, a corrupt economic system that ran protection rackets to boost the PA's cronies, and a military intelligence machine with a dual purpose: to quash the Palestinian people while attacking Israel whenever convenient.

As minister of industry and trade, although it wasn't part of my job, I considered it my obligation to do whatever possible to encourage more jobs for Palestinians. But most of my proposals about joint ventures, which could create more opportunity for Palestinian businesspeople and more jobs for workers, were rejected. The Palestinian leaders blocked anything that risked making their people less dependent on the PA.

The Palestinian Authority wanted everything flowing through Arafat's representatives, who insisted on being the ones to dole out the jobs. Like good racketeers, they demanded a kickback from every Palestinian worker. It wasn't about delivering goods to consumers or providing quality jobs to workers. It was about making the jobs dependent on the authorities, who distributed the goodies to those they wanted to favor.

The PA's minister of planning, Nabil Sha'ath, was my Palestinian negotiating partner. He didn't seem interested in any initiative I championed. I only piqued his interest when I proposed some software ventures. I soon learned that his family monopolized the Palestinian software business.

A big project I inherited from the previous government was building a joint industrial zone on the Gaza border, what became the Karni Industrial Zone. We Israelis planned on creating twenty thousand jobs for Palestinians. All the businesspeople agreed that the zone should be in Israeli territory, near Nahal Oz, to guarantee investors' and managers' safety. Israel would provide the land and the security, and the Palestinians would provide the administration and the workers.

The Palestinian side erupted. They insisted on building the zone on their side of the Gaza border. We gave in and invested much money and expertise to develop a first-class industrial zone. Israeli business leaders were particularly enthusiastic, hoping to make money while making peace. But the PA wasn't interested in thriving independent businesses generating well-paid jobs for Palestinians. Arafat sought to control the factories and the workers' salaries to keep his people reliant on him and his henchmen.

When tensions erupted in 2000 and Palestinian terrorism resumed, our fears came true. Karni became an easy terrorist target. The businesses dried up. Five years later, shortly after Israel disengaged from Gaza, Palestinian mobs torched the factories. Millions of dollars from Israelis, Western investors, the World Bank, and other institutions went up in smoke, proving that the PA preferred fighting the Zionist enemy over improving Palestinians' quality of life.

Obviously, democratically elected leaders cannot behave this way. It's true that leaders in a democracy and a dictatorship share the same goal, to stay in power. The difference is in how they do it. In a developed civil society with free democratic elections, the leaders depend on the people's good graces. To stay in power, they must deliver the goods. That's why peace and prosperity are not mere slogans in democracies, but the keys to elected leaders' political survival. Dictators don't depend on their people; they make their people dependent on them. Peace reduces the pressure they can use to keep citizens in line, while prosperity has to come from Big Brother, not earned independently by citizens. That's why we cannot depend on leaders who do not depend on their people.

Does this mean that democracies can never work with dictators? Of course not. Democracies have recognized dictatorships, cooperated with dictators, and even made military pacts with them. Winston Churchill and Franklin Roosevelt allied with Joseph Stalin during World War II. Churchill and FDR understood it as a tactical alliance against the greater Nazi threat, with no illusions of true friendship. Predictably, just as Stalin had flipped from despising America and England to accepting them as allies in 1941, when Nazi Germany collapsed in 1945 he switched from ally to enemy overnight.

Today, Israel coordinates counterterrorism efforts with Egypt. But the arrangement is tactical and should come with a warning label, like cigarettes. We need each other to fight jihadist Islamism in Sinai and Hamas in Gaza. But Abdel Fattah el-Sisi is a cruel dictator who imprisons dissidents and rules through fear, like all totalitarians. Inevitably, he, too, will be more and more hated by his own people.

Israel should be prepared. True, our peace agreement with Egypt has outlived Anwar Sadat and Hosni Mubarak. But, one day, Sisi may flip abruptly and make us the enemy. It will be particularly easy because Egypt has maintained its decades-long standing as one of the world's leading centers of Jew-hatred. Or, the Egyptian people may overthrow Sisi, just as they deposed Mubarak. If that day comes, we don't want to be Sisi's defenders against the Egyptian people's anger.

Any agreement with Palestinians has much higher stakes because we're so much closer geographically. The more interdependent two countries are, the more each nation's internal dynamics affect the other. The dictator's need to mobilize against an enemy explains why, when a fear society lives next door, beware!

THE THIRD QUESTION: DOES THE FREE WORLD
HAVE A ROLE IN PROMOTING DEMOCRACY?

"*Nu*, OK," my interlocutors keep arguing. "Let's say I agree that Palestinians seek the stability of civil society. And I agree that such progress could improve our security. There's still a problem. They don't want Israel or the West interfering in their internal affairs. How can outsiders affect a country's internal governance?"

Democracies enjoy more leverage over dictatorships than they think, because dictatorships always need to be propped up from without. True, dictators need external enemies to justify their tyranny. But, like true parasites, as they decay, they need to feed off the prosperity of others, which usually means relying on functioning democracies.

Three overlapping ailments deplete these regimes:

- When you reduce your workers to serfs, your economy loses its creativity and then its productivity.

- When you treat your citizens as pawns, you spend more and more money to control the ever-growing number of doublethinkers.

- When you keep your society on a constant war footing against external enemies, your military agenda trumps everything else.

As these maladies spread, dictators' survival instincts look outward. Suddenly, the same country that is useful as an enemy is also necessary as a trade partner. That offers a pressure point clever democratic leaders can exploit to limit the repression and encourage civil society in undemocratic countries.

The Soviet Union was a huge empire with seemingly unlimited resources. It had oil, coal, the best soil for wheat in the world, a huge market, and a cheap labor force. It looked intimidating from afar, with a vast Red Army, ballistic missiles, the KGB, those impressive victory parades, and an aggressive Communist ideology that seemed to mobilize everyone. From within, we knew it was unproductive, corrupt, and teetering. We knew how much it wasted controlling its people.

By the late 1950s, the Soviet leaders were caught. They wanted to continue struggling ideologically with the imperialist world while cooperating economically with its capitalists. They started posturing, claiming that trade and good relations were keys to the new struggle for world peace. Yet, while talking peace, Soviets sent missiles to Cuba, tanks to Budapest and Prague, and soldiers to Angola and Afghanistan.

Through the policy of linkage in the 1970s, some Western visionaries exposed this hypocrisy, making all cooperation with the Soviet Union conditional. The Jackson-Vanik amendment and the Helsinki Accords proved that democracies have tools against totalitarianism that can work. The Soviet Union had to modify its rhetoric from supporting world revolution to supporting peaceful coexistence. Then, it had to find opportunities to showcase its new, more humane approach. Practically, it had to give citizens more freedom while behaving less brutally on the world stage. Spiraling downward, each reform reflected the regime's increasing weakness, then further weakened it until it collapsed.

Logically, the free world should have had a much easier time imposing conditions on the Palestinian Authority. In accepting that the leaders of the Palestine Liberation Organization would form the PA, Israel gave the PA legitimacy, international recognition, power, and buckets of money. The United States armed and trained Arafat's security forces. Yet the West never used the pressure points it created. Initially, the free world could have recognized Arafat's guerilla group, the PLO, as the Palestinians' official representative only after it recognized Israel's right to exist as a Jewish state in peace. Why didn't the PLO have to delete its call to destroy Israel in its charter and change its rhetoric, even when Arafat spoke in Arabic? Why didn't all the international aid go directly to initiatives improving Palestinians' living conditions and nurturing civil society, rather than lining their leaders' pockets? Why didn't the education system Westerners helped develop educate toward democracy, not terrorism?

It's beyond frustrating—it's downright criminal—that the free world had all this leverage and never used it. Instead, from the moment Israel and the free world installed Arafat, he became untouchable, because the courtiers of public opinion orthodoxy decided the alternative was worse.

And that is why Western leaders kept silent as Arafat spoke of peace to the West but talked jihad against the Zionists to the East. On May 10, 1994, just months after signing the Oslo Accords, Arafat, speaking in a mosque in Johannesburg, admitted that holy war "will continue." It's not "the permanent State of Israel! No! It is the permanent State of

Palestine," he scoffed. "You have to come and to fight and to start the Jihad to liberate Jerusalem."

Nearly two years later, on January 30, 1996, Arafat met secretly with Arab diplomats in the Grand Hotel in Stockholm. Aided by Arafat's Palestinian Authority, Hamas had launched a series of suicide bombs. "We Palestinians will take over everything, including all of Jerusalem," Arafat promised the diplomats. He added, "We of the PLO will now concentrate all our efforts on splitting Israel psychologically into two camps," with the clear aim "to eliminate the State of Israel and establish a purely Palestinian State."

CLINTON AT WYE

A typical example illustrating how the West coddled Arafat, protecting him from constructive pressure, occurred in October 1998. I was part of the Israeli team at the three-way Wye River negotiations with the Palestinians and the Americans. On the Saturday before the negotiations began, I was sitting with Prime Minister Benjamin Netanyahu when President Bill Clinton dropped by to visit. Bibi invited me to explain my vision of democracy to Clinton.

The Arkansas-born Clinton is a real southern charmer. He zooms in on you, staring into your eyes, smiling, nodding, mentioning your name, quoting part of what you said back at you word for word. He makes you feel that what you have to say is the most important thing in the world to him. But although he may be the world's greatest listener, he doesn't necessarily pay attention to what you said. He's the great appeaser. He makes you feel heard, then continues doing whatever he planned on doing.

On this relaxed Shabbat afternoon, I had time to explain my theory to the president about how dictatorship works and how the free world could influence the Palestinians to build civil society as the essential precondition to peace. I emphasized how important it was to stop Arafat's double-talk, saying that Arafat must proclaim clearly to his people in Arabic that the PA is changing its charter and recognizing Israel. It was tragic that, five years after Israel recognized Arafat and the PLO upon signing the Oslo Accords, Arafat and the PLO had not yet recognized Israel's basic right to exist. What should have been the first Palestinian step in the peace process was still being treated as some kind of maximalist Israeli demand.

After we spoke for an hour, President Clinton agreed to push Arafat on this first step. Encouraged by Clinton's promise, the Israeli delegation listed that demand first in the negotiations. Clinton pressured Arafat, who agreed to change the charter and recognize Israel to his own people if Clinton made a formal visit to Gaza. As I left the negotiating room, I passed the assistant to the president for national security affairs, Sandy Berger. I told him, "You see, Arafat agreed to change the charter. Now you have to make sure this happens."

Instead of congratulating me, Berger was furious. Turning abruptly, he chased me down the corridor, frantically accusing us Israelis of having "put a gun to Arafat's head." Berger vowed that he would convince Arafat not to go through with it, because it would weaken him against his radical Islamist terrorist rival, Hamas. Then, Berger scurried off to convince Clinton that the United States needed to protect Arafat.

The result was a fiasco. Arafat eventually got his presidential visit. Six weeks after the frustrating Wye negotiations, in December 1998, Clinton made an official visit to Gaza. Five years too late, the Palestinian National Council voted to eliminate the clauses in its charter vowing to destroy Israel—sort of. In what the *Chicago Tribune* called a "masterpiece in constructive obfuscation," Arafat spoke to the Palestinian National Council about changing the charter. When his forty-five-minute speech ended, as applause broke out and many were distracted, hands were raised to appear like the delegates were approving the change. In the confusion, Arafat found a way to deny anything significant occurred while giving the Americans something to celebrate. But we in the Israeli government were not fooled. His public statements were insultingly vague. His forked-tongue deception continued.

Sandy Berger's hysteria confirmed my fears that the free world would not press Arafat to keep any other commitments. Arafat's argument—"If I am forced to fulfill the obligations, that will weaken me and I will be defeated by Hamas"—always shut down the Americans.

Years later, Berger publicly confessed, "I was wrong!" So did some other Clinton administration officials. "There needed to be mutual recognition; that was not in the original Oslo," Berger admitted. "There needed to be a renunciation of terrorism from Arafat; that wasn't in the original."

Critiquing the Americans' strategy, Berger recalled in an oral history, "I've often said that sadly, the Palestinians did not have a Nelson

Mandela at the moment in history when they needed somebody who could pivot from being a revolutionary and the leader of a movement to being a statesman and the leader of a country. Arafat was simply not capable of doing that."

Like many others in the free world, Berger continued to believe that all we had needed was the right personality in the right place: Mandela versus Arafat. It's easier to reduce complicated policy matters to personalities than to implement the right strategy instead of the wrong one.

TRUST A PALESTINIAN DISSIDENT

I understand that no one unifying theory can navigate all of life's complexities. The peace process is not some exercise in physics or mathematical logic. But I remain frustrated. Few politicians were willing to debate these ideas, let alone experiment with implementing them. They couldn't bypass the big, thick wall of resistance, built by groupthink from nearly every security, intelligence, and diplomatic expert. That wall still stands.

No one should rely on outsiders, like me or any Israeli, to say what Palestinians think or want. But no one should listen to Palestinian dictators either. Those of us committed to peace and democracy should listen to our true allies, those insider-outsiders, the dissidents, the brave Palestinians who have fled from doublethink without fleeing their homeland.

The model Palestinian dissident is Bassem Eid, the human rights activist and my friend for the last twenty years. Bassem is warm and ironic and brave. He defied the Palestinian Security Services and the West's conventional wisdom by criticizing Arafat when he was alive. Today, he criticizes Mahmoud Abbas, also known as Abu Mazen, publicly at home.

Back in 1995, shortly after the Americans and the Israelis had installed Yasir Arafat, Bassem started telling the inconvenient truth. At the time a senior researcher for the Israeli human rights monitoring group B'Tselem, Bassem could already detail the PA's "extra-judicial punishment, abduction of residents, illegal arrests, prolonged detention without any judicial scrutiny, refusal to allow legal representation, refusal to allow regular family visits, and use of torture techniques such as beatings, painful tying-up, threats, humiliation, sleep deprivation, and withholding of medical treatment."

Bassem noticed an interesting pattern. When he catalogued Israeli human rights violations for B'Tselem, he was popular: international organizations embraced every report. But when he started monitoring the PA's human rights violations, many foreign friends abandoned him.

Bassem sinned by undermining the Palestinian leaders who, the experts had decided, would make peace with Israel. His testimony showed that the PA controlled through fear. Without minimizing the complex, painful clashes between the Israeli army and the Palestinians, he violated the usual storytelling in another way. In the world Oslo created—and especially following Israel's Gaza disengagement in 2005—90 percent of Palestinians live under day-to-day Palestinian control. That limited Israeli soldiers' interactions with Palestinians, meaning that the regime squeezing Palestinians most directly was the PA, and later the Hamas dictatorship that emerged in Gaza.

Following the Olso Accords, Israel's army withdrew from most Palestinian cities. That move allowed the Palestinians to be as autonomous as possible. The rise of Palestinian terrorism in the early 2000s forced Israel to reimpose some restrictions, mostly city-to-city checkpoints and occasional raids within the towns. But it is the Palestinians' own leaders who have tried controlling the Palestinian mind and soul. Palestinians who live under Israel's full military rule have the freedom to criticize Israel harshly, even celebrating terrorists who murder Jewish children. It's in the Palestinian public squares where Palestinians must doublethink and support a regime they detest, even if it's deemed their own.

By 2003, after nearly three years of watching Arafat spur Palestinians to become suicide bombers, Bassem was even more distressed. "Instead of talking about peace and life, instead of supporting coexistence, instead of fulfilling the consciousness of human beings, Arafat is calling for death," Bassem mourned. "It appears the nearly 2,500 Palestinians and more than 700 Israelis who were killed during this intifada are not enough to fulfill Arafat's political interests."

It's remarkable. Bassem's words parallel so many other dissidents' words about the dictator's need to lead through fear and prop up the regime by targeting the ideal enemy.

Bassem and I have become close over the years, participating in various conferences and writing some articles together. Occasionally, I have also tried to help him secure funding for some of his democracy-building initiatives. When he started a modest program teaching democracy in some Palestinian schools, the European Union governments were investing in programs building Palestinian civil society. A representative of the

Italian government told me how much he respected dissidents for the role they play as reformers. I proposed that his government fund Bassem's program.

"It's a very good idea," the diplomat replied. "But what is Mr. Eid's relationship with Abu Mazen?"

"I don't know exactly," I answered, knowing Bassem was about to lose the funding. "But I can't imagine that the relationship is very warm. Eid is a dissident who criticizes the PA dictatorship."

"Well then," he said. "It will be a problem. The EU has decided only to support projects Abu Mazen supports, in order not to weaken him."

Asking for permission from Abu Mazen before funding democracy projects like Eid's would have been like the West refusing to cooperate with Andrei Sakharov without Leonid Brezhnev's approval.

More recently, Bassem has turned his sights on the brutal rule Hamas imposes in Gaza. "The people who died in Gaza were sacrificed by their own leadership: Hamas," he proclaimed publicly in 2015. "The one who imposed three wars on Gaza was Hamas. In every country the governments use their missiles and rockets to protect its people but Hamas was doing the opposite, using its people to protect its missiles and rockets."

Bassem says, "I don't care if I'm called a traitor," understanding the dictator's faux-patriotic tricks to suppress dissent and demonize opponents. "Any Arab who stands up and criticizes his own leadership is called a traitor for Israel. I am trying to find ways to improve daily life for my people and to ensure a better future."

Every conversation I have with Bassem reinforces my sense that a true liberal cannot worship at the shrine of the dictator. I often think about it when I find myself in the disappointment standoff. "I have to tell you how disappointed we on the Left are with you," a leading Israeli liberal says. "When you came here, you were a liberal champion of human rights. But you betrayed us and the cause of human rights."

"I have to tell you how disappointed I am with you and the Left," I reply. "When I came here, I was joined at the hip with the liberal camp in the fight against dictatorship. Suddenly, I discovered that the first sign of being a good Israeli liberal was loving Arafat, bribing Arafat, defending Arafat, and giving him a free pass to do whatever he wished to his own people. You are the one who betrayed the cause of human rights."

11

DEVASTATED BY THE RABIN ASSASSINATION

On Saturday, November 10, 1997, as soon as the Sabbath ended, I rushed to Tel Aviv. I was going to a painful, public commemoration. It had been two years since Prime Minister Yitzhak Rabin's assassination on November 4, 1995. Tens of thousands would gather at the site where this crime took place, now renamed Kikar Rabin, Rabin Square.

Israel has suffered many tragedies since I arrived in 1986. But this murder of our prime minister by one of our own may have been the worst moment I witnessed, and one of the most dreadful incidents in Israeli history. When I first heard the bad news, I felt our entire Zionist enterprise was crashing.

YITZHAK RABIN, THE FIRST SABRA PRIME MINISTER

I had a warm personal relationship with Rabin, though I never idealized him politically. I first heard "Yitzhak Rabin" as one of those magical, romantic, ever-so-Israeli-sounding names of the 1967 war heroes, like his partner Moshe Dayan. Rabin's name came to us in the song "Nasser Michakeh LeRabin"—Nasser, Egypt's dictator, "awaits Rabin," who was Israel's chief of staff. The song was sarcastic enough to capture our imaginations, and simple enough for our teachers to use in our underground Hebrew classes.

Many of our American Jewish "tourist" friends told us of meeting Rabin when he was Israel's ambassador to the United States from 1968 to 1973. He had charmed many of them, played tennis with some of them, and worked behind the scenes to help free Soviet Jews with most of them. As ambassador, he befriended the Refuseniks' foe, Henry Kissinger, who prioritized détente with the Soviet Union over human rights, and our hero, Senator Henry Jackson, who prioritized human rights, including our freedom of emigration, ahead of the warming diplomatic relationship détente sought.

Following the popular backlash against Golda Meir after the Arab armies surprised Israel on Yom Kippur 1973, Rabin became prime minister. He was the one to approve Israel's heroic hostage rescue in Entebbe. Just as we magically linked Rabin's name after 1967 with Moshe Dayan's, after 1976 we Jews behind the Iron Curtain linked his name with Yoni Netanyahu's—Bibi's brother who fell fighting to free the hijacked Jews in Uganda.

When I arrived in Israel, Rabin was not one of those Johnny-come-lately politicians suddenly interested in Soviet Jewry. He was happy to continue helping, when and if he could be useful—especially if he didn't have to socialize too much. We first met at a formal program, after I had been in Israel for about three months. Characteristically, he went tieless and sockless, wearing those open-toed, "biblical" Israeli sandals.

After that, we met periodically, at official events championing Soviet Jewry and at social events organized by mutual American friends. Unlike most politicians, he was informal, understated, a man of few words. He was happy when catching up with real buddies and unhappy when working the crowds. When he spoke, he was direct, down-to-earth, sometimes abrupt, a real Sabra from Leon Uris's *Exodus*. When our Zionist Forum lobbied for Israel to recognize the Soviet Jewish veterans who had fought during World War II, Rabin, as defense minister, understood. He helped us finance a monument on Mount Herzl.

As I entered politics, I would end up working with—and sometimes criticizing—Rabin and other Zionist heroes. But, overall, no matter how frustrated I might have been at any given time with any of them, I always felt incredibly privileged to be working side by side with these larger-than-life pioneers. I never forgot that people like Rabin, Shimon Peres, Ariel Sharon, Benjamin Netanyahu, and Ehud Barak were building Israel, defending it, and leading it while I was still worrying about my professional career in the Soviet Union, cemented in doublethink, and hesitating about whether to cross the line toward dissent so I could embrace my Jewishness and my freedom.

By December 1987, Rabin's name was mired in controversy. What the Palestinians labeled the First Intifada had begun, with many young riot-ers challenging our soldiers, mostly by throwing stones and lighting fires rather than by shooting guns or blowing up buses. Rabin was defense minister during this first, confusing Palestinian rebellion against Israeli rule. He declared that the IDF would respond with "force, might, and beatings." Soldiers claimed he ordered them to break the protesters' arms and legs.

I was not naive. I knew we were facing serious waves of violence. It was clear to me that stones could kill or maim for life. And I knew that during these ever-escalating confrontations, bones could be broken and brutal force could be used. But that was violence as the consequence of the battle, not at the leader's command. As defense minister, Rabin was not a sergeant speaking to his soldiers in the heat of the battle. He was one of the country's leaders, speaking in our name. His words embar-rassed me.

Rabin later said he didn't remember using that expression. He claimed that, at worst, he may have been using army slang to say, "Don't shoot, but subdue them," and that it was heard incorrectly. But the defense min-ister's words are not heard with subtlety. I knew of soldiers disciplined by the army—some kicked out, others imprisoned—who thought they were acting as Rabin ordered. The mixed messages left them feeling double-crossed.

When he ran for prime minister in 1992, Rabin promised to help new immigrants as an essential part of his Zionist mission. "Aliyah is one arm of my Zionism," he told us once, raising his arm for effect, "and security is the other." By 1993, frustrated that the Labor Party had broken all its promises to assist immigrants, some of us in the Zionist Forum met him after our big broom protest. He tried sounding interested, but he seemed preoccupied. That September, I realized what had happened: Security had trumped immigration. The secret negotiations that culminated in the Oslo agreement had begun.

Rabin never seemed to buy Shimon Peres's utopian illusion of a "new Middle East." In an embarrassingly childlike book by that name pub-lished in November 1993, months after negotiating the Oslo Accords,

Peres predicted that neighboring dictators would suddenly accept Israel's right to exist so they could concentrate on delivering peace and prosperity to their people.

Rabin bought into a different delusion: that Arafat could be "our dictator," only targeting the right enemies, not us. Both visions struck me as simplistic and dangerous.

Although well aware of my critique, Rabin nevertheless invited me to join the delegation to Oslo city hall, where he received the Nobel Peace Prize in December 1994 along with Shimon Peres and Yasir Arafat. I declined politely. Much as I shared the desire for peace, I couldn't toast a process I feared would bring disaster. And I couldn't backslide to my former life of doublethink by joining the civilized world in applauding Arafat, the master terrorist still wearing combat fatigues.

Nevertheless, despite disliking Oslo, I despised the anti-Oslo campaign's harsh rhetoric. The now-infamous posters—with Rabin wrapped in a kaffiyeh, or Rabin's face above an SS uniform—were particularly despicable. In those early days of the Internet, we weren't used to that kind of photoshopping. That made the offensive images even more memorable and unacceptable.

I knew the accusations that Benjamin Netanyahu was behind such imagery were groundless. But neither Bibi nor his Likud Party did enough to denounce such viciousness, or to distance themselves and their political campaign from it. I was discovering that many Israeli politicians, when they've crossed red lines, apologize for overstepping the day after Election Day, having benefitted from the votes their demagoguery attracted.

OUR NATIONAL CATASTROPHE

November 4, 1995, made whatever criticisms I had of Rabin absolutely irrelevant. I confess, I wasn't paying that much attention to the increasingly ugly debate about Oslo. We in the immigrant community were absorbed in building our own political party, which became Yisrael B'Aliyah. Anticipating the elections everyone knew were coming—and would occur in May 1996—we were swept up in the excitement of the new democratic experience of political campaigning. On any given night, we might be brainstorming about slogans, planning strategy, or participating in a seminar about political organizing.

During one of those evening seminars, the telephone rang. The caller shouted, "Turn on the television!" That was how I heard that a fellow Israeli had shot our prime minister. It was a catastrophe. I feared we were sliding into the abyss. Suddenly, our electoral efforts seemed unimportant, all our policy divisions seemed small. I couldn't shake this feeling that everything we had built was threatened.

It took two thousand years to move from dreaming and praying to building the state. Jews then joined a deep debate, arguing how to make the new Jewish democracy feel like a safe home for all. The debate was difficult and passionate, yet we had no choice but to fight it out. Then, one person came along and decided he was God. Trashing all the rules, he shut down the debate by murdering our leader.

I wasn't interested in trying to understand the killer's motives. He deserved an old-fashioned herem, total excommunication, along with life in prison with no hope of parole. Still, I figured, we are Jews, the world experts at turning national tragedies into nation-building opportunities. I expected that we would turn this crime into a renewed sense of unity, resilient enough to absorb the daily political debates with a little less shouting and a little more listening to one another. Unfortunately, partisan furies proved much stronger than my metaphysical hopes.

At Rabin's funeral, the sloganeering didn't express my nonpartisan fear that democracy was endangered; instead, it emphasized the Left's fear that Oslo was endangered. Listening to the eulogies by President Bill Clinton and Shimon Peres unnerved me. "Now, it falls to all of us who love peace and all of us who loved him to carry on the struggle to which he gave life and for which he gave his life," Clinton said, calling Rabin "a martyr for peace."

The funeral turned into an event consecrating the cause of Oslo. Rabin's legacy became a headstrong rush into "peace now," without recognition of the growing doubts he had and the pauses he advised. In their grief, good, sincere people politicized the tragedy. Somehow, the only way to mourn Yitzhak Rabin was to support the Oslo peace process blindly.

Likud's unexpected victory in 1996 further fouled the atmosphere. The morning everyone realized that Shimon Peres had lost, the finger-pointing escalated. Peres's disappointed supporters blamed Netanyahu and Likud for the rhetoric that killed Rabin. "Gam ratzachta, v'gam ganavta," some Peres supporters cried, echoing Elijah the Prophet's charge against Ahab and Jezebel about murdering, then seizing land: "First you murdered, then you stole" the election.

Although only a few made this awful accusation publicly, many from the pro-Oslo camp believed it privately. Nearly everyone on the Israeli Left blamed anyone on the Israeli Right for Rabin's death—and anything else that went wrong with the Oslo peace process. This orthodoxy ignored Rabin's worries, in the last weeks of his life, about Hamas's bombs and Arafat's lies threatening the fragile peace. All of Rabin's growing doubts were buried with him. Peres's gullible version of peace became the only virtuous game in town.

Politicizing the death in this way was a gift to the extremists on the Right, a free pass to those who wanted to avoid soul-searching. It was easier to deny the ridiculous accusation that they had killed Rabin than to answer the hard questions: Did we cross the line? Did we dehumanize our opponents and our leaders? Did we contribute to the lynch-mob atmosphere? I believe that a fuller moral accounting at the time might have avoided some of the problems now with extreme rightists whose fury often turns them anti-Zionist.

At the ceremony commemorating the first anniversary of Rabin's murder, the new prime minister, Benjamin Netanyahu, was the main speaker, naturally. Many Rabin and Peres people cringed, just as naturally. As the official ceremony ended at Rabin's grave site on Mount Herzl, I lingered, looking at Shevah Weiss. A professor who became a politician, Shevah preferred talking with me about Russian history and other intellectual interests to fighting over politics. He had served as Speaker of the Knesset under Rabin. I respected him as one of the Labor camp's most rational and positive thinkers.

As people filed passed Rabin's grave, Shevah stayed longer than most. He stood there, stricken, as his eyes stared blankly. After the ceremony, he asked me, in agony, "Natan, do you also feel like these speeches, this whole ceremony, is an unbelievable farce? It cannot be real. Who thought they could kill our dream?" I felt nauseous. His "they" scared me. This normally cool, analytical intellectual sounded like he believed a coup d'état had occurred.

My grounded, thoughtful friend saw our government, and the coalition I had joined, as forces of evil celebrating their victory over the forces of good. We, from Bibi on down, were cast in this us-versus-them framework as the villains in an old-new Jewish Shakespearean tragedy: the Brutuses of Israel.

The vile killer's crime was monstrous. No doubt the Right's hysteria demonizing "the Oslo criminals" helped inflame the assassin. But rather than trying to de-escalate and humanize their opponents, many good people were reescalating and dehumanizing, treating their political opponents as the enemy and any political debate about the peace process as a betrayal. Showing how this spiral of mutual demonization can always spin out of control, right-wingers started peddling conspiracy theories blaming Rabin's assassination on the Security Service that protected him.

I know many people feel the assassin killed the hope for peace along with Rabin. I believe they are wrong. The killing of Rabin was an evil act of historic proportions intended to derail Oslo. I believe the assassin's plans backfired. *Retzach Rabin*, Rabin's murder, artificially extended Oslo's shelf life.

The Oslo peace process showed its true nature as the Oslo war process long before Rabin's murder. Contrary to most people's memories, Hamas's suicide bombings preceded this awful crime. But the assassination made Oslo holy, untouchable. A political debate became a theological one. It was as if we were desecrating Rabin's name and validating his murder whenever we demanded progress from the Palestinians, protected ourselves from terrorism, or questioned Oslo's flawed assumptions.

The polarized debate left me feeling more torn politically than ever. I shared the widespread, deep despair about Rabin's murder. But I also shared the Right's skepticism about the Palestinian regime and the failing peace process, which the Left renamed "Rabin's legacy."

A NEW FAST DAY?

During the first year of mourning Rabin, and especially after I joined the government, I kept wondering how to wrench Rabin's murder out of its new partisan orbit. On the first Rosh Hashanah after Rabin's assassination, I was struck once again by how religious Jews plunge from the joy of the New Year's celebration to a fast the day after. Called Tzom Gedaliah, Gedaliah's Fast, this minor dawn-to-dusk fast mourns a moment 2,500 years ago when some Jews killed a Jewish leader, a now-forgotten governor of Judah, after the Babylonians destroyed the First Temple. The

Talmud says the fast teaches "that the death of the righteous is likened to the burning of the House of our God."

I thought about our rabbis' wisdom. Few remember just why Gedaliah was killed. But the fact that Jews killed their leader justified a cautionary, penitential fast. The cleansing would teach people that essential, eternal lesson.

In the Gulag, we political prisoners also used fasts to make moral statements and remind ourselves of what was important to us. Every December 10, the Soviet Union ignored International Human Rights Day. By fasting that day in prison, we made it meaningful and memorable. I decided to fast on the first anniversary of Rabin's murder, without waiting for our rabbis. I did not make a big deal about it.

By the second anniversary in 1997, the polarization had intensified so much that some people did not want to attend the official commemorations, because our government and our prime minister would lead the events. Rabin's relatives and Labor Party friends controlled the biggest memorial, in the heart of Tel Aviv. No Israeli government representative was invited to speak at that independent event.

When a colleague at the Ministry of Industry and Trade, who was also a Labor Party activist, discovered that I fasted on the anniversary day, he asked, "Then why don't you come to our rally?"

"It's unfortunate," I replied, "but no one from the government was invited to participate."

A half hour before Sabbath began, I received a phone call saying that Leah Rabin was inviting me to attend the rally as "a friend of the family."

So, there I was, driving to Tel Aviv, wondering what to say. Should I speak in the name of the government? I had no mandate. Should I speak as "a friend of the family" and echo the politicization of Oslo? Of course not. Should I criticize the pro-peace-process approach? Yes, but gingerly, sensitively.

Then it occurred to me to go back to the Entebbe rescue of 1976, which linked the two powerful names of Rabin and Netanyahu in history and heroism. I would speak about how our tragedies, not just our victories, should unite us. The one criticism I would offer would be to say that many people mourning today, from all across the political spectrum and all over the country, did not feel welcome at this rally.

None of these subtleties mattered. The moment it was announced that the minister of industry and trade from the Netanyahu government would be speaking, the booing started. As I approached the podium, facing one of the largest crowds in Israeli history—over two hundred thousand—boos, whistles, and catcalls overwhelmed me.

Some later insisted that a minority of attendees shouted. Looking into the darkness, I could only see a first row of faces and hear tremendous noise. I could barely hear my own voice. It felt like two hundred thousand people wanted to drown me out and shout me down.

One main speaker, Ehud Barak, rushed to help. I waved him off. I didn't want to look like I needed rescuing or that I feared my own people, my fellow Israelis. I made my speech.

I spoke very slowly, as deliberately as I had in my closing speech to the court in Moscow in 1978. Back then, I wanted to help my brother Leonid memorize every word, hoping the world would hear me. This time, I wanted to speak over the din, hoping anyone might hear my words.

I have stood in front of hundreds of thousands at solidarity demonstrations and felt empowered. I have stood in front of small, loud, hostile crowds, who shouted slogans in a KGB-organized expression of the people's anger, and also felt empowered. Now, standing in front of this huge Israeli crowd, I felt drained. I worried: Had Rabin's murderer killed our dialogue? Would we ever be able to mourn together, or even talk together, again?

As soon as I finished, Barak approached the podium. Trying to be my advocate, he emphasized my time in the *tsinok*, the punishment cell, which always fascinated him. But his reaction suggested the attacks were personally against me, when they weren't.

"Aren't you sorry you came?" journalists asked me as soon as I walked down from the stage.

"On the contrary," I replied. "It reminds us how much work has to be done."

People kept asking if I had hard feelings. I had sad feelings. A tragedy had happened to our people and we weren't learning from it.

The next day, Rabin's sister, Rachel Rabin Yaakov, called me. Rabin's son, Yuval Rabin, visited me with his youth movement Dor Shalom, or Peace Generation, to discuss how to renew our democratic dialogue.

For his part, my prime minister needled me. That Sunday morning, I attended the weekly cabinet meeting. Bibi sent me a note: "Natan, are you flirting with the opposition?" I knew what he was doing. He was often suspicious, testing loyalties even of old friends. His suspicions would grow with the years. Back then, he expressed them with a lighter touch.

I wrote back curtly emphasizing one word: "Nonsense."

I still mark the anniversary of Rabin's death by participating in bridge-building discussions with activists and students. The educational efforts often echo our approach to Tisha B'Av, the national-religious day of mourning, commemorating the Holy Temples' destruction in 586 BCE and in 70 CE. On Tisha B'Av, many Jews fast too.

My fear is that, if Rabin's murder remains tied up in Oslo peace process politics, it will be forgotten when the peace question becomes irrelevant in twenty, thirty, or fifty years. In 1977, everyone seemed to know what the Helsinki Accords were. But the Soviet Union fell. Today, if you mention Helsinki, most people give you a blank stare or rush to Google it.

Instead of building the commemoration of this tragedy of biblical proportions around current political events, we should ritualize the memory, as the rabbis did with Gedaliah's murder. Let's focus on the eternal moral lesson about continuing to raise our voices, flap our arms, and clench our bodies when debating, without turning violent or even giving up on one another.

Meanwhile, I fast every year, hoping one day it will become a national fast day, uniting secular and religious Jews, Left and Right, "to establish that the death of the righteous is likened to the burning of the House of our God."

THE PEACE TENSIONS MAKE ISRAEL LOOK WARLIKE

Any Israeli prime minister elected in 1996 would have had to rebalance Oslo, including Yitzhak Rabin, had he lived. By then, most Israelis recognized the dangers resulting from this process. Palestinian terrorists would murder more Israelis in the five years after Oslo than in the five years before it. The Dizengoff Street bus bombing in Tel Aviv, the Kfar Darom bus attack, and the Jerusalem Bus 26 bombing all preceded Rabin's assassination. Two suicide bombings on Jerusalem Bus 18, along with another bombing at Dizengoff Center and several other attacks, preceded Netanyahu's election. If you ignored such facts, it was easier to blame Israel, especially from afar.

But Netanyahu was elected to clean up the mess. After winning the election by a margin of barely thirty thousand votes out of three million cast, Netanyahu faced the democratic dethroner's dilemma. The victorious opposition takes power with a broom to sweep out some old policies. But most policies are like mold, not dust: you can't just wipe 'em away.

It was an impossible juggling act. Our new government had to fulfill Israel's legal obligations to the Oslo peace process, to the Palestinians, and to the international community. Yet none of us around the cabinet table believed in Oslo, albeit for various reasons. We agreed, however, on one goal: we wanted to neutralize the new and worsening dangers.

Back in 1996, as he formed his government, Netanyahu believed that the only way out of this Oslo trap was to slow the process down. By examining each obligation the previous government had undertaken—one by one, one step at a time—we could see if the Palestinians were reciprocating. By necessity, the government was forced to be tactical, not strategic.

Although we all looked united against Oslo, behind the scenes it was obvious the members of the coalition were split. I was one of those who regretted Israel's control over millions of Palestinians and wanted it to end as quickly and as safely as possible. Increasingly, even many traditional security hawks accepted the inevitability of a Palestinian state at the end of the process, as long as it remained unthreatening and demilitarized.

Others on the Right believed that, with more than twenty Arab states already existing, there was no reason to create another threatening Arab state, especially on Israel's historical and biblical lands. But taken to its logical extreme, this stance would require millions of Palestinians to live permanently under Israeli control—or leave their homes.

Of course, members of both factions considered my talk of democracy naive. But the security hawks and I at least shared a common language and a common endgame. For me, the never-Palestinian-staters crossed a line. If Israel controlled millions of people permanently, without giving them full democratic rights, we would indeed lose our right to call Israel democratic.

This tension would burst into the public after the Wye River negotiations of 1998, eventually dooming Bibi's first government. Today, while the never-state maximalists are increasingly marginalized, this debate erupts anew whenever we come close to any kind of negotiations.

Frustrated by Rabin's murder and Peres's narrow loss, the international media blasted Netanyahu whenever he resisted Western pressure. With Oslo deemed sacred, we were under even more scrutiny. Reporters branded any skeptics of this failing process as anti-peace. It was easier for critics to blame Netanyahu's intransigence than to imagine Rabin following a similar path. Increasingly, critics viewed our strategy gap as a values gap. We had no faith in Oslo, so they lost faith in us.

In their pursuit of peace, many sincere people fell for the Palestinian manipulations, making Oslo's "land for peace" formula a one-way street. Israel relinquished territory. Arafat didn't deliver on his promises, yet their pressure on the Israeli government grew. Negotiating with Arafat was like a shopkeeper paying protection: the more you pay, the more the thugs demand—or else!

"What do you want from him?" Oslo's apologists said. "You can't expect more. Yasir Arafat risked his life by signing onto Oslo. Israel is the powerful one. Israel must end the occupation and end the conflict." Year by year, that sacred commemoration of Rabin's murder became a day of recriminations in Israel and the Diaspora.

Mutual exasperation grew, even as American Jewry's pro-Israel consensus held and American support for Israel increased. Along with their Israeli counterparts, many American Jewish liberals had a hard time believing that, finally, there was a chance for peace, yet Israel wasn't pursuing it enthusiastically and proactively. Although a minority, these internal critics became louder, bolder, and more likely to be covered by the media. Many Israelis resented that, after they had taken such risks for peace, some Jews abroad couldn't give Israel credit for trying.

LET'S PLAY CHESS, NOT CHECKERS

We spent many cabinet hours brainstorming about how to redirect the growing pressure on Israel toward the Palestinians. Remembering how the Moscow Helsinki Group monitored Soviet human rights policies in the 1970s, I proposed launching a trilateral committee of Americans, Israelis, and Palestinians to monitor incitement on all sides. The committee met regularly until Ehud Barak downgraded it. Shortly thereafter, the Palestinian suicide bombing campaign made the whole initiative look ridiculous.

But the process backfired long before that. Rather than exposing Palestinian rejectionism, the monitoring process exposed the free world's unwillingness to distinguish between democracy and dictatorship. Whenever we detailed official Palestinian incitement at the highest level or in educational curricula against Israel, the Palestinians quoted anti-Palestinian rhetoric from the most marginal edges of Israel's right wing. "You see?" Arafat's people said. "Both sides have their extremists." Confusing democratic debate with dictatorial indoctrination, guilt-ridden Westerners nodded meekly.

Such moral equivalence was farcical. Comparing the official propaganda a dictator must use to incite hatred with the fringe voices a democracy must tolerate to be free is like a jury acquitting a known arsonist because random sparks can also start fires. To maintain the illusion, you have to compare word for word, without noting that some words come from the leaders at the center of the regime and others come from unpopular, marginal extremists.

I opposed making more concessions without a committed peace partner. I insisted on tying withdrawals to Palestinian progress. Those stands put me to Bibi's right in some debates. I even voted against one phase of territorial withdrawal.

"How can we decide what we're giving away and what we're keeping without an endgame?" I asked. "In chess, you build your strategy by understanding where you want to end up from the beginning and determining what moves will get you there."

When I explained my approach in cabinet, Raful Eitan, the former chief of staff, joked, "It's so complicated. Let's play checkers instead."

"That's precisely our problem," I said. "Arafat is playing chess, willing to sacrifice some pawns—make some concessions—while still seeking Israel's destruction. We're just playing checkers, thinking short term and tactically, hoping that somehow it will end well."

Looking abroad, I worried that Israel and our friendly critics were watching two competing movies. Israelis felt caught in a recurring horror show of violence perpetrated by Palestinian bad guys. Israel's critics saw a preventable tragedy, provoked by an Israeli extremist assassinating the saintly Yitzhak Rabin and worsened by Israelis electing uncompromising right-wing governments dominated by the real villains, the settlers. Long before the harsh debates about Barack Obama, then Donald Trump, divided the Jewish community, the lack of a healthy dialogue between the Diaspora and Israel fueled these growing tensions.

Netanyahu ended up in an excruciating position. The Right kept pressing him to cancel the Oslo Accords—blindly, as if Israel's leaders did not feel bound by their predecessors' international agreements. The Left kept pressing him to keep advancing Oslo—blindly, as if Palestinian leaders felt bound by the agreement. Bibi's first tenure as prime minister ended after three years amid this political standoff. When Israel's most decorated general, Ehud Barak, defeated Netanyahu in 1999, pundits declared Bibi's career over; he vowed to return.

EHUD BARAK'S LABORATORY

When I joined Ehud Barak's government, I found myself in a unique laboratory, a broad right-to-left cabinet. Barak himself was an interesting, wide-ranging cultural mix. Israel's number-one soldier—as his best-selling biography called him—he had also studied physics, mathematics, and economics at Hebrew University and Stanford. This skilled and courageous war hero, who had led many spectacular counterterrorist operations, was also a refined piano player and sharp logician who loved disassembling and reassembling clocks effortlessly.

Barak was famous for loving puzzles, and seeing reality as a series of codes to decipher or puzzles to put together. All that time I spent in the punishment cells playing chess in my head caught his imagination. I could see that his disciplined mind kept trying to figure out, "What did you do?"—meaning what would he do.

Barak assembled a cabinet that was stunningly diverse. The National Religious Party was to the right of Likud. The ultra-Orthodox Ashkenazim and Mizrahim from United Torah Judaism and Shas were to the right religiously of the NRP's Religious Zionists. And Meretz was to the left of Barak's own ruling Labor Party.

In this unique bridge-building laboratory, I enjoyed finding common ground with allies from across the spectrum. The Interior Ministry was a huge ministry that was involved in almost everything in Israel to do with land, municipalities, and the personal status of citizens and noncitizens. It was therefore a bonus of my job in Barak's government to work closely with almost every minister.

When I was easing the process for entering Israel and getting citizenship for those not covered under the Law of Return, when I was redrawing municipal boundaries to help Arab villages become more functional, or when I removed the restrictions preventing many Arabs who had worked overseas for many years from returning to their Jerusalem homes, the left-wing members of the government applauded. And when the Education Minister Yossi Sarid of Meretz said he wanted to build new schools for Bedouins in "unrecognized villages," within twenty-four hours my team and his were already translating this political proposal into reality. Yossi was also the rare cabinet minister who didn't roll his eyes and actually perked up whenever I linked the pursuit of peace with democracy and human rights.

At the same time, the right-wing members of the government applauded when I helped establish and improve communities throughout the Land of Israel. In 1999, I was surprised to discover that there had been no new civilian settlements established in the Negev desert in fifteen years. We worked hard to plan, develop, and launch new communities there in the south and in the north too. My allies on the Right and I also knew we had to slow Barak down in his rush to complete deals with the Palestinians and the Syrians at almost any price.

The fact that all these different camps were at one table created a unique opportunity for dialogue. At the same time, it helped define the boundaries of the Zionist democratic tent. It was obvious that, for at least some of my partners on the Left, the Jewish state was only a tool improvised to escape persecution. They viewed Israel's Jewish character as a passing phase on the way to a normal state for all its citizens. To them, even the Law of Return, the central symbol binding Israel to every Jew throughout the world, was a temporary measure that would eventually fade into irrelevance.

For some of my partners on the Right, Israel's democratic character was the optional tool, improvised for establishing the state, that should only remain if convenient. After all, they reasoned, there are many democracies in the world, but there's only one Jewish state.

While most of us ministers, like most Israelis, remained squarely within the Jewish-democratic tent, we could see how, for some, "Jewish" was a temporary adjective, not a defining noun, and for others "democratic" was the adjective. Ultimately, then, my Barak cabinet experiences also highlighted some of the limits to our dialogue.

Still, this laboratory could have kept experimenting, testing to see which issues enabled these different Zionist voices to build some kind of consensus. But this government was short-lived, doomed by Barak's impatience in trying to disassemble and reassemble the Middle East puzzle in record time.

LINKING HUMAN RIGHTS AND PEACE WITH SYRIA

With President Bill Clinton set to leave office in January 2001, Barak kept his eye on the political calendar. He set the Democratic convention in the summer of 2000 as his deadline for peacemaking, before Clinton became a lame duck. Trying to fix the Middle East in a technical way—in a too-brainy, not-soulful way, just like he fixed his clocks—Barak was anxious to reach quick, sweeping peace deals with Hafez al-Assad and Yasir Arafat.

Understanding Barak's aspirations, during the coalition negotiations I insisted that a special letter be attached to the coalition agreement. The letter specified Yisrael B'Aliyah's position that Israeli concessions to Syria required openness, transparency, and democracy in the country. I believe it is the only formal document in Israeli governmental history making any kind of territorial withdrawals or other diplomatic progress contingent on our opponent achieving substantive human rights progress.

Everybody, from left to right, mocked my party's naivete. But Barak knew that if a peace treaty came to a vote, he would have a problem with me and my party. I watched him trying to figure out how to get us on board.

Early in my tenure as Barak's interior minister, Shimon Peres's confidante S. Daniel Abraham approached me. Abraham—a self-made and generous billionaire who founded SlimFast—was an Oslo enthusiast. I had heard that he had often lent his private plane to ferry Peres's team secretly to Norway for the negotiations that produced the accords.

"I want you to meet Syria's future leader, who will help modernize the Arab world," Abraham said. "He thinks exactly like you. He wants to bring democracy to the Arab world, quickly. He believes in human rights. He's modern, sophisticated. He studied in London. He surfs on the Internet." Abraham wanted to fly me to Paris secretly to meet this wunderkind and glimpse the new Middle East he, Peres, and now Ehud Barak were midwifing.

"How do you know this guy is Syria's next leader?" I asked mischievously.

"Well, he's going to inherit it from his father," Abraham replied.

I winced. So much for democracy. After his father died, Bashar al-Assad "won" the election in July 2000 with 99.7 percent of the vote. Today, he is known as the butcher of Syria, who mass murdered and even gassed his own people.

I chose to skip Paris.

EHUD BARAK'S ONE-MAN RUSH FOR PEACE

Barak seemed to envy the success of Peres, who had secretly negotiated the original Oslo deal in Europe when he was foreign minister, presenting it fully cooked to his prime minister and fellow Labor Party member, Yitzhak Rabin, and to the American president, Bill Clinton. In the spring of 2000, a reliable source in Washington warned me that Barak was secretly negotiating a new deal in Europe. Despite serving as interior minister and sitting in the security cabinet, I hadn't heard about the talks or the deal.

I felt I had to do something. I challenged the prime minister during a cabinet meeting. Barak dismissed the rumors as wild. I agreed that many of the ideas I was hearing about seemed far-fetched. But multiple sources had fed me details about troubling proposals that had already been tabled. They entailed dividing Jerusalem, giving away most of the Old City including the Temple Mount, and withdrawing from almost all the 1967 territories.

Under Barak's proposals, the Jewish Quarter and the Western Wall would be surrounded. If Palestinians controlled the Temple Mount, the Kotel would be a lonely prisoner, encircled from the left, the right, and above, as the Al-Aqsa compound looms over the Western Wall. Jewish worshippers would be vulnerable to rocks raining down on them from on high. One scheme would even bus Jews to visit our holiest site under United Nations or an international commission's auspices.

In cabinet, I told Barak that although I served nine years in prison for being an American spy, the charges were false, so it never bothered me that I hadn't mastered what agents call tradecraft. "I never thought that I would one day need those skills as a minister in my own government to build an international network to find out what my own prime minister is proposing to the Palestinians."

After rechecking the details of the proposals with my sources, I wrote the prime minister a letter and copied other key ministers, detailing the concessions to Arafat that Barak had already made.

Cornered, Barak suddenly went public. He said he was going to Camp David at the Americans' invitation to complete an agreement with the Palestinians. Trying to placate me, he proposed I join him in the United States. "Look, Natan, we in the country are badly split," he said. "But if it all works out, I will bring peace. Even if you and your friends will not like it, it will be a real, final peace that the Israeli people want. And if Arafat refuses, at least our people will be united and fully supported by the world."

"There's no way you will bring peace by demonstrating how desperate you are and offering up our most precious assets, especially Jerusalem," I warned. "Readiness to give everything to a dictator, when he needs to go to war against us for his own survival, is a major sign of weakness. You will only bring the war closer."

Beyond the pressing questions of military strategy and diplomacy, this was about identity. Jerusalem isn't just a piece of real estate. It has been our capital for three thousand years and is so central to our story that the very movement to return to Israel, Zionism, is named after Mount Zion, in Jerusalem.

In 1967, when the Israeli colonel Mordechai Gur announced that his troops had reunified Jerusalem, he said, "The Temple Mount is in our hands" and repeated it a second time in his excitement. This *tikkun* (repair) of Jewish history was so powerful that it roused us in Russia. We didn't know what the Temple Mount was. We barely knew what Jerusalem was. But, suddenly, the newest headline in our ancient story returned us, the lost Jews of Russia, back to the Jewish nation.

Years later, I learned that Jerusalem's liberation wasn't just a profound event for the beleaguered Soviet Jews. It roused American Jews, too, from the Jewishly ambivalent to the Jewishly engaged. The excitement they felt in winning back Jerusalem surprised many of the most American-ized Jews. Israel's triumph deepened "a very personal existential sense of the particularity of what it is to be a Jew, the specificity of being a Jew as a member of an ethnic community," the Reform theologian Eugene Borowitz explained in 1977. When "Old Jerusalem was captured and was somehow, to use that marvelous word, 'ours,'" he wrote, "it hit us with an impact which we couldn't imagine, and suddenly we realized the depths of roots we had in a very specific place."

"There has been a mysterious power in Jewish history which again and again came to crush occasional indifference to Zion and Jerusalem," Rabbi Abraham Joshua Heschel, the mystic and teacher who marched with Martin Luther King Jr., wrote in *Israel: An Echo of Eternity*, chronicling his trip to Jerusalem weeks after its reunification. "Whenever we tend to be forgetful, history sends us a reminder. . . . In those great days we discovered a spiritual underground in the hearts of the Jews of America."

The war shocked Jews: They had thought they were universalists, but suddenly felt proudly particularistic. They had thought they were individualists, but suddenly felt they were one—united, interconnected, not alone. Heschel recalled, "We sensed the link between the Jews of this generation and the people of the time of the prophets."

Jerusalem, the Temple Mount, and the Western Wall all play starring roles in our story. They have been the building blocks of our identity for the last three thousand years, connecting Jews across time and space, fusing past, present, and future. Jews could live for thousands of years, united in sorrow by the story of being forcibly exiled, and united in the hope of return. Our story sits at the core of our identity. I was not willing to throw it away.

The fact that Ehud Barak was making such an indiscriminate move unilaterally and secretly bewildered me. I chided him for trying to bypass the security cabinet, the government, the Knesset, and the Jewish people. "This is a dangerous process you are risking," I warned, "and I believe a vast majority of the Jewish people, sitting in Zion and abroad, will not be able to accept this."

While I was confident in my ideological stance on Jerusalem, I again worried about my responsibility to my party. We had united over quality-of-life immigrant issues, sidelining any disagreements we might have over philosophy or the peace process. Finally, we were running the all-important Interior Ministry, as another founding member of Yisrael B'Aliyah, Marina Solodkin, filled the critical role of deputy minister of immigration and absorption. Would my colleagues be willing to risk our long-sought practical power for yet another fight over the peace process?

We discussed it and all agreed, from right to left: resignation was the only option. Marina, our resident lefty and a passionate advocate for immigrants, read my correspondence with Prime Minister Barak. She said, "I sign off on every word."

We were the only coalition partners to resign before the Camp David negotiations began that July 2000. At the time, I wondered why we, the party of new immigrants, bolted first, before the more established ideological parties, such as the National Religious Party, Shas, and David Levy's Gesher Party. I think it is because we immigrants were the most recent newcomers to the Jewish story. For us, the connection linking our identity with the liberation of Jerusalem and the Western Wall was fresh. We hadn't been around long enough to take it for granted. Maybe we were also the most protective of Jerusalem's centrality to the Jewish story. After all, our renewed identity, our old-new connection to our people's ancient capital, had propelled each of us forward in the journey home.

EXCHANGING A CABINET SEAT
FOR A PROTEST TENT

Before Barak jetted off to Washington on his way to Camp David, I informed him that Marina and I were resigning from the cabinet and our party was leaving his coalition. When the summit deadlocked, Barak started working the phones, trying to save his coalition. He called me and said, "I am sitting here alone and thinking about you alone in your punishment cell in the Gulag. I think of all those decisions about life and death you had to make yourself. And I feel a great sense of responsibility to make these decisions about war and peace, myself."

"I just heard on the radio that Arafat said that before he makes any concessions on Jerusalem, he is going to consult the leaders of the Muslim and Arab world," I replied. "Because, he said, 'Jerusalem belongs to all of us.' Why don't you go to New York and convene a conversation among Jews there? Ask them what they think about giving up the heart of Jerusalem, which is most central to our identity."

Barak had no interest in listening to anyone. He didn't consult the Jews of New York. He didn't consult his own government. He didn't consult anyone else. He tried negotiating single-handedly.

Arafat didn't even respond with a counteroffer. Believing Barak was weak and the Jews divided, Arafat instead responded with that ugly bout of terrorism that Palestinians called the Second Intifada and that killed one thousand Israelis. When I resigned, I warned Barak that, just as the 1967 victory had strengthened the Jewish people and deepened the Jewish bond with Israel, his proposed changes would weaken the Jewish people and diminish their ability to identify with Israel.

I moved into a protest tent in front of the prime minister's residence in Jerusalem. I demanded a national unity government. All kinds of people visited the tent, some to support me, others to try swaying me. An impressive delegation of generals lobbying for peace showed up. Led by Shlomo "Cheech" Lahat, the former Tel Aviv mayor and major general, the generals told me, "You and your friends won a heroic battle back in the Soviet Union, but we won the battles here. We know our enemies very well. And we know that Barak will bring peace. You must support him."

"I know how dictatorships work," I replied. "Arafat needs war for his own survival. All we are showing him is our extreme weakness at this moment. There is no way Barak will bring peace with his proposals."

The generals came well equipped, with Israeli TV camera crews filming their lobbying efforts all over Jerusalem, the City of Peace. After their segment aired, Israel's most beloved news anchor, "Mr. Television," Haim Yavin, visited me to follow up. He arrived late on a Friday afternoon. All my fellow protesters had gone home to prepare for Sabbath. I was about to leave.

"What happened to you?" Yavin asked sympathetically, directing the cameraman to sweep the empty tent. "I remember the day you arrived in Israel, the whole country was with you. And now, you sit here alone in the empty tent. The whole country is with Barak because everyone wants peace. Don't you feel abandoned?"

A few days later, Barak returned from Camp David empty-handed. Most of the other coalition partners soon resigned. Within two months, Arafat and the Palestinians had launched their war of terrorism against Israeli civilians. Within eight months, Barak was out of office, repudiated by the Israeli public for his failure.

The morning after Ariel Sharon defeated Barak, winning 62 percent of the vote to Barak's 38 percent, Haim Yavin interviewed me once again. This time, I participated in a panel discussion in his TV studio about the upcoming coalition battles. Not wanting to embarrass him, I waited until I was off camera to say, "A few short months ago you told me I was alone. You said Barak will bring peace. Today, Barak's alone. Practically the whole country abandoned him. And we are stuck in a war. Maybe there's something I know about Arafat that you didn't take into account then?"

"But Natan," Haim said, "if only you had stayed with Barak, it could have been different." I imagined that famous picture from Camp David, where Barak was pushing Arafat into the negotiating room. If only I, with my bookworm's muscles, had been able to join Barak, Israel's most decorated war hero, in pushing Arafat to sign the agreement, then we would have peace.

I had so many "if only, then" conversations like this. It was much easier to decide that one ingredient or condition in the experiment was off than to question the underlying hypothesis, even amid such dramatic failure.

CLINTON'S CHANGING BLAME GAME

Eventually, President Bill Clinton saw through the Arafat charade, having hosted him thirteen times in the White House, more than any other foreign visitor. But Clinton continued to personalize the problem. When violence erupted, Clinton flipped, blaming Arafat for the breakdown of the Oslo peace process and the Palestinian turn toward terrorism. In their last Oval Office meeting in January 2001, when the oleaginous Arafat called Clinton a "great man," the president yelled, "I'm a colossal failure, and you made me one." Clinton later told the world that when Arafat spurned Barak's Camp David offer in July 2000, he had rejected "the best peace deal he was ever going to get."

By 2010, with Netanyahu back in power, Barack Obama in the White House pressing Israel, and the former first lady Hillary Clinton as secretary of state vainly trying to advance the peace process again, Bill Clinton reinterpreted the past. "An increasing number of the young people in the IDF are the children of Russians and settlers, the hardest-core people against a division of the land. This presents a staggering problem," he told reporters. "It's a different Israel. Sixteen percent of Israelis speak Russian."

As proof of his thesis, Bill Clinton mentioned a conversation he and I had had with Ehud Barak during the Camp David peace negotiations in July 2000. Clinton described me as the only Israeli cabinet minister who rejected the sweeping peace proposal. "I said," he recalled, "Natan, what is the deal" about not supporting the peace deal. Then Clinton remembered me saying, "I can't vote for this, I'm Russian. . . . I come from one of the biggest countries in the world to one of the smallest. You want me to cut it in half. No, thank you."

Bill Clinton cleverly replied, "Don't give me this. You came here from a jail cell. It's a lot bigger than your jail cell." He added that, compared to most Russians, I "was nice about it, a lot of them aren't."

I like the line. I appreciate the backhanded compliment. It's a good story with good humor that undoubtedly entertains the ex-president's many well-paying audiences. It also blames Israel, ever so elegantly, for the ongoing stalemate.

Unfortunately, the conversation never happened. I was never at Camp David. I was sitting in that protest tent, not in Clinton's presidential retreat. I never had the opportunity to discuss the plan with President Clinton.

When I first heard his accusation, I was angry. I feared the finger being pointed in Israel's direction, and I resented the ethnic stereotyping of me and my fellow Russians as thuggish. Having reread Clinton's entire interview, though, I think I understand what happened. He probably remembered our long conversation at the Wye plantation in 1998. He was essentially correct in that I opposed the Camp David negotiations two years later and was the one minister who resigned before Camp David, although others followed afterward. Clinton probably conflated my presence at Wye in 1998 with a discussion asking Barak where I was at Camp David in 2000. Following American logic, I'm a human rights activist, which means I'm a liberal, which means I should be pro peace, which means advocating maximal concessions to anyone. The truth is, in 2000 as in 1998 and from Oslo's start, I knew that Arafat would never bring freedom to his people, an essential element of a sustainable peace.

The multiple shocks—Barak's sweeping concessions at Camp David being met by no counteroffer, followed by Arafat's return to terror—stripped Barak's government of its credibility with most Israelis. The result was an electoral anomaly in 2001, Israel's only special election pitting two prime ministerial candidates against one another without broader Knesset elections. When Ariel Sharon beat Barak, Sharon invited me back into the cabinet as deputy prime minister and minister of housing and construction.

THE 1990S:
SPREADING FREEDOM, NOT DICTATORSHIP

It's hard to remember now, but the 1990s were a decade of hope and miracles. The Berlin Wall fell peacefully. The Soviet Union collapsed peacefully. The Iron Curtain was raised peacefully. Germany reunited, South Africa's apartheid regime vanished, and even Northern Ireland seemed on its way to peace. As one problem after another was solved peacefully, the world became impatient to solve the Israeli-Palestinian problem too.

With the Rabin assassination, a Jew, an Israeli, a Westerner seemed to kill the entire peace process and hope itself. We were blamed, not Hamas and its suicide bombers or Arafat and his gangs of killers. Increasingly, many in the world, including many liberal American Jews, grumbled. They wondered why Israel couldn't magically make this persistent problem disappear along with the Cold War and so many other challenges. Many started asking, "What is wrong with you?"

I saw things differently. What made Oslo different from all the other '90s miracles? They advanced democracy; Oslo advanced dictatorship. In Eastern Europe, Russia, and South Africa, freedom surged ahead. This peace process depended on keeping the Palestinians unfree. Being enslaved by your own dictator is still slavery. Obviously, history didn't guarantee happy endings in all those places, but in the Middle East, we doomed ourselves from the start.

Although it looked like it was going with the flow of history at that moment, Oslo went against the stream of the 1990s. Whether it was Peres's naive "new Middle East" dream, assuming terrorists would transform into pacifists, or Rabin's cynical "he's our dictator" approach, Oslo violated the spirit of the times and people's natural desires. Perhaps now, as terrorism has become a fact of life and many Westerners worry about democracy, people are ready to start understanding why this reckless plan was doomed from the start.

12

A DISSIDENT IN POLITICS

I entered politics with a mandate to focus on domestic Israeli issues, with my personal history propelling me toward Diaspora affairs. As a member of the security cabinet, I had to figure out how to contribute to debates about Israel's security too. Whenever the generals and intelligence analysts lapsed into military speak, I watched everyone around the cabinet table get nostalgic for their days of service, while I pretended to keep up with the insider's onslaught of army acronyms.

My military service consisted of three weeks of civil defense training. My age and height qualified me for perpetual stretcher duty, helping others become good soldiers as they dragged my "corpse" around. Despite such inadequate training, from the start of my government service, I got a firsthand look at the Iran threat and the worry it generated. But it happened almost by chance.

I FINALLY BECOME A SPY IN RUSSIA

In January 1997, I visited Russia for the first time since my liberation. This could have been a normal working trip as Israel's new minister of industry and trade visiting our new post-Soviet friend. Instead, it became an emotional and symbolic journey, closing many circles for me.

In February 1986, I left the Soviet Union with four KGB escorts as a prisoner stripped of his citizenship for bad behavior. Eleven years later, I returned to Russia as an Israeli minister, with staffers and a large delegation of Israeli entrepreneurs, welcomed with red carpet receptions in half a dozen Russian ministries. In 1980, my father had passed away without seeing me even once after my arrest. Now, I could visit his grave and see the one way I had been able to contribute to his burial from my prison cell: I had proposed the line that was etched on his tombstone, Psalm 25:13, "His soul will lie in peace and his seed will inherit the Land of Israel."

In December 1989, the Soviets banned me from Andrei Sakharov's funeral, still considering me a traitor. Now, I visited Sakharov's grave, met old comrades and cellmates in Sakharov's now-iconic apartment, and presented an official photograph to the Sakharov Center, an image of the Israeli memorial to him that I helped establish. Sakharov Gardens lies at Jerusalem's entrance. That makes Israel the only country that mentions my mentor's name daily, in constant updates about the nearby traffic jams.

In 1976, I snuck two journalists around Moscow with smuggled cameras, dodging the secret police, to film the dissidents' struggle. The "slanderous fabrications" of the "illegal film" so infuriated the Soviets that they wove the movie into my indictment two years later. The prosecutors showed the film, *A Calculated Risk*, during my trial to illustrate how I "assisted" Communism's enemies. In 1997, I took a busload of international journalists covering my trip on the same freedom tour. I traced where we had organized, protested, and been arrested, this time enjoying Russian police protection.

In the late 1970s, I spent a year and a half in Lefortovo prison undergoing interrogations. Twenty years later, I insisted on visiting the prison as a condition of my trip. Avital came with me, and I became the first—and so far the only—public figure to visit my still-functioning alma mater on a sightseeing trip. I also took her to the punishment cell, which the jailers at first said no longer existed.

When Avital and I emerged from the prison and the hellish punishment cell, a crowd of journalists surrounded us. "Why are you returning to this dark place?" one reporter asked. "Isn't it painful for you?"

I answered, "On the contrary. It's so inspiring to return. Think about it. At this very place twenty years ago, the leaders of the most powerful secret service of the most powerful empire in the world at the time insisted it was the end of the Zionist movement, the end of the human rights movement in the Soviet Union, that all our friends were arrested.

They claimed that everything was finished and that if I didn't cave in, I would never get out alive."

I continued, "Now, twenty years later, the KGB doesn't exist. The Soviet Union doesn't exist. Communism doesn't exist. The Warsaw Bloc doesn't exist. Today, two hundred million people from that big prison called the Soviet Union are enjoying their freedom. The world is freer and more secure today. The Iron Curtain has fallen down and Jews are leaving the Soviet Union by the hundreds of thousands. That shows the real power of the Jewish people and our army of students and housewives."

On that trip, my childhood dreams came true. Thanks to the attention the visit received, the Russian-language chess magazine I used to read in my teens from cover to cover, *64*, published my chess games and puzzles. My satisfaction in closing the circle of my chess career so grandly competed with the joy I had in closing another career. After serving so much time in prison on trumped-up espionage charges, I returned to Russia with a secret mission in addition to my official business: working for Israeli intelligence.

Shortly before my Moscow journey, Amos Gilad, the head of military intelligence research at Aman, Israel's military intelligence agency, approached me. He and his associate asked me to arrange a short, confidential session with the highest official I would meet, Russia's foreign minister Yevgeny Primakov. They wanted me to inform him that Israel knew Russian technology was being peddled to the Iranians. "The foreign minister will deny the charge," my briefers said. "But we want them to know that we know, and we want to see their reaction."

They started explaining to me what to say and what not to say. After rounds of drilling me in their nuanced dos and don'ts, I stopped them. "To avoid any mistakes, dictate to me exactly what you want me to say and I will deliver the message word for word."

My official meeting with Foreign Minister Primakov went well. This cultured academic with deep intelligence ties welcomed our trade delegation warmly. We enjoyed a wide-ranging conversation about improving our cultural, economic, and diplomatic relations. The weakened, post-Soviet Russian Federation wanted to celebrate historic new beginnings with Israel.

When our short private meeting began, I changed the tone abruptly. I told Primakov that all these good intentions would go nowhere if

Russia continued helping Iran develop lethal ballistic missiles that could reach Tel Aviv. "We will have no choice. We will have to fight Iran and we will win. But nothing will be left of this friendship both our countries clearly desire."

Primakov seemed to sigh in relief. He probably feared I was going to challenge him about some unpleasant Soviet-era episode that was beyond him. This question was easy. As expected, he dismissed it. "I'm sorry, Natan Borisovich," he said. "Someone is misleading you. We are not interested in supporting Iran's aggressiveness. We are definitely not interested in hurting Israel. And we are not exporting military technology to Iran."

Pulling out my cheat sheet from my pocket, I spelled out how X firm in the north delivered Y materials in the autumn of 199Z and facilitated Iran's ballistic missile production. I watched carefully as he took notes on the specifics.

I had run through the information my briefers pumped into me, but I was enjoying myself. "Look, I can't tell you any more than what I already said," I added, improvising. "But, as you know, I am a graduate of MFTI, your top scientific institute in this field. I can understand that without this particular equipment, Iran could only launch scrap metal wildly in our direction. It's your technology that makes them dangerous to us."

Still sputtering denials, Primakov repeated, "I'm sure you are wrong but I promise to look into this."

Two days later, just hours before our flight home, Avital and I were making a farewell tour of the souvenir shops on the Arbat, Moscow's historic shopping center. Someone from the Israeli embassy tracked me down with a message that had been relayed to our ambassador. Primakov wanted to see me immediately.

The Russians knew I was only a few hundred meters from the Foreign Ministry's headquarters, which made it easy for me to peel off discreetly from the shopping for twenty minutes. Minutes later, I was back in Russia's majestic Foreign Ministry building, one of Stalin's famous "seven skyscrapers," which sits on Arbat Street. "We want to be open with you because your friendship is important to us," Primakov said. "We looked into this. You were right. But we want you to know our government was not involved. A private firm violated our security protocols," he claimed. "We will punish the sinners and make sure it never happens again."

When I returned to Israel, my new friends from military intelligence were waiting impatiently for the Russian response. I told them word for word what happened during the two meetings. Like good spooks, they showed no emotion and vanished.

The next day, the chief of staff, Amnon Lipkin-Shahak, called. "Thank you, Natan. You rendered a great and unique service to our country," he said.

WORKING THE RUSSIAN BACK CHANNEL

I was glad to have helped, and I didn't expect any more such calls. But somebody in our intelligence bureaucracy probably decided I was an expert on the Russian mentality and an asset in dealing with such issues. I was invited to top-secret briefings about Russia and Iran. My security clearance was upgraded to the level of the defense minister. Eventually, I became unofficially the minister with a special responsibility for Russian relations.

Altogether, I learned far more than I expected about the danger of the Iranian threat. Most of our neighbors used Israel as a whipping boy, the external enemy every dictator needs. The Islamic Republic of Iran, however, is a totalitarian Islamist regime obsessed with fighting America and destroying Israel. The traditional basis of the Cold War standoff—the fear of mutual assured destruction—for Iran is not a minus but a bonus. The apocalyptic dimension in Iranian Islamists' ideology views the possibility of their own people dying "as an incentive, not a deterrent," explained my late friend, Princeton's legendary Middle East expert Bernard Lewis. They seek this "free pass to heaven."

While working the Russian back channel, I also collaborated with America's vice president Al Gore on the US-Israeli initiatives to stop proliferation. After rounds of negotiation, we scored a big success during one visit to Ukraine in 1998. One of Ukraine's state-owned enterprises, Turboatom, produced giant steam turbines for nuclear power plants. It had a multimillion-dollar contract to sell two turbines to the Iranians. Ukrainian president Leonid Kuchma and his security adviser Volodymyr Horbulin canceled the order.

I called Vice President Gore from Kuchma's office, trying to show the Ukrainian president that we grateful Israelis would continue urging the Americans to thank the Ukrainians with new contracts and jobs. A few years later, Ukrainian diplomats complained to me that the Americans never followed through on their financial promises.

We never succeeded with the Russians. Russian technology continued flowing to Iran, even as we cooperated with Boris Yeltsin's government on other security matters.

In 1998, the head of the new Russian KGB organization, the FSB (Federalnaya Sluzhba Bezopasnosti, or Federal Security Service), visited Israel for the first, and so far only, time. I was asked to host Nikolay Dmitrievich Kovalyov—who had joined the KGB in 1974—at an intimate official dinner in the Mishkenot Sha'ananim neighborhood in Jerusalem. The date added to the surrealness of the situation: we dined on July 14, 1998, the twentieth anniversary of the day I denounced the Soviet court and received my thirteen-year sentence.

I enjoyed reminding guests like Kovalyov about such milestones. They liked to look impassive when I needled them. Then they would declare, "It's all behind us."

"Well, maybe then it's time to open up the archives, so other Refuseniks and I can read our KGB files," I replied, pressing my advantage. Kovalyov promised to look into the question.

I didn't expect much, especially since he lost his job to Vladimir Putin almost as soon as he returned from Jerusalem. I joked, "That's the price a KGB man pays for visiting Israel."

PUTIN'S PRESENT

During my next visit to Russia in February 1999, I met Putin in his new office in the infamous Lubyanka, the former KGB headquarters that now housed its successor, the FSB. I expressed my usual concerns about Iran and Russian technology. I objected, as usual, to the anti-Semitic statements some new Russian leaders made. I warned that, historically, such rhetoric gave extremists a green light and encouraged violence.

Rather than deliver the usual loyalists' denial, claiming Russia had no anti-Semitism, Putin answered cleverly. "Look, some stupid people say and do stupid things," he admitted. "But make no mistake about it. We fear pogroms more than you do. For you, it's a few people being beaten here and there; for us, it's a loss of control. If one group succeeds in taking the law into its own hands, do you have any idea how many other groups might follow? So don't worry, I will not permit any violence against Jews."

As the meeting ended, Putin surprised me again. "I know you requested to see the materials of your case," he said. "If you want, you can see them right now." Dumbfounded, I walked with my staffers to the imposing office of the former KGB head Yuri Andropov. It had been turned into a shrine to his memory. So there I was, about to read my court files, right by the desk of the man who had authorized my arrest and the arrests of many of my friends. I plowed through the papers I had last read in 1978 for trial prep: fifteen thousand pages in fifty-one volumes.

Postponing my return to Israel for a day, I continued reading. Sitting there all day, reading those files, I kept shaking my head and smiling. I was sorry Andropov couldn't come back from the dead, see all the buzz around me in his office now, and then return to the Kremlin Wall Necropolis in Red Square.

By the time I met Putin again, he was president. Slowing Iran's rush to go nuclear and get ballistic missiles remained Israel's priority. In my reports describing my meetings with Putin and other Russian officials, I emphasized that I believed Russia didn't want Iran to have nuclear weapons. The Russians feared their own Muslim extremists in Chechnya and elsewhere. But it was also obvious to me that Putin was playing Iran as a card to force American acceptance of post-Soviet Russia as a superpower. Russia seemed ready to continue helping Iran get close to going nuclear, without crossing the line.

Putin and other Russian leaders always emphasized that the Europeans—especially the Germans, the French, and the Dutch—were making big money selling technologies to the Iranians. "Why shouldn't we Russians profit too?" they wondered. "We won't repeat Ukraine's mistakes."

FACING THE IRANIAN THREAT

When Ariel Sharon became prime minister, I lost my informal role as the back channel to Russia. When it came to any pressing strategic questions, Sharon relied on a small group of foreign policy advisers who resented outsiders.

But Arik was always fascinated to hear about my conversations with Putin and other Russian leaders about Jewish issues. He was especially interested in Putin's reaction whenever I pushed the Russian leader about the fate of the Jewish oligarchs who had fallen from grace the moment he felt they were no longer completely in his camp. It didn't matter to me whether they were wealthy or not. It mattered that the man serving me tea was violating their human rights. I doubted my interventions would help, but I knew I had to try.

At the same time, I developed close ties with some key American officials. So the Iran briefings continued, usually to deliver messages to our closest ally. Along with other Israelis, I kept trying to convince the Americans that Iran was the real number-one threat to the free world and was growing more dangerous. This discussion began long before the United States invaded Iraq and continues today.

In Israel, there's a broad, multiparty consensus among politicians and security professionals that Iran poses the biggest threat to our country too. The debate revolves around the most effective way to protect ourselves: militarily, covertly, or economically through sanctions. During this often harrowing debate, one person stood out. The legendary diplomat Uri Lubrani, Israel's last ambassador in Iran, predicted the shah's fall in the 1970s. Until his recent death in 2018, Lubrani kept anticipating regime change in Iran. He kept in close touch with Iranian dissidents, in Iran and worldwide. Predictably, Lubrani's approach made him an isolated Don Quixote–type figure. Just as predictably, I endorsed his strategy, as did Bernard Lewis, who insisted, "There is only one solution to the Iranian threat, and that can only come from the Iranian people."

Lubrani and I became such good friends that I always kept a bottle of the special vodka he liked at our home. We often discussed the unique situation in Iran, which had a middle class that should be primed for dissent. "The Islamic Republic of Iran reminds me of the last years of the Soviet Union," Mikheil Saakashvili told me when he visited Israel as Georgia's president in 2004. "Every official there speaks so critically about America in public—and just as glowingly about America in private." I kept quoting this insight to others. But Lubrani and I were among the few Israelis who appreciated such an analysis. It meant that Iran, like Gorbachev's Soviet Union, had reached that final phase, when even the elites become doublethinkers.

GEORGE W. BUSH: THE DISSIDENT PRESIDENT

Although my belief in linking human rights and international relations found few takers at home, I found a surprising champion abroad:

President George W. Bush. Despite being raised as a member of the American Establishment, despite a background in oil and baseball, Bush understood the dissident mentality and vision in profound ways.

I first met Bush when he visited Israel as a presidential candidate. To be honest, I wasn't impressed. He knew nothing about the Soviet Jewry struggle. He knew nothing about his father's contribution to freeing Jews from Russia and Ethiopia. Shortly after our meeting, Bush sent me a formal thank-you note. His more personal PS added: "By the way, my parents really do know you and remember you fondly."

After al-Qaeda terrorists attacked the United States eight months into the Bush presidency on September 11, 2001, I applauded Bush's tough stance against terrorism. I expected little on the democracy front.

On April 4, 2002, days after the Israeli army launched Operation Defensive Shield against the Palestinians' terrorist strongholds, President Bush addressed the situation. In his White House speech, as expected, Bush demanded we withdraw immediately. He added, however, that the Palestinians needed democratic leadership as a prerequisite for serious negotiations. "They deserve a government that respects human rights and a government that focuses on their needs, education and health care, rather than feeding their resentments," he insisted.

These were difficult times. Amid the sound and fury of battle, it would have been easy to miss the president's pointed message. Not me. I felt like pinching myself as I read it. Finally, after nine years of being dismissed as a romantic—with even close friends rolling their eyes whenever I talked about Oslo, peace, and democracy—the ground shifted. The president of the United States spoke in the Rose Garden about Palestinians, peace, and democracy.

Days later, I flew to Washington to address the public rally supporting Israel's defensive operation against terror. Commenting on CNN, I applauded Bush's surprising, exciting, overlooked remarks welcoming democracy as the best force to secure peace with the Palestinians.

During my trip, I met Bush's national security adviser, Condoleezza Rice. The president's speech had received much notice, she said, but I seemed to be the only one who acknowledged his freedom agenda. "We're going to pay more and more attention to this approach now," she explained. Inspired by the administration's new commitment, I decided to write up a Marshall Plan–style proposal I had been thinking about, linking increased aid for Palestinians and investment in their economy with clear marks of democratic progress in building civil society. Just as much of the world had turned toward capitalism and away from socialism in the 1990s, I hoped the world might turn toward democracy in the twenty-first century.

My final proof that this president identified with dissidents and understood that Western leaders must support their work to build democracy came when I heard Bush eulogize Ronald Reagan in June 2004.

Attending the funeral in Washington's National Cathedral was a strange mirror-image moment: I seemed to be leading the Israeli delegation to the funeral. In fact, I was defying my prime minister's direct order not to attend. When I heard that Ronald Reagan had died at ninety-three, I assumed a high-level Israeli delegation would go to the funeral. I submitted an article to the *Jerusalem Post* honoring Reagan's exceptional moral clarity in denouncing the Soviet Union as the "evil empire." While writing a condolence letter to the Reagan family, I spoke with someone from Sharon's office. No one from the government was flying from Israel to honor Reagan. I asked why not and received some vague technical explanation.

I called Israel's president, Moshe Katzav. "Natan, you are right. It's not good for Israel not to be represented there. I am ready to go. But I don't want to defy the prime minister. He has to ask me to go." I called Netanyahu, who was minister of finance. "Of course, it's a mistake," Bibi said. "Let's both go. I will call Arik and arrange it."

When I arrived home, Avital offered to join me, to show her gratitude to Reagan too. Bibi then called, warning, "Arik absolutely opposes our going. It's too awkward for me to cross him on this." Reporters were constantly scrutinizing the intense Arik-Bibi rivalry, looking for trouble. "But I will back you if you still want to go."

Confused about all this resistance, I entered the car with Avital. On the way to the airport from Jerusalem, I called the cabinet secretary, Israel Maimon, to inform him that I would end up missing the usual Sunday cabinet meeting. Maimon soon called back to say, rather formally, "Prime Minister Sharon directs you not to attend President Reagan's funeral." Sharon was sending his ambassador in Washington, Danny Ayalon, to represent Israel. That was it. Many other ministers had wanted to go, Maimon said. "If you go, it will cause jealousy and confusion."

I called Attorney General Elyakim Rubinstein. Fortunately, the drive to Ben-Gurion Airport takes time and could accommodate all the back-

and-forth calls. "If the prime minister directs me as a member of the cabinet not to attend this kind of function, can I go nevertheless as a private citizen?" I asked. "I'm not asking for permission. I only want to understand the law." Rubinstein said the prime minister could fire me anytime. Beyond that, I was free to go.

I then called Maimon to inform him that I was taking a few personal days to attend the funeral as a private citizen. I directed our travel agent to pay for our two tickets from our personal account.

As I entered the National Cathedral, someone handed me a ticket Reagan's family had reserved for me. Before I knew it, I was sitting in the front of the church, right behind Margaret Thatcher and Mikhail Gorbachev.

At the first cabinet meeting after my return, one minister noted how gratifying it was to see "the Israeli delegation"—me—seated so prominently at the funeral. This confirmed our "special relationship" with the United States. I glanced at Arik, who was silent. I replied I was honored to represent Israel there, to give this hero who had helped bring down Communism and free Soviet Jews the farewell he deserved.

Eventually, I discovered the most plausible explanation for Sharon's grudging behavior. In his 2014 biography of Sharon, the former editor of *Haaretz* David Landau noted that when Israel invaded Lebanon in 1982, Reagan was furious. Sharon knew that much of Reagan's criticism of the war was directed at him as defense minister. He never forgave Reagan for his angry pressure to withdraw and saw no reason to honor him.

By contrast, when eulogizing Reagan, President Bush had praised him for calling "evil by its name," adding that "there were no doubters in the prisons and Gulags, where dissidents spread the news, tapping to each other in code what the American president had dared to say."

"My God, Bush is quoting my article," I thought to myself, moved again by finding an ideological comrade in arms after so long.

The dissident-as-democratic-champion idea had caught Bush's imagination. His eulogy confirmed that, finally, someone powerful was listening to my analysis about how to defeat fear societies.

MY FRIENDSHIP WITH PRESIDENT BUSH

I was more surprised when Bush emerged as one of my book's first readers. Nine days after his reelection in November 2004, Bush hosted me at the White House. I was already in the United States to promote *The Case for Democracy*. Peter Osnos, my publisher and a former *Washington Post* reporter who had helped me in Moscow, had shared galley proofs with Tom A. Bernstein, a friend of President Bush's and former partner of his in the Texas Rangers baseball club. Bernstein then passed the book to Bush.

When Bush and I discussed the book, he zeroed in on a metaphor my coauthor and I had used, comparing a tyrannical state to a soldier pointing a gun at a prisoner for hours on end. Eventually, the soldier's arms tire. He lowers the gun, and the captive escapes. The dissident Andrei Amalrik had used that metaphor in 1969, when he wrote his courageous essay *Will the Soviet Union Survive Until 1984?* Now, the president's interest brought Amalrik's metaphor back to life.

Bush said, "I always felt that freedom is not an American invention, but a gift from God to all people. You succeeded in explaining it rationally."

I appreciated Bush's graciousness, although I was no longer falling for his "I'm just a simple guy from Texas" act. His commitment clearly ran deeper than my book. He admitted, "That thinking, that's part of my presidential DNA."

I told Bush that he was a true dissident. Rather than following the polls, he remained true to his beliefs and fought for them. Dissidents are lonely, I cautioned, but history is ultimately on their side. Countering the condescending claim that the Palestinians weren't ready for democracy, I recalled how many of the armchair experts used to decree that, while democracy is wonderful, our cause as dissidents would never shake the Soviet Union. I said he was acting in the tradition of Henry Jackson, Margaret Thatcher, and Ronald Reagan, linking foreign policy to human rights.

The Oval Office meeting wowed me. But I started worrying that I had violated diplomatic protocol. Israeli ministers are not supposed to meet the US president without informing the prime minister. I called Sharon. I reported yet again that Bush was going to focus on this democracy agenda and that it might be time to link any further concessions for peace to concrete Palestinian steps toward civil society. Arik remained unenthusiastic, saying, "We will discuss it when you return home." He was in the middle of a massive power struggle to push the Gaza disengagement through Likud and the cabinet. I had already condemned the move, and Arik was waiting to confirm Bush's support.

I returned home with my first box of books and gave a copy to Arik. "It's good that you convinced Bush about things that don't exist," he said sarcastically. Sharon was not about to let anyone distract him from his disengagement plan.

When I resigned from the government to protest the disengagement, I wrote President Bush a long letter explaining my actions. Bush responded, emphasizing that he shared my beliefs in democratization and that we would remain kindred pro-democratic spirits. Still, as president, he had to trust his friend "General Sharon."

My warm relations with President Bush complicated my relationship with many American Jews. Today, many liberal Jews, like most Democrats, hate President Trump so intensely that they forget how much they detested Bush. At the time, the hatred was absolutely vitriolic. Then, as now, many American Jews could not even thank the president when he backed Israel enthusiastically, while many Orthodox Jews could not criticize the president because he was so pro-Israel. Then, as now, some of Bush's harshest Jewish critics assumed that if this despicable president was so pro-Israel, there must be something wrong with Israel.

I liked quoting Bush's line that "freedom is not an American invention; it's a gift from God." This universal expression struck me as something that every liberal Jew should applaud. So I was stunned when I used the line while addressing an important Jewish organization and the room turned hostile. "How can you be friends with that man?" one obviously secular woman, who looked like she had not been inside a synagogue for years, snapped at me. "Don't you understand that his god is not our God?"

I didn't even understand how his stance on democracy wasn't our stance.

I did, however, understand the growing frustration with Bush as his presidency was bogged down in the Iraq War. In 2007, when a *Jerusalem Post* reporter asked me to assess Bush, I called him "a lonely dissident for democracy." He deserved great respect for raising the democratic question at a critical moment in world history, in the true dissident spirit.

At the same time, a president should be bold, yet not so bold as to be lonely. I criticized the way Bush coddled the Palestinians and the way he, like most presidents, couldn't comprehend that the charming, generous Saudis feared democracy even more than they feared Iran.

Underlying my analysis was my fundamental disagreement with President Bush's faith that once citizens were voting, they were free. A free society is necessary for truly free elections to take place. Bush's faith in elections left him unprepared for the chaos in Iraq and for the Hamas takeover in Gaza.

Nevertheless, I admired Bush's consistent support of democratic dissidents. I estimate that Bush met with more than one hundred dissidents from around the world. It didn't matter to him where they fought for freedom. It could be against regimes that were hostile to the United States, such as North Korea and Sudan, or competing powers such as Russia and China, or so-called friendly dictatorships such as Egypt. Bush put so much pressure on Egypt to release the democracy activist Saad Eddin Ibrahim from jail, including suspending aid increases, that Egypt's dictator Hosni Mubarak refused to visit the White House during Bush's second term.

Today, through his George W. Bush Presidential Center in Dallas, Texas, Bush has Republicans and Democrats working together to support dissidents worldwide. The bipartisan nature of his Human Freedom Advisory Council, on which I serve, is particularly impressive during these partisan times. Unfortunately, neither of his two immediate successors, Barack Obama and Donald Trump, have followed through on Bush's core commitment to fighting dictatorships by boosting dissidents.

When Obama won the presidency in November 2008, I shared in the electric excitement that swept much of the liberal world. I wrote an op-ed saying that the world understood that Obama intended to revolutionize American policy and distinguish his presidency from Bush's. Amid all the inevitable changes, I pleaded with Obama to follow in Bush's footsteps by supporting democracy, by personally meeting with democratic dissidents and looking out for them.

I had one discussion with Obama during his presidential run, in March 2007, when I visited Washington to invite President Bush to address our dissidents' conference in Prague. To broaden our coalition, I invited leading Democrats to join us too. Although he was too busy with his freshly announced candidacy to travel that far, Senator Obama responded to my call immediately and graciously invited me to his Senate office.

Obama impressed me with his Clintonesque charm, presence, and enthusiasm. We discussed the importance of the fight for freedom within fear societies. When I raised the question of Iranian dissidents specifically, he spoke passionately about his support for these heroes. Unfortunately, as president, Obama repeatedly prioritized engaging with dictatorial regimes over challenging their human rights records. In Cairo in June 2009, Obama spoke beautifully about democratic principles, about respecting women, about championing human rights. Yet, somehow, in that lengthy, well-publicized, carefully drafted speech, he ignored Hosni Mubarak's oppressive actions, including the pro-democracy bloggers, critics, and journalists the Egyptians had thrown in prison.

Even worse, Obama faltered during the critical moments of Iran's Green Revolution in 2009. According to Iranian dissidents with whom I later spoke, millions of Iranians were at a tipping point, wavering, poised to cross that critical psychological line between doublethink and dissent. At that moment, Iranian democrats needed an American administration ready to state unequivocally that it supported their goals and stood firmly at their side. Barack Obama let them down.

Obama's priority was reaching an agreement with Tehran over its nuclear program. He feared alienating the regime by supporting the dissidents. His passivity at this key juncture poured cold water into an almost boiling pot; he discouraged revolutionary fervor precisely when he could have encouraged meaningful change. When I confronted Michael McFaul, Obama's senior adviser on democracy issues who later served as ambassador to Russia, he claimed the administration feared for the Iranian dissidents' safety. American support would make it easier for the mullahs to tag these dissidents as traitors.

I recognized this argument from my Soviet days. That's what politicians in the free world usually say when they don't want to upset their totalitarian partners. Dissidents, who have already crossed the line, have nothing to lose and want the help. It was later revealed publicly that Obama also blocked the CIA from supporting the dissidents secretly. In *The Iran Wars*, the veteran foreign affairs correspondent Jay Solomon blames Obama's moves on his "obsessive commitment" to negotiations.

When Donald Trump was elected, he, too, wanted to distance himself from his predecessor. Nevertheless, he followed Obama by abandoning dissidents. Trump has taken America's human-rights-free foreign policy to absurd new depths. His assertion that North Koreans support Kim Jong Un with "great fervor" undermined America's moral standing, sabotaged North Korean dissidents, and legitimized an evil dictator. Trump's shocking refusal to confront President Vladimir Putin over Russia's blatant interference in the 2016 US presidential election highlights his mysterious unwillingness to protect Americans' democratic rights, let alone Russians' human rights or others' democratic aspirations.

There are vast differences in tone and substance between Barack Obama and Donald Trump. Yet both have moved the world away from human rights linkage and back to a cynical realpolitik. Obviously, Bush's pro-democracy policies didn't work out in Iraq and Afghanistan. But he deserves credit for the consistency of his vision and the tremendous support he offered dissidents.

A DISSIDENTS' JAMBOREE IN PRAGUE

Some might wonder: Why bother with the dissidents? Why consult them? How much influence can they have? Dissidents are always a small minority. They often look weak and disconnected.

But democratic dissidents play two key roles in their societies. First, they function as a litmus test. Understanding the split between true believers and doublethinkers, they can identify the invisible armies of doublethinkers, even when the regime looks strong from the outside. Having broken out of the dictator's forced illusions, they can help outsiders see past the façade. And second, they can be the agents for change, helping societies transition from fear to freedom.

In 2007, I initiated a unique meeting of democratic dissidents in Prague. I cohosted it with former Czech president Václav Havel and former Spanish prime minister José María Aznar in the nearly 350-year-old baroque Czernin Palace. This grand palace served as Nazi headquarters during World War II. KGB agents pretending to be Communist revolutionaries probably pushed the democratic martyr Foreign Minister Jan Masaryk to his death from his office window there in 1948. The Warsaw Pact, the Soviet military alliance competing with NATO, dissolved there in 1991.

Amid all that history, the meeting offered glimpses of a hopeful future. It was thrilling to be in a room with democratic activists from five continents. In one corner of the room was Lyudmila Alexeyeva, my cofounder of the Moscow Helsinki Group, who was still fighting for civil society in Putin's Russia. Near her was the chess superstar turned dissident Garry Kasparov. We were joined by old friends and veterans of the human rights struggle like Saad Eddin Ibrahim from Egypt, Mithal al-Alusi from Iraq, and the Palestinian Bassem Eid, as well as dissidents I met for the first time from China, Belarus, Syria, Libya, Lebanon, Iran, and Sudan.

I had invited President Bush to address the conference. Most of his advisers objected. When I followed up with a White House contact, he told me not to worry. "There is only one person in the West Wing who wants Bush to come to your conference. Fortunately for you, it is the president." In addition to delivering formal remarks, Bush met privately with every dissident. I knew how crucial these meetings were.

Despite coming from seventeen different countries, we spoke the same language of freedom, the language of human rights. We had all known—or still knew—the worlds of repression, of fear, of doublethink, and of nonviolent democratic dissent.

Later, the Western world would be surprised by the Iranian Green Revolution, which we kept predicting in Prague. Similarly, with the same accuracy the dissident-prophets in the Soviet Union had shown, the activists in Prague predicted political earthquakes shaking the dictatorships of Mubarak in Egypt, Qaddafi in Libya, and Assad in Syria in the next three to five years.

Listening to them, watching them, I could feel history in the making. It confirmed my sense, and Bush's, that the free world's greatest weapon in this struggle is the awesome power of its ideas.

MY PARALLEL UNIVERSES

The dissidents I met in Prague in 2007 got me thinking about that other forum where I had sat for the majority of the last nine years: the Israeli cabinet. Sometimes, even during the most mundane discussions, I would still get excited by the thought that here we were, shaping history. I would imagine how many generations of Jews would have found the whole scene of a Jewish democracy in action fantastic. Even during the hottest arguments with my most aggressive rivals, even after the most disappointing votes, I never lost the feeling that with these people, my comrades in arms, we were inventing new paradigms for the Jewish future.

Nevertheless, thinking of my two worlds together was jarring. Freedom-fighting dissidents and Israeli politicians exist in parallel universes but rarely speak to one another. And serving in government showed me just how difficult it could be to balance my outsider impulse and my insider standing.

When I was minister of industry and trade, building economic ties with China was becoming increasingly important. In 1997, as a Foreign Ministry official briefed me before I hosted a Chinese leader, I asked about political repression in China. "Do we know just how many political prisoners they have there?" I asked.

"We don't have that kind of information—and we don't talk about that," he said nervously, looking away from me. "We leave it to the Americans."

During our meeting, I followed the economic agenda—almost. As we finished, I said I had to add one item. I said that as a political prisoner in recovery, who was freed because people around the world were concerned about my case, I was concerned about the status of political prisoners and prisons in China. My Foreign Ministry briefer turned white, then red, then white again. But the Chinese official, unruffled, answered politely. "My dear Minister Sharansky," he said, "I'm afraid you've been misinformed. Come, visit China. I invite you to join me and we will visit our prisons together. You will see they are civilized—and for criminals, not dissidents."

I felt badly ambushing my Foreign Ministry colleague. And I understood the government's angle: trade with China was growing, from $50 million a year in 1992, to $1 billion in 2000, to $15 billion today. But I felt worse for millions of Chinese political prisoners.

Somehow, that invitation never came—and the Foreign Ministry never again invited me to host Chinese visitors.

The split evoked my Soviet past, when I was in the worlds of the Zionist activist and the human rights activist. Too many people told me I had to choose between the two. I chose both then—in the real world, in my democracy, it was harder to balance.

Today, Israel's success in maintaining the only democracy in a sea of Middle Eastern tyranny undermines the power of its totalitarian neighbors. At the same time, democratic dissidents fighting for freedom while proudly perpetuating their people's traditions are paving the way for new modes of relating to one another, cooperating with one another, and maybe even starting a real peace process. I hope that history will prove, once again, that we don't have to choose between the world of our identity and the world of their freedom. We can help one another defend both.

13

WATCHING THE DIALOGUE DETERIORATE ON CAMPUS

On April 15, 2002, I was demonstrating in Washington, again. This time, I was there officially as Israel's deputy prime minister, representing Prime Minister Ariel Sharon and the Israeli government. I joined one hundred thousand Americans, mostly Jews, rallying to support Israel's Operation Defensive Shield.

As many of us had warned, Ehud Barak's sweeping concessions at Camp David in July 2000 didn't bring peace. Instead, Yasir Arafat launched a renewed, vicious war of terrorism against us, starting in September 2000, what the Palestinians called the Second Intifada. March 2002 was especially bloody. Terrorists murdered 130 Israelis, including thirty killed by a suicide bomber during Passover seder at the Park Hotel in Netanya.

For seventeen months, bombs had been blowing up in cafes and buses; people were being shot while driving, commuting, jogging, and drinking coffee. Schoolchildren in our neighborhood, as elsewhere, were killed. I found myself attending funeral after funeral, paying shiva call after shiva call. I watched parents bury their children and children bury their parents. Closer to home, my secretary was injured in a bus bombing that killed one person right near our office. My hurt, terrified secretary was "lucky"—in the twisted vocabulary we developed—because she survived.

Every time I heard a boom, I scrambled, running around until I located my wife and my daughters. I sighed in guilty relief that they were OK, knowing that someone else would be mourning. And they were. Friends died. Friends lost limbs. Friends lost relatives and other friends.

In this atmosphere, saying goodbye to your spouse and your kids in the morning took on a special meaning, an extra touch. We always feared this goodbye might be the last one. As the terror mounted, so did Israelis' demands that their government protect them more effectively.

Under the Oslo agreements, Israel had withdrawn completely from Area A, leaving no military presence in the seven heavily populated Palestinian cities of Nablus, Jenin, Tulkarem, Qalqilya, Ramallah, Bethlehem, and Jericho, along with 80 percent of Hebron. Yasir Arafat's Palestinian Authority exerted full civil and security control there. All had become centers of bomb making and terrorism.

The day after the Passover massacre, the security cabinet met. We stayed up all night, debating what to do. With the violence escalating, and hundreds already dead, we had no choice. Launching Operation Defensive Shield, we dispatched troops to destroy the terrorists' infrastructure. We hit them where they planned their attacks and produced their bombs.

Because these terrorists were hiding in the heart of Palestinian cities, we decided that Israel would not use heavy weapons. We would not drop bombs or mortar shells on populated areas. The IDF would send soldiers house to house. We understood the choice we were making. Trying to limit Palestinian civilian casualties risked Israeli lives.

The worst fighting erupted in the casbah of Jenin. This cramped refugee camp of 13,500 people next to the city of Jenin was the base for at least a quarter of the terrorists who had murdered our citizens. There, amid intense house-to-house fighting, Israeli soldiers killed fifty-five Palestinians. Most died still clutching weapons in their hands or with their weapons lying nearby. Because we went in so close, Palestinians ambushed our soldiers, killing twenty-three. Those were the facts. Now the real story finishes and the Big Lie begins.

First, the Palestinians told reporters specific little lies: that soldiers tied up a Palestinian before shooting him, that soldiers used children as human shields, that soldiers bulldozed dozens of Palestinians into a mass grave. Next, Palestinian leaders like Saeb Erekat made wild charges of five hundred dead and thousands buried alive.

Then, came the experts, confirming what they expected to find. Richard Cook, the head of operations for the United Nations Relief and Works Agency for Palestine Refugees in the Near East (UNRWA), called the devastation the IDF left in Jenin "much greater than I expected." A British professor of forensic medicine, Derrick Pounder, arrived with Amnesty International. After performing his first autopsy, he was already corroborating what reporters then called "evidence of atrocities by Israeli troops in Jenin refugee camp."

The limited investigation did not stop Pounder from pronouncing that "claims that a large number of civilians died and are under the rubble are highly credible." Using speculation, not evidence, he continued, "It is not believable that only a few people have been killed, given the reports we have that a large number of people were inside three- and four-storey buildings when they were demolished."

The UN condemnations were particularly harsh. Even a fair-minded mediator, whom I knew well and respected, Terje Rød-Larsen, called Israel's actions "morally repugnant." He said that Jenin was "totally destroyed," and added that "expert people here who have been in war zones and earthquakes. . . say they have never seen anything like it."

Within two weeks, Rød-Larsen was downplaying these exaggerations. By then, however, it was too late. By the time the Israeli version was corroborated thoroughly and the Palestinian lies exposed publicly, the facts no longer mattered. The Jenin Massacre of the Truth had become the accepted story. As one veteran BBC correspondent, James Reynolds, admitted, "Those two words"—Jenin and massacre—became linked. "First impressions are very important. And perhaps, despite all the other reporting at the end, they are never rubbed out."

The Washington rally, held as this modern blood libel spread globally, was a typical Jewish event. So many people felt so strongly about attending the rally—which was organized in a matter of days—that too many speakers spoke for far too long. Normally, when placed on an overly ambitious speakers list, I enjoyed being the guy who kept it short. A few well-chosen lines are better remembered and deeply appreciated.

This time, however, I broke my rule. Even as the rally organizers whispered to me on the podium, "Finish up, Natan, really, really," I shared my firsthand account of the battle of Jenin in context. I detailed for the crowd the reasons why Israeli troops entered the casbah, the ethical decisions we made before the operation, the constraints we imposed on our soldiers, and the high price we paid.

I took my time because I felt we were at a delicate turning point. This wasn't the first accusation against Israel of a gross human rights violation. Since 1948, historians have been fighting about what happened when irregular Irgun forces attacked the Arab village of Deir Yassin and dozens of Arabs died. In 1982, the official Soviet newspapers we received in Chistopol prison blasted Israel for perpetuating the Sabra and Shatila massacres. Years later, I learned how Israel's military, judicial, and political systems had tried clarifying which Israelis failed to stop the Christian Phalangists from killing Palestinians in Lebanon, with Ariel Sharon being fired as defense minister as punishment.

This time, I didn't need to rely on historians or military investigators. I had witnessed everything from my cabinet seat and participated in the delicate decision-making. If decent people could believe such outrageous lies about us and actively spread them, I thought, then the situation had turned very dangerous indeed.

On the Washington Mall, I faced an easy audience. Looking into the crowd, I saw many of my comrades from previous battles: those who had visited us in Moscow, those who had marched with us for Soviet Jewish freedom in Washington, and those who had helped us start the Zionist Forum and launch Yisrael B'Aliyah. Despite their nervousness, despite the need to reassure them that these accusations were lies, it looked as if we were all united again, struggling for Israel's right to exist.

But the more I looked into the crowd, as the rally went on and on, the more disturbed I was by this familiarity. If I recognized so many from my generation, I started wondering, where were the next generations? Where were my friends' kids? How were they reacting to the "Jenin massacre" lies?

That's the reality I confronted a year and a half later, when I visited North American college campuses. A new film, *Jenin, Jenin*, used doctored footage and heartbreaking "eyewitness" interviews to present the Palestinians' Big Lie as the total truth. Although the truth had already been exposed in detail, this harsh, impressionistic film embarrassed thousands of young Jews.

Here, then, was the double double cross. Sacrificing for peace and ending up with war was bad enough. That's your enemy's fault. But sacrificing for peace and being broadly blamed for causing the war was doubly infuriating. That's your friends' fault too.

MY MARSHALL PLAN

As terrorism worsened, the need to respond constructively and take re-sponsibility grew. The world was pumping billions into the Palestinian Authority with no strings attached and no benchmarks of progress. I genuinely felt badly for the Palestinians who suffered financially as their leaders stole most of the international aid for their personal use.

I started wondering if the Palestinian territories could be run in a way that would transition to democracy and build economic independence. After April 2002, when President Bush identified democracy as the best tool against Palestinian terrorism, I thought we finally had a chance to make the PA a test case for Bush's vision.

In late spring 2002, I proposed a new Marshall Plan for the Middle East. I modeled it loosely on Secretary of State George Marshall's post–World War II initiative, which helped rebuild Europe while protecting its democratic institutions. "Here's our chance," I told Ariel Sharon, "to cultivate Palestinian civil society, dismantle terrorism, and offer a model for the world, all done under the auspices of the United Nations, the United States, Israel, and the Arab countries that recognize Israel."

These parties would direct huge resources toward the Palestinians. But every grant would be conditional, linked to specific, measurable progress in four areas:

- Economic independence: promoting Palestinian businesses that were viable, profitable, and protected from Arafat's racketeering

- Refugee camps: closing down the slums and committing to im-proving the Palestinians' quality of life in new villages, while eliminating this powerful symbol, exploited over decades, of Zionism's supposed criminal nature

- Education and incitement: using the schools to cultivate dem-ocratic values while ending calls for violence against Jews in the media, the mosques, and the schools

- Dissent: encouraging more democratic voices, which required the free world to pressure the PA to stop punishing candid critics.

Over the decades, as the West has propped up the PA with billions, experts have launched numerous plans to help build a Palestinian state. My proposals differed from the pack because all the reforms, every joint venture and investment, would advance one central mission. Every Western dollar would strengthen individual Palestinians' independence. Not one penny would strengthen the dictators. The return on investment had to be institutions fostering a free, healthy civil society, nothing else.

After three transitional years of such rebuilding, with a civil society starting to blossom, elections would yield a new government, dependent on its people and accountable to them. Peace negotiations between representatives of two peoples, when both sides depend on the well-being of the electorate, have a real shot at success.

The Israeli press pooh-poohed such a quixotic project. So I did what every Israeli who wants to get heard does: I pitched my article in America, in this case, to the *Wall Street Journal*. Democratization, I argued, must boost the people's freedom, not their oppressors' power. The West must wean the Palestinians from their leaders, not tighten the leaders' grip on the Palestinians. Rather than sloppily bombarding dictators and terrorists with more cash to steal, the free world should be disciplined and strategic. It should encourage joint ventures with independent businesspeople while funding genuine civil rights organizations, independent trade unions, bold women's organizations, and democratic student groups. These are the counter forces that build freedom instead of one-man rule.

Israeli experts vetoed my naive ideas. Our generals, intelligence people, and diplomats kept telling me that dreaming of civil society among the Palestinians was utopian and would never happen. Our European, American, and UN friends kept running money through Arafat, then Abu Mazen—bankrolling the problems that needed solving.

When I opposed the initial Oslo peace approach, Yossi Beilin, Shimon Peres's deputy foreign minister, told me, "Natan, developing democracy will take decades. Nurturing a Palestinian civil society is a twenty-, thirty-, or forty-year project. We are bringing peace now. We're going to have peace in the next three to five years."

There's the failure. The buzzword was "peace process." But the real approach stemmed from the impatient, unrealistic slogan "peace now."

Here we stand, thirty years later, with more tension, more suffering, more victims and much more hatred. Despite all the hype, the peace process hasn't started yet. It will not come from one American president or another. It has to emerge from within Palestinian society.

THE END OF YISRAEL B'ALIYAH

In the brief period between the Washington rally and my first campus confrontations, many political changes occurred at home. In January 2003, Israel held elections again. It ended up being Yisrael B'Aliyah's last electoral round. As some of us expected, the more our party succeeded in integrating Russians into Israeli society, the less the Russians needed us.

Terrorism became an unanticipated accelerator. The intense, ideological, life-and-death debates pushed aside our quality-of-life issues. Our attempt to unite right and left collapsed as the two sides clashed ever more brutally. In 2003, only two of us, Yuli Edelstein and I, were elected to the Knesset.

Number three on our list was Marina Solodkin. Marina was a constituent-services miracle worker. When she started, she was a relatively recent immigrant, having landed in Israel in 1991. We thought we would teach her a thing or two. Instead, she schooled us in the art of being loyal to the electorate, spending her days and nights answering mail, visiting the poor and disgruntled, and fighting bureaucratic misfires or abuses.

I felt I owed it to our most loyal voters to keep her in parliament. I resigned from the Knesset shortly after the elections, yielding my seat to Marina, who was next on our list. Keeping Marina in the Knesset acknowledged that, even as Yisrael B'Aliyah faded away, we, its leaders, remained committed to its core voters. Under Israeli law, giving up my seat did not prevent me from serving in the cabinet.

Our party accepted Ariel Sharon's proposal to merge with his ruling Likud Party. As a result of our agreement, I joined the cabinet with a more modest position: minister of Jerusalem and Diaspora affairs.

In truth, whatever big excuses history provided, whatever rationalizations we had, and whatever witticisms we remembered about our party committing suicide by succeeding, the 2003 elections delivered an unpleasant blow. It's never fun to lose.

Looking back, I realize that the timing of our party's demise offered me a great gift. During the next two years I had no party responsibilities, no Knesset responsibilities, and no big ministry to run. My newfound freedom liberated me to concentrate on the issues that interested me, especially Israel-Diaspora relations and the connection between freedom and security. Over the next two years, I would write my book with Ron Dermer explaining my disagreement with the Left and the Right about their attempts to divorce any questions of democracy from a quest for peace, and I would concentrate on the growing fight against the New Anti-Semitism.

A CAMPUS TOUR IN 2003

I visited thirteen North American university campuses in the fall of 2003. This was not a typical lecture tour. I did not just want to speak at large public meetings. I sought intimate forums to learn what students, especially young Jews, were thinking about Israel, and how the growing campaign against Israel affected them. At my first campus visit, a student told me after my speech, "For me, as a liberal Jew, it would be better if Israel didn't exist."

I heard that at York University in Toronto, which had granted me an honorary doctorate in 1982 in absentia, then presented it to me five years later. The ceremony in 1987 had turned very emotional very quickly, as I was surrounded by many Toronto students who had been so involved in the struggle for Soviet Jewry. In those days, the fight for freedom and our national pride in our people and our country overlapped: our liberalism and Zionism reinforced one another. Now, half a generation later, this student—along with many others—was ashamed and announcing a divorce, separating his liberal identity from his Zionism.

The timing of this York student's sweeping repudiation was particularly upsetting. Israeli troops were fighting daily to protect us. Israeli civilians were still targeted by the waves of terror Arafat unleashed. Yet, when we defended ourselves, the pro-terror propaganda against us intensified.

Especially as America's global war on terror continued after September 11, 2001, we in Israel's security cabinet felt we were on the forefront of a shared Western fight. We were defending ourselves while trying to minimize the suffering of civilians caught in the cross fire. Officers from the United States, the United Kingdom, and elsewhere kept visiting Israel to learn how to ethically fight this often shadowy, asymmetrical war. Yet, to hear young, idealistic Jews on many campuses nevertheless echo the false accusations, charging Israel with committing war crimes, was painful and infuriating. Such a disconnect suggested that our lines of communication were malfunctioning and our identities were clashing.

During this trip, I met many enthusiastic Zionists too. These Jews defended Israel on campus proudly. One could sense the Birthright bounce, the positive impact the new Taglit-Birthright Israel program was starting to have on campus. Thousands of young Jews resented the gap between the complicated but idealistic democracy they visited and the evil monster the Jewish state was made out to be by so many.

I enjoyed meeting those Israel activists. But I was particularly curious about the Jews who felt caught in the middle. Some felt a deepening tension between their commitment to liberal ideas and their loyalty to Israel. They commanded the most attention. While some radical, left-wing Jews felt embarrassed by Israel, many more Jews were embarrassed to go public about their support for Israel and Zionism.

During a frank conversation with some Jewish students at Harvard University, one Harvard Business School student admitted feeling caught. She feared signing a petition against the anti-Israel boycotters. She feared joining pro-Israel organizations. She feared identifying as a Zionist. The Harvard campus was so anti-Israel that open identification with the Jewish state could cost her, she believed, and damage her academic future. She knew of at least three professors with influence over her final grades who would probably view pro-Israel activism unkindly. The risk was simply too great for now. "Once I am established in my career," she said, "I can start speaking on behalf of Israel."

I could not believe it. I wasn't in Moscow; this was Cambridge, Massachusetts. This wasn't a fear society; this was Harvard University, supposedly the center of free thought, of openness, liberalism, and professionalism. The student had made it to one of the world's top business schools, but she felt compelled to hide her political sympathies there. She reminded me of me, when I was a student at a similar elite institution in the Soviet Union. She was a doublethinker, as I had been in those days, thinking one thing, saying something else to fit in, get along, and get ahead.

Another pro-Israel liberal studying at Columbia University told a similar story. When he campaigned for Israel, he lost too many friends, he said. Once he abandoned Israel politics and instead pushed organic farming, he was popular again. He, too, was an Ivy League doublethinker, who traded his commitment to his people for popularity with his peers.

A few years later, in 2010, the pollster Frank Luntz invited thirty-five MIT and Harvard students, Jewish and non-Jewish, to discuss Middle East issues. Without prompting, some of the non-Jews started attacking Israel's "war crimes" and America's "Jewish lobby." The fifteen Jews mostly sat silently, absorbing the abuse, for hours. Luntz noted that, in the post-modern world, "kids on the left" in particular "have been taught not to judge. Therefore those on the left will not judge between Israel and the Palestinians."

But something more disturbing happened. When Luntz debriefed the Jewish kids, alone, they defended Israel passionately. He asked why they had not done so to a seemingly friendly audience. Essentially, they told him that because people knew they were Jews, they had to choose their words about Israel carefully. Everyone assumed they were biased no matter what they said.

Watching the video highlights of this encounter upset me. Jews were enjoying a golden age on American campuses. Never before had there been so many Jewish students and Jewish professors, Jewish studies programs and Jewish college presidents. Yet these Harvard and MIT Jews acted like Soviet Jews in so many ways. In the Soviet Union, always conscious that you were a Jew, you kept your internal censor on. You knew your words and actions would be judged differently. Now, on these elite campuses were the early warnings of a hyper-judgmental, suffocating, campus-based fear society, rife with anti-Zionism, the New Anti-Semitism, where people who thought they were the freest Jews in history didn't feel fully free.

This Jewish skittishness in the world's strongest Diaspora community made me grateful for my new freedom in Israel. There, I no longer felt the need to go through such mental gymnastics, worrying about what others might say when I spoke up.

In fairness, this silenced majority, these doublethinking students, faced a carefully orchestrated campaign. Nearly every time I rose to speak in public, I spied what became a familiar sight: well-dressed students in kaffiyehs sitting toward the front, ready to ask tough questions. Sometimes the questions were pointed but fair. Usually they were hostile and vaguely referenced some form of violence the questioner had endured. I am sure some questioners indeed suffered. But the questions often had the same phrasing, with many questioners on different campuses recalling precisely the same personal trial.

These exchanges occurred more than a decade before students started talking about triggering and microaggressions and intersectionality. Jews today are often blocked at the intersection, not welcomed as feminists or LGBTQ activists if they insist on being Zionists. Even then, these anti-Zionist bullies were monopolizing the public space, short-circuiting real debate, shutting down conversation with emotional appeals. I could feel a clear division between those Jews anxious to learn from my responses and those who just wanted the whole problem to go away.

I enjoyed going back and forth with critical students. Without tough questions, without some vigorous debate, no students would change their minds. Without a real dialogue, the harsh imagery of *Jenin, Jenin*—offering accusations greater than the facts—would continue massacring the truth and alienating liberal Jews from the Jewish state.

The most extreme left-wing students, Jewish and non-Jewish, shut down any discussion. At Rutgers University, I was schmoozing with students just before starting my lecture, entitled "Human Rights, Justice and Democracy—A Jewish Approach." Suddenly, *smush!* I was hit in the face with a cherry cream pie. While temporarily blinded, I heard someone yell, "End the occupation! Free Palestine!" My assailant was a Jew who helped found Central Jersey Jews Against the Occupation.

I was hustled backstage. I wiped my face. One of my embarrassed hosts gave me his jacket, two sizes too big. Quickly returning to the podium, smiling broadly, I said, "New Jersey cooks very good cakes. I hope that one was kosher." The audience cheered.

The attack backfired. This radical's violence upset the crowd. Fearing an audience backlash, the usual propagandists slunk out of the auditorium. The loud anti-Zionist demonstration outside, uniting hipsters with black-hatted Neturei Karta Israel haters, dissolved. The crowd that remained was so sympathetic I thought some people might volunteer to join the IDF that night. But there was no real debate either. The opportunity for education had been lost.

The day after I visited Rutgers, vandals spray-painted swastikas on the walls of the local Hillel House and the university chapter of Alpha Epsilon Pi, a national Jewish fraternity. In the meantime, the self-proclaimed liberal professors, who had organized an intense Internet campaign against me as representative of a "Nazi, war criminal state," continued their attacks.

HAUNTED BY THESE NEW JEWS OF SILENCE

After I returned to Israel, I wrote an article called "Traveling to the Occupied Territories," meaning the campuses. My spokesperson pitched it to *Maariv*, Israel's main daily newspaper. The young editors there doubted the essay's relevance to their readers, especially because of its length. Indulging me as a minister, they promised to take it to the editorial meeting Sunday morning.

That Sunday, during our government cabinet meeting, I was called out for a pressing phone call. It was Amnon Dankner, *Maariv*'s legendary editor in chief. His more provincial junior colleagues had said "no" based on their made-in-Israel tunnel vision. He, however, had been the Jewish Agency spokesman in the 1970s and then a Washington correspondent. "Natan, I am running the whole essay," he said. "Not because you're a minister, but because of the message. This is shocking. I had no idea the situation was this bad."

It seemed that few leaders of the organized Jewish community in North America realized it was that bad either. During my campus tour, I tried to meet with Jewish Federation officials in each city I visited. Through our discussions, I saw that in many cases the campus was a no-man's-land for Jewish organizations.

For example, when I met with my friends from the San Francisco Federation, they had many complaints about Ariel Sharon's governmental policies. This was typical of that group. After some back-and-forth, I responded, "I understand your frustrations. Some of your criticisms I accept, some I believe are unfair. But let's look at something closer to home."

I wanted to discuss the harassment of Jewish students at San Francisco State University. It was well known that in May 2002, pro-Palestinian demonstrators had menaced Zionist students at a pro-Israel rally there, chanting, "HITLER DID NOT FINISH THE JOB" and "GO HOME OR WE'LL KILL YOU." The pro-Palestinian group on campus distributed posters of a dead baby with drops of blood, adorned with the words "SHARON," "PALESTINIAN CHILDREN MEAT," and the sick explanation, updating the medieval blood libel, "SLAUGHTERED ACCORDING TO JEWISH RITES UNDER AMERICAN LICENSE." I had tasted a dose of the Jew-hatred there the day before.

I asked, "Do anyone of you contribute to San Francisco State University?"

A number of hands shot up proudly.

"Would the president of the university take your call?" A smaller number of hands shot up, even more proudly.

"Do you know that, of all the universities I have visited, that university is the most hostile to Israel? Even Hillel—the Jewish students' organization—is banned from campus. And Hillel leaders have been trying to meet with the president for over a year. They only had a chance yesterday, because I, as an Israeli minister, simply brought them into my meeting with him."

As I detailed the way Jewish students felt bullied, the leaders looked shocked. They admitted that they thought of students as out-of-towners. They defined the Federation's mission as tending to their local community's institutions.

The problem was complicated by the growing number of voices within the Jewish community saying that any hostility toward Israel on campus was Israel's fault. When the New York Jewish newspaper the *Forward* translated my article and ran it, the headline read "Tour of U.S. Schools Reveals Why Zionism Is Flunking." That title twist pointed the finger at us, rather than the campus occupiers.

Despite its misleading headline, my article triggered many responses. More and more parents were noticing that the growing anti-Israel obsession in the universities echoed traditional Jew-hatred. Today, there's a much greater awareness of the problem. Since 2002, the campus has become the center of attention for the organized Jewish community, as well as many new independent pro-Israel organizations.

When summarizing the trip, I told Ariel Sharon that the North American campuses had become the most important battlefield outside of Israel for the future of the Jewish people.

THE BANNER OF HUMAN RIGHTS
IS TURNED AGAINST US

I could not shake off a heavy feeling. I was haunted by the all-too-familiar look on the faces of these new Jews of silence, who felt they had to keep their feelings of solidarity with Israel underground to fit in. I felt thrown backward in time, seeing too many resemblances to the totalitarian world of doublethinkers I had fled. I was also troubled by the look of the smaller minority of Jewish anti-Zionist zealots, denouncing Israel with a venom I had never seen before from fellow Jews.

Although the physical attacks united us as Israelis, the ideological attacks risked dividing us as a people. Our attackers had not only seized the banner of human rights from us, they had turned it against us. I kept wondering how it had happened, and so fast. When I first visited campuses in the late 1980s, I felt at home. All my identities seemed to be in sync. Far away from the Moscow tensions, where many people kept asking me to choose between the fight for Soviet Jewry and the fight for human rights, I enjoyed meeting students who seemed to see no daylight between their liberalism and their Zionism. The struggle for the Jewish state, the struggle for Soviet Jewry, and the struggle for human rights overlapped for them, as for me.

Only a decade and a half later, it now seemed that students felt forced to choose between supporting Israel and campaigning for human rights. Many critics scoffed when I, as an Israeli minister, lectured at their university about human rights.

Admittedly, the optics around Israel and the Palestinians looked particularly bad when viewed from an American campus. And it wasn't just an image or public-relations problem. Objectively, we really faced—and still face—a serious human rights challenge. Not only is Israel a democracy imposing military control on an unwilling population, but it's a country that has repeatedly had to fight terrorists hiding in densely populated civilian areas. Yet, wasn't it also true that we remained the only democracy in the Middle East? Weren't we the ones often imposing restrictions on our army to wage this difficult war in the most moral manner possible?

When I spoke to sympathetic Jewish audiences, who were obsessed with this gap between our democratic intentions and our tarnished reputation, one question kept coming up again and again: "Why is Israel so bad at public relations?"

Israeli *hasbara* obviously had its massive failures. But there was a deeper shift taking place. Those who wanted to destroy us had hit pay dirt. The ideological climate was now more welcoming to their worldview. Israel's harshest enemies' worst lies took root because they were now being planted in fertile soil, as the once liberal campus turned against the very foundations of liberal nationalism.

POSTMODERNISM DEVALUES
ISRAEL'S CURRENCY AS A DEMOCRATIC STATE

One of the first books I read after leaving the Soviet Union had warned about the new risks to freedom emerging from the university's "politically correct" culture, a phrase everyone was just starting to learn in 1987. *The Closing of the American Mind*, by the University of Chicago philosopher Allan Bloom, noted, "There is one thing a professor can be absolutely certain of: Almost every student entering the university believes, or says he believes, that truth is relative." Students wanted to live in a "problem-free world." Learning from the students of the 1960s, who were now their professors, they started seeing Western values as the source of many of the world's problems, not the basis for common solutions.

Bloom explained what, to me, was the astounding reaction of right-thinking liberals, who condemned President Reagan's speech calling the Soviet Union an evil empire. Bloom's students preferred to talk about a "tension between values," which was more fluid, "than the tension between good and evil," which was too categorical, burdened by its "cargo of shame and guilt." They sought freedom from this judgmental rhetoric personally and politically. "One does not feel bad about or uncomfortable with one-self" when any conflict or imperfection could be solved with "just a little value adjustment," rather than having to sift right from wrong.

Over the years, I kept on thinking about that book as I saw the power and intensity of this new brainwashing build. If everything was relative and all identities were equally flawed, if every Western country was car-icatured as being defined by "dead white males" guilty of imperialism, racism, and colonialism, even the Western commitment to human rights didn't matter much. No wonder our future leaders were asking, "What right do we have to impose our values on others?"

Reading Bloom's book helped me understand so many Western liberals' continued resistance to raising human rights issues during America's strategic negotiations with Mikhail Gorbachev's Soviet Union and when I had sought allies for our big march on Washington. Back in the 1970s, our battle for linkage had been fought against cynical practitioners of realpolitik like Richard Nixon and Henry Kissinger. Now, progressive forces were rejecting linkage ideologically.

It was depressing to hear students in the world's most sophisti-cated universities echo the Soviets' most primitive propaganda, treating imperfect democracies as no better than perfectly awful dictatorships. The Soviets had always enjoyed undermining the democratic West's moral authority against their immoral regime by essentially saying, "You have your conceptions; we have ours. You make sure everyone can say whatever they want; we make sure everyone can eat whenever they need."

This assault on democracy hurt the West, hurt America, and particularly hurt the most vulnerable democracy, Israel. While this approach confused Americans, it clearly hurt Israel. If democracy and human rights were only relative values, then Israel's standing as the only democracy in the Middle East counted for nothing. Year by year, we watched Israel lose its currency in the world as a democratic state.

Even our pride in Israeli democracy started backfiring. Radical liberal voices wondered, "Who needs Zionism importing the liberal democratic ideas of the West to the East?" One French liberal Jewish professor, sounding as if he had just popped out of Allan Bloom's book, told me that the Zionist idea was wrong, because East is East and West is West, meaning "Western" Jews, with their westernized ideas, should stay out of the Middle East.

POSTMODERNISM DEVALUES ISRAEL'S CURRENCY AS A NATION-STATE

By 2003, I saw how much more dangerous these ideas were. The West had indeed won. The Soviet Union had died. But like some mysterious spirits leaving the body as the heart stops beating, certain Soviet and Marxist ideas that undermined Westerners' confidence in the power of their foundational ideas seeped into the atmosphere. These ghosts of dead Communist ideas were shaping the next hot new intellectual trend, postmodernism.

Although my professor friends love arguing about what postmodernism means, I think the label works here to summarize this broad rebellion against many defining modern, Western ideas and achievements that trace back to the Enlightenment of the 1700s. As the label suggests, postmodernists were always more sure about what they opposed than what they believed.

We all agreed that the Western mind didn't start closing in America but in Europe. After the trauma of World War II, many Europeans started blaming centuries of endless, pointless religious and national wars on traditional identities and the resulting prejudices. Postmodernists imagined utopia as filled with individuals, not groups, and freed of any borders, let alone nations. John Lennon's famous song "Imagine" epitomized postmodernism's political dream:

> *Imagine there's no countries*
> *It isn't hard to do*
> *Nothing to kill or die for*
> *And no religion too*
> *Imagine all the people living life in peace*

This postmodern vision attacked the fundamental building block of our world order, the nation-state. In the 1800s, nation builders from George Washington to Giuseppe Garibaldi romanticized their nations. Now, trendy academics taught that Western nationalism was a corrupt tool that created false barriers between people while imposing genuine suffering on the powerless. This belief struck another ideological blow against Israel. In a world where all boundaries were bad, its role as the nation-state of the Jewish people was no longer valued.

A leading postmodern historian, New York University's Tony Judt, who proudly proclaimed himself "suspicious of identity politics in all forms, Jewish above all," declared in 2003 that "the problem with Israel" is that "it arrived too late." Writing as if we didn't live in a world with 191-plus independent nation-states, he claimed that Israel "has imported a characteristically late-nineteenth-century separatist project into a world that has moved on, a world of individual rights, open frontiers, and international law. The very idea of a 'Jewish state'—a state in which Jews and the Jewish religion have exclusive privileges from which non-Jewish citizens are forever excluded—is rooted in another time and place. Israel, in short, is an anachronism."

What a difference from the 1950s and 1960s, when Israel was the poster child of the post–World War II, postcolonial era as a functioning Jewish democratic state. Back then, a young Londoner named Tony Judt felt inspired to volunteer on a kibbutz. Now, Israel earned no points for being democratic, and no points for being a proud nation-state, promising all citizens individual rights while expressing the majority's culture in the public square.

Israel's timing wasn't off—the postmodernists' timing was. In the Soviet Union, we dissidents struggled against a regime that enslaved people by erasing their identities. We felt that the liberal-democratic nation-state offered the best framework for defending human rights. Yet just as most Soviet dissidents were falling in love with this idea of the nation-state, some Western liberals started rejecting it.

Postmodernism poisoned the atmosphere surrounding Israel quickly, especially because Israel was a small, liberal, democratic, nationalist outpost with a big Palestinian problem. Sloppy vocabulary proved damning. In Ukraine, the word "occupation" often gave us chills. It was the word that evoked the Nazis, mass killings, death camps, the brutalities of world war. I realized that whenever most Europeans heard the word, they kept thinking of the Nazis, whose desire for conquest resulted in their smothering, genocidal straitjacket of an occupation. Few critics bothered to understand the complicated historical background of Israel's occupation, including Jews' deep ties to the biblical lands. Even more unfairly, these bashers ignored the dangerous, difficult dilemmas Israel faced in its struggle for survival. It's that background that created Israel's on-off, here-and-there, spotted control over Palestinians.

Similarly, when some Americans heard about the Israeli-Palestinian conflict, they instinctively translated it into black and white, casting the Palestinians as the oppressed blacks and making Israelis the racist southern whites. All these sloppy comparisons reinforced one another. In a rush to demonize Israel, radical leftists saddled the country with the great crimes of the West.

The Palestinian suicide bombing campaign in the early 2000s reinforced these misimpressions about Israel's occupation. Good people on campus and in editorial suites assumed that those willing to kill themselves to kill others must be really oppressed, so tortured by Israelis that they had no choice but to lash out as they did. As the longtime secretary general of Amnesty International Martin Ennals proclaimed back in 1974 about the Palestinians, "Terrorism comes because human rights are not granted."

In January 2002, after Wafa Idris smuggled a bomb into Jerusalem while driving a Red Crescent ambulance and blew herself up in a shoe store on Jaffa Street, I remember reading in the *New York Times* that this evil act was "a sign of the growing desperation of Palestinians." In England, the *Guardian* would write that Idris, whom Palestinians celebrated as their first female suicide bomber, sacrificed "herself on the altar of Palestinian freedom."

Meanwhile, I also read our intelligence reports. It turned out that Idris's husband divorced her after a miscarriage made her unable to have children and she had refused to let him take a second wife. Deemed a "disgrace," she faced a cruel choice. To restore her family's honor, she could either be killed by a relative or kill Jews. Such typically Western romanticization of Middle Eastern brutality created the cruel irony. While under terrorist attack, Israel became, after South Africa reformed in the early 1990s, the last remnant of Western colonialism, imperialism, and racism.

HOW PALESTINIAN NATIONALISM
BECAME ACCEPTABLE IN A POSTNATIONAL UNIVERSE

The postmodernists' logic required Olympic-level mental gymnastics. The biggest leap occurred because the postcolonial rebellion after World War II resulted in many national movements in the developing world. Clearly, postmodernists couldn't reject those nationalisms.

What to do? Improvise.

Postmodernists sang "Imagine" only about Western democracies. At the same time, they gave the world's victims a pass on so many fronts. Postmodernists learned from Marxism to divide the world between the oppressors and the oppressed. While the nationalism of the oppressor is always evil, the nationalism of the oppressed could be a useful progressive force during some historical periods. Viewing the world through this distorting lens, postmodernists defined powerful Western democracies as inherently bad and the powerless nations of the world as always good.

With that, and considering Israel's genuine challenges controlling millions of Palestinians, two more switches occurred. First, Israel became defined as only a white, Western, Ashkenazi project, ignoring its dark-skinned Mizrahi majority as well as Zionism's East-West fusions. Israel also became the symbol of all that is bad, as both a proud nation-state and a supposedly white, Western, colonialist, racist imposition into the Middle East, oppressing the local natives. Second, the Palestinians became the world's most coddled victims, even getting a free pass when their leaders spread terrorism throughout the world and oppressed their own people.

POSTMODERNISTS MAKE DEMOCRATIC ISRAEL
THE BIGGEST OBSTACLE TO WORLD PEACE

In the postmodern universe, if there is one absolute value, it's the value of peace at any price, leaving everyone with "nothing to kill or die for." The Oslo agreement played into those illusions. Calling it a peace process meant that any supporters of Oslo were pro-peace. That made any critics of Oslo—or of the supposed peace partners' regimes—anti-peace by definition.

Frustration as Oslo collapsed, after such high hopes, made Israel's situation even more difficult. With Israel the stand-in for all Western sins, it became responsible for "killing . . . the Middle East peace process," in the words of Tony Judt, expressing the opinion of many of his postmodernist colleagues.

Having grown up in a totalitarian regime that somehow found favor with many Western intellectuals, I have seen how people delude themselves once they decide how the world should work. In the Soviet Union, talk about the "struggle for peace as the highest value" camouflaged the real struggle against the West, as well as the Communists' clever attempts to mobilize pro-peace activists in the West against their own governments.

As with the word "occupation," the word "peace" can be used to describe very different situations. The Soviets were quite successful at keeping domestic peace by imposing mass slavery. Those of us who became dissidents did what we did because we saw through the Soviet half-truths, which used lovely words to hide ugly situations. Defenders always emphasize the appealing half that's true, overlooking that there's an equally large part that's a lie.

We knew the real value was not peace at any price but peace with freedom. Now, years later, it was disappointing to see, even after the Soviet Union fell, that the old Communist peace con worked. Too many sincere, peace-loving people wanted to believe that the struggle for peace can be isolated from the nature of the regime and the freedom every citizen deserves to enjoy.

When I traveled abroad or hosted foreigners for various seminars and conferences, I devised a little parlor game for journalists and diplomats to expose these half-truths and careful manipulations. "Who are the enemies of peace?" I would ask.

I would list three or four Arab strongmen along with Israel's prime minister. Then I would say, "Rank these Middle Eastern leaders' commitment to peace."

Hosni Mubarak, Egypt's dictator, always won; he was the champion of peace. Over the years, I learned that Hafez al-Assad of Syria, was "trustworthy" and "ready to make peace." From 2000 on, I heard about how cultured, enlightened, and open Assad's son Bashar was. After all, he was an ophthalmologist. After 2003, Muammar al-Qaddafi earned the compliment, "He gave away his nuclear weapons." I usually heard that Yasir Arafat "was doing his best, but he's got serious opposition," until the terrorism of the 2000s made that pose farcical. After Arafat died, the same rationalizations returned to excuse Abu Mazen's behavior.

Benjamin Netanyahu and Ariel Sharon (until he withdrew from Gaza) were consistently condemned as the worst enemies of peace. I would respond that, as the only democratically elected leader of the lot, the Israeli prime minister must want to deliver peace to his voters. My contestants would shrug their shoulders and explain to me that "democracy has nothing to do with peace in the Middle East."

Suddenly, the international community seemed to be wired backward: Israel was seen as bad and Palestinian terrorists were seen as good. The polarities were reversed. Israel's great qualities—as a democracy in the Middle East surrounded by dictatorships, as a Jewish state providing a home after centuries of wandering, and as a proud country defending itself against immoral enemies—were transformed into character flaws perpetuating Israel's great sin, the occupation.

Most of these intellectuals didn't wish to destroy Israel. But our enemies who did want to wipe us out discovered they could hitch a ride on postmodern newspeak. The postmodernists provided the road map. Palestinian terrorists and Iranian Islamists followed along, escalating with postmodern rhetoric, from attacking the occupation to negating Israel entirely. The language was similar even if the conclusions differed.

A key bridge builder here was the Palestinian academic and high priest of postmodernism Edward Said, for decades one of Columbia University's most famous professors. His influential book *Orientalism* launched thousands of Western guilt trips, with the blame always placed on "us," never on "them." In that spirit, he treated Israel as a colonialist project, denying its legitimacy as a Jewish state.

In his book *The Question of Palestine*, Said warned Yasir Arafat and the Palestinians that if they remained caught in a local conflict between Arab and Jew, they would lose. Instead, he showed them how to exploit the modern media's "generalizing tendencies" to link their local conflict to the broader fight against Western racism, colonialism, imperialism, and supremacism—what he called "Orientalism."

With such accusations spoiling the atmosphere, the institution that in 1947 recognized the need for a Jewish state, the United Nations, became the forum that best illustrated how postmodern rhetoric eased so naturally into anti-Zionism.

Perhaps the most dramatic example occurred in the summer of 2001. After years of planning by the United Nations and the human rights community, the UN World Conference Against Racism in Durban, South Africa, meant to be a major step forward in the global fight against racism, turned into a festival of Israel bashing. Delegates to the main conference and the nongovernmental organizations' parallel meeting repeatedly singled out Israel as the main cause of racism internationally.

Although she ultimately condemned the brutal attacks on Israel and Jews, the UN human rights commissioner who presided over the conference, Mary Robinson, had spent years bashing Israel in postmodern terms. The well-respected president of Ireland from 1990 to 1997, Robinson too quickly replaced the traditional, liberal understanding of human rights as objective and fundamental with a Soviet-tinged postmodern notion that the Western concept of human rights was flawed.

Robinson would later recall that, "when I started back in September of 1997" with her UN job, "I was quite taken aback by how many leaders of developing countries told me, 'Don't you know human rights is just a Western stick to beat us with. It is politicized, nothing to do with real concern about human rights.'"

She acknowledged, "There was an element of truth in that."

Over the years, Robinson became well known for excusing Palestinian violence while exaggerating Israel's flaws. In May 1998, she defended Palestinian riots as "peaceful assembly." During the contentious lead-up to the Durban conference, she compared "the historical wounds of anti-Semitism and of the Holocaust on the one hand" with "the accumulated wounds of displacement and military occupation on the other."

With that kind of moral equivocation at the top, anti-Israel propagandists hijacked the conference. Yasir Arafat felt comfortable coming to what was supposed to be a world anti-racism conference and blasting Israel's "racist, colonialist conspiracy" against Palestinians. He claimed that "the aim" of the Israeli government "is to force our people to their knees and to make them surrender in order to continue her occupation, settlements and racist practices, so as to liquidate our people." The result was the Durban debacle, defining Zionism as racism.

The accusation was already decades old, but it's worth comparing then and now, because the charges landed in a dramatically new environment. In 1975, when the UN General Assembly passed Resolution 3379, calling Zionism racism, our small community of Zionist activists in Moscow was deeply concerned. Soviet law did not ban Zionism, but it did outlaw racism. We feared that the UN declaration gave the Soviets a new pretext to claim they were punishing our Zionist activity as "racist," to weaken any Western protests. The Soviet campaign against us now seemed to have international approval.

Yet, hearing word of the free world's support—through the KGB jamming—reassured us. America's ambassador to the United Nations, Daniel Patrick Moynihan, denounced this "infamous act." Israel's ambassador Chaim Herzog ripped up the resolution in the General Assembly. Most important of all, the free world voted against the resolution almost as one. So at least we could be confident that the free world was on our side. Soviet propaganda would not fool them.

In December 1991, as the Soviet Union was collapsing, the UN General Assembly actually rescinded the resolution. This was only the second time in its history that the United Nations undid an earlier decision.

Alas, ten years later, a massive ideological hijacking occurred. If the first time the United Nations equated Zionism with racism, the West treated it like a match falling into a puddle of water, this time, thanks to postmodernism, it was like a match falling into a barrel of oil. What Moynihan had called a "Big Red Lie" had entered into the international bloodstream. Whereas in 1975 the free world had mocked the attack, a quarter of a century later many postmodern leaders and thinkers from the free world joined the onslaught.

THE NEW ANTI-SEMITISM INVADES THE ACADEMY

Postmodernism proved to be a great petri dish for growing the New Anti-Semitism—an irrational hatred against Israel resting on traditional

Jew-hatred—and transferring it to the academy. What I started calling "islands of Europe"—universities throughout the world—became the ideological control centers for this attack. The result was what we could call the academic intifada.

Now, Israelis could do no right and Palestinians could do no wrong. I visited some of the departments of Middle Eastern studies, many funded by Saudi oil money. Martin Kramer's 2001 exposé of the anti-American and anti-Israel bias in Middle Eastern studies departments, *Ivory Towers on Sand*, would note that as early as 1979, *Science*, the journal of the American Association for the Advancement of Science, would run a headline, "Oman, Qatar, and the United Arab Emirates Are Worth Studying." These countries and the Saudis, he explained, funded academic departments seeking an "instrument of control" over "American public opinion." Today, tens of billions of dollars later, these aggressive donors enjoy even more influence.

These departments were particularly shameless in spreading pseudo-scientific theories presenting Israel as the last colonial state, whose very existence was immoral regardless of borders, a state that should not exist. Their idea of a panel discussion usually involved three or four critics of Israel—ideally one of them an angry Israeli representing the most marginal, unpatriotic views in Israeli society—vying to outdo one another in Israel bashing. These absurdities only made sense when I viewed them through the lens of *The Closing of the American Mind*. The liberal, nationalist, critical academy I first encountered a decade or two earlier would have resisted these distortions.

I kept being reminded about one story Bloom told about students dodging moral responsibility. He asked his students, "If you had been a British administrator in India, would you have let the natives under your governance burn the widow at the funeral of a man who had died?" Here was an opportunity for students to defend the fundamental Western value of protecting a human life. Yet most students, Bloom reported, "either remain silent or reply that the British should never have been there in the first place."

This attitude, when transplanted to the Middle East, was striking. These postmodernists would always rationalize Palestinian terrorism by pointing to the "indigenous people's" need to fight colonialism. And if Israel, a country that sees itself as part of the free world, could not behave like Switzerland, the natural conclusion would become that Israel "should never have been there in the first place." This new assumption, lurking in the background, explained how that student at York could tell me that, for him as a liberal Jew, it would be better if Israel didn't exist.

CLASHING SURVIVAL STRATEGIES

The fact that the pro-Palestinian, postmodern attack against Israel came waving the banner of human rights made the situation for young Jews particularly difficult. Nevertheless, it explained another mystery: how this ideological assault, of all the ideological assaults we've endured over the millennia, threatened Jewish unity so profoundly. By targeting the Jewish nation-state in the name of Diaspora Jewry's core values and Zionism's liberal aspirations, it puts Israel on the defensive with many Jews, not just non-Jews.

Truthfully, most Jews in Israel and abroad, from left to right, rallied around Israel during this traumatic time, with support, sympathy, and donations flowing to the state. But the intensity of the attack in places that mattered most to Diaspora Jews—academia, the media, and international organizations—using values that mattered to them, showed a worrying vulnerability. Framing Israel as a human-rights abuser was like sending a guided missile aimed at the most sensitive souls in American Jewry. And the growing number of ideological casualties indicated that the polarization would only get worse.

Over the decades, human rights—and *tikkun olam*, repairing the world—came to be the defining Jewish value for many liberal American Jews. In fact, the idea of human rights traces back to the wisdom of the Torah, saying all of us are created in God's image. Thirty-five hundred years later, the Zionist movement wove that biblically rooted, liberal, democratic tradition into Israeli political culture. Nevertheless, the notion of human rights plays a different role in the survival strategies of the two largest Jewish communities in the world today, American Jewry and Israeli Jewry.

We can feel deeply connected as a people and believe that we all share one common Jewish journey, but we have to acknowledge that choosing to live in the United States or Israel means choosing to live a Jewish life in two dramatically different environments. One chooses life as a member of the minority in a free democratic society, where it is easy to abandon your Judaism. The other chooses life as a member of the majority in a Jewish democratic state surrounded by hostile dictatorships seeking to destroy it.

American Jews understand defending freedom as preserving a liberal state that won't interfere with their individual or collective self-expression. Defending identity, for them, means fighting assimilation while keeping Jews committed to Judaism, in a country where they are welcome to fit in as Americans while fading away as Jews.

Israelis feel compelled to defend their freedom by fighting against numerous enemies seeking their destruction while keeping the state functioning. Defending identity, for them, involves integrating many different Jews into one old-new Israeli Jewish nation.

The Bible introduces us to two heroes who represent contrasting aspects of our heritage: King David and the prophet Isaiah. Each represents a distinct survival strategy. Each symbolizes different routes to Jewish identity. Although a psalmist and harpist, David started out as the young shepherd ready to kill wolves—and giant Philistines—when forced. He ended as the king who, through cunning and charm, united our nation. He represents the impulse to build and defend a sovereign nation in our own homeland.

Isaiah represents our ethical imperative and our message of peace, universalism, and social justice: dreams of lions lying down with lambs. The book of Isaiah also embraces particularism, but modern rabbis and teachers emphasize its liberal dimensions.

While every Jew inherits both lineages, the two communities' political cultures have different emphases, like two competing political parties balancing priorities. Israelis represent the Davidian party, ready to use brute force to protect Jewish sovereignty when necessary. Liberal American Jews are Isaiahans, most moved by the prophetic teachings, including harsh critiques of power, particularism, and the status quo. Davidians need not negate human rights but won't prioritize them either. Isaiahans, however, place human rights front and center, both for their sake and for others'.

Davidian Jews also exist in America and Isaiahans in Israel. As with David and Isaiah themselves, both impulses live within every Jew, expressed in different proportions. Just as how, in healthy democracies, passionate debate between rival parties ultimately strengthens the national character, so, too, a constructive debate between Davidian Israelis and American Jewish Isaiahans could strengthen our people. But it rarely happens.

The greatest collision was over the Palestinian question. What Davidians—in Israel and abroad—considered to be a postmodernist, apologetic farce betrayed the basic Jewish patriotism that every good Davidian values. What Isaiahans—abroad and in Israel—considered to be Israel's too-violent defense of its "indefensible occupation" betrayed the basic liberal Jewish values every good Isaiahan cherishes.

It saddened me that the greatest gap seemed to be opening up between the young, idealistic soldiers serving their country and some of American Jewry's young, idealistic students imagining a better world. True, when I joined Birthright groups on Mount Herzl, I saw Israelis in military uniforms and Diaspora participants in their civilian garb honoring Israel's fallen together. But we were hearing more and more stories about the angry, strikingly unpatriotic minority of Isaiahan rebels. The growing fear was that they were not only grabbing the headlines but defining the future of American liberal Jewry.

Even when they were on the fringe, these voices were amplified by intense media coverage and communal hand-wringing. In April 2002, when Israeli troops, at the height of their defense against terrorism, finally surrounded Yasir Arafat's compound, a young Jew from Brooklyn, Adam Shapiro, visited the notorious terrorist and became an international star. Taking the Isaiahan position to the extreme, Shapiro said he was not acting as a Jew but "as a human being, as an American who has grown up with freedom—seeing what's happening, the injustice, and wanting to do something about it."

Shapiro was a rare enough Jew to garner headlines in 2002. But within a few years, my colleague at Shalem College Rabbi Daniel Gordis would describe how many young rabbinical students, raised in universities when Israel was besieged by Arafat's terrorism, were turning on Israel. One shopped for a tallit that was not made in Israel. Another added the creation of the state of Israel to a list of Jewish moments to mourn. Some even celebrated their birthdays in a bar in Ramallah, posting pictures of themselves online in front of posters "extolling violence against the Jewish state on the wall behind them, downing their drinks and feeling utterly comfortable."

Putting the PR concerns aside and focusing on our peoplehood problems, I kept wondering, "How could the voice of Israel be heard among Jews through all this sound and fury?" On the grand scale, only through a more effective, honest, even formalized dialogue, appreciating our differences and learning from one another, could we stay together despite being programmed to see things so differently.

Clearly, Israelis underestimated the damage that resulted within the Jewish community from appearing to be against the liberal understanding of peace, human rights, and social justice. And a growing number of young Jews underestimated the real problems Israel faced, with their natural loyalties to their fellow Jews increasingly jammed by the specific propaganda campaign against them and the broader climate of opinion critical of nationalism and Western exceptionalism.

It was also a lost opportunity. In a healthier Jewish political culture, Isaiahans and Davidians would compare their differences to the distinctions between rival political parties in a country's parliament. One party champions freedom, the other emphasizes identity; one highlights liberalism, the other nationalism. Even while clashing intensely, each faction should be appreciated as the constructive guardian of a valuable dimension of our heritage.

Impassioned but constructive debate between Isaiahans and Davidians would keep rebalancing these important forces. It could even forge exciting, new, Maimonidean golden paths for Israel and Judaism. But because Israelis and Diaspora Jews don't share the same political stage, and because we often turn nasty when arguing these days, we each fail to benefit from the other's distinct point of view. The tensions between us fester.

SOME CONCRETE RESPONSES TO THIS EXISTENTIAL CHALLENGE

Clearly, improving the dialogue or even just learning to see our differences in context would require a dramatic communal adjustment. More immediately, I looked for concrete steps that I, as a politician, could take to help.

Most practically, as Diaspora affairs minister, I initiated a program through the Jewish Agency to start sending *shlichim*, emissaries, to this new ideological battlefield of the campuses. The idea was to deploy young Israeli army veterans, who were usually socially liberal and passionately patriotic like most of their peers. They offered a personal touch and a richer perspective to a topic that many students and professors loved to oversimplify. This initiative would become my flagship program at the

Jewish Agency years later. Today, Israel Fellows work with students on more than one hundred campuses worldwide.

As we started the program campus by campus, my message to the emissaries was clear: don't waste your efforts trying to convince our enemies that Israel is better than they think. "That's not your role," I told the *shlichim*. "Your role is to show young American Jews that they have nothing to be ashamed of in Israel. They can disagree with one policy or another of the Israeli government, one politician or another, but Israel and Zionism are much bigger than this stand, that politician."

As prime minister, Ariel Sharon showed great interest in addressing these internal Jewish tensions. He agreed that we needed to fight for a new Jewish unity within and a new moral clarity worldwide. Looking outward, he also agreed that old-fashioned Jew-hatred had helped fuel the terrorist attacks against Israel and the ideological assaults justifying the violence.

With his backing, I expanded my role as minister of Diaspora affairs to serve as minister against global anti-Semitism too. I turned a small, consultative body that had operated out of the Prime Minister's Office into the Global Forum for Combating Anti-Semitism. This major international conference in Jerusalem convened the key players in the fight against the New Anti-Semitism. This conference, which still convenes regularly, became my springboard into a larger international fight against this old-new bigotry.

14

SEEING THE NEW ANTI-SEMITISM THROUGH 3D GLASSES

In the Soviet Union, it was obvious to all of us that anti-Semitism was the dictator's friend, a natural weapon in the hands of our oppressors. From czarist times to Communist times, whenever the authorities needed a scapegoat to reinforce their control over the population, the Jew was the perfect target.

Seeing how autocracy and anti-Semitism went so well together, I just assumed that anti-Semitism and modern democracies would be incompatible, especially after the Holocaust. That's why watching Jew-hatred survive Communism's collapse and move to the free world, just as I got there, has been one of the profound disappointments of my life in freedom.

A second lesson I learned from my youth has actually held and proved depressingly useful. All of us in the Soviet Union understood that anti-Semitism and anti-Zionism meshed together naturally. Hostility to the Jew and the Jews flowed seamlessly toward Israel, the collective Jew. The Jewish state just broadened the target for the Jew-haters, giving them much more cannon fodder. We could all see how de facto restrictions on accepting Jews in Soviet universities were justified by the need to restrict Zionist influence. When official Communist Party propaganda criticized Israel, the cartoons used all the classic Jew-hating images, depicting Israel as the Yid with a big nose, fangs, and long, hungry fingers. Beyond that traditional anti-Semitism, Israel was an all-purposed and useful target. When Soviets persecuted Jews for being nationalists, we were Israel's agents; when Soviets persecuted Jews as cosmopolites, we were advancing the international Jewish conspiracy, with Israel at the center.

That's why, throughout the 1990s, it was easy for me to see familiar traces of anti-Semitism in many attacks on Israel. Making such a link was heresy. The conventional wisdom throughout the West denied the very idea that criticism of Israel could be connected to any form of anti-Semitism.

Whenever I or anyone else suggested that some attacks on Israel resurrected the old Jew-hatred, many political leaders and intellectuals acted as if I had uttered some four-letter word. Some young Jewish radicals resisted the argument too. "You're paranoid," I kept hearing. "You see anti-Semitism in everything. You're trying to stop legitimate criticism of Israel by connecting it to anti-Semitism, which is obviously evil." Or, "We're not anti-Semitic, just anti-occupation."

It's true, I thought, we are paranoid. We've earned the right to be, after thousands of years of persecution. The old Soviet dissident punchline, probably echoing Joseph Heller's *Catch-22*, applies: "Just because you're paranoid about being chased, doesn't mean you're not being chased."

I realized I would need convincing proof to justify my parallels between anti-Semitism and anti-Zionism, even to many Jews. Unfortunately, by 2002, when the attacks on Israel's very existence cascaded as we defended ourselves against Palestinian terror, these parallels became even more obvious and abundant.

There are, of course, all kinds of words, images, comparisons used to criticize Israeli policies. But when I saw how frequently modern anti-Zionists compared Israelis to Nazis, it rang a bell: the Soviets equated Nazism and Zionism in speeches, cartoons, books, and pamphlets. These lies were even presented as part of academic research. In 1982, a forty-seven-year-old Palestinian, Mahmoud Abbas, received a candidate of sciences degree—a Soviet PhD—for writing "The Other Side: The Secret Relationship Between Nazism and Zionism." He defended his work at the prestigious Institute of Oriental Studies of the Soviet Academy of Sciences. Considering the deep hatred the Soviet people had for Nazis after World War II, these false comparisons and imagined conspiracies helped demonize the Jewish state.

Now, in the free world, I was seeing newspapers publish cartoons of Israeli soldiers or leaders that looked exactly like the anti-Jewish caricatures in Nazi Germany and anti-Israel posters in the Soviet Union. One cartoon in the liberal British newspaper the *Independent* turned Israel's prime minister Ariel Sharon into a grotesque monster eating Palestinian children, their blood drooling from his lips as he asks, "What's wrong? You've never seen a politician kissing babies before?" That was bad enough. But then it won the British Political Cartoon Society's political cartoon of the year award.

When the Nobel Prize–winning Portuguese writer José Saramago visited the Palestinian Authority in 2002, his choice of words was also familiar. He said Israel imposed "the spirit of Auschwitz" on the city of Ramallah and that "this place is being turned into a concentration camp." Just spending one minute in the Nazi Auschwitz would have confirmed that there was no comparison. He was deliberately libeling Israel.

There was another familiar line of attack against Jews that I recognized. On the fifth line of the Soviet passport, there were up to 150 different nationalities that could be mentioned. But when someone said, "He has a fifth-line disease" or "a fifth-line problem," everyone knew that meant Jew. In other words, behind the Iron Curtain we Jews were treated by a different standard than anyone else.

There were 191 countries in the United Nations as of 2002. Each had its own founding story, political system, and collective set of sins, because no country is perfect. Yet, somehow, Israel was the problematic nationality there, the only country subjected to the harsh double standards we Jews knew all too well. Only Israel sat as a permanent agenda item on the UN Human Rights Committee, subject to more condemnations than all other countries combined—including dictatorships—no matter how many killing fields popped up elsewhere, no matter how many despots actually committed ethnic cleansings.

I once challenged the UN high commissioner for human rights Louise Arbour about this anomaly. Arbour was a former professor at York University and a serious, idealistic Canadian jurist. "There is only one country that is on the permanent agenda for condemnation, Israel," I said. "How can you allow this double standard?"

Arbour admitted the situation made her uncomfortable. It all came from the member states, not from her, she insisted. Russia, China, and some African and Asian members had agreed among themselves to keep

Chechnya, Tibet, Darfur, and Arab human rights abuses off the agenda. Each respected the others' claims out of self-interest. The only country this horse-trading didn't protect was Israel.

"Yes, it's very logical," I acknowledged. "But it only proves that anti-Semitism can sound very logical." I told her about a book I had at home "with one thousand czarist-era laws treating Jews differently, legally. Each has its own logical-sounding explanation, especially to the Jew-hater. It doesn't make it less anti-Semitic." It just makes it a double standard.

In the Soviet Union, Jews were the only group chosen by Joseph Stalin to be subjected to a high-profile article by him arguing that our historic community was not really a nation. That meant that there was only one nationality among the 150 that, despite appearing on the Soviet ID's fifth line, was so illegitimate that any requests for specific Jewish national institutions were usually dismissed.

Now, in this new democratic world I had entered, there seemed to be a permanent debate about only one country's legitimacy: Israel. All these upsetting parallels between my old world and my new world helped me see the three main tools that anti-Semites use against Jews and anti-Zionists use against Israel: demonization, double standards, and delegitimization.

So there you had it. Traditional anti-Semitism for thousands of years has demonized Jews as children of Satan, as suckers of young Christian blood, as poisoners of the well, as power-hungry financial manipulators. Jews were repeatedly subjected to double standards, from expulsions in the Middle Ages to university quotas in the modern world. While early Christians attacked the legitimacy of Judaism as a religion, centuries later, when identities went national, xenophobes attacked the legitimacy of the Jews as a people.

Now, seeing the same principles applied to the collective Jew and the pillar of modern Jewish identity, Israel, it was clear to me that we were not just facing anti-Zionism, but anti-Semitism.

THE THREE DS

Mulling this over, I thought of the 3D movies I enjoyed as a child. Without special two-toned glasses, the picture was blurry. With the glasses, the screen came alive, and you could see everything clearly. If traditional anti-Semitism demonized, delegitimized, and pathologized the Jew—often treating Jews as the biggest threat to all that is good in the world—you could start seeing how the New Anti-Semitism did the same to Israel. Similarly, if you did not wear the right glasses, the line between legitimate criticism of Israel and anti-Semitism could become blurred, so that you failed to even recognize this ancient evil, these age-old poisoned darts, much less fight it.

I wanted to help draw those lines by articulating specific criteria to identify when hostility toward Israel turned anti-Semitic. That's when my brainstorming partner and coauthor in this and so many ventures, Ron Dermer, helped me package the pattern. We started writing articles about demonization, delegitimization and double standards, using this 3D analogy. "It's time to put on those 3D spectacles," I insisted, "to distinguish between legitimate criticism of Israel and the New Anti-Semitism."

Starting in 2005, Europe marked the day of Auschwitz's liberation, January 27, as International Holocaust Remembrance Day. This was three months before the Jewish Holocaust Remembrance Day, which is commemorated in the spring on the anniversary of the Warsaw ghetto revolt against the Nazis.

As Diaspora minister, I proposed that we use Auschwitz liberation day in Israel as Let's Fight the New Anti-Semitism Day. Working with the army and the schools, in public forums and other educational organizations, we addressed this old-new threat.

Moving beyond Israel, a new college-based, pro-Israel organization, StandWithUs, integrated the 3D test into its educational platform. Abe Foxman and the Anti-Defamation League he led soon followed. Once new campus leaders emerged, the international network of Jewish student centers, Hillel, accepted it too.

Still, we discovered that defining the criteria was the easy part. It was much harder to convince others to apply the formula. The big challenge remained the politicians. Many still claimed we were trying to suppress criticism. How could we get them to realize that criticism of Israel can sometimes be anti-Semitic?

AN UNEXPECTED ALLY FROM THE LEFT

I found a most unlikely ally to help me convince people they needed to recognize how the world's most plastic hatred had been molded into a new form. Although Joschka Fischer was my age, and we each had had an activist awakening around 1968, we couldn't have been more different. A German, Fischer became a Far Left radical in the late 1960s, swayed by Karl Marx and the calls for revolution that were suffocating us in Moscow. People in his circle turned toward terrorism. Fischer participated in several street battles with the radical Putzgruppe, an abbreviation for Proletarische Union für Terror und Zerstörung (the Proletarian Union for Terror and Destruction). By 1977, the radicals' violence disgusted him, including their involvement in the Entebbe hijacking, which targeted Jews. Denouncing terrorism, he joined Germany's Green Party, and eventually served as Germany's foreign minister and vice chancellor from 1998 to 2005.

Naturally, Fischer was a big fan of the Oslo peace process and Shimon Peres's new Middle East. But on June 1, 2001, while visiting Israel, he jogged by the Dolphinarium, a disco on the Tel Aviv beachfront. A few hours later, a Hamas terrorist walked into a line of young people waiting to enter the club and blew himself up, killing twenty-one, sixteen of them teenagers. Fischer, who believed that the German nation had a sacred obligation to lead the struggle against anti-Semitism, was shaken. He promised to help. He saw that, in this new criticism of Israel, the old prejudices were playing a role.

By 2002, the new Jew-hatred could not be ignored. The Organization for Security and Co-operation in Europe (OSCE)—an organization with roots in the Helsinki Accords of the 1970s—addressed the spike in synagogue vandalism, harassment of Jews, and anti-Semitic incitement in Europe. But most liberal politicians wanted to stick to fighting swastikas and Holocaust denialism, ignoring the Israel connection.

After an initial 2003 OSCE meeting in Vienna focused too rigidly on traditional anti-Semitism, Fischer volunteered to host the next meeting in Berlin on April 28 and 29, 2004. He made sure to invite me, as Israel's Diaspora affairs minister, to address the conference. It attracted over six hundred participants to Hitler's former capital. I proposed my 3D test, explaining that it was essentially the same criteria traditionally applied to identify anti-Semites.

Many politicians feared opening the Pandora's box of Israel, the Palestinians, and the Middle East conflict. But I benefited from some timely outside help. In addition to Fischer, whose trips to the Palestinian Authority convinced him that anti-Zionism and anti-Semitism reinforced one another, I had the pro-Palestinian movement. Its rhetoric was so drenched in Jew-hatred, I simply shared cartoons, newspaper headlines, articles, and video clips.

Thanks to Fischer and others, the 2004 Berlin conference had what seemed like a minor breakthrough but was actually a big deal. The official notes of the conference—approved after heated debates—reported that "an important number of delegations agreed that criticism of Israel can, at times, serve as a cover for anti-Semitism or be motivated by it, although all delegations also stressed that criticism of any government's policies, including Israel's, is legitimate and an essential feature of democratic political systems."

Lurking behind the weak phrasing was a powerful turning point. This conference was finally ready to accept that some forms of Israel criticism can be anti-Semitism. After years of resistance, the international community was targeting the New Anti-Semitism—the shift from singling out the Jew for a special, obsessive hatred to singling out Israel, the collective Jew, for the same special, obsessive hatred.

After Berlin, I turned to our American allies. Continuing to use the Helsinki channel, I returned to the independent government agency established to monitor the fulfillment of the Helsinki Accords: the US Helsinki Commission, formally known as the Commission on Security and Cooperation in Europe. The commission's chairman, Republican Chris Smith, and the ranking Democrat, Tom Lantos, vowed to target this New Anti-Semitism. After my testimony on June 16, 2004, my American friends accepted the language of the three Ds, then took the lead in Congress and the State Department.

On October 8, 2004, Congress passed the Global Anti-Semitism Review Act. Responding to the "sharp rise in anti-Semitic violence," Congress authorized the State Department to monitor the problem, catalogue incidents worldwide in a detailed report, and appoint a special envoy for monitoring and combating anti-Semitism. The preface to the bill stated, "Anti-Semitism has at times taken the form of vilification of Zionism, the Jewish national movement, and incitement against Israel."

The Europeans lagged behind. Eventually, the International Holocaust Remembrance Alliance (IHRA) incorporated the 3D test into what is now the most widely accepted official definition of anti-Semitism in the West: "Anti-Semitism is a certain perception of Jews, which may be expressed as hatred toward Jews." In offering official examples, the guidelines state that "manifestations might include the targeting of the State of Israel, conceived as a Jewish collectivity. However, criticism of Israel similar to that leveled against any other country cannot be regarded as anti-Semitic." Other examples included

- making mendacious, dehumanizing, demonizing, or stereo-typical allegations about Jews as such or the power of Jews as collective;

- denying the Jewish people their right to self-determination, e.g., by claiming that the existence of a State of Israel is a racist endeavor;

- applying double standards by requiring of it a behavior not expected or demanded of any other democratic nation; and

- using the symbols and images associated with classic anti-Semitism (e.g., claims of Jews killing Jesus or blood libel) to characterize Israel or Israelis.

Again and again, we could see how the three Ds were baked into the document.

Today, more and more European countries are adopting that IHRA definition, incorporating all three Ds. In 2019, President Donald Trump's executive order embraced that definition too, which unfortunately made it off-limits for some Trump haters. With anti-Semitism rising—in old and new forms, targeting Jews and targeting Israel—we need the 3D spectacles. Only by seeing clearly can we fight it effectively, on the Left and the Right.

The shift was profound for another reason. Beyond saying that some forms of criticism of Israel can be anti-Semitic, the three Ds taught that not all critiques were bigoted. Unlike many campus speech codes, the three Ds helped carve out room for legitimate debate while highlighting when attacks crossed into illegitimate criticism. Mapping such boundaries identified legitimate territory too. This process was crucial for many liberals, especially Jewish students. Justifiably, they wanted the freedom to criticize the Israeli government without feeling stifled or like they were abetting the world's Jew-haters.

TRADITIONAL ANTI-SEMITISM
ON WESTERN SATELLITE TV

At the OSCE Berlin conference, I singled out the *Al-Shatat* TV series to illustrate how modern Israel-hatred fed modern Jew-hatred. I discovered this twenty-nine-episode series for Hezbollah's Al-Manar network reluctantly, on one of those rare days when I was trying to escape with my wife to one of our favorite guesthouses, far from the public eye. Yigal Carmon, the inexhaustible, Arabic-speaking former intelligence officer who advised both Yitzhak Shamir and Yitzhak Rabin before founding the Middle East Media Research Institute (MEMRI) in 1998, called me excitedly. MEMRI, which translates Arabic media for the West, began when Carmon translated one of Arafat's pro-jihad speeches into English, and journalists attacked him for destroying their illusion. "You're just not going to believe this, Natan," Carmon told me. "This time they've outdone themselves. It's a kind of bloody anti-Semitism far beyond all three of your Ds."

Indeed shocked by what I saw when I returned to Jerusalem, I often showed a clip from the series when speaking. A short sequence of evil Jews cutting a Christian child's throat over some uncooked matzah ended with the blood of this poor, innocent boy spurting all over and filling the screen. Its crudity and brutality made most viewers gasp. Carmon informed me that because Eutelsat, the European satellite operator, carried this Hezbollah station, this series had been widely distributed throughout the continent.

The obscenity of the images struck even the most uninformed viewer. More sophisticated spectators understood how such lies had helped kill Jews en masse in the past. Following the clip, I often showed cartoons like the one of a bloodthirsty Ariel Sharon. This demonstrated how far beyond acceptable debate many in the modern media were going and how they were dredging up deep, traditional Jew-hatred. When I showed the film clip to the cabinet, my colleagues were speechless.

A few months later, I attended a Germany-Israel dialogue about anti-Semitism. I decided to show the film clip to supplement my speech, which I would deliver during the conference's main banquet. One of my cabinet colleagues, Justice Minister Tommy Lapid, objected. "It's too depressing, Natan," he said. "It's a festive dinner." The organizers were more flexible. When they could not get a video screen into the dining hall, they showed the video outside, before my formal dinnertime talk.

The video shocked the participants. "That is what some of your Arabic-speaking citizens are seeing," I warned them. Quoting the newspaper I had read on the plane while flying to the conference, I said, "Look, anti-Israel demonstrators in your cities are shouting 'Israelis are not human,' further demonizing us." Lapid watched, wide-eyed, as the diners shifted uncomfortably.

At the conference, the French Jewish leader Roger Cukierman asked me for the video. The world wasn't so digitized then, so I gave him my only copy. When he returned to Paris, he showed it to the French prime minister, Jean-Pierre Raffarin. Raffarin worked with the parliament and the courts to block the series from French satellite TV to avoid further inflaming France's Muslims against the Jews.

I confess, I did put a damper on the conference's most elaborate meal, with its fine china and overwhelming array of German meats, serving hundreds of diners from Europe and Israel. Rather than eating all that sausage and Wiener schnitzel on the fine china, my senior adviser Vera Golovensky and I received two kosher airline meals, wrapped in endless layers of plastic and foil. We sat there unpacking them, filling the beautifully set table with our trash. This was too much for the aggressively secular Lapid. Shuddering and pointing at my dismal meal while still fuming about the video, he muttered, "Clearly, you're not suited for polite society."

Of course, it was polite society I was aiming at.

MY SECOND AND FINAL
RESIGNATION FROM THE CABINET

It was harder for me to resign from Ariel Sharon's cabinet in 2005 than from Ehud Barak's in 2000. Arik and I had worked closely together for years and were friends. A Zionist with a strong commitment to the Jewish people, he supported my fight against the New Anti-Semitism wholeheartedly. He often was the only minister to take home the materials I brought to cabinet meetings tracking the new Jew-hatred. Like Amnon Dankner of *Maariv*, Sharon was surrounded by well-intentioned young Israelis who didn't appreciate the importance of a robust Jewish people as much as we did.

The ugly anti-Semitic demonizing of Sharon unsettled him. "Congratulations, you have outdone Bibi, Shimon, all your rivals. You are the anti-Semites' favorite target," I said, trying to laugh off the attacks. He grimaced, unamused.

Arik was smart, determined, and patriotic. But he guarded his power jealously and was too image conscious for his own good. A crude example of how hard he tried to control matters with an iron fist, while oscillating between playing Mr. Tough Guy and Mr. Nice Guy, occurred during the delicate Wye negotiations in 1998. I attended, along with Prime Minister Netanyahu, Defense Minister Yitzhak Mordechai, and Arik.

When Bibi asked our opinions about Yasir Arafat's demand for a seaport in Gaza, Arik, who was then foreign minister, tried bullying his boss. "How dare you even discuss it?" he yelled. "Do you know what a threat that will be to our security?"

A few hours later, the first official three-way session with the Palestinians and the Americans took place. It was a closed meeting. The Americans kept requesting that we avoid reporters during the talks. They insisted that our assistants wait for us in a building next door.

Swaggering amid all the polite, if awkward, exchanges, Sharon conspicuously refused to shake Arafat's hand. I then watched him go to the doorpost of our conference room, wave over an aide, and report his antics to his assistant outside. Within minutes, Sharon's favorite reporters were circulating the story of how this Israeli hero had "bravely" rebuffed the terrorist, quoting Arik saying, "Shake the hand of that dog? Never."

But a funny thing happened in the room itself. The Palestinians raised the issue of the seaport. Remembering the fireworks, Netanyahu turned to Sharon to answer, as he was the new foreign minister and had also served as minister of energy and water resources for almost two years. Sharon had so enjoyed proving how tough he was when yelling at the prime minister that morning, Netanyahu was happy to let him repeat the performance before an international audience.

Sharon looked straight at the Palestinians and bellowed, "If you want a seaport, you come to me." Netanyahu, Mordechai, and I couldn't believe our ears. Frustrated, as soon as we left the room, I snapped at him, "Why didn't you shake Arafat's hand? It would have cost us a lot less."

Seven years later, Sharon's plan of disengaging unilaterally from Gaza and northern Samaria highlighted his weaknesses. He wanted to show everyone that he was the boss, and that he could act unilaterally. He hoped to improve Israel's image and his own. And, as when Bibi gave him the floor at Wye, he liked to emphasize that having responsibility changes what you see. The world looks different when you're looking at the prime minister's chair from outside versus when you're sitting in it.

Unlike Barak, Sharon didn't go behind our backs as ministers. He just bulldozed through. He believed he could find favor with the international community—and liberal Jews—by destroying twenty Jewish communities flourishing in Gaza.

I considered this disengagement plan irresponsible and immoral. Much as I liked Arik, I knew he had no patience for my theories. I continued to believe, as I wrote him in my resignation letter, "that every Israeli concession in the peace process must be made contingent upon democratic reforms on the Palestinian side." Instead, this "plan will lower the chances for the establishment of a free Palestinian society, and will even provide terrorist elements with a supportive wind" and "increase terrorism."

"Don't you understand that the world has been against us for so long?" Sharon explained. "Now, the world will be with us. If at any time over the next ten years, the Palestinians dare launch anything from Gaza, we will be able to carpet-bomb them—and no one will object because we did our best to separate from them."

"You won't have ten years, Arik," I replied. "You won't even have ten days."

I knew, even though Sharon was ignoring his generals and withdrawing from every inch of Gaza, that it would not be enough for the Palestinians and that our critics, including those within the Jewish community, would still not be satisfied. The issues ran deeper and the new Big Lies were just too tempting. Not only would we remain occupiers, but when we were soon forced to defend ourselves against Hamas's assault from Gaza, the region would become "the world's largest concentration camp."

Out of courtesy, I informed Arik of my intention to resign two weeks before I left. "I want you to stay in the government," he said. "It's OK. You can continue voting against the disengagement." He didn't need me for that; he had the votes. "But we need you. You take us as a government to the places we never were before and where we should be."

I just could not continue. Foreseeing that this disengagement policy would create another terrorist base to attack us, once I had done everything I could to stop it as an insider, I had reached my limits. I could not be a partner in a government that implemented another self-defeating move.

Netanyahu heard of my plans and called me. "Natan, why don't you wait and we will resign together?" Bibi didn't want to abandon the dramatic reforms he was implementing as treasury minister. He was also planning a comeback as prime minister and wanted to stoke the right-wing base without losing the middle. "Bibi," I replied, "if you want to stop disengagement you have to resign now. Three months from now it will be too late."

I resigned.

But I had learned a thing or two in politics. When I resigned in 2000, newspapers all over the world accused me of betraying the peace. Most people did not want to hear my claim that I feared Arafat was snookering Barak. This time, I decided to try getting my arguments published first.

Having informed Sharon in advance, I gave the *New York Times* an exclusive interview a few hours before I sent my official letter of resignation. The article appeared just as I resigned. It explained, "Mr. Sharansky, whose ideas on the promotion of democracy have been endorsed by President Bush, said he objected to the lack of linkage of the Gaza withdrawal to specific reforms to create more freedom in Palestinian society." The article went on to say that I "also objected strongly to Mr. Sharon's intention to separate the Israeli economy as much as possible from the Palestinian one, arguing that Israel will not find real security in physical borders or walls, but only in a Palestinian state that is truly democratic and free, politically and economically." I was quoted saying, "Their problems are our problems," while calling for economic cooperation.

Arik and I maintained our relationship, despite all the pain during those days of disengagement. Unfortunately, we were deprived of the chance to sit and really compare notes about the decision, the process, and its impact. Four months after the disengagement, Sharon suffered a massive stroke that left him in a coma for eight years until his death in 2014.

Immediately after I resigned, I flew to Germany for the Bilderberg meetings in Rottach-Egern. Every year, between 120 and 150 people designated as world leaders are invited to this getaway to discuss the world's problems off the record. It's a happening for the world Establishment. Inevitably, it showcases the conventional wisdom of the moment, which in August 2005 cheered the Gaza pullout.

Shortly after I arrived, in that Murphy's Law for conferences, I bumped into the one person I was hoping to avoid. James Wolfensohn, the head of the World Bank and a generous Jewish philanthropist, was close to Bill Clinton and an enthusiastic member of the Bilderberg club. We had always had friendly relations. But, just a few weeks earlier, he had been appointed as a special envoy for Gaza disengagement by the Quartet on the Middle East—the group of major powers, plus the United Nations, deeply invested in the peace process. "Oh boy," I said to myself. "I'm going to get it."

"Natan, I saw your interview in the *New York Times*," he said. OK. This friendly, silky smooth Australian American financier was starting in neutral. Good opening gambit. But then he really surprised me. "Of course I agree with you. You're absolutely right. We have to work together economically and I share your concerns about democracy. But," he added as I relaxed, "we have to trust Sharon."

I don't really know if Wolfensohn believed that disengagement would improve matters or not. Like many others, he hoped Sharon knew something he didn't. Wolfensohn worked extra hard to make sure the deal succeeded economically for both sides. A few months after we met, Wolfensohn raised $14 million from generous Americans to buy three thousand greenhouses from the Jewish farmers in the Gaza Strip and pass them on, intact, to the Palestinians. This way, the Gazans could continue the work the Jews had done in making the desert bloom.

During those difficult days before the pullout, Mort Zuckerman called me. "I am contributing to Wolfensohn's effort. What do you think?" Mort asked.

"I can't complain if these unfortunate Jewish farmers who are being expelled will get more compensation from all of you," I said. "But if you think this will help peace—or the Palestinian economy—just watch. Give it a couple of months. They'll destroy the greenhouses on purpose, for political reasons."

I was wrong. They didn't wait that long. Within hours, Palestinians had started looting the greenhouses, destroying them as symbols of Zionist imposition on their homeland.

Predictably, within days of the Gaza disengagement, the rockets started flying. They haven't stopped. In June 2007, Hamas seized control of Gaza in a violent coup that dislodged the Palestinian Authority. Gaza became the biggest terrorist base threatening Israel. Terrorists have launched thousands of missiles and imposed years of trauma on the neighboring communities. Over five years, from 2009 to 2014, Israel would have to mount three major defensive military operations. Israel would endure intense criticism for attacking civilian areas that Hamas had turned into rocket-launching pads targeting Israel's citizens.

The disengagement didn't help chances for peace. It didn't help the Jews. It didn't help the Palestinians of Gaza. And it didn't help improve Israel's relations with American Jewry. Now it's Gaza that sticks in the throat of many Israel critics, including many American Jews on campus. People even insist that the Gaza we withdrew from completely is still occupied.

THE IF-ONLY-THEN-ERS' CARTOONISH HISTORY

A few years later, I asked some of the disengagement's architects what they thought of their plan. In the interim, thousands of rockets from Gaza had bombarded Israeli cities, reaching Tel Aviv. Hamas had seized power, turning the Gaza Strip into a large terrorist base. And the United Nations' Goldstone Report had unfairly pilloried Israel for defending its civilians against the attacks the pullout unintentionally intensified. "Ah," the experts replied, "if only Ariel Sharon had not fallen into a coma shortly after disengagement, then it would have been different."

I hear this wistful phrase—"if only, then"—often. When Israelis say it about Sharon, they usually imagine he would have rained hellfire on Gaza after the first rocket was fired on our citizens. No one knows what he would have done, but it doesn't matter. What matters is that Sharon's attempt to make peace—or to buy Palestinian cooperation and Israeli popularity globally—clearly failed. The only question is which leader might have done a better job aggressively cleaning up the mess.

Most American Jewish if-only-then-ers use the same phrase but seek the opposite result. They demonstrate a deep faith in historical superheroes who can change reality and bring peace whatever the circumstances—whether your partner recognizes your right to exist or not.

If only Yitzhak Rabin hadn't been shot, then Oslo would have worked. If only Bill Clinton and Ehud Barak had muscled Yasir Arafat through the door, or Israel had offered more land, then peace could have been sealed. They then follow through to the logical conclusion: if only Netanyahu, or whoever is leading Israel, would have the courage to follow in Rabin's or Sharon's footsteps, there would be peace.

History doesn't happen in a vacuum, where good people want good things to happen. The magical belief in superheroes differs from dissidents' belief that we can change history. The dissident also believes that individuals acting boldly can make a difference. But the dissident builds success on appealing to the deep desires of people to belong and to be free—not defying them.

I, too, am tempted to wonder, "if only" Andrei Sakharov had lived longer than his sixty-eight years, what would have happened in Russia. I don't know the answer. But I know that he became the moral role model who helped doublethinkers cross the line to inner freedom. I also know that his impact outlived him, because his major contribution didn't depend on his charisma or presence but on his expansive vision and his harmony with democracy's flow.

I once unintentionally insulted Mikhail Gorbachev at a conference in Warsaw analyzing why Communism fell. Addressing the question "Who are the symbolic figures who brought down Communism?" I answered hesitantly, conscious of his presence: "Sakharov, Reagan, and Gorbachev," adding "the order's important."

"But I released you and the others from prison," Gorbachev told me afterward in private, miffed at his third-place finish. He was more used to Westerners idolizing him, as *Time* magazine did when knighting him "man of the decade" in December 1989. "The 1980s came to an end in what seemed like a magic act, performed on a world-historical stage," *Time* reported. "Trapdoors flew open, and whole regimes vanished." Who was "the force behind the most momentous events of the 80s and the man responsible for ending the Cold War"? Mikhail Gorbachev! Ronald Reagan wasn't even mentioned.

"I understand," I told Gorbachev. "And I really appreciate that you released me, but ..." Like Sakharov, Reagan understood that Communism's weakness came from its systematic enslavement of its people. Sakharov symbolized the pressure on the Soviet system from within, while Reagan symbolized the pressure from without. These reinforcing pressures together forced the system to choose between granting citizens freedom or collapsing.

Gorbachev didn't want to replace the system; he wanted to save it. As a true Communist, he didn't realize there's no such thing as a little freedom. As soon as he decreased the pressure, it all started falling apart. So while Sakharov and Reagan were active agents, pushing the tide of history along, Gorbachev was swept up in it, unsuccessfully trying to slow the process, inevitably half a step behind until it collapsed. Without Gorbachev, I might have spent more years in prison. But without the Sakharovs and the Reagans pressuring the system, Communism might have survived into the twenty-first century.

To the West, Gorbachev seemed to be the ultimate hero because he was the doer, the brave public face of change. In Russia, he was much less popular. To those who believed in the Soviet Union, he was the man who destroyed it. To those who had already become doublethinkers or dissidents, he was the man who tried to save Communism by giving it a face-lift, resisting its demise until its collapse.

A similar insider-outsider gap shapes the legacies of Rabin and Sharon and risks becoming yet another wedge separating the American Jewish liberal conversation from the one among Israelis. Most American if-only-then-ers continue yearning for another superhero to advance the peace, in the footsteps of Rabin and Sharon. Most Israeli if-only-then-ers belong to the growing majority of citizens in the Jewish state who have given up on peace efforts without reasonable partners.

Both sides risk locking themselves into problematic positions. One group says, "There's no partner, but we want peace now. Let's rush ahead and make it happen." The other group says, "There's no partner, so let's wait and do nothing." A substantive dialogue could help. It could bring both sides to meet in the middle and answer the pressing question: How can we encourage the emergence of a serious partner? For this to occur, each side has to take the other side more seriously and be ready to engage constructively.

A TIME TO COMPROMISE AND A
TIME NOT TO COMPROMISE

We created Yisrael B'Aliyah and I joined the world of electoral politics to welcome the voices of Russian immigrants into the Israeli dialogue. We succeeded. Of course, throughout my nine years in politics, improving the dialogue with Diaspora Jewry was always on my agenda, independent of my position.

Looking back on the hundreds of different projects I was involved in during that time, large and small, international and local, economic and social, I especially enjoyed those that connected different sectors: new immigrants and veteran Israelis, Jews and Arabs, religious and secular Jews. While I took pride in advancing affirmative action and removing injustice, I particularly appreciated these programs for being proactive. I always felt that this dialogue, with all of these different groups, weaves the different strands of community together.

That kind of mediating and compromising resonated with the life I enjoyed during my years of struggle in the Soviet Union. When, thanks to Israel, I discovered the rich, chaotic world of the Jewish people, I also found that I enjoyed connecting one group to the other: the world of young demonstrators, the *hongweibing*, with the older, more cautious, *bonze*; the *kulturniki* and *politiki*; the upstart American Jewish activist organizations and the American Jewish Establishment.

I got the nickname of the Spokesman because I enjoyed spending time explaining to Westerners the challenges the Refuseniks faced as we transitioned from doublethink to dissent. I also enjoyed helping my colleagues understand what journalists were looking for and what made good copy for their stories.

Learning how to compromise and build understanding among these various groups was essential. But in the Soviet Union it was clear that there could be no compromise with one organization, the KGB. Any compromise with it meant bringing back the fear: losing your freedom and losing this unique world that can exist only so long you are free.

In Israel, years later, I kept hearing Oslo's defining cliché: "You don't make peace with your friends. You make peace with your enemy." That missed something. You only make peace with your enemies if they are ready to become former enemies and at least partners, if not friends.

That is why I was not ready to support all those concessions that we were ready to give to our sworn enemies, who showed no interest in becoming our former enemies. That is why, in 2005, the prospect of expelling 8,500 fellow Israelis from the homes the state had encouraged them to build, so that Palestinian leaders could establish the world's largest missile launching pad there, was too much. For that, I could not take responsibility. On that, I could not compromise.

When I left the government, as I contemplated my next steps, I knew I would continue working with others on these complicated, pressing, and compelling issues. I also knew that my closest allies would be those who also wanted to strengthen our shared commitment to our Jewish journey together, wherever we may live.

After nine years representing the Israeli government to world Jewry, I shifted vantage points. Within a few years, I would switch perspectives entirely, representing world Jewry to the Israeli government. Deeper problems were brewing between Israel and American Jewry. It wasn't about Arafat or Oslo or Sharon or disengagement or Netanyahu, per se. It was the growing feeling of a more profound disengagement from one another as liberal American Jews and Israeli Jews.

PART III

NINE YEARS IN THE JEWISH AGENCY

15

WHY THE JEWISH AGENCY?

As Benjamin Netanyahu launched his winning campaign in 2009, he invited me to run with him for the Knesset again. I said no. He then offered me a position in his cabinet, if he returned to office as prime minister. I declined. After I also refused his kind offer to become Israel's ambassador to the United States, he asked me what I was thinking. I said, "I was nine years in prison. Another nine years in politics balances nicely. I served in four governments and quit twice. I served in four prisons and never quit. Probably, something's wrong with me in politics."

"So, you don't want any public post?" Bibi replied, sounding annoyed.

"Well, actually, would you support my candidacy for the chairmanship of the Jewish Agency?" I responded. "That position interests me."

Netanyahu was stunned. Usually, heads of the Jewish Agency kept angling to become members of Knesset or ministers in the cabinet or ambassadors in Washington. I was hoping to live in reverse, again. Bibi wondered why. "Do you think there will be another million Jews moving here you can take credit for?" he asked sarcastically.

"I don't know. I doubt it," I replied. "But I can tell you this. You're right. The number-one threat facing Israel is Iran. And you should invest as much effort as you do managing that threat. Still, we Jewish people face another threat: How do we avoid becoming two different peoples, split between Israel and the Diaspora? I have spent much of my life building bridges between them. I've also spent a lot of time working with the Jewish Agency, and fighting with it. I know how unique this organization's position is, as a meeting place between the government and Diaspora. So," I concluded, "while you work on containing Iran, I can work on improving Israel-Diaspora relations."

The Jewish Agency? Many would consider it the last place to fix Israel-Diaspora relations. Critics dismissed it as a bureaucratic dinosaur that had had its moment of glory decades earlier, founding and populating the state. Now, they argued, it should become extinct.

In 1929, David Ben-Gurion and Chaim Weizmann helped establish the Jewish Agency to serve as the provincial government of the Jewish community in Palestine until a state was created. After 1948, the formal government of Israel gave the Jewish Agency the mandate to ingather the exiles, that most sacred of Zionist missions. Now known as the Jewish Agency for Israel, it became the Jewish people's great miracle worker, collecting billions of dollars from all over the world to help settle millions of Jews in Israel.

The Hebrew word for immigration, aliyah, means ascent. Aliyah defined the Jewish Agency's new task. The aura surrounding that word emphasized the modern Jew's privilege, to move up to Israel after millennia of homelessness and hatred.

Like most Israeli organizations during the days of Ben-Gurionite Socialist Zionism, the Jewish Agency was hierarchical. It was centralized. It was turf oriented, always asserting monopolistic control over the aliyah and absorption process. It treated the people it helped paternalistically.

Today, we wince when we learn how the state of Israel imposed its ways on the newcomers, especially the 850,000 refugees from the Arab and Muslim worlds. Jewish Agency representatives dictated where they should live, what they would wear, and how they should earn a living. But the Sochnut, as the organization was called informally in Hebrew, also embodied the positive Zionist values of settling the land and ingathering the exiles, of being down-to-earth and ready to work.

"Before there was Hollandia [the fancy mattress company]—there was Mitat Sochnut—The Jewish Agency Bed," one nostalgic Israeli website recalls. The Jewish Agency bed was clunky, eminently functional, and as lacking in style as every kibbutznik who manufactured it. It was the standard issue, one-size-fits-all metal frame with a thin mattress that Israel's immigrants received at their Jewish Agency–run absorption centers. Today, when Israelis hear people singing the good old-fashioned,

With 250,000 people shouting "Let My People Go," this March on Washington in December, 1987, timed for the Soviet leader Mikhael Gorbachev's Washington summit with Ronald Reagan, launched American Jewry's final and winning battle in the quarter-century struggle to free Soviet Jews. *Courtesy of National Council for Soviet Jewry*

Throughout my nine years in politics and nine years in the Jewish Agency, I had a rollercoaster relationship with Bibi Netanyahu. Our friendship was rooted in the help he gave Avital and me during our struggle in the 1980s, but that didn't prevent either of us from occasionally disappointing the other politically subsequently. In May, 1987, we protested together during Solidarity Sunday for Soviet Jewry in New York.

Robert Kalfus GPO

In 2010, we sat together at the Board of Governors of the Jewish Agency.

Amos Ben Gershom GPO

My short experience in airline hospitality, had me serving as flight attendant during Operation Solomon, Israel's overnight airlift rescuing 14,325 Ethiopian Jews in May, 1991.

In January, 1995, our Zionist Forum for Soviet Jewry initiated a conference in Jerusalem with the Senator Henry Jackson Foundation commemorating the twentieth anniversary of the Jackson-Vanik Amendment. Prime Minister Yitzhak Rabin, who was always happy to help the cause, was the featured speaker—ten months later, Rabin was murdered. Senator Jackson's widow, Helen, pictured here, was a founding member of the Congressional Wives for Soviet Jewry in the 1970s.

The Russians are coming. Yuli Edelstein, a co-founder of the Israel b'Aliyah Party, and I chat with President Ezer Weizman, as newly-sworn in ministers at the President's official reception for the new Cabinet in 1996.

Saar Yaccov GPO

One of the lighter moments during the tense Wye Plantation negotiations in rural Maryland in October, 1998.

Ohayon Avi GPO

While on an official visit to Moscow in February, 1999, to my surprise, I ended up reading the files prepared for my trial, all 15,000 pages in 51 volumes, in the imposing former office of my KGB nemesis Yuri Andropov.

Our party's coalition negotiations with Ehud Barak after his prime ministerial victory in 1999 resulted in our joining his government. To the standard coalition agreement, we added a letter which I believe is the only formal document in Israeli governmental history injecting questions of democracy and human rights throughout the region as a factor in peace negotiations.

Milner Mose GPO

In June, 2007, José María Aznar, the former Prime Minister of Spain, and Vacel Havel, the former president of the Czech Republic, joined me in convening this unique forum of democratic dissidents actively fighting dictatorships in their own countries. President George W. Bush was the featured speaker at this Democracy and Security Conference in Prague.

At the open forums we saw that despite coming from seventeen different countries, nearly three-dozen dissidents spoke the same language of freedom, of human rights.

Courtesy Ondrej Besperat Prague Democracy and Security Conference

My friend of twenty years, the Palestinian dissident Bassem Eid, also attended the Prague conference – although this photo shows the two of us in my office at the Jewish Agency, which I started chairing in June, 2009.

In April, 2009, I joined pro-democracy activists from around the world in Geneva to protest the New Anti-Semitism

Courtesy of UN Watch, Hillel Neuer and Oliver O'Hanlon

In 2016, the
Hollywood actor
Michael Douglas
and I spoke at
Brown University
for Jewish identity
and against anti-
Semitism.

*Courtesy of Genesis
Prize Foundation*

As we addressed a
packed lecture hall,
a few anti-Israel
demonstrators shouted
outside and resisted
any invitation to
engage in a dialogue.

Getty Images

In an ironic twist of
fate, at this rally in July
2016 outside the Chief
Rabbinical Court in
Jerusalem, I ended up
protesting in the Jewish
state for Rabbi Haskell
Lookstein and Rabbi Avi
Weiss, who had led so
many protests to get me
into the Jewish state.

*Courtesy of Ezra Landau
ITIM*

During my nine years at the Jewish Agency, 207,188 Jews immigrated to Israel. I never tired of greeting olim like these —who arrived from France— at Ben-Gurion Airport, always thinking about how many generations of prayers and hopes were standing behind each particular arrival.

Photo by Nir Kafri,
The Jewish Agency

These young, idealistic, Jewish Agency emissaries, the shlichim, are among the best bridge-builders between Israel and Diaspora Jewry.

The Jewish Agency

hopelessly naive Zionist folk songs, they call them *shirei Sochnut*, Jewish
Agency songs, half-disdainfully and half-lovingly.

Over time, needs changed. It was no longer the 1930s and '40s, when
the Jewish Agency made the state, or the '50s and '60s, when it populated
the state. By 2009, the Jewish Agency seemed like an aging war veteran
still living off battles won long ago and increasingly forgotten. Israel's commissars of Zionism pushed the aliyah orthodoxy so heavy-handedly that
Diaspora Jews could trade stories about that "guilt-tripping Israeli tour
guide," asking in heavily accented English, "Why you no make aliyah?"

Some friends looked at me even more skeptically than Bibi did when
they heard of my request. It was as if I had volunteered to captain the
Titanic, after the ship hit the iceberg.

To them, the Jewish Agency conjured up images of charmless copycat
offices along endless, narrowing, dimly lit corridors, with tea ladies wearing Soviet-style smocks moving glacially from underworked office drone
to overqualified political appointee. Each office was simply furnished but
occupied by self-important bureaucrats doing bits of busywork between
ever longer coffee breaks, confident that their bullying employees' union
would protect their now irrelevant jobs.

Having worked closely with the Jewish Agency, and having fought
its leadership periodically, I was familiar with all the complaints about its
outdated, overstaffed, underperforming bureaucracy. Its reputation was
even worse. The first time I addressed the agency's board of governors was
just weeks after my liberation. There was a lot of fanfare and warmth. A
little too naively, but candidly, I told them what many had asked me when
they heard I would be speaking to them: "Why isn't the Jewish Agency
closed yet?"

Prime Minister Netanyahu's impression of the organization was correct. The Jewish Agency remained frozen in its historic mission, defined
as a success or a failure by how many immigrants settled in Israel in any
given year.

Ignoring all the warning signs, I went ahead, because I also believed
in this organization's underappreciated and unique strengths. The staff
was impressively professional, especially during national emergencies.
When the Iron Curtain fell, Jewish Agency representatives had fanned
out across the vast Soviet Union, which covered one-sixth of the globe.
They mobilized hundreds of emissaries, initiated dozens of programs, and

helped settle one million Russian immigrants. Through its board of governors and partnerships with the American Jewish Federation, the Jewish Agency then raised $1 billion in resettlement funds for Operation Exodus.

One of the agency's secrets was its staffers' idealism. From lay leaders on the board to secretaries and cleaning staff, everyone was united by a sense of *shlichut*, of mission, something I rarely found in my various government ministries. These Jewish Agency people focused every day on bringing Jews home to Israel.

Jewish Agency staffers also knew how to recruit, deploy, and manage *shlichim* (emissaries) all over the world very effectively, creating a living Jewish people network. This web of Israelis spreading across the globe brought a human touch to abstract ideas of the Jewish people and Israel, especially for the many Jews who had never visited the country. In 2003, after my visit to North American universities, I had recommended that we send these emissaries to campuses. Naturally, we turned to the Jewish Agency.

Most important to me at that critical transition moment in 2009, the Jewish Agency brought Diaspora Jews and Israelis together as no other institution could. The agency's roundtable, its board of governors, offered a unique forum in the Jewish world, where representatives of Israel's Zionist parties could engage with representatives of Diaspora communities, including the leaders of the Reform and Conservative movements. Intercommunal dialogues that were politically impossible to arrange in the Knesset or through the cabinet occurred regularly through the Jewish Agency.

I believed that, with its unique position uniting the Jewish people and Israel, the Jewish Agency could play a powerful role. We just had to tweak its mission, updating it to fit our changing Jewish world.

Even if the Jewish Agency was a flawed vessel, leading it would be the culmination of my ideological journey, which had started with the discovery of those two basic human desires: to belong and to be free. Professor Shira Wolosky Weiss and I described this vision of how to build identity and community in our 2008 book, *Defending Identity: Its Indispensable Role in Protecting Democracy*. By leading the Jewish Agency, I could implement these ideas with perhaps the most far-reaching identity tool kit in the Jewish world.

I worried about the Western drift away from tradition, community, and roots. I believed the underlying tensions in Israel-Diaspora relations reflected Israeli Jews' and Diaspora Jews' strained relationships to Judaism and Zionism more than some inherent hostility toward one another. In the Jewish community and beyond, I felt we needed a better sense of who we were before we could figure out how to better communicate with each other.

At the same time, Netanyahu's comeback government was forming at a particularly fragile moment. The political situation seemed doomed to deteriorate. Barack Obama had been inaugurated in January 2009, just days after Israel finished Operation Cast Lead. It was another military operation in Gaza that united most Israelis but intensified divisions among American Jews.

During those three trying weeks, J Street, the new "pro-Israel, pro-peace" lobby intimately tied to the Obama administration, pronounced Israel's actions "counterproductive" and a "disproportionate escalation." Rabbi Eric Yoffie, the president of the Union for Reform Judaism and a member of the Jewish Agency's board of governors, responded in the left-leaning *Forward* newspaper. Identifying as a "dove," he charged, "This time J Street got it very wrong." Feeling caught between the extremes, like so many Jews in Israel and abroad, Rabbi Yoffie wrote poignantly, "If some Jewish hawks are devoid of sympathy for Palestinian suffering, not a few Jewish doves have demonstrated an utter lack of empathy for Israel's predicament."

Two months after Obama became president, Benjamin Netanyahu became prime minister again. We all knew that this volatile prime minister–president relationship would strain Israel-Diaspora relations. For me, this only emphasized the Jewish Agency's huge potential as the bridge between Israel and the Diaspora.

Netanyahu agreed and supported my candidacy. Two months later, I was elected chairman of the Jewish Agency, a quasi-governmental agency with a $350 million budget. To continue the momentum of so many of the projects I had begun back in the 1990s, I asked Vera Golovensky to serve as my senior adviser. We had first met when we worked together at the *Jerusalem Report*. Over the years, she served in many capacities as my valued adviser on Diaspora affairs.

I spent the next nine years working with others to change the course of this vast ocean liner by just a few degrees. This relatively small adjustment allowed some people to accuse me once again of committing high treason, this time against Zionism.

ISRAEL-DIASPORA RELATIONS IN THREE STAGES

Sitting in my new office, which was David Ben-Gurion's old command post, changed my perspective once again. Across from it, in Ben-Gurion Hall, I hosted representatives of Jewish communities from all over the world. In the corridor, a parade of portraits of Ben-Gurion and each of his successors greeted me. These paintings reminded me, day after day, to look at the Diaspora through Ben-Gurion's eyes, at Israel through the Diaspora's eyes, and at the way Israel and the Diaspora related through my various predecessors' eyes.

Studying the history of the Jewish Agency, I realized that in this building the Israel-Diaspora relationship had evolved through three distinct stages. First, we negated one another, discounting the other community's future. Next, we saved one another, convinced that each could not survive without the other. Rich Diaspora Jews saved Israel from physical destruction as Israel saved the Jewish people from disappearing.

In the present third stage, even amid growing tensions, both communities have realized that we need one another. Diaspora Jews have started turning to Israel to inspire young Jews in their identity-building quests, while Israeli Jews trust Diaspora Jews as the most reliable allies in the fight against the delegitimization of Israel. My mission was to see how the Jewish Agency could solidify this sense of mutual interdependence, then to try building a healthier dialogue between Israel and the Diaspora.

Stage One: I Negate You

In the first stage, Zionists were desperate to build a Jewish homeland. They expected the Diaspora to disappear, either through assimilation or annihilation, as Theodor Herzl put it. Most Jews dismissed Zionism as the marginal movement it was back then. Even those who admired the halutzim (the pioneers) had a hard time taking their state-building talk seriously.

The great movements of nineteenth- and early twentieth-century Jewry resisted Zionism. The Yiddish-speaking Bundists believed in building a socialist future with their fellow workers of the world, not creating a sectarian Jewish state in the Middle East. Most Orthodox and ultra-Orthodox Jews believed in building up traditional religious practice, wherever they lived. Most Reform Jews believed in a Western European or American future, given that they defined Judaism as a religion that was constantly evolving. Even the American Conservative movement, which ideologically was the most pro-Zionist and peoplehood oriented, produced few immigrants. Most American Jews resented the suggestion that they had any home other than their promised land, the *goldene medina*, America.

During these pre-state days, even as many of its leaders negated the Diaspora ideologically, the Jewish Agency was the key practical bridge linking the Jews of Palestine with world Jewry. In the 1930s, the Jewish Agency sent emissaries to different communities all over the world, especially Europe, many of them through the Zionist youth movements. The movements could be socialist like Hashomer Hatzair and Habonim, revisionist like Betar, or religious like Bnei Akiva. It didn't matter. They all broadcast the same Zionist message about establishing a Jewish state for the Jewish people in the Jewish homeland, Eretz Yisrael. Warning about the growing dangers, the representatives urged the local Jews to come to Palestine. Most European Jews ignored this appeal, then paid for it with their lives.

The emissaries also helped organize aliyah for those who wanted to ascend. Sometimes they practiced in mock kibbutzim, called *hachshara*, in Romania, Poland, and Morocco, but never made it to Palestine. Sometimes they were fleeing persecution and sometimes they were survivors. Sometimes immigration was legal and sometimes illegal. The British policy in administering Palestine changed, but the Jewish Agency emissaries were always there, ready to help.

The emissaries' warnings proved prophetic. The Holocaust showed how vulnerable stateless Jews were. This realization turned most Jews into Zionists, broadening the definition to mean "supporter of the Jewish state" not just "current or future citizen." Most Eastern European Bundists had been murdered. The Orthodox and Conservative movements in America supported Israel enthusiastically, but with moral support and money, not mass immigration. Reform Jews Zionized, accepting peoplehood and the need for a state. The ultra-Orthodox still resisted theologically but adjusted pragmatically to the growing realities.

Stage Two: You Count On Me

Supporting Zionism became as Jewish as being bar or bat mitzvahed, especially after Israel's establishment in 1948. With a now functioning

formal government in the country, the Jewish Agency advanced the next
key Zionist mission: ingathering the exiles. Beyond working with immigrants before and after their arrival, the Jewish Agency channeled
world Jewry's generosity in this essential nation-building project. While
rolling up their sleeves, opening up their wallets, and trying to solve
the many problems facing the state, Jews in Israel and the Diaspora
sidestepped whatever ideological divides might emerge regarding who
should live where.

Remembering American Jewry's failure to save European Jews during
the Holocaust, Diaspora Jews vowed, "Never again." They were ready to
muster whatever financial and political power was needed to save Israelis, the poor and weak but inspiring new members of their Jewish family.
Israelis also remembered European Jews' failure to save themselves during
the Holocaust. When Israelis said "never again," they understood that the
only way to save the Jewish people was by building their state. This dynamic shaped the second stage in Israel-Diaspora relations of saving one
another.

Both groups of saviors met and worked remarkably well together
within the Jewish Agency's board of governors. By the time I started
attending the board meetings during my absorption activism in the late
1980s, the ideological passions on both sides had cooled. Still, you could
always sense the clashing crystal balls just under the surface. Most Israelis involved were heavy-duty Zionists, certain the Diaspora was doomed.
Therefore, all Jews should make aliyah, while those who didn't should donate as much money to Israel as possible before assimilating fully. Most
of the Americans involved were lite Zionists. Although devoted to saving
Israel, they knew aliyah was not an option for them, and better not be for
their kids.

Despite being rooted in mutual condescension, this relationship produced excellent results. The national institutions were cursed with convo-
luted bureaucratic structures. The approach to immigrants was often too
paternalistic. Nevertheless, working together, this mix of politicians, organizational professionals, and volunteers settled millions of people while
raising billions of dollars to build Israel.

I saw this mix of competing motives and focused cooperation in the
two last waves of Israel's aliyah of rescue, the immigration of one million
Jews from the former Soviet Union and of one hundred thousand Jews
from Ethiopia.

16

RELIVING MY EXODUS
WITH ETHIOPIAN JEWRY

The story of the Ethiopian aliyah illustrates this second stage of Israel-Diaspora relations, with the Jewish Agency at the center. I'm not peddling rose-colored history. Through the immigrants' rights party Yisrael B'Aliyah, while leading various ministries, and at the Jewish Agency, I was involved in many initiatives to help Ethiopian Israelis overcome the problems they faced on arrival. Some of their challenges were typical immigrant heartaches. Many others resulted from the huge gap between material and social life in Africa and in Israel. Some of these problems were worsened by the racial prejudices of some Israelis.

The story of the Ethiopian Jews' adjustment to Israel is a fascinating one, far beyond the scope of this book. Because this book concerns the dialogue between the Jewish people and Israel, this chapter examines the Ethiopians' immigration, not their integration.

I first heard about Ethiopian Jewry through the static of the Gulag. When not in a punishment cell, a prisoner is allowed to read the official Communist Party newspaper. It's an exercise in double-reading. Every Soviet citizen mastered how to decode the propaganda. You read the words, then read the real meaning behind them.

Toward the end of 1984, I read a long article filled with the usual rhetoric condemning Zionist aggressions. This time, Israel had committed a new crime. Apparently, the Zionist soldiers had invaded Sudanese airspace, landed in the airport, and started kidnapping peaceful citizens, claiming they were Jews with a particular name, "Falasha." The Zionists concocted this ruse to recruit more soldiers for Israel's insatiable military machine, which needed more people as cannon fodder.

I was thrilled. I understood that a miracle was taking place. Israel probably had found some long-lost tribe of fellow Jews in Africa and was bringing them home.

When I came to Israel, I heard about Operation Moses, which airlifted eight thousand Ethiopian Jews from Sudan via Brussels to Israel during seven intense weeks in 1984. Many of those Jews, some barefoot and all dreaming of Israel, had walked thousands of miles to reach Sudan.

On our first trip to northern Galilee together, Avital and I stumbled onto a yeshiva near Mount Meron, which included some Ethiopian Jewish students. Watching the students, black and white, learn together reminded me that the black-and-white images I first had of Israel in 1967 couldn't compare to the bold, vivid, colorful Israel I was experiencing. Having spent my childhood seeing Soviet propaganda posters depicting false images of blacks and whites together thanks to Communism, just to embarrass the Americans, it was thrilling to see them together in reality, thanks to Zionism.

The truth about the Ethiopian exodus was more romantic than I had imagined in prison. I felt like I was reading an African version of Leon Uris's great Zionist novel, *Exodus.* The members of Beta Israel, the House of Israel, were a lost tribe spun off from the Jewish people. Some trace their origins to Moses's time, others to King Solomon's, still others to the first century BCE. They remained cut off for thousands of years. In their time-capsule-like traditions, you could see striking continuities in their kosher dietary laws, Jewish calendar, and prayers, with some variations. But they yearned for what we yearned for, that one word, Jerusalem, which would return us all home from exile.

MY SHORT CAREER AS A FLIGHT ATTENDANT

Nearly seven years after Operation Moses, rumors were flying about another mass airlift. I decided that, if it was happening, I had to be there. I called the Jewish Agency's chairman of the board, Mendel Kaplan, early Friday morning, May 24, 1991. I asked him to get me on one of the planes.

"You don't work for the Jewish Agency. I can't take you as an agency employee," Kaplan explained. "But register as a journalist. If you get press credentials, I'll get you a spot." I called my editors at the *Jerusalem Report*. They approved it instantly. Jewish Agency representatives told me to be ready to be picked up at home that night around nine.

I explained excitedly to Avital that we should start our Friday night Sabbath meal early, because I would be flying out shortly after kiddush, the blessing over the wine. She, too, was excited, saying, "It's *pikuach nefesh*," the Jewish principle allowing you to suspend the Sabbath prohibitions to save a life.

Somehow, as we spoke, she realized that I was going as a journalist. Her face fell. "What? That's *chilul shabbat*," violating the Sabbath. "Journalism is not essential. It doesn't save lives. You must do something useful for it to become *pikuach nefesh*."

I called Mendel Kaplan again. "Can I be a flight attendant or do some other work to help the Jewish Agency team?" I asked.

This time, Kaplan lost his patience. "Natan, you're driving me crazy," he bristled. "We've got a million moving parts on this thing. Call yourself what you want." This way, I could honestly tell Avital I had permission to be a flight attendant.

That's how I started my brief career in airline hospitality. I happily hammed it up on the flight over, fawning over the four Israeli journalists flying with me on the huge empty airplane. I insisted on serving them.

Thanks to American Jewish donors, the CIA, President George H. W. Bush, and other intermediaries, Israel and the Jewish people had bribed Ethiopia's authorities to the tune of $35 million to hit the pause button on the country's civil war. We also paid hundreds of smaller bribes. During that thirty-six-hour cease-fire, Israel would bring home 14,325 Ethiopian Jews.

Over the previous months, hearing whispers that they would be saved if they made it to Addis Ababa, thousands of Ethiopian Jews had trekked from their villages to the capital. The lucky ones came by car or horse. Most walked barefoot. Too many had their loads lightened along the way when bandits stripped them of their possessions. Too many had lost a son, a daughter, a father, a sister, an elder, or a baby amid all the violence brought on by civil war. Now they awaited redemption, from us.

Today, over a quarter of a century later, witnessing this exodus remains one of the most profound moments of my life, up there with the day I ascended from KGB prison to Israel. I have merged my feelings and memories about my own liberation with my feelings and memories of theirs. This is especially true as time passes. The story that I filed for the *Jerusalem Report* that spring captured the excitement of the moment. Much of what follows is adapted from that article.

Immediately after the Shabbat meal on Friday, May 24, I was driven to a military base near Ben-Gurion Airport. Soon after, for the second time in my life, I found myself virtually the only passenger on a huge airplane. Now, as then, there were only four people sitting around me. This time, they were colleagues, Israeli journalists, and we were bound for Ethiopia.

Five years ago, the four companions had been KGB men, my honor escort on the journey from a Soviet prison to freedom. In that moment of release, when, suddenly, after nine years of struggle and prayers, I was lifted from the darkness of the Gulag, I wasn't told where they were taking me. But the sun, like the finger of God, pointed the way: it was a flight to freedom. They had taken away all my belongings—including my prison uniform, which had grown so familiar and comfortable—and given me ungainly and clammy civilian clothes. But I had at the last moment saved one item from the hands of the KGB guards: a little book of Psalms given to me by my wife, Avital, which was my companion in all the years of the Gulag. It kept me warm.

Through the triumphant psalms of King David, God was bringing me the joyous news: You are free and have won. You are going to the Land of Israel. In the coming hours, I would land in Berlin, be reunited with my wife in Frankfurt, arrive in Israel, and pray at the Western Wall. Throughout, I was surprisingly calm and confident—as is a person who has listened for the voice of God and relied on God and watches with rapture and without fear as events unfold, fulfilled according to God's great, unfathomable design.

Now, five years later, as I flew in the dark toward Addis Ababa on an El Al plane whose markings had been painted over, I was suddenly seized by questions and doubts: Why was it so important to me to be on this particular flight to Ethiopia? So much so that I had insisted my editor send me, even on the Sabbath?

Why was I flying toward Ethiopia? Was it because I was intrigued by these Jews who were so different from me? Or was it to understand better the Israelis who were ready to put aside their differences, drop everything, and rush to the rescue of these people at once so remote and so close? Was it perhaps to recover a sense of the purity of the Zionist dream, which in the harsh light of daily life in Israel could sometimes seem more like an illusion?

Let there be no mistake: my first five years in Israel had been full and happy. But they were also years of descending from heaven to earth. The simple, clear lines of the struggle between good and evil had grown ever more blurred, and the cacophony of arguments and doubts made it more difficult to hear the voice of God.

Below, Addis Ababa greeted us with scattered frozen lights, a city under curfew. As I stepped off the plane, I was met by an astonishing sight: A human river in white flowed toward the aircraft. I stood, paralyzed, as the vast crowd streamed through the darkness. They moved unhurriedly. Everyone seemed to be supporting someone else: the men with biblical beards and patriarchal faces; the women in embroidered dresses, surrounded by children. The five-year-olds carried the one-year-olds on their backs. On every forehead, a sticker bearing a number, so that families would not become separated.

The crowd was contained by a rope to ensure that no one would be left in the darkness of the land where they had lived for thousands of years. Israeli soldiers in civilian clothes and Jewish Agency personnel waved flashlights to guide the people toward the airplane. But these were only intermediaries. There was no need to search for analogies. I felt as if God was leading the column, as in the exodus from Egypt.

During the years of struggle for the exodus from Russia, the evocation of the departure from Egypt sustained us Refuseniks, especially at moments of loneliness and dread. As I walked through the Moscow night with KGB tails following, or sat in front of a KGB interrogator who threatened death, or endured hundreds of days and nights in the cold of the punishment cell, I tried to remind myself of the larger picture: Your history did not begin with your birth or with the birth of the Soviet regime. You are continuing an exodus that began in Egypt. History is with you.

It was not always easy to feel this. Sometimes I had to mobilize my whole imagination, summon all my inner resources, to break through the wall of prison. Modern history also came to my aid: Entebbe, when Israel sent planes to rescue Jews in the depths of Africa. The great sacrifice of Yoni Netanyahu, whose picture was on my wall until my arrest, and the daring of those with him. This event was my personal guarantee that Israel would not forsake me, that I, too, would be rescued.

Now these two images fused. Toward us, across thousands of years, Jews moved in an unbroken line from Egypt. This time, I was among the Israelis standing by the empty airplane, in Africa, to bring them out. The whole struggle of the last two decades, of the last two millennia, flowed together until it converged in this one picture.

The waters of the Red Sea part. Two fighting armies stop their war. Ethiopian soldiers resentfully look on as buses of Jews speed through the empty streets and as one Israeli plane after another comes in to take Jews out. With the departure of the last plane, the waters join again, the heavens close, and the war overtakes the country once more. It took slightly more than half an hour to fill the plane's two hundred seats with four hundred Ethiopian Jews.

I set to work as a steward, distributing water and bread. The Beta Israel were obviously hungry but were impressively serene. Each time our eyes met, they were smiling, responsive. Sometimes I held and patted one of the clamoring children so their parents could open food parcels. But this was a pretext. I simply wanted more communication and contact.

Clearly, this was their desire too. They were glad to share their children with me. Both sides looked for all kinds of tasks requiring exchanges. We were overwhelmed by our desire for intimacy.

Through all the events of that night, our passengers showed full trust in the messengers from Israel and were calmly confident despite the astonishing events overtaking them. Again, this implacable confidence in the future reminded me of my own state of mind in the plane that took me from Russia. As I had then, they now experienced a pure rapture and knew no fear.

They, too, left with almost no possessions. I had then two things that they did not: I had shoes, while many of them were barefoot, and I had my book of Psalms. But they themselves seemed like figures come suddenly alive out of the psalms. Their very journey was a psalm of rejoicing.

Their faith seemed to banish our cynicism. I remember somebody started talking politics, but the conversation went flat. It seemed profane in this holy Noah's ark in the air, floating through the clouds.

As the sun rose, we started approaching Israel. The pilot brought the plane low so we could see the land. As he descended, there was some crackling, and the captain announced in Hebrew, "We are flying over

Israel." Quiet. Then the Jewish Agency representative announced in Amharic that below us was the Land of Israel, using their secret word, our word, "Yeruzalem! Yeruzalem!" They started yelling, screaming, crying, cheering. It lasted until after we had landed. This volcano of voices reminded me that one enchanted word connected Jews over thousands of years, from Addis Ababa to Moscow. That word was Jerusalem.

I realized that landing with these Jews gave me the answer to the question of what had impelled me to make this brief, eternal journey. This was the moment I had come for. Here, there was no black or white, educated or unschooled, cynic or idealist, left or right, believer or secularist, immigrant or old-timer. Here was one Am Yisrael, one people, returning to their land, whose applause, singing, and African ululating merged into one impossible and triumphant symphony.

AN ALL-ISRAELI WELCOME

When the first plane landed in Ben-Gurion airport, Israel's prime minister Yitzhak Shamir welcomed the new Israelis. Having choreographed this rescue brilliantly, Shamir said, "They are the remnants of a Jewish community that lasted for thousands of years, who are now coming back to their country. . . . They have come back to their homeland."

Then, another surprise. The early 1990s were rough. Many Israelis had become cynical about Zionism, traumatized by the violence during the Palestinian riots, demoralized by our passivity when Saddam Hussein's Scud missiles hit us during the Gulf War, and dispirited by the aggressively uncharismatic Shamir. Zionism appeared to be a movement whose moment had passed. It had created the state, many concluded, then became an irrelevant relic.

Nevertheless, this day and a half electrified Israelis. As plane after plane arrived, Israelis flowed into Ben-Gurion Airport to greet the new immigrants, a group that now also included five new babies, born during the four-and-a-half-hour flight. Thousands of Israelis also cheered the four hundred buses crisscrossing the country, transporting these new Israelis to forty-nine absorption centers the Jewish Agency had thrown together practically overnight. The euphoria seemed to remind everyone what the state was all about. We took Davidian pride in watching Israel ingather exiles yet again. And we took Isaiahan pride in noting that Israel was the only democratic country actively welcoming black immigrants from Africa.

Joel Brinkley, reporting for the often-skeptical *New York Times*, wrote on May 26, 1991, "At the airport this morning, it was difficult to tell who was more joyful—the barefoot Ethiopians who cheered, ululated and bent down to kiss the tarmac as they stepped off the planes, or the Israelis who watched them aglow, marveling at this powerful image showing that their state still holds appeal, even with all its problems."

REALITY INTRUDES

That was the romantic part of the story. None of it should be underestimated or taken for granted. It began with the stubborn bravery of those Ethiopian Jews, some of whom paved the way back to Jerusalem with their bodies, even sacrificing their lives. It was orchestrated by the creative determination of Israelis, who honored their mandate to help Jews, wherever they were, and ingather exiles, no matter how different they looked or how unfamiliar some of their customs might have become. It needed the full mobilization of world Jewry, uniting Establishment types and activists, as in the good old days of our Soviet Jewry struggle.

But after the romance came the messy realities, which often test the loftiest ideas. Israel's gallant 1991 rescue cleared the waiting list of Beta Israel. All Ethiopian Jews eligible for automatic Israeli citizenship under the Law of Return made aliyah by the end of the 1990s. The story of those heroes who stayed Jewish over millennia and willed their way home would continue now in Israel, presenting its own absorption challenges. But the Ethiopian Jewish saga continued with the Falash Mura, who sought to immigrate but didn't fit the criteria specified in Israel's Law of Return.

There are two paths to Israeli citizenship, beyond being born there. First, anyone can apply to become an Israeli citizen by following standard immigration and naturalization procedures, as in every other democratic country. Or, under the Law of Return, any Jew can immigrate automatically. The state was founded to be the home of every Jew. It's not really up to the government. Every Jew has the right to decide to make aliyah and become a citizen of Israel.

Reeling from the confusing realities of assimilation and the ugly trauma of persecution in Europe, culminating with the Holocaust, the Knesset in 1970 followed Hitler's rules to define eligibility for aliyah. The Nazis targeted anyone with at least one Jewish grandparent, so Israel decided to accept all applicants with at least one Jewish grandparent too, unless they had converted out.

THE FALASH MURA CONFUSION

The poverty, hatred, forced conversions, thwarted dreams, and stormy realities of Jewish life over thousands of years in Ethiopia had created groups of people close enough to the Jewish journey to feel that they, too, had the right to come to Israel—even though they were not eligible under the Law of Return.

The Falash Mura were descended from one group of Ethiopian Jews who converted to Christianity, frequently under duress, starting in the mid-1800s. While most lived apart from the Jews, they never fully separated themselves either. At the same time, their Christian neighbors didn't fully accept them.

Inspired by Beta Israel's redemption in the early 1990s—cynics would say they were jealous of their escape from African chaos—the Falash Mura joined the effort to get to Israel. But those who were five, six, or seven generations removed from conversion, or who lacked a Jewish grandparent, were ineligible under the Law of Return. Legally, Israeli officials could not accept them.

Few Israelis had heard of the Falash Mura until Operation Solomon. Some Falash Mura could prove they had at least one Jewish grandparent and were eligible under the Law of Return. That was easy: they were in. Some had relatives among the two thousand or so who had made their way onto the airplanes in 1991. A few dozen had been rushed onto the last of the planes, despite having been rejected for immigration. While commanding the operation, Deputy Chief of Staff Amnon Lipkin-Shahak had seen these ineligible immigrants lingering in the airport. With the clock ticking, even after being warned that they couldn't prove proper lineage, Lipkin-Shahak declared, "All aboard. We'll sort it out at home. My mission is clear: I won't leave any Jews behind."

But many Falash Mura were left behind. Having trekked to Addis Ababa, there was no turning back for them. They stayed in the city, awaiting redemption. Inspired by the massive exodus, other Falash Mura streamed into the capital, abandoning their villages and giving up their cattle and their livelihoods. Finally, they arrived in miserable urban slums, ready to wait.

Many Ethiopian Jews who had made it to Israel resented the Falash Mura. They considered them fair-weather friends who had dodged Jew-hatred for generations since their ancestors converted. Some Beta Israel suspected the Falash Mura of informing on them over the years. These skeptics feared that, having discovered an upside to being Jewish, the Falash Mura now wanted to cash in on this diluted ancestral connection. At the same time, those who had come to Israel and had Falash Mura relatives argued passionately for their new home to let their friends and relatives come too.

The process of proving eligibility was laborious. This was not a country of standardized birth certificates and formal family trees. With few or usually no documents to rely on, Jewish Agency representatives and Interior Ministry officials would try contacting relatives or representatives from neighboring communities living in Israel for verification. More and more Falash Mura arrived in Addis Ababa. Fewer and fewer would take no for an answer. Rather than returning to their villages, they started living hand-to-mouth in an already poor, overcrowded city. It was a humanitarian disaster in the making.

The Jewish world's experts in aiding physically distressed Jews stepped in, especially the Joint Distribution Committee (JDC). The North American Conference on Ethiopian Jewry proved to be Ethiopian Jews' most outspoken advocate. These and other Jewish organizations helped the Ethiopians in immigration purgatory, whose lives had turned hellish.

Eventually, I no longer viewed the Ethiopian saga from my jail cell in the Gulag or my flight-attendant jump seat on a stripped-down El Al plane above Addis Ababa, witnessing legendary Israel-Diaspora cooperation. By 1997, I faced these complicated questions while chairing the Interministerial Committee on Aliyah, Absorption, and Diaspora Affairs, amid growing Israel-Diaspora tensions about what to do with those of ambiguous status who were left behind. High on the agenda were the compounds that had developed in Addis Ababa, housing 3,500 Falash Mura waiting for answers from the Israeli immigration authorities.

Our committee essentially heard two opposing arguments. The American Jewish organizations and Israeli activists in the field emphasized that these people felt Jewish. They belonged to our people. Many already had relatives among our new Ethiopian Israelis because the communities had intermingled and intermarried.

These people were living under desperate conditions. Time was working against us, we were told. Month by month, crime intensified, prostitution spread, worries about AIDS grew. As the anger, despair, and privation mounted, the gap these people would have to overcome between their old African life and new Israeli one would only grow. "Israel should bring these people home as soon as possible," we kept hearing. "Enough bureaucracy. Make it happen."

A second position, advanced most forcefully by Israeli officials, started with one undisputed fact: they were ineligible under the Law of Return. Each case had to be assessed individually. "If anyone can just come to Israel because they feel close to Israel or want to move here, regardless of lineage or conversion, we make a mockery of the law," the officials warned. "Besides, look at a map. We could be overrun by millions coming on foot from Africa, fleeing all the misery there."

We also considered the opinion of the former Sephardi chief rabbi and founder of Shas, Ovadia Yosef. Give the Falash Mura the benefit of the doubt, he advised. Following a teaching of Maimonides, rabbis historically had a bias toward accepting *zera yisrael*, the seed of Israel. They were happy to welcome back descendants of Jews who were forced to abandon their Judaism under the sword. Lost Jews returning to the fold, or those whose status was unclear, could undergo *giyur le'chumra*, a less rigorous conversion process. It still involved intensive study before a rabbinic court and ended with an immersion in the mikvah, the ritual bath. Once converted, they could receive automatic citizenship.

I consulted with government authorities, rabbis, and American Jewish activists. We reached a compromise that the Israeli government and the American Jewish organizations accepted. We would clear the compounds once. An accelerated process would handle one group after another. They would fly to Israel by regularly scheduled commercial air travel, not with another airlift.

Because they were ineligible under the Law of Return, the Falash Mura would enter under the usual entry law. Nevertheless, they would get the full new-immigrant benefit package. Once they finished the *giyur le'chumra*, which they could start immediately, they could become citizens. Israel would be circumventing the Law of Return as a one-time humanitarian gesture.

Addressing Israeli officials' fears about setting a dangerous precedent, the American Jewish organizations vowed: No more compounds. The JDC and others would not reopen them and wouldn't staff or fund any others. In the future, refugees would be directed back to their villages to apply for aliyah individually, then wait.

"Beware," experienced Israeli officials warned. "Even ignoring all the family reunification headaches, watch how the number of Falash Mura will grow by leaps and bounds because you're encouraging them." More cynical Israelis warned, "You cannot trust these American Jewish organizations. They will keep pushing and tugging at the heartstrings." Nevertheless, we were pleased with our Solomonic solution—as long as it lasted.

AS MINISTER OF THE INTERIOR

Two years later, on my agenda as interior minister was the growing problem of two large compounds. One smallish one was in Addis Ababa. The other, almost ten times larger at twenty thousand people, was in Gondar province. In 1997, just four months after the JDC shut down its Ethiopian operations as per our agreement, it started building that first Addis Ababa compound. American Jewish activists involved in the Ethiopian struggle had exerted tremendous pressure on the organizations to return. "JDC, as a humanitarian organization, cannot ignore the plight of hungry children," Michael Schneider, executive director, explained. As more distant descendants of Jews emerged, more compounds were improvised, more applicants left their villages for the city's slums, and more heartbreaking appeals were logged. Initial estimates of ten thousand Falash Mura tripled, to at least thirty thousand.

The American Jews' demand was familiar: "Don't waste time with your bureaucracy. Bring them as soon as possible." In a typical appeal, the executive vice president of the United Synagogue of Conservative Judaism, Rabbi Jerome Epstein, said, "The Jews have always been a people committed to mercy. . . . We have faith that the State of Israel will continue in this tradition and will manifest values that serve as a beacon of light to other nations."

This time, even if I had wanted to continue airlifting everyone from the compounds to end the problem, I would not have received my colleagues' support. I had no credibility left on this issue. The immigration officials' warnings had proved to be true. And we had learned that American Jewish organizations would sacrifice any promise they had made to the government if they endured enough pressure from their members.

I decided to visit the compounds in Ethiopia. I couldn't imagine making these difficult policy choices from thousands of miles away. I had to see the conditions these people endured. "No. Israeli ministers are not allowed to visit those compounds," our Foreign Ministry warned me. "If you go it will mean that the state of Israel has a special obligation to these people. Even our ambassador to Ethiopia doesn't visit." Here was one more taboo I had to break.

I flew to Ethiopia anyway in April 2000. I visited both major compounds. I traveled to some of the villages these people had left. I sat in on several immigration interviews.

I have visited slums all over the world. In 1994, I was part of the team of international observers monitoring South Africa's first democratic election. I chose to monitor the election in the South African prisons and the Soweto township. After seeing parts of Soweto, I left convinced I had just seen the most distressing slum I would ever see.

Some of what I saw in Ethiopia was worse. The villages these people came from were frozen in the Stone Age. Entire families were crowded into tiny, ramshackle one-room huts made of mud, dung, and straw. Many lacked windows. Even if these people were lucky enough to have a small coal stove, they often lacked money for the coal. Food came first, although they often lacked money for that too. Kids in one Addis Ababa school I visited had been fainting from hunger until the North American Conference on Ethiopian Jewry started feeding each student bread, one piece of fruit, one vegetable, and some protein every day.

Amid the dirt and smells and disease and hunger and misery, it was easy to understand why people would grasp at any chance to run away, to the compounds and to Israel. Inside the compounds, the JDC's miracle workers brought order: sanitation, medical care, and three meals a day.

Amid all this chaos, the Falash Mura were starting their Jewish lives, coached by Jewish and Israeli activists. They were studying Judaism. They were learning Hebrew. The men were putting on tallit and tefillin—prayer shawls and phylacteries—while praying in the synagogue. They even mastered the art of baking matzah, unleavened Passover bread, within the eighteen minutes you need before the dough rises.

At the compound's school, I spoke to some of the students in Hebrew. I watched the students say the hamotzi prayer over the bread they were given. I saw one "first grader" sitting patiently with the kids—he was twenty-six years old and anxious to learn.

When I sat in on one family's immigration interview, the group of seven had grown by one since their previous meeting. The newcomer was a young girl who had just married into the family. She claimed she was eighteen but looked twelve. "This is typical," the Jewish Agency representative told me. "She comes from a village with no Jews, not even Falash Mura. Once we accept her, look how easy it will be for the process to get out of control. She will be able to invite perhaps a dozen close relatives through family reunification. That's why we have to be vigilant. But look at her, look at them. That's also why it's so hard to say no."

"I hope we'll succeed as quickly as possible in bringing all Jews to the Land of Israel," I said, choosing my words carefully when I addressed about 1,500 of the Falash Mura in one camp. Most of the men in the crowd who cheered wore kippot; most of the women were wrapped modestly in shawls.

During my visit, a BBC reporter interviewed me. I was proud of what we were doing with Ethiopian Jewry. Israel was the only democracy welcoming African immigrants with such open arms. When I agreed to the interview, I thought, "The BBC is usually hostile. This time, finally, I will be on their good side."

Not quite. "I understand," the reporter said, "that you Israelis are ready to bring non-Jews from Russia because they are white and not ready to bring Jews from Ethiopia because they are black."

I don't like to lose my temper or let reporters see they've gotten under my skin. This time, I did both. I accused him of anti-Semitism. After all we did, and considering what nobody else in the world was doing, how could he still pick on the Jewish state? Even after our dramatic airlifts, and with the confusion about each person's status, we still made exceptions for those who were not eligible to immigrate to Israel. Yet we were racist?

If anything, it was the opposite, I explained. Officials stretched the law to welcome these people to Israel. "No Russian or American or French applicants for aliyah who were ineligible under the Law of Return would have received such special assistance," I said. "Russians who could prove their roots from three generations back and who tried hard to get permission to make aliyah were being refused constantly. And Falash Mura brought to Israel sometimes were even eight generations removed."

"What are you getting so angry at me for?" the reporter responded. "I was quoting what American Jewish organizations say about you guys."

Most "American Jewish organizations" were saying no such thing. But some angry activists who wanted to pressure Israel were. That was enough to diminish all of Israel's good work. It was infuriating that, over the years, crying racism became the standard go-to argument among Israeli politicians looking for a quick headline when criticizing the government on this complicated issue. With this falsehood bandied about so loosely in Israel, no wonder American Jewish liberals and other Western critics overlooked Israel's efforts and ended up crying racism too.

I returned to Israel. It was clear, even without resorting again to an "aliyah of *compoundim*"—compounds—that we had to process many more applications, much more quickly, in both Ethiopia and Israel. As interior minister, I secured extra funds for the Jewish Agency to hire more staffers. There was no magic bullet. Still, we increased the flow of immigrants from a few dozen a month to a few hundred. Eventually, we plowed through the list of seventeen thousand.

Between the time I visited in the spring of 2000 and when I started leading the Jewish Agency in 2009, more than twenty-seven thousand Falash Mura became Israelis. Nevertheless, another "final" list lingered, this time of 8,200. When I asked cabinet ministers, "Can we just finish this already? Can we just let them all in at once? After all, they are the last Jews in Ethiopia," they usually scoffed, "You already brought us the 'last 3,500' twenty years ago. How many times can the last plane from Ethiopia land?"

TENSIONS WITH AMERICAN JEWS
OVER ETHIOPIA

While my Israeli colleagues dismissed me, my Diaspora friends kept lobbying me. Before I joined the Jewish Agency, and certainly after, representatives of the Jewish Federations of New York, Cleveland, Chicago, Boston, and elsewhere kept the heat on about the continuing crisis. "We're getting a lot of pressure from our donors," they would say. That usually meant one or two influential people who really cared about the Ethiopian problem. Then the executives would raise their bigger concern: "Israel, which should be so proud of what it has done, is instead giving itself a black eye on this issue. Our people just don't understand this," they continued. "How can you turn away needy people—who have a Jewish connection—from the Jewish state? Isn't that why Israel was founded?

Some of our people feel that you treat the aliyah from Africa differently than the aliyah from Europe."

They correctly saw me as their ally. I always advocated for an accelerated immigration process. But this permanent suspicion, contrary to all the facts, that the Israeli government was somehow prejudiced against Ethiopian Jews because of their skin color, irritated me. At a certain point, I started needling some critics in response.

"You believe they are part of the Jewish people," I would say. "And you seem very concerned about them. Why don't you take some into your communities?" I asked, ever so innocently. "Not one thousand, not one hundred, just take ten to set an example and show your sympathy."

The reaction was usually a mix of surprise, confusion, and indignation. "Um, they aren't asking to move to America. They want to return to the Jewish homeland, Israel," they would often reply. "You're a Zionist. You and Israel want them in America?"

"No. I want them in Israel," I would respond. "But Israel didn't want Soviet Jews going to America. Nevertheless, back then you made a big effort to welcome them."

Their next argument usually was, "They will be absorbed into a different reality. If they move to Israel they will stay Jewish. If they come to America, many will stop being Jewish and embrace their black identity instead."

"Isn't that the kind of assimilation process many of the Jews from the former Soviet Union experienced?" I would continue.

Whenever I would get into one of these tiffs, my staff members would ask, "Why are you starting up with them? Do you really want them to lure Falash Mura to America?"

I didn't. But I was annoyed by American Jewish activists' insinuations that racism shaped Israel's immigration policies. I wanted to turn the tables on them and have them compare their own attitudes toward Russian whites and Ethiopian blacks. We all needed to recognize that different communities at different times demand different policy choices.

True, it was messy. Israeli officials in the twenty-first century were applying the Law of Return, which reacted to the plight of European Jewry during the Holocaust, to a lost tribe in Africa, with its own 2,500-year history of persecution and survival strategies. American Jews were often thinking about their idealized vision of Israel, rather than about Israel's legal constraints. We all lacked the mutual trust we needed—let alone a functional forum—to resolve these problems constructively.

Nearly three decades after Operation Solomon, the Ethiopian purgatory continues. It must end. It would have ended more quickly and elegantly if Israel and the Diaspora could always pull off the kind of miraculous cooperation that produced Operation Solomon. That May of 1991, Israel and world Jewry together exercised raw power to do the right thing. The Jewish world united to help Israel do what it was founded to do, to save Jews.

Since then, suspicion has grown on both sides. Some American Jewish activists have a gut feeling that racial considerations have influenced the Israeli government's approach to the Falash Mura. They are annoyed that, instead of being the source of pride it was supposed to be, Israel has offended their liberal values. Meanwhile, many Israeli government officials resent that they are supposed to undermine the solid legal foundation for ingathering the exiles—the Law of Return—and move into murky legal and political territory just to indulge American Jewish sensibilities.

Today, the primary victims of this mutual mistrust are the Falash Mura waiting in Ethiopia. Those who get to Israel still end up waiting too long for permission. Others who have refused to take no for an answer just wait endlessly, expecting Israeli policy to change yet again.

This localized episode exemplifies the problems inherent in a mutually condescending relationship based on "we're saving you." In the crudest distillation of the conflict, Diaspora Jewish activists essentially were saying: "We give you all the support you need, how dare you embarrass us?" And Israelis essentially were saying: "We're giving you a state—don't make our work even harder for us."

At this second stage of the Israel-Diaspora relationship, with both sides saving one another, each of us considered ourselves the senior partner and the other clearly the junior partner. The road to the third stage of mutual dependence, when we realize that we needed one another as equal partners, remained to be paved.

17

REFORMING
THE JEWISH AGENCY

Because We Need One Another

In 1948, when the state of Israel was established, many Diaspora Jews felt that their poor relative needed saving. The state had to ration oil and food in the 1950s as the population more than doubled from immigration. With enemies surrounding it, and what looked like chaos within, Israel became the great charity case of the Jewish world.

By the 1990s, Israel was one of the world's most rapidly developing countries. Its traditional, centralized, socialized economy was modernizing, becoming the launchpad for a start-up nation. Israel's standard of living was starting to match Europe's. The one million Russian immigrants were bringing in new skills, professional experience, and a sophistication in basic sciences, enhancing Israel's competitiveness. In 2000, Israel's economy started its amazing winning streak, averaging 3.3 percent growth every year, outdoing most European countries.

Israel started passing most of a society's essential road tests. It was heading in the right direction in terms of social justice, tolerance, education, fairness, prosperity, and freedom, while acing the test that assesses confidence in today and tomorrow: the pregnancy test. Israel's birthrate of 3.1—2.2 per secular woman—is the highest by far in the OECD. The last time Western Europe averaged 3.1 births was in 1931; for the United Kingdom and France, it was 1889.

This optimism helps explain why Israel ranks higher on the world happiness index than the United Kingdom, Germany, the United States, Belgium, and France. Israelis also have a strong sense of family and tradition. Israel is the only major Jewish community growing quickly today, a rare place where nonreligious Jews succeed in passing on a strong sense of Jewish connectedness to their children and grandchildren.

At the same time, Diaspora Jews, especially in America, underwent their own transformation. Jewish communities outside Israel were richer, prouder, stronger, and freer, with each generation of children more American, more Canadian, or more British than their parents. But in the 1990s, Jewish demographers started pointing out a trend, especially in America, that many parents and grandparents, including some of my friends, were already experiencing in their own homes. As each succeeding generation became more American, rates of Jewish commitment dropped dramatically. The sociologist Steven Cohen observed that young adults were "significantly less involved in Jewish life in terms of communal affiliations, ritual practice, and even friends." They were more distanced from Israel too.

AND YOU SHALL TELL
YOUR STORY TO YOUR CHILDREN

If Hebrew school didn't excite, if the bar or bat mitzvah didn't inspire, if synagogue left them bored, what else might work? Well, wasn't there a generation of kids whose parents played an important role in the unique struggle for Soviet Jewry? They enjoyed a success of biblical proportions. Could this story, now a part of their family history, engage them? You can't just inherit that feeling of belonging or the connection to old stories. Kids only take it personally and feel it easily through the hard work of their parents.

In our family, we have two seders every year, despite living in Israel where most people have one. One is the traditional Passover seder. This celebration of freedom remains one of the most popular Jewish traditions. More than 70 percent of American Jews and 97 percent of Israeli Jews reported attending a seder last year. Every spring, each family repeats the story of our exodus from Egypt.

A central mitzvah, commandment, that night is, "Thou shalt tell that story to your children." Children are invited to ask questions, and the discussion proceeds from there. When we read about the four sons, we learn that the Wise One asks, "What does this means to us?" The wisdom lies in understanding that each person is supposed to take Passover personally, imagining that we were just freed from slavery that night. The Wicked One distances, asking, "What does this mean to you?"—and not "to me" or "to us"—separating from our people, from our story. The Simple One is easy to understand. But the growing threat in the Jewish world today is the fourth child, who does not even know how to formulate the question.

Our family's second seder usually occurs about six weeks before the traditional one. It marks the anniversary of my release from the Soviet Union and my reunification with Avital, on February 11, or the Hebrew date of Bet Ba'Adar Aleph.

Our more personal seder always revolves around our children's questions. Avital and I answer them, as I wear the kippah a Ukrainian cellmate made for me in the Gulag from the rough cloth used to line my boot. When my daughters were younger, they would ask about my best friends in my punishment cell, the spiders. They would ask how we used Morse code to communicate from one cell to another. And they were always fascinated by how we spoke through the "toilet phones," sticking our heads deep inside the bowl after draining it of water. As they grew older, their questions became more sophisticated. They would ask Avital how she knew what was happening to me, and how I knew what was happening at all. They wondered how it was possible that so many people around the world wanted to help.

As they matured more, they probed deeper, asking how we started building our lives together after a twelve-year delay and what lasting impact it had on us. "Was it hard to resume normal life after Abba's release and your reunion?" they asked Avital—all too shrewdly.

Now, we are on round two, telling the grandchildren our story. These days, our children and their husbands help their children ask the questions. Our children do a better job of answering them, finding a common language linking all three generations. Today, with the grandkids still young, we are back to playing with spiders and talking through toilets. We haven't graduated yet to mobilizing masses or communicating between forcibly separated spouses.

A few years ago, I tried retelling them the story of the Soviets as a new Pharaoh who sentenced me to jail. But I lost them as soon as I used the Hebrew word for jail sentence, *tzav ma'asar*. *Tzav* also means "turtle." "Turtle!" the kids yelled. "Pharaoh sent Grandpa a turtle." Before I could get flustered or frustrated, my daughters, with years of experience as educators in youth movements, stepped in. "Quick, kids, under the table!" they yelled.

"Now, get out," they commanded, while blocking the way. "That's what happened to Sabba"—to Grandpa—they explained. "He wanted to get out, and go to Israel, but they locked him in a small room and didn't let him go." The kids looked up, worried.

"Don't worry, he got out, because Savta"—Grandma—"started yelling too. At first no one listened to her, but she traveled all over the world, asking Jews to help. When the Jewish people joined in, you know what happened?" my daughters asked.

The kids shook their heads.

"Well, let's try," they said.

Everyone shouted: "Let my grandpa go to Israel! Let my grandpa go to Israel!" It worked. My daughters and sons-in-law let my grandkids go.

That short, punchy, Twitter-esque message was just what the kids needed to know then. The Passover seder teaches about God's power in helping us by choosing us, liberating us. My personal seder teaches about God's power in helping us when we each stand up individually and work together as a people.

So far, for our first two generational cycles, all this storytelling and re-membering has worked well. My oldest daughter, Rachel, says that one of the things that helps is that we told the story in fragments. She explained, quite insightfully, in *Tablet* for Passover 2020, that "like the authors of the Haggadah, my parents never tried to offer us polished versions of their story." She believes "this lack of editorial intervention. . . made their story so impactful." Avital and I "didn't treat it as their story to tell and to give, but rather as building blocks that we could use in the stories we told to ourselves," then—fragmented—to their kids. "With every new question and every new answer, my parents' experiences seeped into my own sense of self." Ultimately, of course, how it will work in the next cycles, time will tell. But it will not happen by itself.

For the past thirty years, Avital and I have been asked again and again, together and individually, to tell our personal stories and the story of the broader struggle for Soviet Jewry. One particularly popular request is that we speak to young bar- and bat-mitzvah-age kids, either one-on-one or to their class. It's difficult to say no, especially when a former comrade in arms—from Russia, North America, Europe, Australia, or Israel—asks. Inevitably, whenever our friends who fought with us relive the struggle through our retelling, they get very sentimental. It triggers a flood of memories. They often leave teary-eyed.

Over the years, as their children listened to the story, we could see it had already turned into history. Most kids lacked the emotional connection with our struggle their parents felt. At first, we were shocked. How could parents not have told their children about the determination they showed, the risks they took, the sacrifices they made? The smuggled letters, the angry protests, the secret trips to Russia? Tens of thousands of people spent years of their lives in the movement. Hundreds of thousands, if not millions, attended demonstrations. And they simply forgot to tell the next generation about their devotion and about our shared victory.

Gradually, we stopped being so surprised. We got used to the ignorance. Now, we are asked to speak to their grandchildren. You can see it in the kids' eyes: most don't feel anything. They don't want to upset their grandparents. They are willing to sit patiently, indulging them. Avital and I can always resort to the time-tested anecdotes that wake kids up, about Morse code and toilet phones. But it doesn't seem to mean much to them.

At a certain point, pitying those kids and ourselves, we had had enough. We were tired of burdening this captive audience. Now, when asked to speak to young teens or to their classes, Avital and I propose, "First, let them read a book, any book, about the struggle. Let them come with questions. We will be happy to answer." Since we added this condition, the number of speaking requests has dropped drastically.

This little experiment suggests that the parents or grandparents need to give it a personal touch for the next generation to feel connected. Without the elders' massive investment, those in the younger generation don't take the leap to make any part of history a part of their identity. There are too many other distractions. It's too easy to see it all as distant.

By contrast, look at these same kids' faces, and their older siblings' eyes, when they visit Israel. They're engaged. They're excited. They're discovering something they have been told is theirs for years, but they never appreciated before. That's what drives Birthright.

THE BIRTH OF BIRTHRIGHT:
THE MODEL THIRD-STAGE PROGRAM

Toward the end of the 1990s, Charles Bronfman and Michael Stein-hardt, two well-known North American billionaires, approached me with a "crazy" idea. It had been bubbling up for a while now, thanks to Yossi Beilin and others. I had known Bronfman as a generous funder of many initiatives, including our Zionist Forum. His wife at the time, Andrea Bronfman, of blessed memory, had been among the leaders of the Montreal Group of Thirty-Five, determined Canadian housewives who spearheaded the fight to free Soviet Jews. I knew Steinhardt, a gravelly, grumbly street kid who made really good, less well.

"We noticed that our kids and their friends are more interested in being Jewish after they visit Israel," they told me. "We want to guarantee that every Jewish kid born anywhere in the world will get a free trip to Israel. We want the Israeli government to pay a third of the costs. Local communities will pay a third. And the last third will come from private philanthropists, us and our friends."

I eagerly became their cheerleader and government lobbyist. For more than a year, I played the role of matchmaker, connecting these visionary donors with various Israeli officials. Many in the government considered this strange idea anti-Zionist. It upset the natural order. "Are you mad? Why are you supporting them?" some ministers scoffed. "You want Israe-lis taxed even more so rich American Jews can bring their children here for free? They can afford it. They should be sending us money."

Although only a few million dollars were requested in Birthright's first years, Israel's budget was so tight that any new allocations triggered massive government bickering. I believed this new program was worth fighting for. I believed in bringing young Jews to Israel on intensive pro-grams, while appreciating the symbolism of the gesture. The state of Israel would be investing in developing the identity of Jews who remained in the Diaspora, not just those ready to make aliyah. That kind of leadership could represent a revolutionary shift toward a more mutual relationship.

Bronfman and Steinhardt were a new breed of guerilla philanthro-pists. They did not wait around for the Establishment's approval. As the government and the Jewish Federations dithered, the billionaires charged ahead. Before getting the green light, they already had established a foun-dation, a steering committee, a top educational team, and a basic recipe for the free ten-day trip for eighteen-to-twenty-six-year-olds, which participants more or less still follow today.

Meanwhile, for more than a year, I continued my lobbying within the government. It wasn't easy. Sometimes, when speaking to old-fashioned aliyah-focused Zionists, I talked their talk, asking, "How else are we going to recruit immigrants in the future if we don't introduce them to Israel today?" But despite many studies proving the Israel experience's effectiveness, most ministers remained unconvinced or uninterested.

One minister got it. Fortunately, he was the prime minister. Netanyahu understood that the money would be well invested in strengthening our unity as a people and that the dividends would pay off in the future.

I was proud to participate in the historic meeting at the Prime Minister's Office with Charles Bronfman and Michael Steinhardt. We watched with excitement, and some nervousness, as Prime Minister Netanyahu signed the letter that turned this fantasy into that great Jewish identity-building project, Taglit-Birthright. Instead of looking at the Jewish people as a tool to build Israel, we were using Israel to build the Jewish people.

The first group arrived at Ben-Gurion Airport in December 1999. For the first three years of the program—as Israel ran through prime ministers from Netanyahu to Barak to Sharon—the small sums the government allocated kept coming under cabinet attack. Again and again, I would confer with Bronfman and Steinhardt, then lobby the prime minister and finance minister to protect the funds.

Eventually, something clicked. The program's importance became so obvious, it became politically incorrect to oppose it. The budgetary requests ballooned as the program expanded, but the government support grew too.

By 2006, Birthright had inspired tens of thousands of young Jews, but it was still relatively small. It wasn't yet the standard Jewish rite of passage Bronfman and Steinhardt had first imagined. The founders dreamed that, at birth, every young Jew would get a certificate to be redeemed after the age of eighteen, promising an Israel trip as one's "birthright."

That December, Miriam and Sheldon Adelson started scaling up the program dramatically when they stepped in to "buy out" the waiting lists. During Israel's sixtieth anniversary in 2008, they and their family celebrated by donating $60 million to Birthright.

Their donations sent twenty-four thousand young Jews to a country Sheldon's taxi-driving father was too poor, then too unhealthy, to ever visit. Since then, Birthright has operated on a much larger level, as a $100-million-plus program, bringing forty thousand to fifty thousand young Jews to Israel annually. This program shows that cooperation is possible, even in our polarized world. Funders of the Jewish Left like Charles Bronfman and Lynn Schusterman work together with funders of the Jewish Right like the Adelsons, appealing to young Jews from across the political spectrum.

Malcolm Hoenlein, the outgoing executive vice chairman of the Conference of Presidents of Major American Jewish Organizations, has often said that the struggle for Soviet Jewry saved a generation of American Jews from assimilation. The same can be said about Birthright. It became the biggest and most successful educational project uniting the Diaspora and Israel. It also became the most prominent example of American Jewry's strategic switch. The Diaspora was no longer just saving Israel; now the Diaspora needed Israel to save it too.

By 2009, Birthright and Masa, a Jewish Agency internship and learning program for five to twelve months, were bringing tens of thousands of Jews to Israel annually. As of this writing, more than 750,000 young Jewish adults have participated in Birthright—including one hundred thousand Israelis through *mifgash* encounters with their Jewish peers.

THE SECRET TO THE ISRAEL EXPERIENCE'S SUCCESS

The statistics speak for themselves, especially because, as good businessmen, Bronfman and Steinhardt invested in elaborate mechanisms to track the results to see the return on their investment. Twenty-plus years after Birthright's founding, mountains of surveys show that 85 percent of participants considered the trip a life-changing experience. Seventy-four percent feel a connection to Israel, and they're 40 percent more likely to feel that way than nonparticipants. However you judge being Jewishly involved, Birthright helps.

Educators, who know how difficult it is to change young minds, wonder: What's your secret? How can so many participants have a life-changing experience in just ten days of touring, including travel time?

Over the years, I have spoken to thousands of Birthright participants, in formal speeches and informal chats. I always get this eerie sense of recognition. The way they speak about the program's effect on them, and the looks I see on their faces, throws me back to the 1967 war's effect on me and my Soviet Jewish peers. It's immediate. They discover, as we did, all at once, their roots, their people, and their country.

Of course, we're not the same. Our assimilation was forced upon us. Most of them, or their parents, just drifted away. Most have always known they were Jewish and just never cared about it. It's harder to overcome intentional indifference than imposed ignorance.

While appreciating the past, Birthright participants also discover an excitement in the present they had never associated with being Jewish before. It's not Judaism as some kind of suburban country club for middle-agers. Instead, they feel they belong to this young, exciting family and a wise, ancient nation. In Jerusalem and Tel Aviv, in the Negev and the Golan, Israel is cool and fun. On Birthright, they just get to experience this first surge, this initial injection of energy. Nevertheless, the strange new feeling that there's something deeper in their identity, in their birthright, is liberating and truly thrilling.

If Birthright offers this sweet first taste, Masa provides a meatier meal. Established before I joined the Jewish Agency in 2003 as part of a fifty-fifty partnership between the government and the agency, Masa is the clearinghouse for two hundred or so different programs, lasting from five to twelve months, for eighteen-to-thirty-year-olds. They study, teach, volunteer, or intern, finding meaningful interactions in Israel.

I enjoy speaking to Masa participants after they have been in Israel for a few months. I start by asking, "What are your complaints about Israel?" With the range of options Masa offers—from teaching English in Arab schools, to volunteering in Tel Aviv slums, to studying in a yeshiva in the Jewish Quarter of Jerusalem—it attracts participants from across the political and religious spectrums. The participants' experiences usually reinforce whatever political or religious inclination led them to choose their program. After all, they are often with like-minded—and strong-minded—people. I hear lots of political criticism. I hear that Israel has abandoned Judaism or that the rabbis dominate Israel, that Israel is too hard on the Palestinians or that Israel has turned soft.

"Now tell me," I ask, "what does Israel mean to you?" During hundreds of conversations I have had with Masa participants, religious and nonreligious, left and right, I hear roughly the same answer. They say, "I found a family here. I feel more comfortable expressing my views here than anywhere else in the world. Here, I am loved not for my politics or my achievements, but because I belong."

As one young woman explained to me, "You know in Israel when the cab driver, after grilling me about three generations of my family history, wishes me 'shabbat shalom' on Friday, I feel that he really means it. When the New York cabbies mutter, 'Have a nice day,' it means nothing."

As Jewish identity thinned in America, American Jews discovered Israel as a tool to thicken their Jewish selves. It was no longer about saving Israel, but about using Israel to increase the chances that your grandchildren will be Jewish tomorrow by finding meaning and passion today.

The Jewish world beyond Israel faces an assimilation epidemic. Small communities are disappearing, big ones are shrinking. Having visited dozens of Jewish communities, I have only seen two sets of brakes that can counter assimilation: faith and Zionism. To stay Jewish, you either connect to tradition or to Israel. As with all systems, if you can use both, they reinforce one another. If you have neither, statistically speaking, your grandchildren have very slim chances of being Jewish, wherever you live, in France or Mexico or Australia or America.

REALIZING WE NEED YOU TOO

Israel could afford to finance programs strengthening Jewish communities because Israelis were no longer the poor relatives. On the contrary, Israel was flourishing. The outside media treated the country as if it were on the verge of collapse, but we Israelis lived a different story. We made the desert bloom and welcomed the exiles home. We were leap-frogging ahead of one European country after another economically, while becoming the eleventh happiest country in the world. We weren't defined by boycott, divestment, and sanctions (BDS) and delegitimization, but by drip irrigation, USBs, Waze, Mobileye, ReWalk, PillCam, Check Point's firewall, rooftop solar water, and cutting-edge, life-saving medical research.

When he founded the modern Zionist movement, Theodor Herzl expected that the creation of the Jewish state would eliminate both anti-Semitism and the Diaspora. Though he was prophetic when it came to envisioning Jewish statehood, on this, so far, he has been wrong. Despite all of Israel's successes, establishing a state didn't eliminate anti-Semitism or the Diaspora. In fact, anti-Semitism survived and spawned a new offshoot, the New Anti-Semitism targeting Israel, with its demonization, delegitimization, and double standards. Despite being strong, stable, and successful, Israel was the only country in the world forced to defend its very legitimacy, constantly.

When the Forum Against Anti-Semitism was first formed out of the Prime Minister's Office, it advanced Israel's mission of helping world Jewry, in this case by defending Jews. Once I turned it into the Global Forum for Combating Anti-Semitism, world Jewry was defending Israel.

This same transformation occurred on campuses. We all realized that strong connections between Jews and Jewish communities worldwide were in Israel's interest. So, as a secondary payoff, all these Jewish identity-building programs boosted Israel enthusiastically. Soon, on every campus, ambassadors for Israel, from left to right, religious and secular, Israeli-born emissaries from the Jewish Agency and full-time students, were not just defending Israel but celebrating it. They didn't do it out of some kind of guilt or obligation, but out of a need to defend themselves and this place that was so central to their identities.

This process was repeated in other parts of the Jewish world. It wasn't easy for many Israelis to stop expecting the Diaspora to assimilate away, or to start supporting these Jewish identity programs. The justice minister and deputy prime minister from 2003 to 2004, Tommy Lapid, entered politics as a classic Zionist, hostile toward religious Judaism and disdainful of the Diaspora.

Lapid's life story wired him to scoff at all these Jewish identity programs and the worries about whether the world liked us. Born in Novi Sad, Yugoslavia (present-day Serbia), in 1931, as a boy he watched the Gestapo take his father away. Lapid and his mother survived the Budapest ghetto, but he lost his faith in God and the world there. He became a Herzlian Zionist, defining "the whole Zionist idea," he later wrote, as a guarantee that "every Jewish child will always have a place to go."

Whenever cabinet discussions turned to any religion-and-state issue, Lapid liked to pronounce, "I am a better Jew than the Lubavitcher Rebbe himself, because I live in Israel." He loved to note that our kids serve in the Jewish army, and the Rebbe never did. Lapid bristled whenever I mentioned yet another identity-building program, saying, "A modern government shouldn't pay for old-fashioned missionizing activities."

Yet, when as minister of justice he had to counter the delegitimization of Israel, he started appreciating our Jewish partners abroad. When I launched my initiative to learn about the New Anti-Semitism every International Holocaust Remembrance Day, Lapid surprised me. Speaking in the Knesset, he quoted my report from my campus trip. As he descended from the podium, he turned to me and said, "It's good that you took us there. It's good that we are reaching the students. We need them fighting for us."

Lapid and many other Israelis had to adjust. They had to appreciate Israel's new needs, then see the Diaspora's potential. Diaspora Jewry was no longer just Israel's piggy bank and population bank, but, like every good family member, Israel's first line of defense and perpetual sparring partner.

We were entering the third, more mutual stage of Israel-Diaspora relations, wherein we still save each other but we need each other too. Strong Diaspora Jewish communities stopped being threats to the aliyah tallies in the short-term, becoming long-term investments in future advocates and immigrants.

Some went so far as to suggest dropping the term "Diaspora," just as previous generations stopped calling the Diaspora "exile." The term still works for me. Diaspora suggests that we are dispersed, which we are. Acknowledging the Land of Israel as the historic homeland does not stop us from respecting one another. Besides, "world Jewry" includes Israel, so "Diaspora" distinguishes between Israel and the other Jewish communities scattered globally.

Most important, just as many Diaspora Jews realized they needed their Israeli family in their great battle against assimilation, many Israelis—especially in government—realized that, even in these flush times, they needed their Diaspora Jewish family in the great battle against those questioning our very right to exist.

Despite the headlines that emphasize our distance, surveys keep showing that 80 to 90 percent of Israeli Jews understand instinctively that we need one another, practically and existentially. A state of Israel that is just a state of all its citizens and not the Jewish people's homeland risks losing its legitimacy. More than seven decades into Israel's existence, the state's legitimacy shouldn't be questioned. But our enemies are constantly questioning it, because they understand the stakes involved.

The international community has repeatedly recognized the Jewish people's fundamental right to a nation-state in the Jews' historical homeland. Israelis only emerged after May 1948, meaning that they don't have the rights to the Land of Israel—the Jewish people do. The Jewish people received the Balfour Declaration in 1917. The Jewish people won the vote in the United Nations in 1947 granting the legal right to establish a state. After defying exile and oppression, after longing for the Land of Israel for two thousand years, the Jewish people came from dozens of countries to rejoin the Jews who never left.

If we only talk about the Israeli people—a state of all its citizens— what distinguishes Israel from certain colonial projects that have vanished from the earth? The difference between Israeli identity and Jewish identity is the difference between the fact of existence since 1948 and our eternal right to exist. The difference is between citizens who live on a piece of land and speak the Hebrew language and the descendants of a people who, after being scattered globally, returned to their historic homeland, with broad-based international approval.

That's why, even during the starkest disputes about the Diaspora and Israel in cabinet, my ultimate argument remained the same. "But Israel belongs to all the Jews in the world," I would say, "and we have an obligation to keep it as a home for all the Jewish people." No matter how heated the fight might have been about implementation, no one ever questioned that core principle.

REFORMING THE JEWISH AGENCY

When I became chairman, the Jewish Agency for Israel already was running some third-stage identity-building initiatives that acknowledged the new interdependence uniting world Jewry. Launching Masa and funding Birthright helped Diaspora Jewry. Sending young emissaries to campuses to fight the New Anti-Semitism helped Israel. But ideologically and structurally, the Jewish Agency was still in the second stage. The board of governors consisted of Israeli and Diaspora Jews still out to save each other. And while the Jewish Agency was organized into three major departments—aliyah, education, and Israel activism—encouraging aliyah remained the core of its mandate. The agency therefore evaluated every program based on its contribution to aliyah, no matter how artificial the connection might be, especially when justifying programs to the government.

The three departments functioned more as competing corporations than as one integrated organization. This structure unintentionally encouraged emissaries from different departments to waste time and precious resources on turf wars, pitting, say, the community-focused education emissary against the Israel-oriented aliyah emissary.

Noting the years I spent fighting for Soviet Jewish emigration, many in the Jewish Agency expected me to strengthen the aliyah focus. Instead, I brought down the walls dividing the three departments. I merged them into one integrated, cooperative organization while making an ideological shift: strengthening Jewish identity became the agency's central mission.

My logic was simple. Most of the 3.5 million Jews the agency had helped settle in Israel came on the aliyah of escape. Since 1948, Jews had fled Holocaust-torn Europe, anti-Semitism-scarred Arab countries, Communist regimes, and African dictatorships. We would continue helping any Jews escaping persecution, be they the oppressed Jews of Iran, Yemen, or anywhere else. But today, most Jews live in free communities. Those who move to Israel make an aliyah of choice. Deciding to live in the Jewish state expresses a desire to be more intimately connected, hour by hour, day by day, to Jewish history and Jewish life. As I liked to quip to our board of governors, "To have more immigrants, you must have more Jews," meaning more connected Jews.

The aliyah of escape required speed; aliyah of choice required patience. The best way to encourage aliyah was by strengthening Jewish identity. The best way to fight assimilation or oppose the anti-Israel boycott or encourage more activism and community building was by strengthening Jewish identity.

This shift tested a central Zionist idea: our shared sense of peoplehood. We couldn't approach identity building as a sham, just waiting for those in the Diaspora to wise up and move to Israel. We had to ask ourselves, "Can you love them wherever they live, even if they never leave?" For me, the answer was easy. My commitment to Israel sprang from my sense of Jewish peoplehood as family, not the other way around.

THE IDENTITY REVOLUTION

One can ask, is this only branding? After all, it's the Jewish Agency's programs that count. Do they serve our people or not? To prove that we weren't just switching slogans, I often compared it to the Copernican revolution. Until the 1400s, the Earth sat in the center of every map of the universe. All the planets and stars circulated around it, just as they appeared to be doing when we looked up in the sky.

Copernicus put the sun in the center. As we know from modern physics, all the movements are relative. Nevertheless, suddenly, all the equations describing the planets' paths became simpler. Before that, complicated equations describing each planet's orbit had to be tailor-made. Once Copernicus realized the planets all circled the same center, scientists could use one elegant equation to describe the trajectories.

Similarly, once the Jewish Agency put strengthening identity at the center, it was easier to explain the logical connection between different programs and assess their impact. The agency's main tool in strengthening Jewish identity was the *mifgash*, the grassroots, mutually beneficial encounters between Israeli Jews and Diaspora Jews. This *mifgash* would take place in Israel, in communities all over the world, and on neutral turf, with global Jews united in common cause.

We would build a spiral of such Jewish experiences, with Jews at various ages and stages of their lives involved in these *mifgashim*. Rather than revolving everything around one question—When are you moving to Israel?—the spiral of experiences invited young Jews to find their place in an ever-escalating process, interacting with Israelis along the way. It could start by meeting Israelis: as counselors at summer camp, emissaries on campus, tour guides on a Birthright trip, or neighbors and colleagues during a Masa internship in Israel.

Different people could decide for themselves how far to go on this spiral and where to get on or get off. Some would go all the way and make aliyah. Some would be active in their community. Some would get involved in pro-Israel advocacy. Some would send their children to get a basic Jewish education. All this fed the Jewish Agency's central purpose of nurturing the global Jewish family.

In going beyond traditional, one-size-fits-all identity building, we developed new programs to address people's interests, capabilities, and trajectories on their particular Jewish journeys. So, for example, the Jewish Agency opened up Masa in 2004, with forty-five programs offering participants the choice to work or study. By the time I left, we offered nearly two hundred different pathways for Masa participants, from studying to cooking to dancing to teaching English to participating in cutting-edge social and communal experiments.

In our identity-centered world, once-competing programs became complementary. When first launched, Birthright and Masa fought each other so intensely for support from the government and philanthropists that the program administrators refused to share information. Today, they cooperate. Birthright runs Masa program fairs so the ten-day participants can easily transition to longer-term internships or study opportunities.

It became clear that there were many students who seek a post-Birthright experience but are unwilling to spend a full year in Israel. In response, we created Onward Israel, a six-to-ten-week Israel program, so these students could also find their place on the spiral.

Most dramatically, this identity-centered world updated that classic Jewish Agency type, the *shaliach*. For decades, the *shaliach*—the emissary—was the ultimate living, breathing Zionist stereotype. This representative Israeli's first historic role, long before the state began, was to encourage aliyah and to save as many Jews as possible by bringing them to Israel.

In this new stage, we tried to eliminate the historic tension between a strong Israel and a strong community. To the contrary, we Israelis were now interested in building the community. The new mission changed the *shaliach*'s role to encompass building individual identities, reinforcing the connection Jews felt to Israel, and representing Israel in different contexts.

Not surprisingly, we saw that, once emissaries were no longer just aliyah recruiters imposed on communities, communities became more welcoming. New types of emissaries started appearing to fit our identity-building approach, in synagogues, in schools, and in Jewish community centers. They joined the traditional emissaries in youth movements, in summer camps, and in an ever growing number on campus. The number of *shlichim* almost doubled, and the average age dropped from thirty-eight to twenty-six.

A new program brought in younger bridge builders, *shin-shinim*, from the Hebrew abbreviation for Shnat Sherut, the national service year. More and more young Israelis started doing a year of national service before their army service, often in neglected or peripheral communities. As these volunteer, educational, or social work internal gap-year programs proliferated in Israel, we in the Jewish Agency asked, "Why not send some of these young idealists abroad?"

Army officials were skeptical about this program at first, hesitant to give draft deferments for a boondoggle in cushy Jewish communities overseas. Over the years, commanders have seen how much more mature returnees are, and some high-ranking officers have noted the experience's profound impact on their own children. The program expanded from twenty-five to more than two hundred participants during my tenure. It keeps expanding. More and more communities are requesting to host these Israeli teenagers, while more and more Israelis are volunteering. The program is remarkably cheap—because these youngsters usually rely on home hospitality—yet often life-changing for Israelis and Diaspora Jews alike.

One post-high-school, pre-army volunteer told me that throughout her "entire life" in Tel Aviv—all eighteen years of it—she had received less exposure to Judaism than in her first three months in Toronto. In the increasingly popular expression, "she left as an Israeli and returned as a Jew." Once back in Tel Aviv, she would share these new perspectives with her friends.

The Jewish Agency's emissaries in each city started working as a team, often meeting regularly, even if they worked with assorted organizations. Different departments stopped competing with one another. We imagined one big identity assembly line, culminating in aliyah for those who chose that path.

We soon realized that a more sophisticated approach required more sophisticated training. The traditional two-week orientation seminar for emissaries was not enough. We needed a school for them, which we founded and which I continue to head.

With this new understanding of Israel-Diaspora relations as a two-way street, when emissaries finished their jobs representing Israel to the Diaspora, their bridge-building missions would continue as they represented Diaspora sensibilities to Israelis. Israelis could best explain to other Israelis that the different Jewish denominations were not different escape routes toward assimilation but different pathways toward communal expression and worship. This new, deeper understanding might help defuse some of the tensions around controversies, such as the ongoing struggle over who can pray at the Western Wall.

To help keep these young Israeli voices interested and engaged, our Shlichut Institute in Jerusalem expanded to work with people post-*shlichut*, improving follow-up once their jobs abroad formally ended.

All these different kinds of encounters welcomed members of different Jewish communities around the world to feel part of the bigger Jewish story. In speaking to one another and sharing new experiences, Diaspora Jews and Israelis could enrich their Jewish identities by adding new dimensions they wouldn't have otherwise experienced. Diaspora Jews could see what it's like to have a more natural, integrated Jewish identity, free of neurosis, second-guessing, and doublethink. When young Diaspora Jews met Israeli soldiers, they realized what it means to take responsibility for your people, to belong to and contribute to something big, sweeping, and noble—Jewish history itself. At the same time, Israelis discovered what being Jewish feels like when you are in the minority, not the majority. Judaism seems different when it is really a choice to affiliate, not simply assumed, and when there are pluralistic Jewish expressions, not Israel's all-or-nothing approach to religion.

Thanks to all these interactions, hundreds of thousands of better-informed and more engaged Jews have become our most effective ambassadors, explaining the Diaspora to Israelis, Israelis to the Diaspora, and Israel to the world, while championing all kinds of projects shaping Jewish civil society.

Similarly, responding to the desire of young Jews who wanted to help people beyond Israel, we launched Project TEN. This international development program operates volunteer centers in Ghana, Mexico, Uganda, South Africa, and Israel to help the needy while raising a new generation of global Jewish activists. We envisioned a serious program of Israelis and non-Israelis working together and learning together about the sources of *tikkun olam*, repairing the world. By studying, they would understand that they are volunteering in that region not in spite of their Jewishness but because of their Jewishness.

Avital and I visited these idealists in Durban, South Africa, and in Uganda. We were moved to see young, post-army Israeli women bringing smiles to the faces of neglected children, and to see an Israeli-style youth movement emerging in the world's grimmest slums. Many participants reported achieving a better understanding of what people were talking about when they talked about peoplehood.

When some government officials heard we were sending Israelis and Diaspora Jews to developing countries, they hit the roof. "Isn't *tikkun olam* a pretext to run away from Zionism?" they asked. "Why go to a third country and not to Israel?"

My standard answer was always the same: "Don't you expect the Jewish Agency to work wherever there is a Jewish community? The 'republic of *tikkun olam*' is teeming with Jews. Often, they see their idealism as an escape hatch, helping them run away from what they believe to be their 'narrow' Jewishness. This is the opposite."

Once again, in our polarized age, a fundamental value that should have united left and right, religious and secular, became a flash point. Liberals kept trying to make it their exclusive property without reading the entire phrase: "Tikkun olam be-malchut shaddai," repairing the world in God's kingdom. In response, conservatives, including Israeli politicians, mocked such an important Jewish value because, as interpreted, it tracked too closely with the trendiest liberal agenda of the moment rather than expressing eternal Jewish values.

Tikkun olam, in proportion, was and is a central Jewish idea, but it is not the only Jewish value. It's also a central Zionist idea, but not the only one. Something is off when Jews divorce *tikkun olam* from their Jewishness. And something is off when Jews embrace *tikkun olam* instead of their Jewishness.

With our new approach, we looked more systematically and sympathetically at Diaspora communities, assessing how to help. I saw the advantage of outsiders looking at a community through fresh eyes when I visited Toulouse, France, where a terrorist had killed a thirty-year-old teacher and three children. I visited this embattled community twice. Once, with the prime minister and other officials, I went to pay respects. Another time, I just looked and learned. The Islamist terrorist had cased the Ozar Hatorah school a few times, discovering its vulnerabilities. I, too, saw that the electric gates didn't close and the security cameras didn't work. But when I asked school officials about these lapses, they replied, "We have no money for this."

We in the Jewish Agency launched a special project to protect synagogues and other Jewish community buildings throughout the world. It was a great symbolic moment. The two major donors came from New York and Moscow, the Helmsley Charitable Trust and the Genesis Fund. Enhancing the sense of global partnership, Israelis offered their unique counterterrorism expertise. We spent over $11 million fortifying Jewish buildings in fifty-eight countries during the first four years.

We expected to spend most in developing countries, yet Europe and Latin America had the greatest need. On Yom Kippur 2019, when a German terrorist attacked the Halle synagogue, the security door and cameras we purchased stopped him—saving seventy people inside.

CLOSING TWO CIRCLES
FROM THE GOOD OLD DAYS

Still, reorienting the Jewish Agency ocean liner wasn't easy. It required tremendous efforts on the part of lay leaders and professionals. The board of governors debated the reforms for months. Then, the professionals had to restructure the agency, a multimillion-dollar operation, developing new understandings and methods in seminars and workshops.

Some Jewish Agency veterans, backed by some old-school government allies, worried that aliyah seemed to have lost its central place. I was accused at one cabinet meeting of undermining the agency's core mission. "You are diminishing this unique Zionist institution," the minister of aliyah and absorption charged. "It's no longer an agency of aliyah but the Ministry of Tourism."

The director general of the Prime Minister's Office agreed. "Why should the Israeli government fund some kid in New York rather than our kids in Kiryat Malachi?" he once challenged me. "Why should I, as the government, care about them?" Fortunately, Prime Minister Netanyahu supported our reform.

With every program now fitting into a broader vision and with emissaries and departments cooperating, not clashing, the figures soon started speaking for themselves. Each new emissary and each new program expanded our reach exponentially. Even the average annual aliyah rate nearly doubled, from seventeen thousand when I became chair of the Jewish Agency to over thirty thousand when I left.

Many factors beyond our control shape any individual's desire to emigrate. Still, our programs were inspiring more alumni to choose Israel. When 85 percent of Masa graduates from the former Soviet Union made aliyah, when nearly 100 percent of immigrants had gone through some Jewish Agency Israel experience or another, we knew the spiral was propelling some people, and Israel, forward.

In building the agency's more mutual "we need one another" approach, I was closing two circles from my Moscow days. First, recalling the dropout wars, I was again linking identity and freedom, championing a Zionism based on choice while refusing to play the traditional role as a command-and-control commissar of Zionism.

By bringing down the artificial walls between the world of Jewish education and the world of aliyah, I felt we reached a new equilibrium on the *politiki-kulturniki* question. When we face physical destruction, we must be *politiki*, plunging into practical political work to save individual Jews. But looking at the long run, fortunate as we are to have most Jewish communities located in democracies, we were able to be *kulturniki*, learning, developing, and building identity, strengthening our global Jewish family.

Of course, there's more to build. We certainly have to work harder to develop a constructive dialogue between Israel and Diaspora. But rather than being a dinosaur lumbering toward extinction, the Jewish Agency returned to the center of the Jewish world, once the platform for the third stage of relations between Israel and non-Israeli communities was up and running. Once again, the agency was addressing the key questions vexing the Jewish world, questions about how to stay Jewish and how to stay together as one family, despite being spread throughout the globe.

18

BRIDGE BUILDING
HITS THE WALL

The Kotel Fiasco

Despite our attempts to strengthen our Jewish family, some issues still threatened to tear us apart. I spent a great deal of time trying to manage the growing tension between Israel and the liberal streams of Judaism.

The Jewish Agency's board of governors is known to be a particularly difficult body to lead. Its members are delegates from different Israeli political parties and Diaspora Jewish organizations. As a result, many competing agendas are represented around the table.

This mosaic, which made our board so frustrating to run sometimes, was also what made it so significant. Whenever the governors convened, this roundtable amazed me. I would think, "Where else in the Jewish world does such a broad variety of Israeli politicians and Diaspora Jews have direct dialogue and make decisions together?"

The participation of the leaders of non-Orthodox movements on the board of governors was particularly important. From my years in politics, I knew how difficult it was to organize any formal negotiations between Israel and the leaders of the liberal streams. Ultra-Orthodox politicians were ready to dissolve a coalition if they felt the government was recognizing liberal movements in any way.

From my first days at the Jewish Agency, I urged Netanyahu and his cabinet secretary Zvi Hauser to tap into this unique resource. We could try addressing some of the issues that kept popping up between the Israeli government and the Diaspora. Hauser and I cochaired an informal mechanism we called "the roundtable." It included representatives of the Israeli government and members of the board of governors from the non-Orthodox streams.

We used this roundtable to push the Interior Ministry into talks with representatives of the different denominations. For too long, the Interior Ministry was a black box. Clerks there determined the validity of an immigrant's conversion as the first step to citizenship. The criteria were mysterious and could change from clerk to clerk, minister to minister.

Our lobbying created a transparent process for granting citizenship to converts. We agreed on specific benchmarks for approving conversions and for appealing rejections. "This is how we should be working together in the new, more mutual, stage of Israel-Diaspora relations," I thought. Not just building identity together, and not just sniping at one another in the media. This kind of problem-solving roundtable among equals had great potential.

Decades ago, when David Ben-Gurion made the status quo agreement with the ultra-Orthodox, he expected most religious Jews to disappear soon. His feeling that he was on the right side of history made it easier for him to compromise with his fellow Jews. Any concessions he made were temporary, he believed. Today, many Israelis assume that liberal American Jews will soon assimilate away into oblivion. Sadly, predicting their partner's doom now has too many on both sides thinking, "Why bother accommodating them? It's not worth risking any political capital."

What changed? Decades ago, for all the ideological rigidity of Ben-Gurion, the ultra-Orthodox, and American Jews, they were all deeply insecure too. After the Holocaust, the entire Jewish world was reeling. After 1948, Israel was fragile and embattled for decades. Despite the many American Jews with creature comforts, it took decades before they truly felt at home in America and not on probation.

Today, Israel is robust. American Jews feel deeply American. It's wonderful that so many Jews today feel secure in their own homes. But that unprecedented mass comfort has produced at least one unpleasant side effect: today's arrogance epidemic. Arrogance may be the great character flaw of our time. It surges when we silo ourselves in social media echo chambers that define everything we say as good and everything they say as evil and offensive. Only a conversation that helps us know one another better can overcome this arrogance.

"ONE WALL FOR ONE PEOPLE"

My hope that we could overcome our characteristic arrogance encouraged me when the prime minister called me a few years ago, during yet another violent confrontation over women praying at the Western Wall. Once again, Jews were fighting other Jews at the Jews' holiest site. Once again, the world press highlighted photographs of these ugly clashes. "I can't stand looking at these pictures anymore," Bibi said. "You have ties to the various factions. Can you find out if they would be willing to negotiate?" Then he coined the phrase that became our guiding light throughout years of negotiations: "It should be one Wall for one people."

The Western Wall was the right place to start. The issue of who could pray there and how was getting lots of attention and generating lots of emotion. But even though it touched on sensitive matters of religion and state, this challenge looked easier to solve than most. The questions involved practical arrangements regarding where to pray. They didn't require sweeping ideological concessions or theological shifts from either side, as the conversion question and other flash points did.

At the same time, I believed that solving the issue could have major symbolic significance. The battle over the Kotel stirred fears of Jewish division, because this wall has symbolized Jewish unity for so long in so many ways.

The Western Wall—Kotel means "wall" in Hebrew—is the only surviving structure from the Jews' magnificent Holy Temple, first built by King Solomon in the tenth century BCE. Today's Kotel, the remaining retaining wall from the Second Temple, rebuilt 2,500 years ago, represents the two faces of Jewish identity: the religious and the national.

The Kotel is Judaism's holiest place. Although Jews believe that God is everywhere, praying at that site gives a boost, a feeling of being extra close to God. Here is where the Jews parked the Mishkan, the Tabernacle, after wandering for so many years. Here is where the high priest used to enter the Holy of Holies, in a ceremony so significant we reenact it every year on Yom Kippur, our holiest day. Here was the pilgrimage place where Jews had the mitzvah, commandment, to "walk up" from all over the world three times a year, celebrated today by the holidays of Passover, Shavuot, and Sukkot.

This religious site is also the most potent national Jewish symbol. The Kotel represents King David's power, King Solomon's wisdom, the Maccabees' heroism, the exile's anguish, and the redemptive joy of our recent return to Zion, including the 1967 Six Day War miracle.

That religious-national duality makes the Kotel the world's most popular Jewish attraction. It is the most well-attended synagogue and most visited national monument. It attracts ten million worshippers a year. The Kotel unites religious and secular Jews in shared memories and dreams. A number of the Israeli army's best-trained soldiers swear their oath to defend our state there. New immigrants often get their identity papers in ceremonies at the Kotel.

Alas, the two sides of this one wall are often underappreciated. One American Jewish leader complained to me about all the uncivilized skirmishing surrounding the Kotel. "Why do you Israelis make such a fuss about that darned wall?" he asked. "In America, there's no controversy around the Lincoln Memorial."

I responded, "Well, no one tries inserting written requests to God into the cracks of the Lincoln Memorial, either."

At the same time, I heard a constant complaint from ultra-Orthodox politicians. They grumbled, "What chutzpah! No one would dare mob the Vatican demanding a Protestant prayer space there."

I often replied, "Saint Peter's Basilica is a religious Catholic space. Garibaldi didn't use it to build an Italian national identity."

At the Kotel, we feel united as a nation, or at least we should. After Jerusalem's reunification in 1967, the Israeli government quite naturally gave the Chief Rabbinate control over the Kotel. The rabbinate managed other holy sites too. The move followed the Ben-Gurion line of thinking, that the synagogue Israelis didn't attend was an Orthodox one.

It was also logical for liberal Jews to start protesting their inability to pray in their own way at this most sacred national Jewish site. Since 1988, the Women of the Wall have been protesting the Kotel's emergence as "an ultra-Orthodox synagogue." For three decades, at Rosh Hodesh, the beginning of every Jewish month, this coalition of Orthodox and liberal feminists convenes at seven in the morning at the Kotel. Some women pray wearing kippot and tallitot, skullcaps and prayer shawls, which most Orthodox Jews believe are exclusively for men's use. The women also demand the right to read from the Torah on the women's side of the Kotel plaza, which, they note, is only one-fifth the size of the men's side.

Some ultra-Orthodox have responded violently over the years. Sometimes, the police intervene to protect the women. Other times, they arrest the women for praying there, for violating *minhag hamakom*, the local custom.

At one particularly tense moment, the Kotel's rabbi, Shmuel Rabinowitz, insisted the police protect the local custom by arresting any woman who read the Hallel—the songs of praise—too loudly. The police did his bidding. When I heard about the arrests, I was furious. I called the local police commander, who quickly explained that it was up to the "Rav."

I summoned Rabbi Rabinowitz to my office. He started justifying himself by quoting Supreme Court decisions, which he believed gave him the power to authorize such arrests for disturbing the peace. "I don't care," I exclaimed. "In a few hours, American Jews will start waking up. They are going to read that Israel, the Jewish state, is the only place in the world where women are arrested for praying 'Hallel.'" He didn't care.

Then I called Bibi. He cared. The police released the women immediately.

SEARCHING FOR COMMON GROUND

As the controversy escalated over the years, it came to symbolize the Jewish world's religious schisms. It spilled over into the Knesset, the Supreme Court, one cabinet meeting after another, and the Jewish world's pews, papers, websites, and dining room tables.

Following Bibi's request, I took the issue to the board of governors. We started brainstorming, seeking common ground. It soon became clear that to get the ultra-Orthodox on board, we had to meet abroad, away from Israel's crazy political dynamics. Jerry Silverman of the Jewish Federations of North America hosted an informal cabinet of religious leaders in New York, including ultra-Orthodox leaders and the heads of the liberal denominations. We decided to start there.

I flew to the United States to convince both sides that a compromise was in their best interest. "You don't want your prayer disrupted," I told the ultra-Orthodox leaders. "And you're in the minority here. If we don't solve this, public opinion in Israel and abroad will turn against you sooner or later, or the Supreme Court will force you to share the central prayer space with others. Why don't you try calming passions now, while you still have control with the government's guarantee? Otherwise, you risk losing it all."

"Let's be honest," I told the Reform leaders, "you don't have any political power in the Knesset. Your power in the *New York Times* does not mean all that much in Jerusalem. If you can get a proper, respectable place for prayer at the Kotel, which will be yours to run in cooperation with the government, this could be a breakthrough. You will have a toehold of legitimacy in the Jewish state."

Violating the norms of Israeli politics, I openly put these arguments to both sides. It was important that we all knew from the start what was involved, without backroom deals. After three months, I told the prime minister, "I believe I can bring everyone to the table, provided we all agree in advance that any compromise would be based on two principles. First, the Chief Rabbinate will continue controlling the central prayer space. Second, the non-Orthodox will have an equally comfortable place for prayer at the Kotel, which they will run independently, with the government's assistance." Bibi accepted both conditions.

Nevertheless, finding a compromise took three and a half excruciating years. The negotiations, led by the cabinet secretary, eventually included me, Jerry Silverman, Rabbi Rabinowitz of the Kotel, and leaders of the major denominations from America and Israel, as well as the Women of the Wall. The leaders of the liberal movements in Israel and the Women of the Wall were permanent members of the negotiating team, bringing important pragmatic perspectives.

The process wasn't pretty. Voices were raised. Tables were pounded. Walkouts were threatened.

What was under discussion? With ultra-Orthodox control of the Kotel's main prayer space accepted, we were debating what kind of alternative space we could make for non-Orthodox prayer. What would it look like? Who would control it? Would there be a common entrance?

Previous Supreme Court decisions had forced the government to designate the area further south along the Western Wall, to the right when facing it, for egalitarian prayer. The entire section is called

Robinson's Arch, because in 1838 the biblical scholar Edward Robinson identified the stones jutting out of the retaining wall as part of a grand staircase Jewish pilgrims used to climb up to the Temple thousands of years ago.

The area set aside for prayer was small. Access had to be restricted to such a delicate archaeological site. Archaeologists dug down, layer after layer, until they found some huge sacred stones, knocked off the walls by soldiers, that had not been touched since the Romans destroyed the Second Temple 1,900 years earlier.

The stones of the continued wall were just as holy as the stones of the traditional Western Wall, but this area had no amenities. It lacked the basics an outdoor synagogue needed, from a place to store Torah scrolls and prayer books to bathrooms and easy access for disabled visitors. Some liberal Jews held services there occasionally, but it was not open 24-7 like the Kotel. You could only get there during limited time periods, with limited numbers of participants, by special permission secured through the larger Davidson archaeological park authorities.

This being the Middle East, any real development of the place faced great resistance. The archaeologists worried about the antiquities, while the Jordanians were still trying to convince the Arab world that they were protecting the entire Temple Mount area. When we started boosting Robinson's Arch as an alternative, the Hashemite Kingdom of Jordan issued a special statement condemning my supposed attempts to establish a new "illegal" settlement at the base of the Muslims' holy Al-Aqsa mosque.

No matter how much we upgraded the prayer space, it would never be equal in size or height to the traditional prayer space. It was sunk far too low, and the antiquities, while romantic in their own way, were not movable. The only way to showcase the equality the non-Orthodox deserved was to have one main, united entrance.

That, too, triggered a power struggle. Perhaps one gate should flow to the main plaza, with liberal Jews then searching for their marginalized space on the side? Or should there be separate entrance gates?

The question of visibility proved explosive. The liberal leaders insisted that people arriving had to encounter two equally legitimate, equally accessible choices. They didn't want the "real Kotel" overshadowing some seemingly second choice. Liberal Jews demanded visibility as a mark of respect. Refusing to "sit in the back of the bus," they maintained that they would not feel equal if it did not look equal.

At the same time, some ultra-Orthodox leaders demanded new barriers, so no religious Jews would have to witness the egalitarian prayer services. If liberal Jews entered furtively through a tunnel, that might work. As one rabbi told me, if such an "abomination" wasn't hidden from the public eye, it could "harm the Jewish soul."

Finally, intense clashes broke out over governance: Who would be in charge of the egalitarian prayer space? The ultra-Orthodox worried that the Reform Jews might start playing music on the Sabbath, ruining the day's quiet atmosphere. Liberal Jews feared being dependent on the whims of ever-changing Israeli governments.

All this debate took place in an inflamed atmosphere. Ultra-Orthodox rabbis, and even some government ministers, kept making public statements during the negotiations, insulting the "Reformim" as assimilators, heretics, hijackers of real Judaism, and threats to the Jewish future. Some questioned whether they truly were Jews. One influential rabbi even said he would rather see every stone in the wall destroyed than see one desecrated by "witnessing" Reform prayer there.

Some liberal leaders demanded the elimination of the Chief Rabbinate, accusing these rabbis of keeping Judaism in the Middle Ages. Liberals' "separate but equal" and "back of the bus" rhetoric unfairly compared their legitimate grievances in free, democratic Israel with the fear, humiliation, powerlessness, and oppression African Americans suffered at the hands of white Southern racists.

As usual, the prime minister was caught within a democratic dilemma. While Israel's silent majority probably favored an egalitarian space at the wall, the question wasn't important enough to most Israelis to risk the government's stability over. Only the ultra-Orthodox prioritized this fight. They cleverly and legitimately exerted their democratic leverage as a passionate minority of absolutely unyielding voters on this issue. They wanted their government partners worrying, aware that they would topple the coalition to protect the Kotel.

The negotiations dragged on. Elections came and went, as did the first cabinet secretary, Zvi Hauser. The new cabinet secretary, Avichai Mandelblit, made me nervous at first. Mandelblit's English was crude, in a situation that demanded finesse. He didn't seem to grasp the complexity of the debate, which resisted simplistic slogans or solutions.

Fortunately, my first impressions were wrong. Mandelblit demonstrated patience and an impressive openness to all the different arguments. He kept us moving ahead, step-by-step, with his characteristic caution and wisdom. Even his leaving worked out well. When Netanyahu appointed him to become attorney general, Mandelblit's pending departure created an artificial deadline that accelerated the negotiations.

Bibi took these negotiations very seriously. Whenever we risked hitting some dead end, we turned to Bibi, who proved remarkably creative. At one impasse over the access question, he invited the key leaders to come to Jerusalem. It was two days before Rosh Hashanah, the Jewish New Year, a terrible time for husbands or wives to be traveling anywhere, let alone halfway across the world. But everybody showed up, and Bibi's ingenuity impressed us.

We were, however, still tangled about the entrance. Bibi suggested bringing in an architect. Then, harking back to his days as an MIT architecture student, he introduced his own ideas for managing the space. Feeling fanciful, he said, "What about a bridge in the air?" Proposing a flying staircase suspended over the Robinson's Arch pit instantly created headaches for his team of mediators. They knew the ultra-Orthodox wanted the entrance sunk under the earth, meaning a tunnel, not something suspended flamboyantly high in the air.

This tedious negotiating process generated something that could have been revolutionary: newfound mutual trust between Prime Minister Netanyahu and liberal American Jewish leaders. They appreciated how much he invested in the process. He appreciated how willing they were to stretch and to pressure their communities to give the negotiations a chance. With everyone coordinating positions, periodically sending similar media messages to their constituencies to be patient, relationships flourished and common ground emerged.

It didn't come naturally. I was working hard to strengthen positive feelings on both sides. I believed something unprecedented was happening. A new dialogue was developing.

THE KOTEL COMPROMISE

Slowly but surely, we reached a four-part compromise. The agreement, which the ultra-Orthodox accepted silently, but agreed not to veto, stated:

1. The Chief Rabbinate would maintain its monopoly in the main, "official" area, running the wall as an Orthodox synagogue with no protests and no interference.

2. The liberal movements would get their Robinson's Arch upgrade, with a major renovation establishing a comfortable, legitimate but alternative prayer space for as many as 1,200 people, where men and women could pray together as they chose.

3. Although other demands to broadcast equality proved impossible to meet, a shared entrance to the site would emphasize the notion that all enter the area as equals, regardless of where they might pray.

4. A special administrative committee would guarantee the liberal movements' autonomy at Robinson's Arch, even as governments changed. The committee would include representatives of the liberal movements in an unprecedented partnership with government representatives.

On Sunday, January 31, 2016, the government voted on the proposal. It was Mandelblit's last day as cabinet secretary. He and Bibi wanted to wrap up the issue on his watch. Feeling the time pressure, Netanyahu held the meeting while I was in Los Angeles. In the spirit of compromise now afoot, he violated the usual security protocols. Bibi invited me to wake up at 3:30 a.m. and participate by Skype. Calling in like this was unprecedented; it required a laptop in the cabinet room, even though we usually weren't allowed in with cell phones. I explained to the ministers how important this issue had become to Diaspora Jewish leaders. Ultimately, Netanyahu's pressure determined the vote. Fifteen of twenty ministers voted yes.

At our next board of governors meeting, which began February 21, we celebrated our achievement. Our guest of honor, Mandelblit, had already started working in his delicate new job. As attorney general, he would eventually indict his old boss, Netanyahu, for bribery, fraud, and breach of trust.

After the celebrations, Mandelblit called some of us aside, including the Reform and Conservative leaders, Rabbi Rick Jacobs and Rabbi Julie Schonfeld. "Give me two weeks more of quiet to let this settle in," Mandelblit pleaded. "We need to lay the foundation here carefully. Please don't celebrate too loudly." Mandelblit understood that the ultra-Orthodox representatives needed time to sell their concessions to their people and try tamping down any rebellions.

We all agreed, including Rick and Julie, who then hurried to another meeting. The next day, I read jubilant headlines from the Reform movement describing the agreement as the "foundation" for a new pluralism and the start of a "quiet revolution." So much for discretion, or "quiet."

American Jewish organizations often plan back-to-back missions. Right after the Jewish Agency board meeting that February, some three hundred members of the Central Conference of American Rabbis visited Jerusalem. As a result, the morning after Mandelblit asked for a low profile, all three hundred Reform rabbis appeared at a special meeting of the Knesset's Committee for Immigration, Absorption, and Diaspora Affairs. The leaders of the movement naturally celebrated the Kotel compromise loudly and enthusiastically.

The ultra-Orthodox erupted. Newspapers publicized this "declaration of war." One member of the Knesset proclaimed, "No one has succeeded in desecrating the Western Wall for thousands of years." He would not allow this government to break the streak. Demonstrators gathered outside the houses of Haredi ministers, who were also harassed in synagogue.

The Reform movement's giddiness allowed some bureaucrats in the Prime Minister's Office to blame the Reformim when things soured. It was a pretext. It was obvious that the pressure on the prime minister would grow following the cabinet's decision, especially because he had to implement the compromise.

Netanyahu seemed ready to stand up to the pressure—until he wasn't. Throughout the next year, he kept asking for more time to implement the decision, while avoiding a coalition crisis. He promised me. He promised American Jews at their biggest, most public forums, the General Assembly of the Jewish Federations and the American Israel Public Affairs Committee (AIPAC) policy conference. He kept promising he was just about to move ahead. Then, he surprised us.

THE KOTEL FIASCO

If Prime Minister Benjamin Netanyahu wanted to focus maximum attention on the way he betrayed his own good work on the Western Wall issue, while generating the most amount of ill will with the Diaspora, then he staged the events of June 25, 2017, magnificently.

First, his timing was superb. He made sure to freeze the long-negotiated Kotel agreement just as our board of governors conference welcomed hundreds of people from around the world who were anxious to see the compromise implemented. Second, he made his announcement at the only cabinet meeting of the year that begins with a presentation by American Jews, who emphasized how important the compromise was. Third, to feed sensationalist headlines, he sprang it all as a surprise, not even preparing most of his cabinet ministers for the switch. Finally, as if violating the Kotel agreement wouldn't be inflammatory enough, he also tried resurrecting the divisive conversion bill that day.

The board of governors of the Jewish Agency meets every four months. June 25 happened to be the opening of our summer session in Jerusalem, which brought together more than two hundred leaders from all over the world whose patience with Netanyahu was draining away like sand in a dwindling hourglass.

Our opening panel featured four of the thirty members of Knesset whom the Jewish Agency had hosted in the American Jewish community on missions within the last year, many for the first time. The members shared their impressions about the Jewish Agency projects they had seen and the insights into American Jewry they had gained. During the question period, the governors harped on one issue, asking the same basic question in many different ways: When would the government finally enact the Kotel compromise? The government had done nothing with the plan for a year and a half. Bibi kept advising patience, caution, discretion.

For its second night, the board of governors had scheduled a festive dinner hosted by the Speaker of the Knesset to celebrate the fiftieth anniversary of Jerusalem's reunification. Netanyahu would be the guest of honor. We assumed he accepted the invitation to announce the long-awaited launch of the Kotel renovation to a friendly audience that was celebrating the Western Wall's return to the Jewish people in 1967.

That Sunday morning, June 25, as the board of governors convened, the Jewish People Policy Institute (JPPI) presented its annual report to the government assessing the Israel-Diaspora relationship. JPPI's cochairs, Stuart Eizenstat and Dennis Ross, had come from Washington, DC, to submit the report, which was the first agenda item of the cabinet meeting. I had to scurry across town for an hour after our session with the members of Knesset, because the head of the Jewish Agency is invited to cabinet meetings whenever any Diaspora-related issues appear on the agenda.

This leading Jerusalem-based think tank, which the Jewish Agency partially funds, presented a sobering analysis of Israel-Diaspora relations. I was briefed in advance about what its most pressing recommendation would be: implement the Kotel compromise quickly. The report warned that every day delaying the upgrade of the egalitarian prayer space alienated American Jews just a little bit more.

Cabinet protocols dictate that ministers receive an agenda and related briefing papers three days before every meeting. Surprises in politics are more often bad news than good. The Kotel question wasn't even on the cabinet's agenda that day. Still, when I arrived at the Prime Minister's Office, the journalists hanging around outside asked me about rumors that Bibi was about to cancel the Kotel deal. None of the waiting ministers I spoke to knew more than I did.

In fact, the Israel-Diaspora issue they feared that day centered on the Ministerial Commission for Legislation session scheduled immediately after the cabinet meeting. The Shas leader and interior minister, Aryeh Deri, planned to propose a bill at that meeting making Orthodox conversions the only legitimate conversions in Israel. This was the same-old "who is a Jew" bill that had stirred so many bitter fights before. Putting a new spin on it, Deri was claiming it was necessary to stop illegal migrants sneaking into Israel. He had calculated that most of his fellow ministers were ignorant about our past battles over this issue. Still, Bibi had to know better. I was surprised that, having removed this volatile topic repeatedly from the agenda over the last twenty years, he agreed to open it yet again.

Netanyahu, as usual, was running late. When he entered the cabinet room with Deri, it was obvious something was up. The cabinet debate followed the first item, the JPPI report. As Jewish Agency chairman, I was the first respondent. Echoing the report's analysis, I emphasized how dangerous the Kotel delay had become. It was frittering away the trust and goodwill we had cultivated for so long with our best Jewish friends around the world. The prime minister nodded his head in agreement.

For a moment, I allowed myself to feel reassured. After all, we had been working closely on this issue for years.

But, across the table, I saw Deri and Bibi exchange knowing glances. Any seasoned observer of this scene could understand: the deal had been made. Netanyahu would be succumbing to ultra-Orthodox blackmail.

As sensitive yet confused political weather vanes, most ministers responded to the JPPI recommendations cautiously and circuitously. The same ministers, who a year and a half earlier had voted for the compromise, started lecturing me about its flaws, without quite repudiating the agreement.

Watching the growing confusion, Netanyahu finally put his cards on the table. "For me every Jew is important; all Jews are equal," he said. "And I do believe that Israel is the home for all the Jewish people. But," he sighed, "it's essential, with all the challenges we face, that we keep our coalition together, so we can keep addressing our pressing problems, including guaranteeing our security. I still believe we reached a good agreement that should be implemented. But we have coalition partners who think differently. They demand that we cancel the agreement. I refuse to cancel it. Instead, I propose we freeze its implementation."

Freeze? After eighteen months of repeated delays, an indefinite delay marked Bibi's full retreat.

Once their leader had spoken, the ministers followed his lead. An ultra-Orthodox minister started with nasty remarks about how "all the Reformim are J Street." This was code for "liberals who betray Israel." Others were more cautious, echoing Bibi about how much they, too, valued coalition unity.

A Bibi loyalist, Minister of Tourism Yariv Levin, whom I had befriended during our struggle against the Gaza disengagement, declared, "Natan, I learned from you. You taught us that only a strong sense of Jewish and Zionist identities can save Diaspora Jews from assimilation. These people certainly are not Zionists. You more than anyone else know how small our aliyah figures from America are, let alone from American liberals. They are not even interested in Judaism. You told us how few of them send their children to Jewish schools. Assimilation is skyrocketing; they have turned intermarriage into a religion; and, when they vote, as their studies show, Israel is not their first priority. It's not their second, nor their third. And during the last eight years, when it came to the most difficult issue where we need their help, stopping Iran's nuclear program, they were not with us. Yet now we are supposed to risk our coalition for them?"

Levin was one of the better-educated observers of the Diaspora. He could back up each attack with American Jewish polls and identity studies. He did not dismiss the Reformim, as some others did, in ugly ways. Yet the research had been around for more than a year and a half. Why didn't he and the others who voted with Bibi make this argument in January 2016, when the cabinet first approved the compromise?

Deri added, "I will say this here, but won't repeat it outside. People who are not loyal to Judaism fully will never be with Israel fully either."

Barely controlling my temper, I replied, "It's true that if you look at J Street and harsher critics like Jewish Voice for Peace, almost all of them come from the non-Orthodox Left. But 85 percent of AIPAC supporters are Reform and Conservative Jews. Don't you realize that a majority of American Jews affiliate with non-Orthodox streams?"

I added, "It's fair to worry about their weakening connection and assimilation. But the best way to counteract this is by keeping them closer to Israel. This decision, as well as the attempt to bring back the conversion bill, distances them from us. So now we can't just blame them when we wonder why they assimilate; we will have to share the blame too."

I knew I wouldn't change the minds of those who voted with Bibi then and were voting with him now. But I wanted my objections on the record.

By the time I returned to the board of governors meeting at the David Citadel Hotel, everyone knew that the cabinet had voted to freeze the compromise and that the interministerial judicial committee was advancing the conversion bill. This betrayal infuriated the governors. It was not the first time an Israeli prime minister had caved to religious party pressures to save his coalition. In fact, every prime minister surrendered at some point. But shifting so dramatically after all the negotiations, after all that trust building between the prime minister and the liberal leaders, really stung.

American Jewish leaders felt duped. Year after year, they had used their credibility to quiet their communities. Even when they had started feeling stupid during the months of delays, they had kept insisting, "The prime minister is with us," requesting, as he did, "just a little more time."

Members of the board of governors received furious emails and phone calls. Some donors suspended their annual contributions to Israel. Some local Jewish leaders canceled missions to the country. One board member even proposed boycotting El Al or shunning Israel's leaders until they came to their senses. I had to dismiss such nonsense publicly.

Still, over the next few difficult weeks, I kept hearing echoes of the anguished cry I had heard from a Conservative rabbi when the Kotel compromise first ran into governmental trouble: "How can I fight against the delegitimization of Israel, when the government of Israel delegitimizes me?"

Our emissaries found themselves in a particularly delicate situation during this crisis. Forty-eight hours after the cabinet meeting, I spoke on an emergency conference call with 150 or so young Jewish Agency emissaries, who were serving all over the world. "We now face two struggles," I told them. "First, as always, you're on the front lines and the people you work with are angry. Convey to Israel what you hear. You should represent American Jews and express their feelings of disappointment."

But I also reminded them of their main mission: "Speak strongly against those calling for boycotts of Israel or weakening their support of Israel in any way. Remind them of the core of our identity-building message. Supporting Israel is not some favor American Jews do for their poor cousins, but rather one way of continuing to be a part of the Jewish family. We're a family that cannot divorce. You just cannot boycott yourself."

Our first response was obvious. We voted, unanimously, to cancel the dinner with the prime minister and decided to spend much of our time lobbying in the Knesset against both of Bibi's moves. The head of one of the biggest Jewish Federations proclaimed, "If anyone from home saw me applauding Bibi at this dinner, I would be fired from my job immediately."

In another unprecedented move, the Jewish Agency took out big advertisements in the English and Hebrew newspapers condemning the Israeli government and demanding immediate implementation of the Kotel plan.

Bibi called me amid all this hullabaloo. He, too, was furious. "Why are you being so negative?" he asked me. "I only froze the agreement; I didn't cancel it. And we can go ahead on the most important parts. We can turn the Robinson's Arch area into the prayer space you feel you need. That's what I promised," he insisted. "I never promised to start recognizing the different religious streams."

"Well, cancel or freeze," I said, interrupting him. "That's just playing with words. Who will believe your promises, now that you've canceled your own government's decision? And there is nothing in the decision about recognition. It only says that representatives of those who pray in the egalitarian area will participate in running it. You not only agreed to it, but your agreement was a precondition to the start of these negotiations four years ago. All these years, it was the foundation of the compromise, and you never opposed it. How can you now say you never agreed to it?"

Bibi seemed confused by my remarks. I heard him consult with someone nearby. Then the line went dead.

A few minutes later, he called back even angrier. "You dare say, with your American friends, that we are anti-Zionist—while they, living in the United States, are somehow Zionist? Take those words back immediately."

I guessed that some staffer had crudely summarized our full-page advertisements. Pulling one newspaper from my desk, I asked, "Do you mean this?" and read the text of the ad. It stated that these decisions by the Israeli government had "a deep potential to divide the Jewish people and to undermine the Zionist vision and dream of Herzl, Ben-Gurion, and Jabotinsky to establish Israel as a national home for the entire Jewish people."

"I absolutely stand behind those words," I said, then ended the conversation abruptly.

THE CONVERSION ISSUE REIGNITED

While Bibi's backtracking on the Kotel compromise destroyed five years of work, his government's move that same day on the conversion issue reignited the now seventy-year-old "who is a Jew" battle. For months, we had watched the conversion question escalate dangerously. Twenty years ago, we in the Ne'eman Committee recommended guidelines to make the conversion of immigrants who became citizens of Israel under the Law of Return "welcoming and friendly." Instead, now, the Chief Rabbinate was getting more rigid, demanding that these mostly Russian-speaking newcomers live a strictly Orthodox way of life, both during the conversion process and subsequently.

In response, a group of Orthodox rabbis involved with the inclusive Tzohar movement created their own conversion court, which they cleverly called Giyur k'Halacha, conversion by Jewish law. I hosted their founding meetings in my offices in Ben-Gurion Hall. I was consciously using the Jewish Agency's double status here. This quasi-governmental institution could give them some legitimacy and resources, while as a representative of the Jewish people it could remain independent of the Israeli government's dependence on ultra-Orthodox power politics.

Although all the members of this court were Orthodox rabbis, the government was too afraid of the ultra-Orthodox parties to recognize the court's legitimacy. Further escalating, the Chief Rabbinate started questioning conversion decisions made by Orthodox rabbis abroad, when new immigrants from the United States and elsewhere sought their citizenship under the Law of Return.

Even some of the most prominent modern-Orthodox rabbis, including Rabbi Haskel Lookstein and Rabbi Avi Weiss, found themselves blacklisted; the Chief Rabbinate wouldn't accept their conversions. Israeli authorities were negating some of the Diaspora's most effective Zionist educators, who had prepared generations of young Jews for Zionist activism, including aliyah.

At a rally I attended in July 2016 outside the Chief Rabbinical Court in Jerusalem, I felt like pinching myself. I now had to protest in the Jewish state for rabbis, like Lookstein and Weiss, who had led protests to get me into the Jewish state. While I could appreciate the historical irony, there was something grotesque about it. I did note with satisfaction that many of their former students now living in Israel joined this rally and others.

I looked for an opportunity to raise the issue with the government. When the minister of Diaspora affairs, Naftali Bennett, issued his annual report about new Israeli government initiatives to reach out to the Diaspora, I was invited to represent the Jewish Agency at the discussion. Complimenting the ministry for its many bridge-building efforts, I warned that what one hand of this government was building, the other hand was knocking down.

I noted that the cover of the minister's report featured a photo from the wedding of Ivanka Trump and Jared Kushner. The rabbi who had converted Ivanka and officiated at her wedding was Haskel Lookstein. The rabbi who read the ketubah, the marriage contract, was Avi Weiss.

"The conversions of both rabbis were rejected by the Chief Rabbinate," I said. How well did we think our efforts with American Jewry would work when we were delegitimizing the very people we designated as their symbols?

It was clear that this absurd situation was untenable. We assumed that most ministers recognized that and were ready to correct it. But the leaders of the ultra-Orthodox parties read the political situation better than we did. When they sensed Bibi's weakness on the Kotel issue, they went for a twofer. Minister of the Interior Aryeh Deri decided to bully Bibi into giving the Chief Rabbinate its long-sought Knesset-approved monopoly, shutting down the "who is a Jew" conversation once and for all. Using a ridiculous fig leaf, claiming to fear "illegal immigrants" pretending to be Jewish, Deri served up the old law with the same language in a new package.

On the last day of the board of governors meeting, we took advantage of our presence in Jerusalem and lobbied the Knesset. Here, we benefited from the relationships with legislators we had nurtured since I became chairman by showing them our programs in Israel, America, and everywhere else. We proved to leading non-ultra-Orthodox coalition partners that the conversion bill had nothing to do with stopping migrant workers. Instead, it was a ploy to delegitimize non-Orthodox denominations.

When we met Naftali Bennett and Ayelet Shaked, I told them that, as an Israeli, I was embarrassed that he, as Diaspora affairs minister, and she, as justice minister, had supported this old conversion bill with a new spin without understanding it. They told me I was wrong, insisting, "There's probably some misunderstanding here." They had swallowed Deri's absurd argument that this law was meant only to stop "illegal migrants."

To their credit, they looked into it. A few hours later, after confronting Deri, Bennett called me back. He said, "You were right. This bill won't solve our border problems and will cause all kinds of Diaspora problems. We won't support it." As more coalition partners refused to advance the bill, Deri threatened to bring down the coalition, but didn't.

Two days after my angry exchanges with the prime minister, Bibi called again. As was always the case with him, after he had concentrated on the urgent problem of the moment, he pressed a kind of mental reset button. Our recent confrontation was pushed aside so he could push ahead.

"Look," he said calmly, "I'll do what I can with Robinson's Arch. We can start renovations quickly. And I want to freeze the conversion bill.

But the Reform and Conservative leaders want to change the religious status quo through the Supreme Court. No government can accept that. So I am willing to block the bill in the Knesset as long as they suspend their legal fight."

"And what will be in the meantime?" I asked. "Must they always depend on your goodwill?"

"No. There will be a time limit to this cease-fire," he replied. "I will form a committee with all the sides participating and give it six months to prepare recommendations that will be acceptable to everyone."

My Ne'eman Committee experience taught me that if the "who is a Jew" question is fought in the Knesset or the Supreme Court, we all lose. Only a broad agreement in Ya'akov Ne'eman's spirit could solve the problem. But now, as I had warned Bibi, without any trust left, it was hard to know how the liberal leaders would react. Still, I promised to take his proposal to them.

JEWISH DISTRUST
CATCHES UP TO ME IN MOSCOW

I spent the next two days in conference calls with Prime Minister Netanyahu, Interior Minister Deri, and Attorney General Mandelblit on the one hand, and leaders of the non-Orthodox movements on the other. Finally, on Friday, shortly before the prime minister left for Europe for a diplomatic trip, he declared at Ben-Gurion Airport that an agreement had been reached. The next night, after Shabbat, I flew for a long-planned visit to Jewish Agency–sponsored summer camps in Moscow. A camera crew from Arutz 9, Israel's Russian-language TV channel, accompanied me. They wanted to interview me in various sites around the city for a documentary recounting the struggle for Soviet Jewry.

They brought me to the courthouse where, in 1978, Soviet judges had sentenced me to what ended up being nine years in the Gulag. I hadn't been in the courthouse since. I did not even know where it was located. My captors had driven me there and back, day after day, in a windowless prison van.

Now, the courthouse was being renovated, stripped to its two-by-fours. The construction workers greeted us suspiciously. They warmed up after Googling me and understanding I was not connected to the Russian government. They directed me to the largest room, on the second floor.

Slowly, unsteadily, I recognized my surroundings. I became emotional as I remembered exactly where I had stood. I remembered the table where the judges sat, where my guards stood, where the hostile audience watched. I remembered where my brother, Leonid, sat, memorizing every word I said because the KGB forbade him from taking notes. I remembered speaking very slowly, knowing he would be my only channel for broadcasting my message through Western journalists, who were barred from the courtroom but waiting outside.

I recalled how big the room felt as I turned it into my platform to address the world. When the judge asked me what my final words would be before sentencing, my answer was: "To my wife and the Jewish people, I say *l'shana haba'ah beYerushalayim*, next year in Jerusalem. To the court whose only function it is to read a prepared sentence, I have nothing to say."

Why did I use those words? I figured that, in the long years of isolation to come, the most important thing for me would be to remain fully confident that the Jewish people would continue our struggle. What could be a better guarantee of that than to go back to our ancient oath to Jerusalem?

At that moment, I had full trust in my people. As I was beginning my long journey in the Gulag, I knew I would remain in dialogue with these invisible partners. I would never be alone during our long struggle for freedom.

As I was lost in my memories, my cell phone rang. It was the Prime Minister's Office. Benjamin Netanyahu's assistants were asking me to intervene, because Reform and ultra-Orthodox negotiators were still squabbling over the timing and texts of the letters to be exchanged detailing the commitments of each side in the cease-fire. The liberal leaders no longer trusted the prime minister of the state of Israel, or his aides, enough to promise to suspend court proceedings without getting his written assurance beforehand. All confidence was lost.

Over the next hour, as I kept trying to describe my feelings in 1978 to the Israeli TV crew, the cell phone interrupted me three more times. I was toggling back and forth, commuting instantaneously between my memory of that exciting moment of global teamwork uniting millions of strangers, and the present plague of suspicion and fury among leaders who knew each other intimately and had worked closely on this issue for so many years.

With each piercing ring—shaken from this atmosphere of unity then and pulled into our disunity now—my anger at the prime minister grew. Most of the week, I had been on autopilot, reacting, speaking, strategizing, organizing, and protesting. Here, far away from the frenzy—but not far enough—and time traveling back to the 1970s, it suddenly hit me. I could feel the proportions of our loss, all the wasted good work and goodwill.

Only recently, we had all been sitting at one table. The prime minister could speak directly to the leader of America's Reform movement by phone, and together they could coordinate their media strategies. Now, they didn't even have faith in a written promise from one another.

BIBI AS STATESMAN AND POLITICIAN

Clearly, Prime Minister Netanyahu was to blame. He appreciated the Kotel compromise's importance and its historic nature. Yet, with one decision on one Sunday morning, he had abandoned his own initiative, making a mockery of our efforts and his, including his eloquent statements and solemn commitments to so many. I felt betrayed.

Reporters kept calling me that summer, hoping, finally, to turn me against Netanyahu. But I held to the same line I had for years. I didn't pull any punches when criticizing him on whatever issue might divide us—in this case the Kotel. But as disappointed as I was in him, I disappointed them too. I refused to attack him personally or be pulled into what often seemed to be many reporters' personal vendettas.

On one level, my relationship with Benjamin Netanyahu is simple. He and I have been friends for over thirty years. His relationship with Avital goes back further, to when he served as a devoted strategist during our struggle. Politically, I admire all he has done to free up the Israeli economy. Geopolitically, I respect his wariness about going to war combined with his ability to withstand international pressure for yet another self-destructive unilateral withdrawal.

Yet, with all that, Bibi and I have had intense ups and downs, with moments of great anger and disappointment from both sides. Sometimes, I didn't give him the political support he expected. Sometimes, as in June 2017, he turned on me.

Ultimately, we run on different engines with different fuels: he's a true politician and I'm a dissident at heart. I have no need to detail all my frustrations with this giant, if flawed, historical figure, or to settle any scores here. That is not for this book. But it is fair to speculate about what makes Bibi tick to understand why he abandoned the compromise over the Kotel. The fiasco was yet another example of Bibi being Bibi, allowing the ruthless politician he felt he had to be to upstage the scholar states-man he was raised to be.

As the son of the famous historian who edited the *Encyclopaedia Hebraica*, Benzion Netanyahu, Bibi has a unique understanding of Israel's historic role, its "place among the nations"—the title of his best-selling book. He sees Zionism as the Jewish people's great game changer, having created Israel, the guarantor of our survival. He wants Israel to be a center for entrepreneurship and technology, a stable democratic foothold in the Middle East, and the free world's grand strategic asset in the fight against terror and Islamist mayhem. He was far ahead of most people in recognizing the Iranian threat and far more effective at mobilizing the world's economic power to slow the mullahs' rush to go nuclear.

Moreover, he backs up his good gut instincts with thoughtful analysis and piles of books. Wherever I saw him relaxing at home, flying abroad, or working in the office, I could usually spy some half-read weighty tract about politics, economics, history, or biography that he was racing through. After working sessions on the prime minister's airplane, every-one else goes to rest, relax, or, these days, text. Bibi reads.

Once, I came to talk to him, distracted by some ultimately forgettable controversy that everyone was yelling about so intensely that I couldn't concentrate. Despite being in the center of this storm, he looked up calmly from the scholarly book he was reading, almost hypnotically put-ting me at ease. Instead of reacting to the shouts, he started discussing some deeper question regarding President Bill Clinton and the negotia-tions at the time.

Watching Netanyahu conduct lengthy strategy sessions is like watch-ing an air traffic controller land and launch airplanes simultaneously, for hours on end. His concentration never breaks, he sticks to the conversa-tion, and he keeps everyone on point, even as others fade. Ehud Barak rarely had the patience for these marathon meetings; he made up his mind before the briefings began. Ariel Sharon occasionally dozed off as the experts rattled on. Not Bibi.

On the afternoon of February 4, 1997, we were involved in a long, in-tense security cabinet debate about a pressing military matter. Suddenly, an aide handed Bibi a note. He read it, struck his forehead with his palm, and exclaimed, "Oh." Watching our usually unflappable leader turn ashen, with a pained look on his face, then turn to resume the meeting, I feared some family disaster had occurred. I wondered if his eighty-seven-year-old father or eighty-five-year-old mother had died.

In fact, Zila Netanyahu lived until 2000, and Benzion Netanyahu lived until 2012, dying at the age of 102. The note informed Bibi that two Israeli Air Force transport helicopters had crashed in midair, killing all seventy-three soldiers. It was the worst air disaster in Israeli history. As I drove home that day, I marveled at how Bibi had calculated instantly that if he announced the news, we never would finish our discussion, because the next few days would be consumed by national mourning. He kept to his strategy, deftly accelerated the discussion, secured the decision we needed to make, then briefed us about this tragedy.

Twenty-three years later, I watched Bibi exhibit similar discipline, developing a thoughtful strategy while explaining it effectively to the public, as the coronavirus menaced the world. In the spring of 2020, facing trial, negotiating round-the-clock, seeking a national unity government, Netanyahu compartmentalized superbly.

While undoubtedly doing whatever he could to remain prime minister, Netanyahu kept functioning successfully as prime minister in a pinch. He toggled back and forth between parliamentary politics and coronavirus statesmanship seamlessly. His approach placed Israel way ahead of nearly every country when it came to closing the borders, shutting down the economy, imposing social isolation, and trying desperately to "flatten the curve" of this terrifying disease's spread. And he proved to be his government's best spokesperson, explaining to the public night after night why every individual needed to take the threat of this plague very seriously.

Even many critics who had called for his resignation, winced at his blatant self-promotion, and detested his parliamentary tricks acknowledged his effectiveness in shaping Israel's response to this deadly disease and explaining it. Throughout the world, many experts saluted his ability to summarize their briefings, comparing him favorably to most other leaders.

Of course, like any politician, he tried to make himself look good too. But I kept defying his critics to identify any strategic steps in fighting the disease that were unwise because they were politically motivated.

Netanyahu fights to win in politics as aggressively as he fights to keep Israel safe. In fact, he equates the two. He believes his staying in office keeps Israel alive, an equation that only grows more significant the longer he stays in power. He is a politician who will do everything to guarantee his party's victory and his coalition's stability.

Netanyahu's calculus as a politician essentially became, "My country needs me. To save my country, I need my coalition. And to save my coalition, I can permit myself to do things today I can correct tomorrow."

I kept watching him cross red lines while campaigning, understanding that he was doing what he believed he needed to do. I had felt squeamish when our clever "nash kontrol" campaign in 1999 fed the us-versus-them divisiveness between Russians and Mizrahim. But that was nothing compared to Bibi's harsh rhetoric on Election Day 2015, when he riled right-wing voters by speaking, demagogically, about the Arabs "voting in droves."

Sad but true: this appalling act worked—so he kept repeating it. It was a winning political weapon. That's why he is an effective politician. Bibi knows polls better than the pollsters and politics better than the political consultants. When he was on the political warpath, he would do practically anything, including, if pressed, insulting Arabs or trying to rehabilitate Kahanist bigots to attract more votes for his coalition allies, as he did in the April 2019 elections.

As the political stalemate dragged Israel into three parliamentary elections from April 2019 through March 2020, Bibi's polarizing strategy kept mobilizing his base. In the March election, he surprised the doubters by winning five more seats than in September, returning Likud to its longtime status as Israel's largest party. It was a stunning comeback, considering that Netanyahu had been indicted and declared politically dead by so many commentators.

Bibi pulled this off, however, not only by running on his impressive economic and diplomatic achievements but by demonizing his opponents. He called every rival a leftist, spitting out the label as if it were a dirty word reserved only for collaborators.

While boosting him, his polarizing tactics boosted the opposition too. The fury against him united forces from extreme left to centrist right. And his anti-Arab rhetoric spurred the usually squabbling Arab parties to get out their vote, big-time. By March, the Israeli Arab party Joint List had an astonishing fifteen seats, becoming Israel's third-largest party.

Yet, in the end, who eked out a "national emergency government," with himself starting off in charge? Benjamin Netanyahu.

Clearly, Israeli society was as polarized as much of the Western world. And Israeli politicians across the spectrum have long shown themselves to be grand masters in demonizing one another. As we have seen, from the moment he won his first election in 1996, Netanyahu was the Israeli media's favorite target. Still, as Israel's leader for a decade, he had a choice. He could have resisted such partisan bullying or exploited it. It's a mark against his historical record that he worsened our divisions rather than trying to heal them.

In fairness, Netanyahu focused on results, not process—viewing politicking as a form of theater and governance as real. He counted numbers—per capita revenues, unemployment statistics, budgetary outlays—and often discounted questions of tone, spirit, and atmosphere. As far back as his 1996 win, Bibi believed in a cleansing day after. You win the contest, then lead; you trash-talk when campaigning, then deliver the goods when governing.

In 2015, April 2019, September 2019, and March 2020, he continued his long-standing policies of working with those he bashed politically, including the Arabs and the "evil" leftists he demonized—the day after. He also continued investing money generously in the Arab sector and pushing affirmative action in education and employment. He did what he believed Israel needed to do now that Israel again had the leader it needed.

That's how he and most successful politicians I have watched justify their harshness. They may sin along the way, but they get the job done of defending the Jewish people and the state of Israel. So they give themselves permission to politick aggressively, regardless of the damage they might cause. And, the day after Election Day, they start cleaning up their own mess.

With Bibi, I saw this ability to flip so quickly, not just with sectors but with people, from fury to full cooperation, from one meeting to the next. His reset button is constantly on. The man who broke David Ben-Gurion's record of 4,872 days as prime minister has spent over nine years of his life managing more crises in a day than most people face in a lifetime. He oversees Israel's foreign relations and domestic relations. He has to grow the economy, steady a boisterous society, and field every problem or idea any minister might raise at a given moment. He deals with staffers, rivals, party members, the public, and the media while occasionally taking a breath. He must be on all the time, facing the weightiest of decisions, the toughest of choices. Even his private life became increasingly public, politicized, and scrutinized. It's an awful job. I cannot understand how he has done it for so many years. Or why he keeps wanting to extend it.

Amid such constant bombardment, you need to zero in on the pressing need of the moment and handle it the best way you can. Inevitably, that risks crowding out what you did, what you said, who angered you, or who pleased you two, three, or four weeks ago, let alone months or years ago. So turning on a dime, from friend to foe or foe to friend, does not mean Netanyahu is fickle. It just shows how he focuses on the crisis of the moment.

Bibi is not in the world of moral lectures or delicate sensibilities, but of crude politics for a noble purpose. If you believe you can do better for everyone, you will do almost anything to anyone because it's for their sake, for the common good. That is why, when he decided it was time to backtrack on the Kotel, he retreated without regrets, writing off his own considerable investment in the deal as collateral damage.

So why did he cave in to blackmail? The ultra-Orthodox demands had not changed for decades. When Netanyahu had fought so stubbornly to pass the government agreement, he knew what he was in for. His readiness to resist the inevitable ultra-Orthodox pressure was built in to his actions, unless his patience ran out.

Cynics have an easy explanation for his turnabout: "What's the difference between January 2016 and June 2017?" they ask. In January 2016, they've decided, Barack Obama was president and Bibi needed to woo the liberal Jews who supported Obama. By June 2017, President Donald Trump was clearly in Israel's corner, liberal Jews were losing power, and Netanyahu was free to roam.

The cynics are wrong. Not everything he does is calculating. In this case, Bibi is a true Zionist. Keeping our Jewish family together around Israel has always been an important component of his worldview. He is still the same leader who gave the political green light to Taglit-Birthright before most others in the government did and who pushed for the Ne'eman Committee's "who is a Jew" compromise.

He's also a realist. Netanyahu never indulged in some naive hope that he could influence Obama by charming liberal Jews. He could see the glint in most American Jews' eyes from the time Obama won the

Democratic nomination in 2008. By June 2009, when, as a new president, Obama visited Turkey, Saudi Arabia, and Egypt—with no plans to visit Israel—Netanyahu knew relations would be rocky. Throughout much of the Kotel negotiations, Netanyahu worked with leaders of the liberal denominations despite his growing resentment over their lack of support during his confrontations with Obama. Putting his frustrations aside, he focused on "one Wall for one people."

Other cynics claim the mounting scandals made Netanyahu ever more dependent on his ultra-Orthodox coalition partners. But in the summer of 2017, I saw no signs that the corruption scandals were distracting him. Bibi has been under such scrutiny for years. It was only in early 2018, when two former advisers turned state's witness that the police pressure started to affect Bibi's politics.

All the political calculations had been there all along; the two sides of Bibi had always been in a tug-of-war. So what happened? Why did Netanyahu—who had resisted Haredi leaders' blackmail over the Kotel since 2013, who in January 2016 forced the ultra-Orthodox leaders to accept the Kotel compromise—jump ship?

It was especially confusing because many of us believed Aryeh Deri and his allies were bluffing in June 2017; they didn't seem ready to resign. In the coming months, I kept returning to that mystery, wondering what had changed in the year and a half between pushing the compromise through the cabinet and giving it up.

19

IRAN AND OUR FEELING OF MUTUAL BETRAYAL

Gradually, I realized that even as some liberal American Jews started trusting Netanyahu's desire to build one Wall for one people, he started losing faith in American Jewish liberals' fundamental loyalty to their people. His tolerance for political risk on the Kotel deal shrank as his frustration with liberal American Jewry grew. It was all about Iran. Just as many liberal Jews felt betrayed by Bibi regarding the Western Wall, he felt they betrayed Israel in blindly supporting Barack Obama's Iran treaty, the Joint Comprehensive Plan of Action (JCPOA).

Shortly after Obama concluded the deal in July 2015, the United States transferred $25 billion to $50 billion in long-frozen funds back to Iran. That included $1.7 billion in pallets of untraceable, non-US currency flown to Tehran. Some of that money flowed quickly to Hezbollah in southern Lebanon. "As long as Iran has money, Hezbollah has money," the group's leader Hassan Nasrallah rejoiced in October 2016. Watching that guerilla group committed to Israel's destruction become a standing army, Bibi told me in frustration, "You understand, liberal American Jews really don't like Israel."

"Of course they do," I replied indignantly. "They're all building their Jewish identities around Israel."

"Nah," he scoffed. "They love an Israel that exists in their imaginations. But the real Israel, which can exist only if we defend ourselves, makes them uncomfortable, because it makes them unpopular with their president. We, however, have no choice. We have to live in the real world, not in the world of their imaginations."

I once had a pain in my leg that the doctor explained was a sign of back trouble. Such radiating pain in different parts of the human body reflects the fact that each individual is one organic system, connected by all kinds of nerves. Similarly, we can see in the Jewish body politic that discomfort or conflict in one area, say, over Iran, sometimes causes pain elsewhere, say, over the Kotel. These hot issues, which led to repeated cries from Israel and abroad about "betrayal" and worse, reflect both the centrifugal and centripetal forces shaping us as a people today. True, the Iran and Kotel fights spun many of us away from one another in fury. But the anger, and the way the issues sometimes blurred or even fed one another, proved just how deeply interconnected we remain with one another and as a people, which is why it is illuminating to explore these controversies.

THE IRAN DEAL HARMS ISRAEL'S SECURITY

The Islamic Republic of Iran's fundamentalist determination to have a "world without Zionism," combined with the mullahs' desperate efforts to develop nuclear power and ballistic missiles, rattled most Israelis. There was a striking consensus among Israel's political, military, and intelligence experts that Iran posed the greatest threat to Israel's existence. From the terrorism against the Jewish community in Argentina to the expanding chaos in the Middle East, most Israelis recognized that the issue went far beyond weaponry. Iran aspired to become a regional superpower and global puppeteer of terror, dedicated to fighting "big Satan," America, while trying to destroy "little Satan," Israel.

Benjamin Netanyahu has been an international pacesetter in fighting Iran. It was clear to me that he considered himself to be on a sacred mission. When Bibi was foreign minister under Ariel Sharon from 2002 to 2003, he tried convincing the West to restrict shipments and technology transfers to Tehran. As treasury minister from 2003 to 2005, he implored the West to restrain Iran with economic sanctions. He orchestrated the big-tent international campaign against the Iranian nuclear and ballistic missile program almost single-handedly.

Bibi's financial attaché, Ron Dermer, launched the campaign in Congress. He mobilized many of Bibi's old congressional contacts to sound the alarm in the United States, then the world. Ron was a young Floridian who in 1995 volunteered to work as a pollster for our new immigrants' party campaign. We became friends. After we won, he made aliyah and eventually became my writing partner.

My only mistake was introducing Ron to Bibi, so Ron could explain the Russian immigrants' impressions of him during the campaign. Bibi left saying, "Whoa, that guy really doesn't like me."

I replied, "He's telling you what the Russian immigrants think. He's a pollster; that's his job." In a second meeting, the chemistry between the two was obvious. Eventually, I lost Ron as a partner to Bibi, although we remain close friends.

When he returned to the prime minister's chair in 2009, Netanyahu had one top foreign policy mission: stopping Iran. There was sharp debate about Iran within Israel, but it centered on how to solve the problem—almost every Israeli agreed Iran was dangerous. Some pushed a military solution, destroying Iran's nuclear development sites from the air. Some trusted the intelligence approach, intervening covertly to sabotage Iranian nuclear development from within. Bibi choreographed the economic strategy, strangling the regime financially while keeping all other options open.

Unfortunately, Bibi's approach to Iran clashed with Obama's. Netanyahu believed the regime was too rotten to be redeemed; Obama believed it might be ready to reform. Even when campaigning for the presidency in 2008, a time when most candidates like to appear extra tough, Obama preferred engaging with the mullahs to pressuring them. More broadly, Bibi—like most Israelis—worried about containing Iran's expansionist foreign policy, because it caused so much regional instability. Obama focused solely on limiting Iran's nuclear capability.

Beyond the strategic concerns, Obama kept disappointing those of us around the world who expect the American president to champion human rights. When Iran's grassroots Green Revolution erupted in June 2009, the protesters looked to America's hip, charismatic, progressive, African American president for help. He let them, and us, down. Obama's betrayal of those dissidents confirmed Bibi's fears about his blind spot regarding Iran's regime.

Before and after the United States signed the treaty with Iran, I joined the concerned chorus warning Americans to be wary. Many of us who survived the Soviet regime kept urging Americans to remember how their country had defeated Communism. In 2013, when pundits and politicians welcomed Hassan Rouhani, Mahmoud Ahmadinejad's supposedly moderate replacement as president of Iran, I wrote an article in the *Wall Street Journal* recalling the Western euphoria over Mikhail Gorbachev. Then, as now, the conventional wisdom proclaimed, "If he seems unprepared to meet our demands today, we must meet him more than halfway so he can meet them tomorrow." But, I pointed out, "tens of millions" of Soviet citizens, including Andrei Sakharov, understood that "only continued Western pressure could, over time, 'help' the Soviet leader and the Soviet system reform themselves out of business." Then, as now, we were called warmongers for advocating strategic pressure. Back then, but not now, "the U.S., to its eternal credit, held firm."

In 2015, the fight heated up as Obama refused to link the negotiations with Iran to its Middle East machinations and abuses. Iran therefore continued spreading terror throughout the region. Iran armed troublemakers like Hamas and Hezbollah, and the negotiations proceeded. Iran threatened countries with genocide, and the negotiations proceeded. Iran called for the destruction of America itself, and the negotiations proceeded.

"Imagine what would have happened," I wrote in the *Washington Post* in April 2015, if, "after completing a round of negotiations over disarmament, the Soviet Union had declared that its right to expand Communism across the continent was not up for discussion. This would have spelled the end of the talks. Yet today, Iran feels no need to tone down its rhetoric calling for the death of America and wiping Israel off the map."

In another *Washington Post* article, on July 24, 2015, I reminded Jews that they "stood up to the U.S. government 40 years ago, and should again on Iran." It was shocking to see that the courageous Jews who had demanded that Richard Nixon and Henry Kissinger make détente contingent on human rights were silent now. We Israelis were reluctant to criticize our American ally. It was awkward to denounce an agreement everyone insisted would bring peace.

The United States had to choose. It could either appease a criminal regime—one that supported global terror, vowed to eliminate Israel, and executed more political prisoners each year than any other country per capita—or it could stand firm in demanding that Iran change its behavior.

I wondered what changed. Being mischievous, I asked in another article, "When did America forget that it's America?" I feared that in today's postmodern world, when asserting the superiority of liberal democracy over other regimes seemed like the quaint relic of a colonialist past, even the United States appeared to have lost the courage of its convictions. Joining the president and their peers, most liberal American Jews easily dismissed Israel's warning about a negotiating approach that never addressed the broad scope of the Iranian threat.

The tensions between Netanyahu and the liberal American Jewish community peaked in early 2015, when he accepted an invitation from the Republican-controlled House of Representatives to address the Congress that March. With most American Jews in favor of Obama and the Iran deal, they were furious that Netanyahu was insulting the Democratic president by coming to Washington without his invitation. "How dare Israel force me to choose between my loyalty to its prime minister and my loyalty to my president?" one activist seethed.

Bibi believed he was sticking to his historic mission to defend Israel from destruction. Certain that Obama's deal would threaten Israel's future, Netanyahu sought out prominent platforms to broadcast his message. All the formalities—who invited whom, when and where—struck him as silly compared to this existential threat.

Looking back, many of his supporters view that speech as Benjamin Netanyahu's finest hour. He did what he does best: define an effective strategy and articulate it effectively to the world. Today, Netanyahu feels even more justified, sure that Iran's subsequent aggressiveness vindicated him. And he undoubtedly takes satisfaction in knowing that it was his persistence that kept the Iran issue on the international agenda, and on Donald Trump's agenda. Yet, many American Jewish communal leaders are still seething about that speech and resent Bibi's persistence. Clearly, even beyond the Iran deal, the speech itself became a core issue that radiated pain.

In the summer of 2015, when most liberal American Jews ignored the Israeli consensus and supported the Iran agreement, Bibi still hoped the realities of this bad deal would ultimately convince them. To the Israeli government and most of the Israeli opposition, the agreement was reckless. It gambled with Israel's security and the West's. As billions of oil dollars flowed back to Iran, hundreds of millions of terror dollars flowed straight to Hezbollah, thanks to the United States. Spending Iran's money liberally, Hezbollah morphed from a ragtag series of terror cells into a well-financed, formidable army, planning terror strikes abroad too. Even as the IDF hurriedly improvised doctrines to defend against this new threat, liberal Jews were grumbling about the Israeli government's continued attempts to polarize the political situation and cross their beloved president.

As furious as I was with Bibi over his Kotel switch, I could understand how irritating all these American Jewish attacks were to him. In the fall of 2016, while visiting Jewish Agency absorption centers in the north, I received a local military briefing. I could not believe how much our security situation had deteriorated in the year since the treaty was signed. Hezbollah's capacity to attack civilians, kidnap soldiers, and barrage Israel with missiles had soared. Even worse, the northern commanders shared a new worry: a possible Hezbollah invasion could cut off the city of Metullah from the rest of the country and hold thousands of civilians hostage. Yet, as I absorbed this sobering news, our American partners in the Jewish Agency requested a brainstorming session during the next board of governors meeting about how to stop the Israeli government from alienating American Jewry by campaigning aggressively against the Iran deal.

The nature of the complaints drained Bibi's patience. He felt that, even when Israel faced the dangerous consequences of the deal with Iran, liberal American Jews ignored these facts because they preferred Obama's vision of reality. These frustrations with the majority of American Jews undoubtedly made Netanyahu less willing to risk his coalition—making him more vulnerable to persistent ultra-Orthodox pressure to abandon the Kotel deal in June 2017.

Of course, Bibi never admitted this connection publicly. But both his ambassadors to the United States, Michael Oren and Ron Dermer, share my belief that there is a direct connection between the position of liberal Jews on the Iranian deal and Bibi's Kotel retreat.

BARACK OBAMA AS THE AMERICAN JEWISH DREAM; IRAN AS THE ISRAELI NIGHTMARE

The debate over the Iran deal posed a classic clash between the two largest Jewish communities' priorities, their competing Jewish survival strategies. For all the divisions in the country, most Israelis agreed with Netanyahu that their three top strategic worries were a nuclear Iran, a nuclear Iran, and a nuclear Iran. And most Israelis also agreed that Obama's Iran deal would only toughen the country against Israel.

At the same time, for most American Jews, supporting President Obama did not just express the fact that two-thirds or more voted Democratic. Barack Obama beautifully incarnated their American dream, that this democracy protected minorities and gave everyone the chance to succeed. It was my dream too.

Obama was the first black president. I remember that thrilling election night in 2008. I, too, was proud that America had finally chosen an African American with what Obama himself used to joke was a "funny name." Truthfully, I felt badly for my kindred spirit, the Republican nominee Senator John McCain, who had suffered for five and a half years in North Vietnamese prisons—he had refused to accept an early release unless every American captured before him was released too. We met when John was still a congressman on my first trip to Washington in 1986. We clicked immediately—like two ex-cons in a convention of preachers—when he looked at me and said, "I understand why you refused to be released on the USSR's terms two years ago."

From the start of the presidential primary campaign, even a tough customer and fierce advocate of Israel like Marty Peretz of the *New Republic* supported Obama, partially because his life story fulfilled the American Jewish dream. Peretz wrote that Obama's election would "give fullness to the paradigm and promise of an open society." Others, to Peretz's left, praised Obama as "the first Jewish president," with Peter Beinart going so far as to write that "Obama reminds Netanyahu of what Netanyahu doesn't like about Jews." Beinart meant liberal American Jews like him. Matt Nosanchuk, Obama's White House Jewish liaison for three years, would say the president has a "Jewish soul" and is "very much in sync with the majority of [the] American-Jewish community—he's committed to social justice and prioritizes issues like civil rights and equality, and he values intellectual discourse."

I witnessed that deep connection between so many American Jews and their liberal president in 2011 when I addressed the Union for Reform Judaism biennial in Washington. That Obama spoke to them only magnified their enthusiasm for the president. Any time his name was mentioned, it felt like waves of electrical impulses were rousing the audience.

The devotion reminded me of the zeal with which the Likud Central Committee welcomed Ariel Sharon or Benjamin Netanyahu on various election eves, serenading each as "king of Israel." Even in 2011, four years before Netanyahu's controversial speech to Congress, whenever Bibi's name was mentioned at the Reform biennial, it was like someone had poured water on the crowd to douse any enthusiasm. I often heard booing too.

By 2015, the mention of Obama's name to many Israelis triggered their most protective, patriotic instincts. From the start, many had doubted Obama, because he promised to "engage" with Iran. They felt let down by his Cairo speech, his early visit to Egypt and Turkey but not Israel, and his silence during Iran's failed Green Revolution. Every testy exchange with Bibi made things worse, with the Iran deal just proving the security-minded skeptics right.

Marty Peretz was soon beside himself, outraged by Obama's "scandalous approach to the Middle East," which included a "coldness to the Jewish nation," a "hostile indifference to Israel." Peretz denounced Obama's "clinical allergy to power." He defined the president as "weak-willed and weak-kneed" in dealing with foreign adversaries, and he concluded, "It is with Tehran that Obama has architected the greatest foreign policy disaster of his administration." Most American Jews didn't flip with Peretz. It was easier to turn against "Bibi's Israel"—which so many progressives hated—instead of the progressive president they loved.

Under these conditions, with American Jews' Isaiahan fantasy about the first African American president being deeply Jewish at heart clashing with Israelis' Davidian worries about the Iran deal, Bibi had a hard time cutting through and making his case against Obama's agreement.

I attended many, many roundtables about the relationship between Israel and Diaspora Jewry during the Obama years. At one, held at the JPPI, Dan Kurtzer, the first Orthodox Jew appointed to serve as America's ambassador to Israel, now teaching Middle East diplomacy at Princeton, insisted, "In order not to lose American Jews, the Israeli government has to change its attitude toward President Obama." I responded, "How would you feel if I said, 'In order not to lose Israel, you should change your attitude toward Bibi'?"

American Jews and Israelis were forgetting that we are siblings, not twins. Each part of our family is not quite ready to acknowledge that we have chosen to live in very different neighborhoods. Most Jews were sticking with their particular survival strategy.

It would have been naive to expect that any dialogue would change the Israeli government's or American Jews' attitude toward Obama. But a healthier dialogue might have helped American Jews take Israeli alarm more seriously. And Israelis could have been much more sensitive to the standing this "first Jewish president" and first African American president enjoyed among American Jews. This kind of exchange could only have occurred if we had first succeeded in lifting the curtain that fell between the factions in this fight and trusted the other side's sincerity.

FRUSTRATIONS GROW BEYOND IRAN AND THE KOTEL

So even though I was angry with Bibi about the Western Wall, I recognized that he captured many Israelis' growing frustration with liberal American Jews. Increasingly, it seemed the only times some Jews brought up Israel was to bash it. At the same time, many American Jewish friends felt that, for all his rhetoric about leading the Jewish people, this prime minister and his electorate kept disappointing, even double-crossing, the Jewish people. Cries of betrayal echoed throughout the Jewish world, no matter who talked about what topic.

I could feel it, for example, in the intense debate regarding the Africans from Sudan, Eritrea, and elsewhere who entered Israel and stayed illegally. With only thirty-five thousand or so illegal migrant workers in a country of nearly nine million people, I thought this problem was solvable.

Trying to mediate, I invited representatives from both sides to my office. The pro side, representing most American Jews and many Israelis, saw Israel's threats to deport these immigrants as a betrayal of Jewish values. After all, hadn't we been strangers in Egypt, on the Lower East Side, in British Palestine?

The con side represented 73 percent of Israelis who were fed up with African migrants illegally overstaying their welcome. We all know that stable, democratic countries have become magnets for refugees and are having trouble managing the nearly infinite need. But Israel is the closest democracy to these distressed countries, as well as one of the world's smallest democracies. Given Israel's geographic proximity to so many millions of desperate refugees hoping to make it to Europe, a lenient policy would inevitably put this small state at risk of being overwhelmed. Seeing these migrants as mostly fleeing poverty, not oppression, Israel's leaders felt that letting masses in too easily would betray their responsibility to keep Israel stable. Once again, many Israelis felt betrayed that American Jews would sacrifice Israel's needs to feel liberal "on our backs."

These clashing symbols were crushing subtleties and obscuring common values. Most Israelis wanted to be humanitarian without being overrun. When I approached Bibi with a plan to absorb one hundred Syrian orphans into various Jewish Agency youth villages, he asked me, "And where will they go two, three, five years from now?" We both knew that under international law, Israel would be obligated to let them stay if they wanted to.

"If we take one hundred today, they'll press us to take one hundred thousand tomorrow," Netanyahu said, emphasizing how small we were and how close we were to so many potential refugees. "But we will happily help not just a hundred but thousands, even tens of thousands in all kinds of ways, without offering permanent homes." Showing Israel's goodwill, Bibi emphasized that under his leadership Israel was already giving urgent medical assistance in our two northernmost hospitals to Syrians fleeing the civil war.

While visiting those hospitals, I had seen how sensitively the doctors and nurses worked, giving hundreds of horrifically wounded Syrians the most sophisticated medical care available often for months on end, before the patients returned to their families. No one asked whose side they or their families were on. These programs kept growing, regardless of cost, with Netanyahu's direct encouragement and Israel's full subsidy. Ultimately, Israeli doctors treated more than five thousand Syrians, no questions asked, until Assad's regime doomed the humanitarian effort.

Of course, such fine-tuning didn't fit the "humane Left" versus "heartless Right" stereotyping that feeds the partisan hostility.

THE NATION-STATE BILL: GOOD AND NOT GOOD

I saw a similar sense of mutual betrayal in the international cross fire over the controversial nation-state bill the Knesset passed on July 19, 2018. The law, which took seven years to pass, badly divided the Jewish world over the central tension of my life: how much do we emphasize our particular identity as a Jewish state and how much do we emphasize our universal democratic commitments in this law—especially because equality and liberty were already guaranteed by other Basic Laws and Supreme Court decisions. By sixty-two to fifty-five, with two abstentions, the Knesset defined Israel as the nation-state of the Jewish people and detailed the state's symbols, capital, language, and calendar.

Once again, instead of having the nuanced debate we needed, partisans reduced the conversation to a clash of false choices. The bill's supporters said they were just stating the obvious, that the force of Zionist history and the citizens of Israel democratically determined that Israel is a Jewish state. Those opposing the bill said it was obvious to them that Israel was no longer interested in being a Jewish-democratic state.

I was invited to be the final speaker at a conference about the bill, shortly after it passed. The organizers assumed that as the head of the Jewish Agency for Israel, I would blast the critics and support the law.

I did, initially. I rose and said, "If you asked me about the law in a word, I would say 'good.'" The pro side applauded enthusiastically. "But," I added—recalling a famous Jewish joke—"in two words: 'not good.'" Everyone turned quiet, confused.

I explained my position. Of course Israel has the right and need to assert the basics of its proud national Jewish identity in a world of postmodern hostility that questions our state's legitimacy. The bill emphasized the state's mission to keep Jews and Judaism alive, physically and culturally. While fulfilling our responsibility to ingather the exiles, expressed in our Law of Return, it was legitimate to have a flag with a Jewish star, to make our Jewish holidays national holidays, and speak Hebrew. When other countries affirm their national identity in similar ways, it's called patriotism; when we do it, it's called racism.

At the same time, the law failed to affirm Israel's sacred symmetry as a Jewish-democratic state. As a Basic Law, it should have reaffirmed the vow in Israel's Declaration of Independence protecting the equality of all of Israel's inhabitants, avoiding this false choice between our identity and our commitment to human rights. It was wrong to leave our Arab and Druze citizens feeling neglected, especially by a Basic Law that took so long to negotiate.

The pro side's experts gave me a long explanation about the complicated dynamics between our government and the Supreme Court, and why the vow of equality I wanted to add was unnecessary. The Supreme Court does that job anyway. Equality was already assured by a steady stream of court decisions, they promised.

They were correct technically, but so wrong symbolically. The nation-state law was unnecessarily asymmetrical, even if there were other counterbalances. Usually in life, if you lack simple answers, take the hint—there's a problem.

To illustrate the mess we were creating, I said, "Ask our campus representatives to explain all these subtleties to the angry crowd using this Basic Law as ammunition to further attack us as an 'apartheid state.' See who actually understands that the law safeguards the state as Jewish, while the court safeguards it as democratic."

Missing the point, and washing their hands of responsibility for Diaspora Jewry, the experts insisted, "That's not our problem. That's your job."

INTERMARRIAGE:
CATASTROPHE OR OPPORTUNITY?

For their part, Israelis were often stunned by the constant media reports emphasizing American Jewry's growing disengagement from Judaism and from Israel. With an intermarriage rate of 70 percent, and still soaring, many liberal American Jews had stopped calling intermarriage a problem. They called it an opportunity. Some even praised it as a blessing.

When the popular novelist Michael Chabon received an honorary doctorate from the Reform movement's Hebrew Union College–Jewish Institute of Religion in Los Angeles, his charge to the graduates seemed to cross yet another line. Calling "endogamous marriage"—marrying another Jew—a "ghetto of two," Chabon dismissed Judaism by saying, "The whole thing's a giant interlocking system of distinctions." Showing no sensitivity to the dangers facing Israel, he dismissed "security" as "an invention of humanity's jailers." He went on, "Security for some means imprisonment for all."

Almost everyone in attendance applauded enthusiastically, except for one Israeli student who walked out in indignation. As many Israelis, both secular and religious, read Chabon's remarks, they found the scene a betrayal of their core Zionist and Jewish identities. Many Israelis active in the Reform movement understood how such antics would hurt their movement's credibility in Israel.

The controversy confirmed many Israelis' fears that Reform Jewry is a halfway house for those ready to leave Judaism. Reform Jews resent this caricature. They see their denomination as a creative way to live as modern Westerners and as Jews simultaneously, from generation to generation.

If we were squabbling over one or two issues, the crisis would have felt manageable. But it seemed that the issues that kept triggering the key charges—"they betray Jewish values" versus "they betray the Jewish people"—were piling up like Russian Matryoshka nesting dolls.

WATCH THAT B-WORD: BETRAYAL

Having been falsely imprisoned for high treason and knowing how many millions of lives were ruined by similar false Soviet accusations, I take words like "betrayed," "treason," and "traitor" seriously. That's why it is so painful to hear so many crisscrossing accusations of betraying Jewish values or betraying the Jewish people.

Everything becomes a loyalty test: Israel's treatment of all migrant workers or Arabs or non-Orthodox religious streams betrays Jewish values. All American Jews' ignorance, intermarriage, and indifference betrays the Jewish people. "How dare you?" so many bellow across the divide, refusing to recognize that their opponents' position might have any validity.

From one side, regarding the Kotel, I heard, "How dare you compare an issue central to our survival, like stopping Iran's campaign to annihilate us, to a minor symbolic issue like the Kotel, which involves Jews who are not ready to live here fighting for an alternative space that is already open to them, even if it's not official!"

From the other side, I heard, "How dare you compare Prime Minister Netanyahu's cynical double-cross, after four years of negotiations and public promises, to our sincere support for President Obama's noble efforts to make peace!" We are in trouble when opposing sides in an argument strike similarly absolutist tones, displaying parallel blind spots.

I did hear some good news hidden in all the arguing. The tensions and fury were problems of the third stage—of being so deeply interconnected. Just as the nuclear family sometimes explodes because relatives are wrapped up so tightly in each other's psyches, Jewish people fight so intensely because we're so wrapped up as one. We get mad with one another instead of giving up.

Decades ago, our need to save one another pushed any differences aside. But when American Jews are sending their kids to Israel for a positive Jewish experience, suddenly, official Israel's negative attitudes toward their Jewish expression becomes very relevant and infuriating. When Israelis turn to American Jews to defend Israel against delegitimization, suddenly, some Jews' negative attitudes toward Israel become relevant and infuriating.

THE UNDERLYING CLASH OVER THE PALESTINIANS

A more basic clash underlies many of these tensions between Israeli Jews and the Diaspora. Many American liberals cannot forgive Israelis for becoming the oppressors in the world's eyes. Meanwhile, many Israelis cannot forgive liberal American Jewish critics for seeing Israelis as victimizers of Palestinians instead of as the victims of Palestinian terror.

The steady drip of Palestinian terror attacks—along with the occasional bursts of warfare and the constant attacks in the media, on campus, and elsewhere—keep reducing the grand Israel story to this one dimension: the Israel-Palestinian conflict. Diaspora Jews expect Israel to inspire them, not disappoint them. Israelis expect Diaspora Jews to defend them, not disappoint them.

It has become fashionable to blame Israel's rigidity in the age of Bibi for the ongoing stalemate with the Palestinians. That caricature overlooks dramatic shifts in Israeli public opinion. The Left won part of the argument: more and more Israelis, even many right-wingers, including Benjamin Netanyahu, admit that it's bad for Israelis to continue controlling millions of Palestinians. But the Right won, too, in part: more and more Israelis, even on the Left, admit we cannot withdraw immediately or unilaterally without a solid agreement with reliable negotiating partners who accept Israel's right to exist.

Most Israelis believe in a two-state solution. The widespread fear that there is no serious negotiating partner on the Palestinian side has discouraged the Israeli prime minister from rushing ahead with territorial concessions. Yet, as that 1970s-era slogan, "peace now," loses ground in Israel, that's precisely what more and more American Jews demand. They blame "Netanyahu's Israel" for "the stalemate" and assume he is a one-stater when he doesn't offer massive amounts of territory as an opening gambit. They demand that Israel solve the problem and end their ongoing embarrassment as quickly as possible.

Israel seems stuck in a post-Oslo pattern: Israel suffers from Palestinian terrorist attacks, often launched from the most vulnerable and populated urban areas. Israel then goes to war while imposing self-restrictions no other democratic army follows. Jews from all over the world fly in, bringing moral support and generous donations. Yet Israel is still condemned as a war criminal for its "disproportionate" response, leaving more and more progressive Jews squirming. When those Jews echo the harsh words of the outsiders, the family ties make the insiders' cries all the more painful.

"You are losing me . . . and many, many people in the Jewish community," a liberal Jew told a group of Israeli members of Knesset at a Boston town hall in 2017. Three years after the 2014 Gaza War had ended, she and many others were still troubled by the disproportionate numbers. "I cannot look the other way," she said, "when three Israeli teenagers are brutally murdered, and the response is to kill 2,300 Palestinians."

The Israeli parliamentarians, from right to left, scoffed, shocked by her one-sidedness. The Knesset members remembered how thousands of Hamas missiles sent millions of Israelis into shelters, including some of their own children and grandchildren. They knew all the military advantages Israel sacrificed—and continues to sacrifice—to minimize Palestinian civilian casualties while fighting terrorists who were secreted in neighborhoods and hiding behind innocents. "If I have to choose between losing more lives of Israelis, whether they are civilians or soldiers, or losing you, I will sadly, regretfully, rather lose you," one member replied. This response to the lost liberal was mostly ignored in America. It went viral in Israel, rousing Israelis fed up with being judged by self-righteous Diaspora Jews.

Twice during my years in the Jewish Agency, Israel went to war to try to stop Hamas from bombing Israeli civilians. Each time, we worked around the clock, making sure bomb shelters were clean, comfortable, even fun. We bused thousands of children away from the regions Hamas targeted, arranging fun days and homes to host them. Our Diaspora partners, particularly the American Jewish Federations, were characteristically generous. They financed these efforts with emergency campaigns yielding millions of dollars.

During the 2014 Gaza conflict, I arranged for one American Jewish leader involved with these humanitarian efforts to be photographed with Benjamin Netanyahu as a thank you. When he proudly sent this picture to his family, his son snorted, "Why would you be photographed with that butcher?"

20

DOES ANTI-SEMITISM UNITE OR DIVIDE US?

Once again, the tensions have played out most dramatically on campuses, many of which have become the places in America where Jews feel most uncomfortable being pro-Israel. But first, some good news. The pro-Israel infrastructure on campus has developed impressively since 2003, when I first visited the occupied territories of American academia. Back then, universities often felt like a no-man's land for the pro-Israel community, with the Jewish Establishment ignoring campus politics. Today, many Jewish organizations recognize universities as key battlefields shaping the future. Back then, Birthright was a small program just starting to send young Jews to Israel. Today, tens of thousands participate in organized Israel experience tours every year, starting with Birthright.

Israel Fellows became the Jewish Agency's fastest-growing program during my years there. Today, this army of emissaries defends Israel on more than one hundred campuses, in sync with the local Hillel Jewish student organizations. Often working with Israel Experience alumni, the emissaries spearhead the counterattack against BDS resolutions, explaining just how unfair—and counterproductive to the peace process—it is to single out Israel for boycotts, divestments, or sanctions. And the results are clear. BDS resolutions have been much less successful on campuses with Israel Fellows, because they build the best defense against them: a generalized awareness of Israel beyond the headlines, as a normal democracy with strengths and flaws, reinforced with a personal touch.

Nevertheless, anti-Zionism has become ever more central to campus ideology. More and more students hate Zionism, even as fewer and fewer know what the word actually means. And more and more Jewish students report being tagged with the label Zionist by progressives who spit out the word as if it were a curse.

The postmodernism we faced in the early 2000s caricatured the nation-state as guilty of bigotry and warmongering. It became fashionable to reject nationalism in favor of a supposedly peace-seeking universalism. Today, those attacks on Israel seem mild. Two new ideological weapons have proved particularly potent against Zionists and Jews: intersectionality and white privilege.

Intersectionality unites all the oppressed groups in the struggle against oppression. Who are the oppressed? People of color, women, LGBTQ people, and . . . Palestinians. And who is the oppressor? Regarding the first three, it's liberal democracies, weighed down by their racism, sexism, and homophobia. Regarding the Palestinians, the oppressors are clear: Zionists and those who live the Zionist dream, Israelis.

The Marxist slogan that hounded me throughout my childhood— "Workers of the world unite!"—has now essentially been replaced by "Victims of the racist, colonialist, imperialist, capitalist, sexist, homophobic democracies unite!" In Marxism, as implemented by Lenin, Trotsky, and Stalin, the bourgeoisie was inherently bad. Whole classes of people—the capitalist exploiters—were enemies. In the court of revolutionary justice, one didn't need to look for proof of specific crimes: all those deemed to be the enemies of the proletariat were on the wrong side of progressive history and obviously guilty.

Following the same logic, intersectionality and white privilege declare those deemed to be oppressors guilty by definition. All those fighting different forms of oppression must unite in the struggle against Western oppressors, which includes Zionists. In a bizarre act of transference, Israel and Zionism have also become guilty of the Western sins of racism, sexism, and homophobia.

BLOCKED AT THE INTERSECTION ON CAMPUS

Today's fight for social justice applies intersectionality's simplistic calculus broadly. In 2016, the Black Lives Matter movement connected the problem of police shootings in Missouri to the Middle East with the slogan "From Ferguson to Gaza." Its platform accused Israel of being an apartheid state. That lie, which racialized the Israeli-Palestinian national conflict and falsely equated it with the one-way oppression in South Africa, makes the Israeli-Palestinian struggle an African American concern too.

Similarly, many campus radicals accept the claim of Mariam Barghouti and other Palestinian activists that "you can't be a feminist and a Zionist." "Calling yourself a Zionist feminist," Barghouti argued, "means granting de facto support to patriarchal domination, as Israel embodies the same roles and techniques that have long been, and continue to be, used against women." While protesting Donald Trump's presidency in 2017, the International Women's Strike platform declared the "decolonization of Palestine" as part of "the beating heart of this new feminist movement."

Some young disaffected Jews, steeped in the white progressive embrace of "wokeness" that champions other groups and denigrates your own, romanticize Palestinians and demonize their fellow Jews, especially in Israel. Others are more pragmatic, or intimidated. "We must each find our path to engaging in this movement and commit ourselves to an intersectional view of our collective fate," said Nancy Kaufman, chief executive officer of the National Council of Jewish Women, before the first Women's March in 2017. Kaufman also endorsed "everyone's" right to free speech, code words for tolerating feminist Israel bashing.

In January 2019, as more feminists boycotted the Women's March for its anti-Semitism, others, like film critic and feminist activist Jan Lisa Huttner, marched anyway. "Given the importance of unity in this case, I refuse to center myself 'as a Jew' in this controversy," Huttner told the Jewish Telegraphic Agency.

Students tell me there's a new initiation ritual on campus. Many young Jews wishing to join human rights groups, especially those supporting feminism, LGBTQ rights, or Black Lives Matter, have been told, "You must condemn Zionism first." In essence, many radical leftists are blocking Jews at the intersection. They say, "We love Jews. It's only racist Israel we hate." The Jews who surrender usually do so silently. That's the point.

On one level, intersectionality makes sense. In the Soviet Union, we democratic dissidents representing different national and religious causes shared a common suffering at the hands of the dictators. But when we united as the Moscow Helsinki Group, we weren't just opposing our oppressors. We based our bond on our mutual interest in defending human rights and fighting for a democratic society for all.

Perhaps most outrageous in today's brave new intersectional world is that being labeled a legitimate oppressed identity comes with an added bonus: a free pass to violate others' human rights aggressively and shamelessly. Palestinian society is homophobic and sexist. The premeditated murder of women, often by close family members, carries an abominable Orwellian name: honor killings. Year after year, these shameful murders constitute as much as two-thirds of the slayings in Gaza and the West Bank. But the Palestinian cause gets a free pass from the West for these crimes, let alone for the anti-Israel crimes of incitement and terrorism.

Here, too, I learned that Marx was not dead. In the modern progressives' fight—as in the Marxist, Leninist, Stalinist world—any atrocities the progressive camp commits cannot be criticized, to avoid weakening the forces of progress.

In 2014, Saudi Arabia sentenced the liberal blogger Raif bin Muhammad Badawi to ten years in prison, one thousand lashes, and a fine. His crimes included apostasy and "insulting Islam through electronic channels." Badawi's website, Free Saudi Liberals, encouraged Saudis to live by his motto: "To me, liberalism means simply to live and let live."

Shortly thereafter, while speaking to coordinators of the Israel Fellows on campuses, I said, "There are thousands of Muslim students on campus who I am sure feel a strong sense of solidarity with Badawi. When they protest, demanding his release, it is extremely important that we join as Jews and cosponsor as Jewish organizations, even if the Muslims or some groups involved have been hostile to Israel. Here's a chance to put our differences aside and fight for human rights together."

A few weeks later I checked in, anxious to hear about the human rights bridge building. The fellows informed me that I'm not much of a prophet. No one demonstrated for Badawi on any of their campuses. The social justice warriors' maxim not to criticize non-Western oppression prevailed. Protesting against Islamist fundamentalism didn't fit the intersectional script; Muslim-against-Muslim persecution muddied the story that white Westerners were always the oppressors.

"Do you want us to initiate protests to free him?" one Israel Fellow asked naively. "No, it won't help Badawi," I replied. "The Saudis will use it to claim he was an Israel agent, and on campus we'll be accused of a 'Zionist provocation.'"

True, four years later, Westerners protested the Saudi murder of Jamal Khashoggi. But he was a *Washington Post* columnist, Saudi Arabia's leadership was close to the unpopular President Trump, and the anger came more from journalists than from students. Badawi remains unknown and neglected. In fact, when my former lawyer Irwin Cotler convinced Canada's prime minister Justin Trudeau to act boldly for Badawi, the rest of the West was silent. And when Saudi Arabia retaliated aggressively in August 2018 by suspending Canadian investments, recalling its Canadian ambassador, and even pulling Saudi patients out of Canadian hospitals, the West remained dormant.

SHAMED BY WHITE PRIVILEGE

The pressure has intensified on liberal Jews because of the new woke accusation that all Jews benefit from white privilege. Here, too, what started as a reasonable insight has been hijacked to demonize Jews. Whites should be sensitized to the hidden bonuses of living in a race-conscious society. Many take their advantages for granted and are not fully aware of the obstacles others face.

But, increasingly, illiberal liberals yelling "Check your privilege," especially on campus, cast all Jews as white European elites who have never suffered any discrimination anywhere. Zionists become white supremacists whose privileged skin color automatically makes them colonialist and guilty of multiple crimes. Decades ago, when whiteness was most valued, Jews weren't considered white; today, whiteness is devalued, so now we're white.

The "framing of Zionism as 'white,' not 'Jewish,' supremacy enables and strengthens the formation of coalitions between all those opposed to Zionist settler colonialism in particular and white supremacy in general," one Al Jazeera essayist wrote in January 2019, noting that the accusation yields propaganda dividends.

Even more than intersectionality, white privilege puts many progressive Jews on the defensive. Fueling anti-Semitic stereotypes that all Jews are rich and powerful, progressives try shaming Jews into feeling guilty for coming from the oppressive ruling elite. Similarly, while caricaturing Israel as the ultimate racist, colonialist, imperialist settler state, radicals view modern Israel, with its new wealth and power, as a fortress of white privilege.

Sometimes, defenders of Israel refute this lie by pointing out how many dark-skinned Israelis there are and how many light-skinned Palestinians there are. Beware this argument; it's a trap. It's like the poor shopkeepers who tried saving themselves from vengeful Bolshevik bureaucrats by yelling, "I'm too poor to be bourgeois." That defense conceded that being bourgeois was a crime. The "we're not all white" counterargument treats whiteness as a form of evil while implying that all people of the same skin color—or gender or religion or nation—act alike and are equally evil or virtuous.

The next stage in this process casts Jews and Israel as tools of the patriarchy, as Palestinian feminists like Mariam Barghouti are cleverly trying to do. Even fighting anti-Semitism has been caricatured as perpetuating patriarchal power. That accusation injects modern ideas about gender into what we have already seen is an ancient struggle. It negates all the Jewish women demeaned and killed by anti-Semites over centuries. Will those trying to dodge that accusation say, "Well, we are not all men?" How far will the loyalty tests based on identity go?

Sometimes, I read these sentences and I'm sure I'm exaggerating. Then I research some more, and it seems our enemies have gone off the rails. In March 2019, the Democratic Speaker of the House Nancy Pelosi endorsed a resolution condemning anti-Semitism, responding to Congresswoman Ilhan Omar's barb that pro-Israel activists were pushing "for allegiance to a foreign country." The Palestinian activist Linda Sarsour defended her "sister," Omar, by posting on Facebook that the resolution exposed "Nancy" to be "a typical white feminist upholding the patriarchy doing the dirty work of powerful white men."

Despite calling herself a feminist, Sarsour rendered all women who opposed Jew-hatred invisible, treating the fight against anti-Semitism as some oppressive tool of the patriarchy. Depressingly, this criticism, echoed by many others, worked. Pelosi backed down and the congressional resolution, which passed on March 7, 2019, condemned all hate. One Democrat called it a "kitchen-sink resolution." Congressman Ted Deutch, a Florida Democrat, asked, "Why are we unable to singularly condemn anti-Semitism? Why can't we call it anti-Semitism and show we've learned the lessons of history?" But that's it. Words don't matter anymore. What matters is who said them.

I recognize all this unforgiving stereotyping, this "good is bad and bad is good" rhetoric. I grew up with it. These progressives risk yanking history backward. Those of us who escaped Communism's grip had to grow into the fundamental liberal belief in individualism. It's sobering to watch so many privileged Westerners flee from it—or at least unknowingly weaponize tools from the class struggle we fled.

"WE DIDN'T COME HERE TO TALK TO YOU!"

In January 2016, the actor Michael Douglas and I toured American college campuses to talk about Jewish identity. When we reached Brown University, some angry demonstrators didn't want to talk, certainly not about Jewish identity. Protesters waved placards advocating the typical BDS demand to boycott Israel. Before our event began, I insisted on going outside to talk to these students, defying my security team's advice.

I approached a young woman in the loud but small crowd of thirty protestors. She was waving a poster proclaiming ISRAEL = APARTHEID!

"With respect," I began, "you are too young to know the real race-based apartheid in South Africa. As a human rights activist who was friendly with Nelson Mandela and was an official international observer of South Africa's first free election in 1994, will you permit me to explain to you what South African apartheid looked like and did? Then you and your friends can decide if the label fits Israel."

The young woman hesitated. She looked to the protest's ringleader. He gave her a sign. Refusing to make eye contact with me, she started shouting, "We didn't come here to talk to you! We came here to demand 'Boycott Israel!'" The others echoed: "BOYCOTT ISRAEL! BOYCOTT ISRAEL!" Now the communication lines weren't just malfunctioning, they were being cut completely, because I was from the wrong country. I got chills.

Her tone, her words, the look in her eyes—I recognized them all. They brought me back to the campaigns of condemnation the Communist Party officials used to run at school and at work. These orchestrated outbursts of groupthink would have people shouting hysterically about Alexander Solzhenitsyn or Andrei Sakharov or some other enemy of the people: "There is nothing to discuss about that book! Of course I

didn't read it! It's all lies! We don't need to read to know how treacher-
ous it is—just look at how happy it makes our enemies. Shame on you
Solzhenitsyn. Shame on you Sakharov. Shame on these renegades. We
Soviet people condemn you!"

Even if I had spoken to her, I suspect it would not have helped. She
wasn't interested in dialogue. We, Israel's defenders, often try discussing
Israel in traditional liberal terms, on its merits, but Israel is now guilty for
what it is, not what it does.

In my university lectures, I often recalled that commanders briefing us
in the security cabinet during Israel's various military operations always
identified excruciating moral dilemmas. Quoting Israel's code of military
ethics, they would detail how pilots aborted legally justified and militarily necessary missions at the last second to save Palestinian civilian lives.
Referencing those moments—or noting that we drop leaflets warning
civilians to leave areas we plan to bomb—should help, but it doesn't. To
our enemies, Israel is both an oppressor and an interloper that doesn't
belong in the Middle East. To them, all our talk about moral dilemmas
is the equivalent of quibbling over a speeding ticket for a career criminal
already sentenced to the electric chair.

Welcome to the world of the unthinking university, where call-out
culture cancels thought. These student activists didn't want to learn, because reality is more complicated than their slogans. And, let's be honest,
we live in a cancel culture. People ghost one another—we used to call
it disappearing—if relationships get complicated or a friend takes the
wrong political position. In this disposable world, it's easier to just delete
your relationship with Israel than to defend it if it is unpopular or occasionally flawed.

Sadly, many professors—especially the intellectuals driving BDS—
are equally closed-minded and quick to judge. Many progressive boycott
supporters usually insist they are fighting the occupation, while ignoring
the frank admission of the BDS movement's founders that, as the Palestinian American activist Ahmed Moor says, "BDS does mean the end of
the Jewish state."

We've seen this before. When the legitimacy of the Jewish state is denied and—in the language of some of the key promoters of BDS—there
is no place for a Jewish state in the Middle East with any borders, that is
delegitimization; that is anti-Semitism. The true aim of many of the BDS
movement's key figures has been the destruction of Israel as we know it.

Indeed, cofounder and leader Omar Barghouti has said so unequivocally: "Definitely, most definitely we oppose a Jewish state in any part of Palestine." How often must they say it before intellectuals believe it?

Too many self-styled progressives today feel comfortable hiding behind noble-sounding titles like Students for Justice in Palestine—a name with genocidal implications as long as so many founders and members of that movement equate a just result with the destruction of Israel.

I confess, I cringe when I hear that name. I want justice in Palestine too. But I come from a world where both the czars and the Communists masked their worst crimes against Jews with noble-sounding words, calling for justice or, another favorite of the Soviets and the Palestinians, solidarity. In fact, throughout Jewish history, many expulsions of Jews from different parts of Europe were rationalized by the supposed pressing need for justice for these local populations.

THE CONTROVERSIES AROUND TRUMP
DRIVE AMERICAN JEWS AND ISRAELIS FURTHER APART

Donald Trump's emergence on the political scene further broadened the gap between the Israeli security-minded street and the *New York Times'* liberal Jewish boulevard. From the launch of his candidacy, Trump's vulgarity, divisiveness, materialism, egotism, and demagoguery disgusted the vast majority of Jews, even those tired of the political correctness he targeted so cleverly. Initially, most of the Republicans I knew joined the Democrats in opposing him. His language was so crude, he made a mockery of words like "presidential," "patriotic," and "dignified." He attacked women, disabled people, immigrants, and Muslims. He attacked heroes like my comrade in arms, Senator John McCain, for being "captured" and imprisoned by the North Vietnamese. Such rhetoric unleashed an ugliness on all sides throughout the land.

"Do you think Trump's an anti-Semite?" I asked one influential Manhattan Republican who continued supporting the Republican Party while resisting Trump. "Of course not," he replied, noting Trump's many close relationships with Jews, including his own daughter Ivanka. "But all the anti-Semites will vote for him. His rhetoric and tone and antics legitimize them."

When Trump became president, it became more confusing. Just as many American Jews so disliked George W. Bush that they couldn't

appreciate his increasing support of Israel against Palestinian terrorists, most American Jews couldn't stand Trump, no matter what he did.
Trump, however, started making moves that struck most Israelis as common sense and that other presidents hadn't done.

By the time Trump entered the White House, the Joint Comprehensive Plan of Action, the Iran nuclear deal, was a fact of life. Refusing to
relent, Netanyahu continued campaigning against it. Most leaders and
international experts, even those who originally opposed it, advised Bibi
to move on, stop complaining, and accept reality.

Then, in May 2018, Trump withdrew from the deal, triggering rounds
of doomsday predictions. The debate over America's Iran strategy will
continue for years, perhaps decades, to come. But we in Israel could see
the positive results within weeks. An isolated, embattled Iran had less
money to bankroll mischief throughout the Middle East. "Trump's Sanctions on Iran Are Hitting Hezbollah and It Hurts," a *Washington Post*
headline in May 2019 proclaimed. Hezbollah's leader, Hassan Nasrallah,
even felt compelled to make a fundraising pitch that March, calling for a
"jihad of money."

Similarly, for decades, the world had pumped billions of dollars into
the pockets of Palestinian leaders, no matter how vile their rhetoric or
violent their actions. Trump said, "Enough." He made a move so obvious you had to be an undiplomatic outsider like him to see its logic: he
made further aid contingent on the Palestinian Authority's willingness
to negotiate.

Trump punctuated his strategic shifts with three bold symbolic moves.
Since George McGovern's Democratic platform in 1972, Democrats and
Republicans have endorsed moving America's embassy to Jerusalem and
respecting Israel's choice to designate that city as its capital. Bill Clinton
signed bipartisan legislation promising to do it, then kept postponing
the move. By 2017, so many presidents from both parties had broken the
promise so many times, it had become a farce. Then, Donald Trump actually fulfilled it. Additionally, since the start of the Syrian civil war, most
Israelis and pro-Israel supporters have breathed sighs of relief that Israel
kept the Golan Heights. Trump finally recognized Israeli rule there.

Finally, in November 2019, Trump's secretary of state, Mike Pompeo,
released a statement declaring that the settlements were legal. It was like
lifting a dark cloud from over us. Since the Carter administration, our
closest friends the Americans had joined the world in finding us guilty

of illegally living on our historic homeland. Even many Israelis who seek a two-state solution were relieved that the United States wasn't invalidating our historical rights to the land they were willing to give away for peace.

These moves culminated with the Trump peace plan, rolled out in January 2020. Ironically, despite showing little interest in promoting human rights or democratic values, Trump proposed a "deal of the century," which had elements that, if implemented broadly, would have reversed Oslo's antidemocratic miscalculation. Resisting the usual temptation to create a Palestinian state instantly, the plan offered a four-year transition period for Palestinian economic, social, and political detoxification, backed by $50 billion.

Clearly, I wish a less polarizing president had made these moves. And I remain worried about Trump's abandonment of the Kurds along with his passivity in the face of Vladimir Putin's ongoing power grab in the Middle East. But the question most non-Americans ask about the American president is "How have you helped me lately?"—so Israelis appreciate wherever Trump helped.

With most Israelis feeling so grateful to Trump, the Israeli government was reluctant to criticize him, even when he acted insensitively toward Jews. In August 2017, neo-Nazis and Southern racists marched through Charlottesville, Virginia. One right-wing fanatic ran over a young counterprotester, killing her. The bigots shouted many nasty slogans, including "Jews will not replace us." Many American Jews feared their worst nightmares coming true as the beasts of intolerance Trump had unleashed toward women, Muslims, and immigrants targeted the Jews too. That's what intersectionality actually should highlight.

Rather than giving America the moral leadership it needed at that moment, Trump first muttered, "There is blame on both sides" and there "were very fine people, on both sides." Subsequently, he tried walking back those comments. His supporters claim he was only speaking about the two sides of the Confederate statue controversy. But it was a sensitive moment, and Trump's words were the wrong words in the wrong place at the wrong time, emboldening the wrong people while demoralizing the wronged people.

Trump's moral muddle in the wake of Charlottesville was the last straw for many American Jews. They rejected Trump's tone, his supporters, and his dog-whistling messages that subtly stirred up Jew-haters. Liberals

linked Trump with the hyper-nationalist Far Right, which pushed identity to the extreme, often targeting and demonizing left-leaning Jews.

In Europe and North America, ultranationalists define themselves by
building walls around their exclusive identities. Beyond whatever local
clashes with liberal Jews have emerged from country to country, these
Far Right activists enjoy targeting Europe's favorite, age-old scapegoat
for being alien and unwelcome, the Jew. That is why the white supremacists and Ku Kluxers marched so angrily against Jews as well as blacks
in Charlottesville. And that is why alt-right, pro-Trump fanatics bombarded at least eight hundred journalists, both Jewish and non-Jewish,
with thousands of anti-Semitic tweets for daring to criticize their favorite
candidate during the campaign in 2016. After Julia Ioffe wrote an article
about Melania Trump, the *Daily Stormer* website attacked her as a "Filthy
Russian Kike" and she received tweets like this: "Whacha doing Kike?
You sure will make a preuurdy lampshade." Ben Shapiro, a right-wing
Never Trumper at the time, was called the "Christ-Killing Kike Shapiro"
and received threats when his second child was born that the whole family would be thrown into a gas chamber.

Amid all this confusion and anger after Charlottesville, the Jewish
world and the world in general needed leadership. As the leader of the
Jewish state, Benjamin Netanyahu should have immediately condemned
Trump's moral dithering in the face of Charlottesville's neo-Nazis.

I called Bibi's spokesperson after forty-eight hours had passed. "Don't
you see how problematic this silence is?" I said.

"Wait another twenty-four hours," he advised me.

Finally, after three days, Netanyahu tweeted a generic statement, say-
ing, "Outraged by expressions of anti-Semitism, neo-Nazism and racism.
Everyone should oppose this hatred." Clearly, Bibi did not want to cross
Donald Trump, whom he kept labeling Israel's "best friend ever."

While many Israelis couldn't bring themselves to criticize Trump,
most American Jews couldn't bring themselves to thank him. The "resistance" repudiated nearly everything Trump did or said. Even when Trump
recognized Jerusalem as Israel's capital, many American Jewish liberals
chided him for a move they themselves had demanded for decades.

Rabbi Rick Jacobs, the leader of the Union for Reform Judaism, told
the *New York Times* that the move was "ill-timed," explaining, "We're very
concerned that the announcement will either delay or undermine the
very, very important resuming of a serious peace process." Debra DeLee,

the president of Americans for Peace Now, said, "Trump is causing severe damage to the prospects of Middle East peace, imperiling lives and degrading U.S. leadership."

Many Israelis wondered how hatred for a term-limited president could trump Jews' eternal love of Jerusalem. When a radio reporter asked me, on air, what I, as the Reform movement's friend, thought of Rick's statement, I called it "awful." "Everything that Trump does is bad, as far as they're concerned. When the leader of a superpower recognizes Jerusalem, first you should welcome it overall, then if you wish to, express disagreement on the nuances."

I especially regretted crossing swords with Rick. Throughout the Kotel negotiations, he, as an open-minded soul, kept looking for compromise. I frequently witnessed his deep devotion to Israel and the Jewish people. He delighted in the little things that make Israel Israel, and the big ideas that created the state. It's true that when it came to Israeli politics, he usually took positions and marched with organizations to the far left of me. But, as I often told our Jewish Agency youth educators, "we need more patriotic Zionists on the left and more human rights liberals on the right."

Rick is also a man of impressive intellectual integrity. I often heard him speak frankly about the problems his Reform movement faces. Proclaiming that "the first step" in healing "is to speak the truth," he has urged his colleagues to "admit the painful truth that in most of our congregations we are failing miserably! By the time they reach twelfth grade, 80 percent of our Reform b'nai mitzvah [teenagers] have dropped out of Jewish life." Such self-critical courage, I regret to say, is rare among Jewish leaders.

Rick called me that afternoon. He urged me to consider his statement about Jerusalem in context. Since his initial comment, he had spoken more positively about the move. Three days after Trump's announcement, he delivered a deeply Zionist sermon at the Reform movement's convention, describing "our love of Jerusalem" as "a powerful dynamic in our communal and individual lives." He made his criticism more nuanced, saying his doubts were "never, never about the concept" of recognizing Jerusalem as Israel's capital "but about the timing of these actions."

Still, I told him, "But all your other lovely statements weren't quoted in the *New York Times*." I was thinking about the historical record. The secretary of state in 1948, George Marshall, tried to stop President Harry

Truman from recognizing Israel, because that announcement represented "bad timing" too.

"You have to make sure," I advised him, "that when they write the American Jewish history of today, they don't say the Reform movement opposed recognizing Jerusalem as Israel's legitimate capital by repeating Marshall's argument about 'bad timing.'"

I was talking American history, but I was concerned about more pressing Israeli political matters. Indeed, half an hour after my conversation with Rick, someone from the Prime Minister's Office called, saying, "You see! These are the people you wanted us to sabotage the coalition for!"

American Jews grumbled: You Israelis insulted our former president, whom we loved. Now you love our current president, whom we hate. Israelis returned the volley: You American Jews loved your former president, who threatened us. Now you hate your current president, who protects us.

American Jews were emphasizing their Isaiahan, more universalistic and liberal Jewish principles. They were defending their vision of *tikkun olam* against a president they perceived as a threat to their most cherished principles. Israelis were emphasizing their Davidian, more security-oriented and patriotic principles. They were defending their vision of Zionism against enemies who threatened their lives and their state.

THE RISE OF THE NEW NATIONALISM

The Trump dilemmas that vex Israel and American Jewry—to criticize or not to criticize, to thank or not thank—fit into a bigger global phenomenon. In many countries, the postmodern assault on identity has unleashed an inevitable nationalist counterreaction, trying to restore a sense of national pride. The old-country expression "One knife sharpens the other" is coming to life. One extreme—denying national pride as the enemy of liberalism—keeps colliding with the opposite extreme—denying liberalism as the enemy of national pride.

Postmodernists pushed the noble ideas of peace and universalism to such an extreme that they negated traditional identities. Similarly, nationalists began with an equally legitimate desire to protect identity and feel pride in their people and comfort in their community. For extremists, however, nationalism can too easily override essential liberal approaches, ideals, and protections for others.

Israel's insistence on being a democratic state with a strong national identity is what makes it so unpopular with postmodernists. But that national pride is exactly what many new nationalist parties find so appealing about Israel. Caught in this cross fire, the politics has often turned messy for Jews. While a growing number of illiberal liberals didn't even want to talk to us, some devious ultranationalists seemed obsessed with embracing us.

The leader of the alt-right, Richard Spencer, delights in blurring the lines and slurring Zionism by seeming to compliment it. Beyond pushing his vision of white nationalism, Spencer has emerged as one of America's most prominent Jew-hating Israel-lovers. While flirting with Nazi imagery and neo-Nazis, Spencer calls himself a "White Zionist," caricaturing liberal-democratic Israel as a model of his exclusionary ultra-ethno-nationalism.

Shortly after Trump's election in 2016, Spencer appeared at Texas A&M University. A rabbi there challenged him to study Judaism's "radical inclusion" and love.

Spencer responded, "Do you really want radical inclusion in the state of Israel?" He claimed that "Jews exist precisely because you did not assimilate to the gentiles. . . . I want my people to have that same sense of themselves."

The rabbi sat down, blindsided and intimidated.

White nationalists seeking legitimacy and anti-Zionist leftists seeking to delegitimize Zionism insisted that the rabbi's silence proved Spencer right and exposed Zionism as illiberal and white supremacist. Actually, the rabbi's silence reflected how hard it is to stay balanced during this age of extremes. But walk down any street in Israel, and you'll see radical inclusion at work. Jews come in all colors and are united by common stories, values, and beliefs. The four-term New York senator Daniel Patrick Moynihan liked to say that because Jews are a rare people linked with a religion, and that by converting religiously you join the Jewish people, Zionism was the least race-based and most biologically diverse form of nationalism.

Zionism's identity cocktail of ethnicity, religion, and geography is one of the many valid mixes underlying modern democracies. But to defend its balance between liberalism and nationalism in debate or in real life is much more difficult today; many prefer veering toward liberalism or nationalism.

Humans are tribal. Distinction isn't always discrimination. A community needs boundaries to be a community, otherwise there's nothing in common to contain it and distinguish it from others. In this way, Spencer was right: Jews survived for millennia by having boundaries, preserving our people. But our nationalism goes with our liberalism and our liberalism with our nationalism. Take one or the other out, and you don't have Zionism. Israel's Declaration of Independence makes the duality clear.

In November 2019, a leaked audiotape captured Spencer yelling about the "Little f—ing kikes. They get ruled by me" and the "little f—ing octoroons," a disgusting slur against African Americans. I wasn't surprised. Spencer saw no contradiction between loving what he decided was the nationalism of Israel and hating the liberalism of American Jews.

These kinds of challenges keep popping up throughout the West. Two decades ago, Jean-Marie Le Pen's party in France, the National Front, represented the rare ultranationalist voice able to gain any power in post-Hitler Europe. Not only did the party—now renamed the National Rally and led by Le Pen's daughter Marine—become strong enough to force a runoff for the presidential elections in 2017, it has been joined by more than a dozen new or renewed national populist parties throughout Europe. In the 2019 European Parliament elections, the right-wing or nationalist parties of Italy, France, Poland, and Hungary won majorities in a quest for a "Europe of Fatherlands."

Many of the new nationalist parties often reject the postmodern liberalism many Diaspora Jewish communities embrace, while some of their supporters are crudely anti-Semitic. Heinz-Christian Strache became vice chancellor of Austria in 2017, buoyed by a network of anti-Semitic fraternities that trafficked in anti-Jewish stereotypes. The fraternities gained traction among hundreds of thousands of Austrians by describing their parents and grandparents as Hitler's victims, not his collaborators. In Hungary, huge billboards attacked the controversial liberal philanthropist George Soros, emphasizing his supposedly "Jewish-looking" nose and chin. A broader whisper campaign warned about Jews and their financial control, and the criticism turned anti-Semitic.

At the same time, these parties appreciated Israel's unapologetic nationalism. While many progressive Europeans led the Israel bashing, nationalist governments in Hungary and Austria joined the fight against anti-Zionism in the United Nations and elsewhere.

Watching the Israeli government befriend these European national-ists, many liberal Jews responded angrily: "How dare Israel support these anti-Semitic parties! Being pro-Israel doesn't excuse being anti-Jewish!"

I attended some of the cabinet and Knesset discussions wrestling with these dilemmas. Some ministers insisted that, in our hostile world, Israel could not afford to alienate these friendly governments. These pragmatists insisted that the real conflicts in these countries were local skirmishes: conservatives fighting liberals, not ultranationalists target-ing Jews. Suggesting that the government ignore local politics, they wondered, "Why should we sacrifice Israel's national interests because the political debate in Hungary or Austria or elsewhere has turned toxic between left and right?"

Pointing to the Hungarian ruling party's infamous poster campaign against Soros, I responded, "I believe George Soros is no friend of Israel, putting it mildly. He proudly proclaims that he is not a Zionist. But when the Hungarians shift from attacking his views to attacking his nose, that's an attack on Jews."

Then, appealing to the ministers, I said, "We all correctly expect lib-eral Jews not to be deceived by those who say they love Jews but hate Israel, like Linda Sarsour. Similarly, it's fair for liberal Jews to expect that the Israeli government should not be deceived by those who say they love Israel but hate Jews."

When the New Anti-Semitism started spiking nearly two decades ago, we developed the three Ds to distinguish valid criticism of Israel from anti-Semitic Israel bashing. Now, with new ultranationalist parties fighting liberals, we need criteria tailored to the Right too. We need to see when critics cross the line between legitimate or even toxic attacks on their political opponents, some of whom are Jewish, and Jew-hatred.

Noticing the recurrent tics on that side of the spectrum, I propose three possible criteria: Do they deny the Holocaust or use it against us? Do they try to outlaw Halachah, Jewish legal practices, like circumcision or ritual slaughter? And, more generally, in their political struggles do they deploy any of the historic prejudices against Jews? When criticizing a Jew, an Israeli action, the Jews, or all of Israel, do they resurrect any of the historic libels that have tormented us for centuries, especially claims of Jews being greedy, seeking financial or political hegemony, trying to control the world, being guilty of dual loyalty, lying, cheating, or having big noses, sharp chins, and beady eyes? Gil Troy proposes calling these the four Hs: Holocaust, Halachah, hegemony, and historic libels.

It's depressing to watch so many Jews fall for the anti-Semites' well-known tricks: "I love Jews; I'm only critical of Israel," or "I love Israel; I'm only critical of those cosmopolitan Jews." But we have enough experience to see how the poison flows from one polluted platform to the other. Look at Islamists in France or the Labour Party in England. There, the anti-Zionism and anti-Semitism blur.

Then look to Jew-haters like David Duke of the Ku Klux Klan, with his rants about "ZOG," the supposedly Zionist-occupied government of the United States. This right-wing white supremacist ended up congratulating a left-wing woman of color, Ilhan Omar, the congresswoman of "it's all about the Benjamins" and "allegiance to a foreign country" infamy. Duke saluted her as someone who hates Israel, and thus hates the Jews. Duke and his far-right Klansmen, as well as the crazed gunman who shot up the Chabad of Poway synagogue near San Diego, prove it once again: those who start by hating Jews, end up hating Israel.

OUR URGENT NEED TO UNITE
AGAINST ANTI-SEMITISM

Too many of us are too happy to attack our political opponents' anti-Semitism while overlooking it among our allies. I've heard Israeli ministers and some leaders of major American Jewish organizations scoff at right-wing anti-Semites as "lone wolves" who lack the reach of left-wing BDS activists. I've heard liberals and leaders of other major Jewish organizations dismiss left-wing anti-Semitism as a fringe phenomenon from either mentally unbalanced people or a few overwrought critics of Israel.

When the *New York Times* columnist Bari Weiss condemned left-wing, right-wing, and Islamist anti-Semitism equally, many Twitter bullies mocked her supposed moral equivalence. A review in *Slate* called her thoughtful book *How to Fight Anti-Semitism* "a bizarre and undercooked exercise in rhetorical bothsidesism, in which she argues that American Jews should be just as worried about college students who overzealously criticize Israel as they are about the aspiring Einsatzgruppen who shoot up shuls."

Partisan Jews and mainstream media organizations could not resist this silly sifting between supposedly benign anti-Semites (their allies) and real, malignant anti-Semites (their rivals). In December 2019, the popular conservative columnist Caroline Glick argued that "whereas white supremacists are political orphans," because "progressive, Islamist and black anti-Semites have become powerful actors in the Democratic Party and converge most powerfully" on campuses, they "present the greatest threat to Jewish life in America."

By contrast, and just as predictably, the left-leaning *New York Times* editorialized that month that "the larger threat to American Jews goes beyond college students sparring over Israeli policy: Violent anti-Semitism is being fomented most significantly by white nationalists and the far right."

Such dismissals—including a *Forward* headline claiming "Anti-Semitism on the Right Is the Only Real Threat to Jews"—ignored many inconvenient facts. First, that same *Forward* edition of November 6, 2019, covered the most frequent expressions of anti-Semitic violence in America. It did not come from Far Right haters or left-wing BDS supporters, but from hoodlums who, the day before, had assaulted and chased a number of "Brooklyn Orthodox Jews" in a "series of nighttime attacks." Denouncing those attacks didn't advance any Jewish faction's partisan agenda. In fact, one prominent radical rabbi, Jill Jacobs, tweeted: "The horrible attacks on Orthodox Jews in Brooklyn & elsewhere likely relate to long-term tensions & don't fall easily into left/right category. Not parallel to white nationalists whose beliefs are based on anti-Semitism."

In 240 characters, Jacobs blamed the victims by using code words hinting that Orthodox Jews were generating "tensions," she sounded frustrated that these crimes didn't fit into her Left-Right paradigm, and she ended by claiming that the real threat, the only genuine anti-Semitism worth worrying about, was from "white nationalists." As a result, too many American Jews minimized these street crimes, until December 2019, when the murders in a Jersey City kosher supermarket and the slashings at a Monsey, New York, Hanukkah party drew attention to the problem of Jew-hatred among some African Americans.

While right-wing anti-Semitism riles up neo-Nazis who might kill, left-wing anti-Semitism encourages Palestinian terrorists who kill Israelis far more frequently. But again, beware, even pointing out these facts somehow legitimizes this ridiculous debate. Instead, we should have zero tolerance for all forms of bigotry against everyone, regardless of the target or the source.

Hate is hate. I despise this insulting, distracting, myopic new fight about whether left-wing anti-Semitism or right-wing anti-Semitism is worse. I can't think of a more intellectually hollow, morally shallow, pointless debate today. No one cares that the disgraced Hollywood producer Harvey Weinstein supported liberal causes; his sexism was quite literally criminal. No one asks if a racist is right-wing or left-wing; if you mistreat or pre-judge African Americans, you are racist, period.

In the swamps of hatred, the mud doesn't change colors, it's neither Republican red nor Democratic blue. Selective indignation undermines the righteousness of indignation, emboldening the haters. From up close, when you're experiencing Jew-hatred, it looks and feels the same, regardless of the haters' background or affiliation.

Consider these recent Jew-hating incidents. Did a left-winger or a right-winger tweet out the sick riddle asking, "What's the difference between a Jew and a pizza—the pizza leaves the oven"? Who was guilty of abusing a young Jewish politician in California with cries of "Fire up the oven"? Who photoshopped the face of a Jewish journalist onto the body of an Auschwitz prisoner? Who made a mock album cover for "Set Fire to the Jews" with a distorted picture of the singer Adele as "Adelef Hitler"? Who knocked the kippah off of a fourteen-year-old's head in Brooklyn? The first tweeter was a left-wing BDS supporter. The second online bully was a neo-Nazi. The third was an inflamed far-right Trump supporter. The fourth was a Students for Justice in Palestine activist. And the fifth was just a hoodlum.

I understand the appeal. When Right fights Left and Left fights Right, it confirms our media-shaped view of the world. Partisans feel virtuous, having scored their ideological points. Right-wing anti-Semitism does feel more threatening to liberals, because it threatens their universalistic survival strategy. Similarly, left-wing anti-Zionist anti-Semitism particularly targets Israelis while threatening Zionism's more nationalistic survival strategy.

All this cherry-picking, choosing convenient enemies and excusing annoying allies, is like fighting a grease fire with water. The fire gets crazier and steam shoots up. You fail to make a difference while politicizing something sacred. When conservatives attack progressives, or liberals attack governments they already oppose, they feel good about the political points they score but don't pack much of a punch. Progressives have to fight the anti-Semitism in Black Lives Matter, which artificially links

Gaza with Ferguson; those allied with Donald Trump have to fight the Jew-hatred in the alt-right that led to Charlottesville.

When partisans have the courage to fight from within, the results are impressive. "I am happy to debate Middle East politics or listen to critiques of Israeli policies. But why should criticism of Israel be key to feminism in 2017?" the millennial writer Emily Shire wondered. When she proclaimed in a *New York Times* op-ed, "I see no reason I should have to sacrifice my Zionism for the sake of my feminism," many previously silenced feminists applauded.

By 2019, the hostility toward Jews among some leaders of the Women's March became too blatant to ignore, especially when several of its leaders supported Louis Farrakhan, a crass anti-Semite who compares Jews to termites. Most notably, the #MeToo founder and *Melrose Place* actress Alyssa Milano joined *Will & Grace* star Debra Messing in boycotting the 2019 Women's March. These two anti-Trump actresses felt the march's leaders were too tolerant of an anti-Semitism only occasionally hidden behind anti-Zionism. Milano declared, "Any time that there is any bigotry or anti-Semitism in that respect, it needs to be called out and addressed. I'm disappointed in the leadership of the Women's March that they haven't done it adequately." Once again, many followed.

Similarly, the fight against boycotts on campus has been much more effective when pro-Israel forces from left to right unite, and pro-Israel progressives can speak sincerely, not cynically, about not feeling safe and feeling othered.

At the governmental level, Prime Minister Netanyahu reacted too hesitantly to Hungarian anti-Semitism. But eventually, Bibi explained to Prime Minister Viktor Orbán why those caricatures of George Soros were disturbingly anti-Jewish. When I met Hungary's president János Áder on a Jewish Agency trip in 2018 to Budapest, he told me, "We respect Prime Minister Netanyahu and the state of Israel. When the prime minister explained that some of the rhetoric in Hungary today upset him, we took his concerns very seriously."

True, Orbán's anti-immigrant rhetoric continued, and most Hungarian Jews remain wary of him and his party. But he avoided such blatant anti-Semitic caricatures subsequently and denounced Hungary's collaboration with the Nazis during World War II as a "mistake" and a "sin."

Liberal Jews in Hungary helped launch the fight against the Soros caricatures and Orbán's Jobbik Party's menacing yet subtle approach to

Jews. But many right-wing politicians easily ignore left-wing complaints because there are few votes for conservatives to be found among liberals. When a respected ally weighs in, it counts more heavily.

IS OUR COMMON JOURNEY IN DANGER?

I have experienced many situations that made it clear: a healthier dialogue can help us address our differences while working together. Better teamwork would have helped us deal with the dropping out of Russian Jews or the immigration of the Falash Mura or the growing tension between American Jews and Israelis during the Obama-Netanyahu brawls.

But, today, when it comes to the question of uniting our efforts against all forms of anti-Semitism, I am not just saying that it's nice to have a dialogue or that we've missed some opportunities to solve problems more easily. We face a national emergency. The fact that this renewed Jew-hatred is stirring partisan divisions between us, not creating broad solidarity among us, tests our very willingness to continue our journey together.

At so many searing moments throughout the long Jewish past of enduring hatred and trauma, anti-Semitism has united Jews. When Syrian authorities kidnapped sixty-three Jewish children during the Damascus Blood Libel, when the French government framed Alfred Dreyfus as a traitor, when the Russian press accused Menahem Mendel Beilis of draining the blood of a Christian Ukrainian boy, Jews of all stripes rallied together, recognizing our common enemy. We were never alone because they never left us alone. But today, with Jew-hatred spiking left and right and going mainstream, our partisan affiliations often blind us to the threats next door.

Anti-Semitism has often been the last bond linking us to our history. It was the great Jewish pressure cooker, throwing us together whether we liked it or not. In my Soviet childhood, my Jewish identity was a dead one. Like a dead language, it existed on paper—in my identity card—without any practical use. Yet, while reading the classics, every mention of anti-Semitism I stumbled across, from William Shakespeare's Shylock to Lion Feuchtwanger's *Jew Süss*, felt like a message in a bottle sent directly to me. It was one more reminder that I belonged to this ancient people and was still targeted by this ancient hatred. I sympathized with these heroes on paper while identifying with them too.

Now, sixty years later, if we cannot even recognize the anti-Semitism targeting the other half of our people, in real time, right now, if our passing political differences somehow wipe out thousands of years of camaraderie and instinctive alarm signals, then our common journey together really is in doubt.

The French philosopher Jean-Paul Sartre claimed in 1946, "The anti-Semite makes the Jew." What he said was true if your identity is as dead as it was for me in the Soviet Union. There, anti-Semites did keep Jews aware of our Jewishness. In that vacuum, we sought solidarity to defend ourselves physically as we desperately sought to assimilate successfully—making Sartre essentially correct.

But when I discovered Israel, history, and the Jewish people, I went far beyond this defensiveness. By embracing my Jewish heritage, I resurrected my identity. A constructive Jewish identity is proactive, not reactive—it's not just about physical survival.

The Jew makes the Jew. That's how I found my extended Jewish family. And that's how I realized what the real answer is to anti-Semitism. The best response to Jew-hatred is not to run away from Judaism but to be a Jew, in every way possible. Joining the dialogue with your people and building partnerships with them in a mutual journey turns your identity from dead to alive.

The Jewish Agency has a project called Partnership. It began in 1994 as Project P2K, building up to the year 2000. P2K became a platform for many cross-Atlantic, people-to-people initiatives, from hands-on projects in welfare and medicine to more ideological seminars on Jewish identity and our people's future. It is now known as the Partnership2Gether peoplehood platform, or simply Partnership.

When I led the Jewish Agency, I noticed that we had no partnerships with the communities in Russia. They lacked the organizational infrastructure that made it easier to link Boston with Haifa, or Montreal with Beersheba. That's why we started twinning schools. We began by linking three Jewish schools in Russia with three in Israel. To our pleasant surprise, it became the hottest ticket in the Israel-Diaspora partnership business. Today, the Global School Twinning Network facilitates over 720 school-to-school interactions, with 1,440 educators involved in teacher-to-teacher programs that reach 28,000 schoolkids, who regularly share their thoughts, hopes, and concerns.

This small project initiates students into the Jewish dialogue. There are many other such programs, including new ones I keep hearing about in Jerusalem encouraging dialogue between ultra-Orthodox and secular Israelis. These efforts reflect great wisdom about uniting by talking. The message is clear: it's best to start building this sense of extended family from an early age.

21

IMAGINE A DIALOGUE OF ONE, A DIALOGUE OF US

Amid so many serious disagreements in today's partisan environment, we're programmed to see cracks and overlook bonds. Even on June 25, 2017, when Netanyahu scotched the Kotel deal and the newspapers shouted "rupture" and "divorce," the commonalities that have kept us together persisted, along with many welcome new ones. That sobering night, when the board of governors seethed about Bibi's betrayal, Gil Troy's son Yoni went out across town to the Shuk, Jerusalem's open-air Machane Yehuda market. He reported in frustration that he could not find a seat, or buy a drink, or eat a snack anywhere.

Why? Because a record number of young American Jews were visiting Israel that summer and building ties, thanks mostly to Taglit-Birthright. Most of them described Israel in two words: "AWE-SOME!" Moreover, despite the justified fury of rabbis and intellectuals about Bibi's Western Wall betrayal, when *amcha*, the people—meaning most Birthright participants, most American Jewish tourists—visit the Kotel, they consider it the spiritual highlight of their trip, and often their lives.

We love to focus on the loudest, angriest extremists who denounce Israel. Nevertheless, poll after poll shows that three-quarters of American Jews agree that a thriving Israel is vital for the Jewish future. The Israeli results and global results are even higher. Jews all over the world visit Israel regularly, while many more exude pride in the traditions, values, and ideas that have kept the Jewish people alive and have contributed to the betterment of humanity in so many ways. The state of Israel was founded to rally every Jewish community together, inviting every Jew to participate in this shared adventure.

It's trite but true: we are family. We don't want to see the Jewish people splinter into disconnected fragments, and it's not just because we don't want Jewish history ending on our watch.

So, are we converging or diverging? In truth, pollsters can tweak questions to uncover more empathy or distrust, more tension or warmth, more estrangement or connection. Two processes are occurring simultaneously. Between Israel and Diaspora Jewry, anger and alienation coexist with cooperation and communication. It's a mistake to underestimate the daily frustrations or the deep bonds.

The bad news (signs of divergence) is countered by good news (interdependence). But the danger is that the good news might contain elements of the bad: this intimacy generates new, often disruptive, demands. As with a spouse—or a cellmate—the more you come to rely on one another, the more intensely you scrutinize each other.

As we've seen, when American Jews started turning to Israel to solve their identity problems, Israel's slighting of the non-Orthodox branches of Judaism suddenly stung more deeply and caused great resentment. In parallel, as Israelis continued relying on American Jews to help them fight boycott threats and UN sanctions, American Jewish criticism of Israel's policies became more pointed and more resented by those criticized. Thus, the new interdependence raises the emotional stakes and escalates minor irritations, especially when mismanaged, into major breaches. If divergence has propelled the two communities further apart in a spiral of distrust—even, some fear, to the point of no return—convergence, wholly welcome in itself but operating at a higher speed and a faster rate than in the past, raises its own risks of collision and damage.

Whether you are optimistic about the Jewish communal future or pessimistic, one thing should be clear: we need a better, more sustained, more substantive dialogue. At the height of the Kotel crisis, amid the usual confusion and anger and frustration that week, amid all the harsh, hurtful words we're so good at piling up, Gil asked me who my enemy was. That week, he was thinking of many suspects. I blurted out instinctively, "Arrogance." This sense, from so many battle stations, that we know better than you, that we chose a better path than you for Jewish survival and therefore don't need you anymore, is poisonous yet spreading throughout the Jewish world.

DRAWING JEWISH PEOPLEHOOD
FROM THREE PERSPECTIVES

More and more, I hear a question I've rarely heard before. Concerned Jews in Israel and the Diaspora are asking: Do we today share a common commitment to be one people, to continue our historic journey together?

Fortunately, I don't have to rely on bendable statistics or fancy theories to sense our peoplehood power. My confidence in our shared future comes from the fact that at this point in my life, I've had an opportunity to view the relations among the Jewish people from three perspectives: the Soviet Gulag, the Israeli government, and the Jewish Agency. My old technical drafting teacher was right—looking from three dimensions captures depth.

When you are in the Israeli government, you're working with politicians who think around the clock about serving their electorate. That, after all, is in the job description, and it is the way for every politician in a democracy to get reelected. Yet, in Israel, these same politicians also invest a lot of time dealing with people who are not citizens of their country and have no voting rights: namely, Diaspora Jews.

Over the last twenty years, despite complaints that Israelis don't care, and amid great pressure to cut unnecessary budget items, Israeli governments have invested more and more money in strengthening Diaspora Jews' identity and communities. In addition to subsidizing Israel experience programs and educational projects abroad, the Israeli government hit a remarkable milestone during my eighth year at the Jewish Agency. The government's subvention dwarfed the North American Federations' contributions to such programs for the first time ever. Israel is now the most generous funder of Diaspora-related Jewish Agency projects, further defying the pessimists.

There's a broad Israeli consensus here. Despite our differences, the members of every Zionist party in Israel agree that every Jew in the world should consider Israel home. That makes dealing with Diaspora Jewry not just part of every politician's mandate, but preserving and protecting the Jewish people remain broadly recognized as central to the state's mission.

While chairing the Jewish Agency, when I looked through the Diaspora's lens, I noted an internal Jewish glue that keeps us together. Even though many Jews criticize Israel harshly, the vast majority know they need Israel if they want to continue the Jewish journey. Some walk away. But most, especially in the last twenty years, have recognized that, unless they are ultra-Orthodox, Israel is the best medium for connecting to their Jewish roots, building their Jewish identity, and giving their grandchildren a shot at remaining Jewish. As I often explain, Jewish tradition and Israel serve as the only functional brakes against assimilation, and it's most effective to use both together.

Finally, examining Israel-Diaspora relations from a more bird's-eye perspective is reassuring. Crises clarify it all. Just as we all fought for Soviet Jewish freedom, when Israel is at war, the Jewish people come together, instinctively. Jews from all over the world put their differences aside, ignore their personal agendas, and mobilize. Suddenly, we are all from Odessa, we are all from Jerusalem, and we were all together at Mount Sinai.

From my experience, putting all three perspectives together—Israel's ongoing concern and growing investment, the Diaspora's new commitment to identity building through Israel, and our shared commitment to the Jewish journey—shows something profound. True, we sometimes seem to be one people divided by one religion. And sometimes we seem to be one people divided by one state. But we remain one people.

Despite the internal bickering, most Jews continue to see themselves as Jews—as a part of a people, worried about growing apart. All these fights, all these Israel-Diaspora flash points, therefore, are warning signs.

JOINING THE JEWISH CONVERSATION

Clearly, not everyone is going to have the kinds of experiences I and others have had that provide all three perspectives. But if becoming too imprisoned in one perspective produces arrogance, how can people broaden their worldviews? Here's where I believe that yelling and screaming helps. Ironically, by jumping into heated, no-holds-barred debate, I have frequently ended up appreciating how deeply committed my sparring partners were to our common goals too. Often, trying to convince others you are right exposes your commitment to maintaining this dialogue and keeping this people going.

These days we rely too much on media that emphasizes our differences and squelches real exchanges: news headlines, Twitter wars, snarky Facebook postings. Today's cancel culture suggests that if you disagree with me, it's over, you're out—even if we're fellow citizens in the same democracy.

By contrast, Jewish tradition teaches that disagreement can be a way of staying in, even if we are spread among the four corners of the universe. It's a "can sell" culture, pressing others as an act of faith in them. We agree to disagree on some matters, only because we agree to agree on some fundamentals, starting with our shared sense of belonging to the Jewish people. Like all voluntary memberships, the Jewish community survives as a dialogue of one, meaning that it persists because we consider ourselves part of the same people. It's also a dialogue of us, because when we disagree, we don't just screech "Traitor! Now you're one of them." Instead, we start to fight.

DEBATING PRESSING QUESTIONS CONTINUES OUR JEWISH JOURNEY

While specializing in belonging through battling, Jews are also pretty good at getting to the very big ideas by going very small. That's the Talmud's bait and switch—so many debates look so trivial, but they ricochet between the picayune and the profound. Similarly, in a functional, substantive, expansive Jewish people's forum, what might start as a dialogue regarding practical, concrete issues can help clarify the big underlying challenges we face in continuing our mutual journey.

When I began my journey with the Jewish people in the Soviet Union, I faced the specific questions I described in this book's opening chapters. Should I join the *kulturniki* or *politiki*? Should the struggle to free Soviet Jewry be the struggle to come to Israel or to leave the Soviet Union? Should I only fight for Soviet Jewry or for human rights more broadly? These questions seemed all-consuming in the moment and deeply rooted in that time and that place. But in fact, these questions were the tip of the iceberg. They brought me into the defining challenges of Jewish life today that continue to spark our ongoing debates.

The split between the *kulturniki* and the *politiki*, which first struck me as a petty argument fueled by fragile egos, was much bigger than that. It was yet another version of the profound and still ongoing debate about Zionism and Jewish culture. Today, the central question is "To what extent does the newly emerging Israeli identity depend on traditional Jewish identity?"

Our intense arguments about dropouts—about whether Israel and the Jewish people should support only those Soviet Jews who went to Israel or Jewish emigration in general—seemed to revolve around the value we placed on free will. But with time, and as I assumed different roles within the Jewish journey, I saw that, too, as part of a bigger question: "To what extent does Jewish identity depend on a connection with Israel?"

I started combining my Zionist activism with my activism as a dissident because of my enthusiasm for my newfound freedom and identity. I wanted to pursue both. With time, I came to see that the centrality of this connection went far beyond my personal experience. In joining the argument about balancing liberty and identity, I was participating in the bigger debate about the nature of Israel as a democratic Jewish state among the nations and the Western debate about liberalism and nationalism.

Though I spent my life seeking answers for specific spin-offs of these big questions, I realized something else was going on too. Ultimately, I have learned that, as important as the answers are, the act of questioning is also critical to keeping us in conversation with one another. The circumstances of this eternal conversation change all the time. Our answers must change with them, within limits. But it is the conversation itself, about our historic national and spiritual agenda, that keeps us connected, dynamic, and alive.

That's why, decades after I first heard the anti-Semitic joke about the Jews surviving the *Titanic* by talking, I still appreciate its wisdom. Participating in the ongoing debate about who we are and what we can be is the best guarantee that we will continue our journey together.

IMAGINE A GLOBAL JEWISH COUNCIL

There's a general recognition that we need better frameworks for constructive dialogue. We have seen the deep thirst for better people-to-people interactions. But there's little consensus about just what format might work. One interesting idea to improve our back-and-forth on the communal scale, which has been bandied about in different forums for years, is some kind of a Jewish people's parliament, a Global Jewish Council.

Israel's parliament meets three times a year. Imagine convening three-day sessions of a Global Jewish Council before each Knesset seating. Imagine delegates from Israel and around the Jewish world debating all proposed laws that the Knesset legal advisers have determined might affect Diaspora interests, with the council issuing nonbinding advisory opinions. Imagine mandating the Knesset to require a special supermajority before passing any laws the parliament agreed might harm Diaspora Jewish interests. This approach would invite those fighting the BDS boycott movement on the front lines in universities and elsewhere to weigh in before Israel passed any BDS-related legislation. It would encourage representatives of the Jewish nation throughout the world to voice their opinions on a nation-state-type bill. It might not change the outcome, but speaking up might cut down on frustrations and reduce our rivals' constant attacks.

In parallel, these delegates would also debate any significant Diaspora Jewish organizations' decisions that might affect Israeli interests, with any potential Knesset resistance being respected enough to require a second look.

Imagine a security committee briefing Diaspora leaders, offering an inside perspective on Israel's security dilemmas and moral choices by interacting with Israel's decision makers, not its PR flacks. Imagine a foreign aid committee launching cutting-edge, unifying *tikkun olam* projects to genuinely improve the world. An education committee could ask tough questions about education in Israel and the Diaspora: Why did American Jewish day schools abandon Hebrew? Why do Israeli schools teach so little about Diaspora Jewry? Why doesn't anyone do a better job teaching Zionism?

Consider how much good a meaningful intercommunal dialogue could accomplish—even without much decision-making power, which would take time to develop. Jews throughout the world could focus on two shared, overlapping goals: maintaining Jewish continuity in each community while keeping Israel secure, stable, and democratic. Rather than accusing one another of violating core Jewish values, we could develop joint projects expressing common visions. The resulting honest, substantive, and meaningful conversation at the heart of the Jewish community could result in fewer Jews taking refuge from Establishment groupthink in marginal or hostile organizations or simply drifting away.

Imagine finally addressing one of the central Jewish frustrations of our time. Instead of enjoying the classic democratic privilege of granting the consent of the governed, both Israeli and American Jews feel burdened by the responsibility of the implicated, saddled with defending positions and actions they don't understand by other Jews living far away from them. The result is too many interactions degenerating into mutual accusations and feelings of betrayal. A redrawn Jewish social contract could better explain why we are connected and what kinds of responsibilities follow. Rather than calling it consent of the governed, call it "belonging to the tribe," emphasizing the advisory, voluntary, yet covenantal nature of the relationship. If Jews better understood why we are involved with one another and had input on at least some big decisions through the council, frustrations would diminish.

Right now, our competing survival strategies risk pulling us apart—even blinding us to common enemies, who don't care if we are conservative or liberal when they call us "kikes" or "oven kindling." A healthy dialogue could tap into these different survival strategies to create more resilient approaches, with Isaiahans helping us speak to the universalists and Davidians helping us speak to the particularists.

We could, for example, build a coalition against the delegitimization of Israel by intertwining the liberal and nationalist arguments, as we did during the should-there-be-a-Jewish-state UN debate in 1947, rather than helping our enemies pit the Jewish Left against the Jewish Right. We could reexamine conversion courses, trying to make them more appealing to non-Jewish spouses while making sure that all rabbis teach about Jewish history and Jewish peoplehood, not just Jewish religion, ritual, and spirituality. We could try developing a combined curriculum, teaching Jews all over the world about the history of the Jewish people. And we could encourage moderates, rather than allowing the polarizing media to pit the loudest, shrillest Israeli politicians and Diaspora activists against each other.

Imagine, if our alienated campus radicals at least had somewhere they could feel heard, and if their embarrassed pro-Israel peers had a place committed to helping them debate these issues. Consider how much better the anguished debate about the Western Wall might have been if it had been conducted with the transparency and inclusiveness of a well-established global body. Similarly, rather than just whining about the intermarriage epidemic, Israelis and Diaspora Jews could brainstorm together about effective educational and spiritual strategies for building a robust Jewish future. We could try solving problems together rather than judging each other as failures.

We won't fix everything, but we could start addressing some issues in healthier ways. And, yes, we could afford to let it get ugly. In fact, it would have to degenerate. Our long, loud history as a people is bound to continue.

In a Jewish education committee, American Jews might cry "Hypocrite!" and accuse Israel's nationalist government of endorsing a global Jewish education for all without subsidizing it. Israelis might say it right back, quoting studies that show that even free Jewish education would only attract 20 percent of the community, adding that American Jews are more into padding their kids' CVs than deepening their Jewish identities.

Fighting on a different dimension, making alliances that transcend countries of origin, conservatives would no doubt cry "Traitor!" They would be furious that liberals are blind to left-wing anti-Zionists who claim to love Jews while demonizing the Jewish state. Liberals would shout it back, outraged that conservatives, including Israel's government, hobnob with right-wing ultranationalists who claim to love the Jewish state while demonizing the Jews. Perhaps, once the shouting ended, we could focus on explaining the criteria we have developed for clear red lines, uniting us all in a zero-tolerance policy toward anti-Semites, no matter how personally charming or politically useful they might appear to be.

Some might ask, "What's the use? What's the point in having us gather and yell at one another? We live in a world with too much noise already. Can such debates ever yield solutions?"

Our rich history of great Jewish congresses in the nineteenth and twentieth centuries offers encouragement. By arguing over our positions more formally and systematically, we sometimes reach compromises, as we did at the early Zionist congresses and the Brussels Conference on Soviet Jewry. One of these gold-standard conversations created the Jewish state, despite sometimes murderous rivalries; the other kept our squabbling movement focused on "let my people go."

Failing something on that scale, we can at least try building community consensus regarding which directions are worth exploring and which ones are dead ends. That was my great takeaway from the Ne'eman Committee's framework. It helped us keep living with our disagreements while establishing the parameters of debate.

Similarly, for all the frustrations around the Kotel battle, the years-long dialogue established useful groundwork for an eventual solution. We narrowed the field of expectations from all sides. When the political situation changes, we will be all set with blueprints detailing a prayer space, which is already functioning but just needs improved access and authorization.

Looking back over my life since joining the Jewish people, I imagine that an ongoing, constructive dialogue like this could have helped during many key moments. Sometimes the dialogue didn't occur because people said, "We have nothing to talk about." Sometimes there was no forum to address the issue. With regular, obligatory, formal discussions, the outcomes wouldn't have been perfect, but they would have been much improved.

There are barrels full of practical questions about this forum as well: who would vote, how would they vote, who could run, just how would decisions be made, and, most important, who would represent the different voices of Diaspora Jewry in this forum? I am often asked, as the outgoing chair, "What about the Jewish Agency?" In fact, an informal dialogue exists between the board of governors and Knesset members. Moreover, the Jewish Agency created what is now the largest caucus in the Knesset, the Friends of Diaspora Jewry.

We could indeed use the Jewish Agency and the Knesset to get this forum started. But in the Jewish organizational world, the best way to kill a new initiative is to start arguing about who gets to sit at the table. As a first step, let's accept the principle, then flesh out the concept. We can yell about the details and personnel soon enough.

RETIRING FROM THE JEWISH AGENCY

As I completed eight years at the Jewish Agency, the board of governors, as well as the prime minister, asked me to serve another four-year term. I thanked them for their faith in me, but I believe that democracy requires renewal and replacement. Twelve years would be too much. I agreed to serve another year as we sought a successor. That addition pleased the mathematician in me, as my nine years in the Gulag and nine years in Israeli politics ended with nine years at the Jewish Agency. Such symmetry allowed me to make my crowd-pleasing one-liner: that having served for nine years in each, I didn't know where I suffered most.

When I passed the torch to my successor, Isaac "Bougie" Herzog, I gave him one piece of advice. I said, "To enjoy your job, not only for nine years but even for one minute, you have to answer one question: Do you love the Jewish people? I don't like hours-long conference calls on cutting programs and managing the bureaucracy of Israel and the Jewish world. But I love our projects and meeting with their participants. You have to enjoy the feeling of being an emissary of the Jewish people and building bridges between Israel and the Diaspora."

Do you love the Jewish people? What does the question mean? Well, for starters, while it is true that the head of the Jewish Agency is never alone, it often felt that I was never at home. I made over fifty trips overseas in my nine years at the Jewish Agency, traveling more than two million miles to dozens of communities in over twenty countries. When we had conference calls in Jerusalem with our emissaries, we could joke that the sun never sets on the Jewish people, with our Australians nine hours ahead of us and our Californians ten hours behind.

When I retired, I felt like I had earned an El Al captain's stripes. Instead I received a model El Al airplane with 207,188 on it, the number of people who immigrated to Israel during my years at the Jewish Agency. I wondered just how many of them I had greeted at the airport. I never tired of coming to the arrivals terminal, no matter how early in the morning or late at night. Every time I saw a new immigrant walk down those stairs onto Israeli soil, I would start thinking about how many generations of prayers and hopes were standing behind that particular *oleh*. I would try imagining just how big a historical and personal circle each new arrival was closing.

The leader of the Jewish Agency has to get a kick out of going to conferences with young emissaries, who became more and more numerous each year and also somehow younger and younger. It's important to enjoy talking with them deep into the night then dancing in a circle with them, around and around, and to enjoy debriefing them when they return to Israel, as they join a unique group of Israelis who can present both worlds.

The government kindly acknowledged our programs' successes. Although the Jewish Agency criticized official Israeli policies as never before over the Western Wall and other matters, the government's budget for our programs nevertheless increased as never before.

JEWS LOOK DIFFERENT TODAY
IN MY HOMETOWN

Sometimes, a moment catapults you from the day-to-day, so you can see some grand logic in your life, closing some circle in a way you didn't quite anticipate but makes sense when it happens.

The town where I was born, Donetsk, did not fare well in the post-Communist years. When I was growing up, what was supposed to be the unbreakable bond between Russians and Ukrainians was symbolized by all the propaganda hailing the unity of the Soviet people. But Donetsk ended up in the middle of the prolonged war between Russia and Ukraine. By the time I started chairing the Jewish Agency, the situation in the area had turned desperate.

Trying to help Jews caught in the war zone, we ended up establishing a refugee center just outside Dnipropetrovsk, now called Dnipro, a few hours' drive from Donetsk.

On one of my visits there, a man approached me in my hotel. "You're Sharansky, yes?" he asked.

"Yes."

"You're the head of the Jewish Agency."

"Yes."

"And you were born in Donetsk," he stated.

Again I nodded, not sure what was coming.

"Me too," he said. "We in Donetsk are very critical of your work."

Really? I was surprised. Usually, as we traveled around this broken region, to the extent people noticed us, they thanked us for helping out however we could.

He said, "I'm not Jewish. We're all suffering too. No one's coming to take me away from this nightmare and to give me a better life. We're all alone here. Only Jews are getting telephone calls from your organization. Only Jews receive invitations to emigrate to another country and get help to move on top of that. So only Jews have somewhere to go. Is that fair? Why are you people singled out?"

Of course I could have told this man a lot about the many Jewish philanthropists and organizations helping the needy all over the world, including the victims of the Russia-Ukraine conflict. But I didn't feel that he wanted a lecture at that moment. He was in trouble. Alas, despite the collapse of the Soviet Union, despite siding with Ukraine against Russia, this man did what people with problems did in the good old days of the Soviet Union: he resurrected the old anti-Semitic paradigm viewing Jews as clannish, as only looking out for ourselves.

But instead of correcting this throwback to Soviet days, I was too busy absorbing the irony of our interaction. "My God," I thought. "That's quite a change from my childhood." Back then, to be outed as Jewish in Donetsk was the worst thing that could happen to you. When someone linked you with the fifth line, outing you as a Jew on your identity card, it meant only one thing: you belonged to the one outcast group. It was a disease without cure, a sentence to a life without hope, an invitation to be pitied because there was no one to help us. Now, that word "Jew" meant that not only someone had your back, but that there was a proud people and democratic state behind you.

"Thank you for telling me this," I said. I was thanking him for reminding me how the world had changed, how Israel had empowered the Jewish people, how that empowerment involved building ourselves up so we could benefit others, and that when you belong to the Jewish people you are never alone.

EPILOGUE

The Israel-Diaspora Chessboard

A punishment cell is a small, dark, cold place where there is no one to speak to, nothing to read, nothing to touch, and almost nothing to eat. Soviet law decreed that no prisoner should be left in the *kartser* for more than fifteen days in a row. Any longer was considered too dangerous to the individual's psyche.

But when the KGB wanted to break a political prisoner, there were no limits. They could keep you in for fifteen days and another fifteen and another fifteen. My longest stretch was 130 days in a row. And I spent 405 days in punishment cells in total.

My aim while inside was to survive mentally and physically while refusing to surrender. So I played chess in my head. I played one game after another, thousands of games. The good news is I always won. In each game, I would identify with one side and try to beat my opponent. I would check all the options that might work for me and consider which ones were reasonable for my opponent.

When the game was finished, I turned the board around in my head and became the opponent. Now I was trying to follow the rival strategy. Each time, I realized there were more and more opportunities for both sides. I had more than enough time to test each possibility. After all, I was not in a hurry—the longer, the better.

In a real game against an opponent, the aim is to win. Here, my aim was to survive. In this game, I was white but would be black in ten minutes. So, after a few hundred games, there was no difference between white and black, all these pieces were my allies in one mutual struggle for survival.

That's how I feel about the dynamics between Israel and the Jews of the Diaspora. Against true enemies like the KGB—or Iran's regime, Hamas, or Hezbollah—we play to win. We take no prisoners and make no compromises. But when we are involved in the debate between Israel and the Diaspora on either side, we are not looking for victory. We are seeking ways to continue our journey together in our dialogue of one—understanding that even when we take two different sides of an issue, we remain part of one people.

It happens again and again. I turn the board around in the middle of a dispute. I try to understand the logic of the other side. Like a good yeshiva student, I seek the *chidush*, the innovation, the new idea—not to beat my opponent but as an opportunity for us all to move ahead.

In a community, we understand there will always be tensions, there will always be struggle. But we want to continue the joint journey through history, and I feel I belong to both camps, to both sides, to both Israel and the Diaspora. At the same time, we also make different choices, live different lives, and play different roles. Having each other's backs does not require speaking in the same voice.

In 2003, I published an article in *Commentary*, "On Hating the Jews." I analyzed the common link underlying different types of anti-Semitism in different countries and civilizations over the millennia. I noticed that Jews have always stood against the tide. We are forever the other, the perpetual dissidents. We were monotheists in the ancient pagan world and unrepentant heretics in the Christian and Muslim worlds. In enlightened Europe's modernizing world, we were traditionalists to some and ultramodernists to others, and, of course, we were Rothschilds and Marxes, both the ultimate capitalists and the ultimate Communists. In the Purim story, the evil Haman sums it up, saying, "There is a certain people scattered and dispersed among the people in all the provinces of your kingdom, and their laws are different from those of other peoples, and the king's laws they do not keep, so that it is of no benefit for the king to tolerate them."

Haman is just one of many enemies over the millennia who justifies his Jew-hatred by emphasizing the Jews' exasperating separateness, their rejection of the majority's customs and moral concepts. This separateness, this catalyzing readiness to be countercultural and think unconventionally, explains why the Jews became what Leo Tolstoy called "pioneers of culture" and "pioneers of freedom."

Today, we Jews stand against two powerful tides sweeping the world. One is the tide of illiberal liberalism. It speaks in the name of universal human rights, but in its extreme form denies the value of a nation-state while seeing Israel as the last remnant of colonialism. But Israel, the democratic nation-state of the Jewish people, insists that its strong bottom-up grassroots national identity, consecrated by the will of the people, gives it the strength to be the only island of democracy in the Middle East.

Opposing illiberal liberalism is also the tide of the new nationalism, which appeals to a lost sense of national pride and helps to mobilize the energy citizens get from belonging. But it, in its extreme form, is illiberal. Most members of the progressive Jewish community oppose this extreme, insisting that their strong liberal society preserves their Jewish identity.

Each community is doing what it does naturally to survive. But when the Jewish world works together, as a Jewish democratic state in the Middle East and as a constellation of minority Jewish communities in Western democracies, we can bring out the best in each other. Benefiting from the best of liberalism and the best of nationalism, together we can champion the joint mission to belong and to be free as both central to human happiness. This synthesis could also help moderate some of the extremes afflicting the West and affecting each of us in our respective communities today. This approach requires a conceptual leap in all societies, accepting that we are complementary, not carbon copies of one another.

Perhaps my obsession with dialogue as a tool for survival is overcompensation for my years of silence in the Gulag, despite having been nicknamed by my older brother "a bloody chatterbox" when we were kids. No matter how lonely I might have seemed to be in my punishment cell, I survived by knowing I had not been abandoned by my people. We will continue as long as we all know that the balancing act goes on, the commitment persists, and the dialogue survives, guaranteeing that once you are a part of the Jewish debate, you are never alone.

THAT UNIVERSAL DESIRE TO BELONG
AND BE FREE

Avital keeps asking me, "When are you going to retire?" I reply, "I did retire, in 2018." She responds, "I didn't notice."

I admit, chairing the Jewish Agency's Shlichut Institute for emissaries, chairing ISGAP (the Institute for the Study of Global Antisemitism and Policy), teaching, lecturing, and writing this book was keeping me a bit busy.

But one day, it all stopped. First, there were no trips abroad. Then, the lectures were canceled. Finally, I didn't even have permission to leave the house—or see my grandchildren.

Relatively early in the coronavirus crisis, when the first Jewish schools closed in New York, the head of one of them, Rabbi Joshua Lookstein— the son of my old comrade in arms Rabbi Haskel Lookstein—asked me to speak via Zoom to students and parents from three of the schools. The topic was how to cope with isolation.

Within days, I had a new gig—as a self-help guru. Shut-ins from Alaska to Australia were asking me for advice. At first, it seemed absurd, even obscene. How could my experience of playing chess in my head in my punishment cell compare to being cooped up in gadget-filled homes wired to the Internet—with computer chess—especially because this isolation is imposed to protect people, not break them?

But it appeared that when people's plans are disrupted, when their long-planned vacations are canceled, when their dreams are undermined, their career plans put on hold, and their movements dramatically disrupted, they often spiral downward. Their feelings of disappointment, fueled by uncertainty, often grow into anger, then fear: What will be with my dreams? What will be with my life? What's happening to my world?

That's something that's familiar to me.

In mid-March 2020, my successor at the Jewish Agency, Bougie Herzog, asked me to summarize the five tips I kept giving in a three-minute YouTube clip. Essentially, my message was that, while sitting alone in your home against your will and following rigid restrictions, you should:

- First, remember that you are a soldier in a bigger struggle, and you have an important role to play in determining whether we win or lose.

- Second, don't try controlling what you can't control—focus on what you can control. You cannot control when this craziness will finish, but, in the meantime, you can take on ambitious plans to challenge yourself. Learn a new language. Read that thick book. Clean your closets—or finally build that new one. Don't let corona bring you to despair.

- Third, don't stop laughing at yourself and the world—it puts everything in proportion.

- Fourth, use your hobbies, like I used chess. This is your time to enjoy life.

- Fifth, always remember that you are part of something bigger than yourself.

Surprisingly, this short clip went viral, reaching so many people all over the world within a few days that it made me wonder why even bother writing this book. After all, the conclusion of this book boils down to the same rule: to have a full, interesting, meaningful life, you have to figure out how to be connected enough to defend your freedom and free enough to protect your identity.

AUTHORS' NOTE

This book, written jointly, uses the life of one man to teach something we both have learned through our different life stories. Both of us have learned that we benefit individually and collectively by entering a dialogue of one, by leveraging our disagreements to keep us as one people. To make our point, this book focuses on the dialogue between Israel and the Jewish people living in communities dispersed throughout the world.

Every story in this book retells an episode from Natan's life about this dialogue, which is why we wrote it in his voice. And, just as in a movie about a villain you inevitably end up sympathizing with, in this book, with stories revolving around Natan, we inevitably ended up sympathizing with him. Still, we analyzed each incident through the prisms of our different backgrounds and experiences.

Every English sentence in this book was written by Gil. But together, we weighed and played with every word and every idea, again and again, sometimes in Hebrew, usually in English, with occasional lapses of Natan into Russian and Gil into professor-speak.

Natan was born into Communist dictatorship in a town called Stalino in 1948; Gil was born into American freedom in Queens, New York, during John F. Kennedy's presidency. Most of the years Natan was surviving in prison, Gil was studying history at Harvard. Despite our vastly different backgrounds, we come to similar conclusions. Israeli Jews and Diaspora Jews live different realities. But most of us want to continue our journey together.

In a healthy dialogue, we challenge each other while looking out for one another. That can teach us what Natan learned during nine years in prison and Gil learned when marching on the streets of New York and Boston to free him. This dialogue is rooted in a 3,900-year-old Jewish conversation balancing the two basic human desires to belong and to be free, now brought to life in the decades-long Zionist debate. Today, that spirited dialogue can help us resist those who deny the validity of nationalism and those who deny the values of liberalism. Getting that balance right is not only important to us as Jews and as Zionists, but to all citizens cherishing human rights throughout the world.

ACKNOWLEDGMENTS

We are both deeply grateful for all the help we have received in writing this book—and are also grateful that each of us can blame the other for any remaining flaws.

Natan feels extremely guilty that there are so many people who helped shape each nine-year period of his life whom he could not single out for thanks in this volume—it would have doubled the book's size, at least. That doesn't mean they weren't important to him or are not remembered. The many, many omissions confirm our claim that this book isn't a comprehensive life and times, but a series of snapshots from one life to make the broader point about our people, the power of community, and the value of dialogue.

Over the course of this collaborative writing project, cherished friends and relatives read the manuscript and offered critical feedback. We thank them in alphabetical order: Linda Adams, David Cape, Rachel Sharansky Danziger, Yossi Klein Halevi, Roman Polonsky, Aviv Troy, Dina Troy, Tevi Troy, Hanna Sharansky Waller, and Noam Zion. Dina Kirshner assisted with fact-checking while Zemira Wolfe-Solomont, Vera Golovensky, and Larissa Ruthman helped in countless ways.

We salute the inimitable David Suissa, editor in chief of the *Los Angeles Jewish Journal*, for brainstorming with Gil about a book title. Our working title was "999," but titles shouldn't be inside jokes. Gil was describing how year after year the KGB told Natan that he was forgotten and abandoned in the Gulag, but he knew he was never alone. "That's it," David exclaimed. "You've got your title. After seventy-five years of 'never again,' we must remember that when you belong to the Jewish people, you are 'never alone.'" We also salute another legendary editor, Neal Kozodoy, of *Mosaic*, who edited our July 2018 essay, "Can American and Israeli Jews Stay Together as One People?" Neal's characteristically thoughtful challenges and excellent stylistic suggestions sharpened our thinking at a critical point in our project, while helping us focus on the broader theme of dialogue, having made our pitch in *Mosaic* for a Global Jewish Council. We also thank the respondents to the piece.

Special thanks to Natan's superb previous coauthors, whose intellectual fingerprints are all over this book, Ambassador Ron Dermer and Professor Shira Wolosky Weiss. Thanks to Steve Linde of the *Jerusalem Report* for permission to quote extensively from some of Natan's earlier articles, especially describing the exodus of Ethiopian Jews.

While this book is the result of a three-year collaboration between Natan and Gil that began in Jerusalem, its publication culminates a four-decade criminal conspiracy between Natan and our publisher Peter Osnos that began in Soviet Russia. In the mid-1970s, Peter was the *Washington Post*'s correspondent in Moscow and an essential pipeline for Natan, along with many other Refuseniks and dissidents—to the annoyance of Russia's secret police. Their friendship has produced one arrest, one near-arrest, stacks of KGB files, and now four books—once Peter was kind enough to shift from journalism to publishing so this criminal collaboration boosting the capitalist countries could continue.

As the founder of PublicAffairs and now a consultant to Hachette Book Group, Peter Osnos has mastered the editor's art of giving his authors just enough room to develop their own voices, while always reassuring them that they, too, are never alone. The always insightful Clive Priddle, publisher of PublicAffairs, once again served as a masterful editor and visionary for one of Natan's books. Beyond this dynamic duo, the crackerjack team that shepherded this book to publication included Clive's editorial assistant Anupama Roy-Chaudhury, a publishing rookie who offered the kind of thoughtful, sophisticated feedback one would expect only from a grizzled industry veteran; the masterful copy editor Liz Dana; the publicity whiz Jaime Leifer; the skilled production editor Katie Carruthers-Busser; and the rest of the Hachette team. A freelancer, Malka Margolies, has expertly worn two hats: as an experienced editor, she read the book thoughtfully, critically, at least twice, and as a publicity guru. In the process, she has not only become a valued adviser but a cherished friend.

Ultimately, we are most grateful for the support and patience of our families—who kept congratulating us on finishing the book, only to discover there was more, and more, and more to be done. Each of us is blessed with a wonderful artist wife, who not only brings beauty to the world and our worlds but joy and meaning to our lives. Both of us deeply appreciate the support, love, and fortitude of both Linda and Avital, as they started fearing that this book might become another nine-year chapter in Natan's life.

Gil also thanks his four children—Lia, Yoni, Aviv, and Dina—for serving as sounding boards as well as cheerleaders, and his two brothers, Dan and Tevi, who are always by his side, no matter how far away they might be physically. Weaved into the dedication are hopes for the good health of his father, Bernard Dov Troy, and deep regret that Gil's mother, Elaine Gerson Troy, only lived long enough to see a printout of the proposed book cover, not the book itself.

Natan also thanks his two children, Rachel and Hanna, their husbands, Micha and Nachum, and his grandchildren—Eitan, Yehuda, David, Avigail, Uri, Daniel, and Ariel—for their supportive and demanding love. They kept reminding him of the importance of writing this book, while reminding him daily that there are things more important than writing a book.

This book, which started around Natan's Jewish Agency desk and was mostly written around Natan and Avital's dining room table, is being finished via Skype, during this strange, unnerving period of mass isolation thanks to the coronavirus. Although one friend teased us that we were cashing in on quarantine with our title *Never Alone*, the fact that the book's call for connectedness and engagement suits this particular moment is not due to any stroke of luck or any authorial sleight of hand. We not only stumbled onto the title over a year ago thanks to David, but we've both been living it our whole lives.

It's the timelessness of this message that neither of us invented that makes it so timely—and explains how the two of us, with such vastly different backgrounds, could end up living as neighbors in Jerusalem. It's a timeless timeliness that harks back to Sinai. This eternal message has survived worse plagues—imposed by nature and by people. But more important, its life-affirming joyfulness gives meaning to our lives, and the lives of millions of others. And it motivated our dedication, to thank our parents for passing on the torch, while inviting our children and grandchildren to carry it forward, each in their own way.

Natan Sharansky
Gil Troy
Jerusalem, May 2020

INDEX

451

Natan Sharansky was a political prisoner in the Soviet Union and served in four Israeli cabinets. The sole living non-US citizen to receive both the Congressional Gold Medal (in 1986) and the Presidential Medal of Freedom (in 2006), Sharansky won the 2018 Israel Prize for exceptional contribution to the State of Israel and the 2020 Genesis Prize for outstanding professional achievement, contribution to humanity, and commitment to Jewish values. He lives in Jerusalem with his wife, Avital. He has two daughters and seven grandchildren.

Gil Troy is a distinguished scholar of North American history at McGill University. He is the author of nine books on the American presidency, and three books on Zionism. Recently designated an *Algemeiner* J-100, one of the top 100 people "positively influencing Jewish life," Troy has appeared as a featured commentator on CNN's popular, multipart documentaries, *The Eighties*, *The Nineties*, and *The 2000s*. He lives in Jerusalem with his wife, Linda. They have four children.

PublicAffairs is a publishing house founded in 1997. It is a tribute to the standards, values, and flair of three persons who have served as mentors to countless reporters, writers, editors, and book people of all kinds, including me.

I. F. Stone, proprietor of *I. F. Stone's Weekly*, combined a commitment to the First Amendment with entrepreneurial zeal and reporting skill and became one of the great independent journalists in American history. At the age of eighty, Izzy published *The Trial of Socrates*, which was a national bestseller. He wrote the book after he taught himself ancient Greek.

Benjamin C. Bradlee was for nearly thirty years the charismatic editorial leader of *The Washington Post*. It was Ben who gave the *Post* the range and courage to pursue such historic issues as Watergate. He supported his reporters with a tenacity that made them fearless and it is no accident that so many became authors of influential, best-selling books.

Robert L. Bernstein, the chief executive of Random House for more than a quarter century, guided one of the nation's premier publishing houses. Bob was personally responsible for many books of political dissent and argument that challenged tyranny around the globe. He is also the founder and longtime chair of Human Rights Watch, one of the most respected human rights organizations in the world.

•   •   •

For fifty years, the banner of Public Affairs Press was carried by its owner Morris B. Schnapper, who published Gandhi, Nasser, Toynbee, Truman, and about 1,500 other authors. In 1983, Schnapper was described by *The Washington Post* as "a redoubtable gadfly." His legacy will endure in the books to come.

Peter Osnos, *Founder*